# Re-Envisioning Service:
# The Geography of our Faith

**ACRS MEMOIRS·VOLUME 3**

# Re-Envisioning Service: The Geography of Our Faith

The metamorphosis of Mennonites and Church of the Brethren in the second half of the twentieth century—like a monarch butterfly dangling before us, wiggling its way out of its cocoon—should not pass by unnoticed. We ask: What are we seeing? What is it that we are witnessing?

These sixteen brief memoirs give no straightforward answers, but they provide insights and lead to a new appreciation of transformative service. A quiet people, virtually hidden from the face of the earth, seek no more than to serve the suffering of their day; but when they return to their cocoons they are unable to re-enter. They have been transformed in ways no longer to be accommodated by the old abode.

The title of this volume befits the contents: Service in its many forms, practiced in the Anabaptist Brethren-Mennonite tradition, is transformative and redemptive for those being served. But for those serving, each day and each epoch re-configures their personal and communal geography of faith. Reading these stories allows us to participate in this metamorphosis.

# *Anabaptist Center for Religion and Society Memoirs*

**RAY C. GINGERICH, SERIES EDITOR**

This series of autobiographical accounts is typically published by Cascadia Publishing House LLC and copublished with the Anabaptist Center for Religion and Society (ACRS), based at Eastern Mennonite University. ACRS/EMU sponsors the series, determines the particular focus of each set of stories, and in consultation with the publisher, volume editors, and authors, is responsible for the content.

Volume 1, 2007, 2009
Making Sense of the Journey: The Geography of Our Faith
    *Robert Lee and Nancy V. Lee, Editors*

Volume 2, 2009
Continuing the Journey: The Geography of Our Faith
    *Nancy V. Lee, Editor*

Volume 3, 2016
Re-Envisioning Service: The Geography of Our Faith
    *Ray C. Gingerich and Pat Hostetter Martin, Editors*

Volume 4, 2017
Making a Difference in the Journey: The Geography of Our Faith
    *Nancy V. Lee, Nancy M. Farrar, Audrey A. Metz, and Kathy D. Fisher*

**ACRS MEMOIRS, VOLUME 3**

# Re-Envisioning Service: The Geography of Our Faith

*Brethren and Mennonite Stories Integrating Faith, Life, and the World of Thought*

Edited by
Ray C. Gingerich and
Pat Hostetter Martin

Foreword by
Stanley W. Green

**Publishing House**
Telford, Pennsylvania

*copublished with*
**Anabaptist Center for Religion and Society
Eastern Mennonite University
Harrisonburg, Virginia**

Cascadia Publishing House orders, information, reprint permissions:
contact@CascadiaPublishingHouse.com
1-215-723-9125
126 Klingerman Road, Telford PA 18969
www.CascadiaPublishingHouse.com

*Re-Envisioning Service*
Copyright © 2016 by Cascadia Publishing House,
a division of Cascadia Publishing House LLC
Telford, PA 18969
All rights reserved.
Library of Congress Catalog Number: 2016032354
ISBN-13: 978-1-68027-005-1
Book design by Cascadia Publishing House
Cover design by Dawn Ranck, with engraving by Jan Luyken

The paper used in this publication is recycled and meets the minimum requirements of American National Standard for Information Sciences—Permanence of Paper for Printed Library Materials, ANSI Z39.48-1984.

Library of Congress Cataloguing-in-Publication Data
Names: Gingerich, Ray C., editor.
Title: Re-envisioning service : the geography of our faith : brethren and Mennonite stories integrating faith, life, and the world of thought / edited by Ray C. Gingerich and Pat Hostetter Martin ; foreword by Stanley W. Green.
Description: Telford, Pennsylvania : Cascadia Publishing House, 2016. | Series: ACRS memoirs ; VOLUME 3 | Includes bibliographical references and index.
Identifiers: LCCN 2016032354 | ISBN 9781680270051 (6 x 9" trade pbk. : alk. paper) | ISBN 1680270052 (6 x 9" trade pbk.)
Subjects: LCSH: Mennonites--Biography. | Service (Theology)
Classification: LCC BX8141 .R44 2016 | DDC 289.7092/2 [B] --dc23
LC record available at https://lccn.loc.gov/2016032354

22 21 20 19 18 17 16    10 9 8 7 6 5 4 3 2 1

*To the Mennonite and Church of the Brethren communities of faith
who offered their sons and daughters a vision of service
alternative to the wars of the twentieth century;*

*To the young men and women of those Anabaptist communities
who heard the beckoning call to serve
in those distant worlds at home and abroad;*

*And to the emergent landscape of Anabaptist institutions and
ecumenical communities now serving as an epiphany of hope
for a new and less violent world.*

# CONTENTS

*Foreword by Stanley W. Green* 11
*Series Editor's Preface* 13
*Editors' Preface* 14
*Introduction by Nancy Heisey* 17

## PART I: RE-ENVISIONING SERVICE AS EDUCATORS

**J. Kenneth Kreider**   23
   *Service to Others: An Awesome Journey*

**Dale V. Ulrich**   45
   *One Life, Many Educational Roles in Service*

**Emmert F. Bittinger**   65
   *Heritage and Promise:*
     *Strands of an Eighty-Three-Year Journey*

**Carl S. Keener**   89
   *The Evolution of My Years: A Stream of Life in Process*

## PART II: RE-ENVISIONING SERVICE AS WRITERS AND PUBLISHERS

**Margaret Jantzi Foth**   115
   *The Road Taken*

**Paul M. Schrock**   141
   *From Reluctant Farmer to Passionate Book Editor*

**Earle W. Fike Jr.**   161
   *Flock Chefing*

Daniel Hertzler  183
    *Coming to Terms with Our Heritage*

### PART III: RE-ENVISIONING SERVICE AS INTERNATIONAL, RELIEF, AND DEVELOPMENT WORKERS

R. Jan Thompson  205
    *From Small Town to an Extended World View*

H. D. Swartzendruber  225
    *My Life and Times*

### PART IV: RE-ENVISIONING SERVICE AS INTERRELIGIOUS PRESENCE

Bertha Beachy  251
    *The Journey of My Life: Crossing Borders, Defying Boundaries*

Kenneth L. Seitz Jr.  273
    *Thirty Years in and out of the Middle East and What Lies Between*

### PART V: RE-ENVISIONING SERVICE AS PEACEBUILDERS

Paul W. Roth  297
    *A Journey of Identity*

Pat Hostetter Martin  311
    *Braiding the Strands of Life*

Earl S. Martin  335
    *Bread Boys and Woodcutters*

Edgar Metzler  357
    *An Autobiographical Stroll Through Sixty Years of Mennonite Peacemaking*

*Appendix by Calvin W. Redekop and Ray C. Gingerich* 377
*Notes on Contributors* 385
*Index* 395

## FOREWORD

The twentieth century witnessed some of the world's most horrific atrocities: the Armenian genocide, World Wars I and II—which included the Nazi Holocaust, the Rape of Nanking, Hiroshima, and Nagasaki. Following World War II came the Cambodian Killing Fields, apartheid in South Africa, the Rwandan genocide, and the ethnic cleansing in Bosnia. The list of nightmares in which hurt and harm on an unimaginable scale were perpetrated against innocent human beings seems endless. Too few, however, are the accounts of people of goodwill who were willing to invest their lives in building a more compassionate, caring and humane world.

The authors of *Re-Envisioning Service* tell deeply personal stories which recount how each distinctively grappled with life's opportunities, enigmas, and dissonances, investing lives with meaning through vocational (and shorter-term) decisions made while building a vision of a more humane world. Readers will gain insight into some ordinary individuals who experience extraordinary lives pregnant with meaning, purpose, and generosity. They pursued a vision of service congruent with the communities of faith out of which they emerged—yet in striving to make a positive contribution toward a more genial world beyond "their own people," they transformed the geography of those communities and, without exception, were themselves transformed.

Whether writing as erstwhile educators, pastors, administrators, writers, developments workers, peace and conciliation consultants, the sixteen authors offer us a multi-lensed perspective through which we are privileged to see how even seemingly slight choices or carefully discerned directions, and even unwelcome disappointments, are woven together so that the trivia of each day's endeavors construct a life of unanticipated significance. In the accounts which follow, the authors document how they overcame obstacles they encountered, learned valuable lessons from those they sought to serve, and developed enriching relationships that expanded their sense of community and belonging into distinctly different geographies and cultural contexts than those in which they were raised.

In these chapters the writers have courageously given us access to lives thick and rich with joys, struggles, memories, dreams, losses, and passions. These stories, told sometimes with humor, occasionally with pathos, but always with humility, bear testimony to the communities of faith which nurtured in them the intrinsic value of pursuing a vision of healing and hope. Though the stories reflect the lives of particular individuals, the stories together give us a glimpse into the Brethren-Mennonite communities from which they came, where this promise of a world renovated by healing and hope was sung and storied, proclaimed from the pulpit, and shared across the kitchen table.

Assuredly impacted by countervailing currents to violence and conflict which gave rise to movements like the Peace Corps and Doctors Without Borders amid wars and divisions that plagued the twentieth century, the writers in this text reveal being profoundly shaped by two additional dynamics foundational for their self-understanding. The Mennonite-Brethren communities in which their deeply held values and beliefs were shaped were collectivist-type cultures in which these communities upheld as the model of a good person someone who was generous, helpful, dependable, attentive to the needs of others, and eager to propagate and work for a kinder, gentler world. This ideal was, moreover, grounded in a resolute commitment to follow Jesus who exemplified selfless service of others.

Since we are shaped and sustained in our own altruistic commitments by stories of those who lived with honorable purpose, the narratives assembled here are worth telling and preserving for posterity. As someone called to lead an organization that challenges and invites people of all ages to learn and serve in many places of pain, brokenness, and alienation, I celebrate that these stories will inspire readers to consider serving a cause greater than personal aspiration or ambition. I pray this text will bless generations yet unborn as these accounts spur them and us to become agents of healing and hope.

—*Stanley W. Green, Executive Director, Mennonite Mission Network*

## SERIES EDITOR'S PREFACE

Too many years have passed since a small Anabaptist Center for Religion and Society (ACRS) committee—the late Al Keim, Lee Snyder, Carroll Yoder, and I—were given the assignment to set the direction for the next volumes in *The Geography of Our Faith*. Quite specifically we wanted to reach out and tap a broader stream of resources than were available under the Eastern Mennonite University umbrella of the first two volumes.

After several sessions of "concept testing" across a rather broad range of possibilities our committee centered on the concept of *service*. This leitmotiv, we rather quickly agreed, is common to Brethren, Mennonites, and Quakers, and would allow us to tap our common Anabaptist historical and theological resources beyond the EMU campus, and even beyond the Shenandoah Valley.

The current volume is the first to test these new directions. We look forward to our readers' responses.

— *Ray C. Gingerich, Editor, ACRS Memoir Series*

**EDITORS' PREFACE**

This third volume of essays from the "Monday Morning Breakfast" series of the Anabaptist Center for Religion and Society (ACRS) distinguishes itself from the previous two volumes in several ways: First, rather than being focused on Eastern Mennonite University faculty who are no longer actively engaged in the classroom, the essays in volume three are organized around the leitmotiv of *service*. In some of the essays this theme is much more in evidence than in others. It should be noted that "service" is quite broadly defined. For some of the authors it is quite literally a rendering of their life's work.

Most are quite aware that theirs was an "alternative service," alternative to "military service"—alternative in method, with alternative support agencies. For others "service" is more outward-looking, giving us an account of how in the thought and in the institutional engagement that intertwined them, life served as a catalyst in a larger movement of the church—namely, the evolution of theology and practice within our religious denominations. Specifically, the changing strategies of being peacebuilders and of being a people of hope in a land that is not ours are most clearly enunciated in the final segment (Part V) of the essays of this collection.

Second, the first two volumes of *The Geography of Our Faith*, particularly the earlier essays of volume one (*Making Sense of the Journey: The Geography of Our Faith—Mennonite Stories Integrating Faith and Life and the World of Thought* (ACRS 2007, Cascadia edition 2009), constituted a series of intellectual memoirs belonging to the genre of "how my mind has changed." The current collection of essays is more vocationally focused and might reasonably be read from the perspective of "how my life's work has transformed me" into the person I now discover myself to be. That is, service is seen less from the perspective of what it has done for others and more with an eye on how those engaged in service have themselves been served—i.e., been transformed. Each of these *shifts* in focus deserves elaboration well beyond what is possible to provide here.

Finally, whereas the storytellers of volumes one and two of *The Geography of Our Faith* were all Mennonites, the current set of essays includes persons of the Church of the Brethren tradition. (Unfortunately we were unable to include Quakers, also included in the planning for this volume.) With several Anabaptist-related groups geographically comingling here in the Shenandoah Valley, where maintaining a pacifist-rooted faith has been neither culturally popular nor without political costs, we hope readers will find these personal accounts in the struggle to be faithful not merely historically interesting but a motivating inspiration toward faithfulness in their own particular vocations today. This is the *geography* of our faith. The metaphor underscores the socio-political landscape in which we live out our deepest commitments in the struggle to realize our profoundest hopes.

The representation of storytellers from the Brethren tradition in this collection should be yet another reminder of our common heritage and cooperative work expressed so well through the Brethren-Mennonite Heritage Center (Crossroads) in Harrisonburg, Virginia. The focus on *service* as an expression of discipleship underscores just how central ethics and vocation are to faith and belief—key elements of the Historic Peace Churches (Mennonites, Quakers, and Church of the Brethren). This focus is also in keeping with the less academic tenor of the current set of memoirs than the tenor of previous volumes.

Our gratitude goes to each of the sixteen contributors of this volume, for their openness in sharing and the vulnerability that encompasses every good memoir.

Thanks to Margaret Foth for her urging to include the abbreviated biographical introductions on the title page of each of the chapters (sketches originally written by Ray Gingerich in his email invitations to the ACRS Monday Morning Breakfasts). We hope our readers will find delight in these sketches. They shed light on the authors' characters—often highlighting dimensions which they themselves were unable to share.

Special thanks go to our publisher, Michael A. King of Cascadia Publishing House, for his continued commitment to storytelling as a way of laying the stones for the larger structure called "community," and for the energy invested in making these essays available to a larger contemporary readership while preserving them for posterity.

Thanks must also be given to EMU for providing a home to ACRS and for lending support, particularly through Fred Kniss and the provost's office. Without this institutional support, ACRS and its ancillary activities could not continue.

—*Ray C. Gingerich and Pat Hostetter Martin, Editors,*
  *ACRS Memoir Series*

## INTRODUCTION: GROWING INTO SERVICE

In the article on "Service" in the *Global Anabaptist Mennonite Encyclopedia Online*, Peter J. Dyck underlines the twentieth century as a time when service became a word that shaped descendants of the Anabaptists. As Dyck saw it, this usage dates from the 1950 decision of Mennonite Central Committee to add "service" to its tagline task, "relief." But historian James Juhnke argues that the connection of peace churches' commitment to service as an idea can be traced back to World War I, when their responses to modern needs to draft soldiers for global war (also called "service") were challenged and tested.

This third volume of *The Geography of Our Faith* series offers wide-ranging accounts of Mennonite and Church of the Brethren women and men facing the call and challenge of service, shaped by World War II, when service in the form of United States government sanctioned Civilian Public Service (CPS) provided an alternative/mirror opportunity for pacifist men of draft age.

Most of the writers in this volume experienced World War II as children or felt its impact on their communities from the adults of the "CPS generation" who raised them or spoke in their churches. New insights emerge from participants here who carried and experienced the evolution of the service vision through and beyond the U.S. war in Vietnam and the Cold War. The inclusion of stories from Church of the Brethren participants provides valuable points of comparison and accounts from parts of the world less familiar to Mennonites.

The farm was the first home for most of those who recount their stories here, and if not their own home, a place where they visited with and were nurtured by close family members. Keepers of the service legacy among descendants of the Anabaptist have noted and wondered about the impact of the move within both Mennonite and Church of the Brethren communities away from their rural and farming roots. Clearly, the spirit and flexibility of farm childhoods provided much of the energy for the first forays into service in new and strange environments as these chapters describe.

Church life is a given for the storytellers and, for the most part, a comfortable and sustaining foundation for their service. Further, the institutional flowering which occurred in the post-World War II period offered frameworks for expressions of their callings, through agencies such as Mennonite Central Committee, Brethren Volunteer Service, Heifer Project, Church World Service, World Council of Churches, Mennonite Publishing House, and Eastern Mennonite Board of Missions. Interestingly, the anguishing over whether the Anabaptist "theology of service" was adequate to the faith we profess, as expressed in some circles during the twentieth century, seemed not to trouble these storytellers who rather expressed a clear, while not simplistic, confidence in the relationship between their faith and their works.

The role played by church colleges in the preparation and orientation to service is a strong interwoven theme among the accounts here. Significantly, the geography of church-related higher education was much broader for Church of the Brethren writers, from the most local, Bridgewater, to the most distant, La Verne (California). For the Mennonite participants, the geography revolves around the tighter educational network of Eastern Mennonite, Hesston, and Goshen Colleges.

The learnings of those who have spent a lifetime in service, of course, flow broadly outward from their church college educations. As reflected in these stories, the writers are gentle in character, bearing wisdom that comes from long practice and continuing willingness to humbly engage the questions that emerge over those lifetimes. Among the rich individual vignettes presented here, readers are offered sharp questions and pulled into an ever richer understanding of service.

Emmert and Esther Bittinger welcomed a German exchange student into their home, when the wounds of World War II were still raw in the United States, and maintained relationships with her throughout the decades. Kenneth Kreider was confronted by an angry Elizabethtown College student in his history class, labeled a communist, and offered a one-way ticket to Moscow because of his views. Margaret Foth, whose most audible public service was as a radio voice for Mennonite women in transition from homemaking to more professional roles, immersed herself in the diverse faith traditions of international students, finding God in new ways in her retirement years.

H. D. Swartzendruber moved from an MCC assignment to work with the World Council of Churches, UNHCR, and the United States Foreign Disaster Assistance Office. Dale Ulrich encountered systemic racism in Baltimore and partnered with the NAACP to publicly protest its presence at a segregated restaurant. Paul Roth pushed through pastoral failure into the work of assisting congregations in the midst of conflict. Bertha Beachy parlayed her bilingual childhood in an Amish family into an ability to enter into Somali culture.

Along the way, these humble servants came to understand and demonstrate that service, for followers of Christ, is not simple. The lifelong commitments they reflect have pushed far beyond a straightforward "other side of the coin" of military service which shaped the churches who first called them. Their willingness to be stretched, troubled, changed, and renewed along the way give us hope. Their examples of leaning-in to the needs of the world inspire us. For that we thank them, and we ask for their blessing and encouragement for the Anabaptist Christian service callings of the twenty-first century.

—*Nancy Heisey, Professor of Biblical Studies, Eastern Mennonite University; Associate Dean, Eastern Mennonite Seminary*

**PART I**

# Re-Envisioning Service
# . . . as Educators

*J. Kenneth Kreider*

---

**Brethren Historian, World Traveler, Anabaptist Leader**

*A professor of history for thirty-five years, Kenneth Kreider has lived a life rooted in service both at home and overseas. As a world traveler, he has embodied what it means to be "Brethren" in the prophetic spirit of Anabaptism. His historical tours to sacred venues of Brethren heritage have enabled him to share his historical knowledge and passion with more than 6,000 people, visiting all fifty states and 106 countries on the seven continents. Here is an elder with a youthful spirit, a treasured heritage, and a life story that reverberates into the present.*

## J. KENNETH KREIDER

# Service to Others—
# An Awesome Journey

### A Solid Foundation

"It's a good thing you're not a woman. You would be pregnant all the time because you cannot say no," my father told me in 1955, as I was preparing to leave home for war-torn Europe. I was in Brethren Volunteer Service (BVS) and planned to take several hundred dollars from my savings along with me to Europe. "You will see so many heart-wrenching cases of need that you will quickly hand out all of your money. Leave it here and when you see a reason why you truly need it, we'll send it to you," was the advice I wisely followed.

Beginning a new life together on a small farm in the middle of the Great Depression meant that my parents had very little money. My three brothers and I knew, however, that any hobo who stopped at our farm would receive a meal. In our family, during World War II, our national enemies were always referred to as Japanese, not what most people called them. Likewise, although none lived in our neighborhood, the N-word was never to be used in reference to the major minority group in our nation at that time. They were Negroes and were to be treated and referred to with dignity and respect. Family devotions around the table occurred every day before breakfast.

I was born on April 7, 1934, in Lancaster, Pennsylvania, and raised on a dairy farm in southern Lancaster County. Life revolved around our local Church of the Brethren congregation, including Sunday morning and evening services and annual two-week revival services.

I can't remember any sermons, Sunday school lessons, or parental discussions regarding pacifism, but when I became eighteen, I knew that I had to register as a conscientious objector to military service. I must have absorbed pacifism as a normal part of trying to live according to the teachings in the Bible—of being a Christian. After all, I could not even kill a dog, cat, or cow; I certainly could not kill—or learn how to kill—a human being.

Tracing my family roots back to Europe, I find Anabaptist or Mennonite heritage on both maternal and paternal sides of our family tree. However, after coming to this continent, marriage and biblical interpretation as to mode of baptism led my family toward the Brethren. I had the very good fortune of knowing and appreciating two parents, four grandparents, and five of my eight great-grandparents. My parents, grandparents, and great-grandparents were members of the Church of the Brethren. I saw no reason to find a different church home.

During my teen years I "ran around" with many Mennonite youth and dated Mennonite girls. I learned that local Mennonite churches excommunicated young men who entered military service. "Kicked them out of the church," is the way teenagers put it. I thought that our Brethren way was better, in that while we taught and encouraged alternative service, we kept those who chose to enter military service in active membership in the church. If young men needed religious support at any time, they certainly needed it when they entered the military.

I have had to reevaluate my teen feeling that the Brethren reaction to the choices of young men was better than that of the Mennonites. When one looks at church membership of Brethren and Mennonites in 1955 and then at 2010, it appears that while membership in the Mennonite family has increased, membership of the Brethren has declined. While recognizing that there are always multiple factors for most events, I am forced to consider that perhaps it is healthy (and biblical) to enforce some degree of discipline.

Another moral issue was that of tobacco. Many farms in Lancaster County were paid for by tobacco. My grandfather Kreider did not smoke and did not want his sons to use the weed. He logically deducted that to be consistent in his teaching he had to cease raising the crop. This sacrifice paid off in that none of his eight children who survived to adulthood and, to my knowledge, only four of his twenty-nine grandchildren used tobacco. Anyone who raised tobacco was not eligible to be a delegate representing my home congregation, Mechanic Grove Church of the Brethren, Quarryville, Pennsylvania, at the denomination's annual conference. With about 96 percent of the membership of the church being farmers in the 1950s, this was a significant requirement (in 2010 about that same percentage of the membership are *not* farmers).

My grandparents dressed in the "plain" way. I was twenty years old when I attended my first annual conference of my denomination in Ocean Grove, New Jersey, and learned that not every female member of the Church of the Brethren wore a prayer covering. I was shocked. My grandmother was convinced that only Brethren would go to heaven. After all, the Brethren follow the biblical examples of triune, forward, full immersion baptism, feet washing, holy communion, head covering for women, etc.

Then her youngest daughter married a man by the name of John Wesley Hagen. Anyone with that name was not Brethren. Not even Mennonite! But he was such a wholesome, decent, genteel Christian and gentleman that by the time she died at age ninety-six (after giving birth to twelve children and spending not one night or one day of her life in a hospital), Grandma had come to the conclusion that perhaps heaven had more room than she had previously thought.

Incidentally, the wedding of his daughter is the only time I ever saw my grandfather Kreider wearing a necktie. It is amazing what little girls can get their daddies to do. For that wedding, Grandma wore her ever-present prayer covering—with strings that tied below the chin, long dress going to her ankles—including the usual cape. I wonder what she thought of Grandpa and his necktie.

Because of the groundwork laid by our Brethren patriarch, M. R. Zigler, working with his companions, Orie O. Miller of the Mennonites and E. Raymond Wilson representing the Society of Friends, the United States government agreed to recognize the legality of people of conscience performing alternative service in lieu of military service. (I well remember driving M. R. Zigler in 1976 to Landis Retirement Home, between Lancaster and Lititz, to visit his longtime friend, Orie Miller. This was the last meeting of these revered patriarchs of our two denominations.)

## Alternative Service to the Military

Remembering that one of the Ten Commandments was "Thou shalt not kill," and finding meaningful significance in Matthew 5:38-48, I registered as a conscientious objector to military service. Although it is not possible to be perfect, I recognized the imperative of those significant words, "You have heard it said of old . . . but I say unto you. . . . " From what little I knew of military service, it did not square with attempting to live as Jesus Christ taught us to live. Fortunately, since I lived in Lancaster County, the draft board accepted my application and granted me the classification of conscientious objector.

Years later my stepsister was an exchange student to Iceland, where she met a young man from Nebraska. They later married. He found meaning in the Brethren teaching of nonviolence and also registered as a conscientious objector. The draft board in Nebraska had never had such a claim and was not about to allow such a claim to besmirch their patriotic image.

Denied on local and regional levels, he pushed the claim to the highest state level. As he addressed the review board he said, "You think you are deciding whether I go into the military or not. You are not deciding that. I have decided that. I am not going to participate in military activities. You are deciding whether I go to jail or not for my belief. If you put me in prison you will have to feed and keep me—and you will have to feed and keep my wife and baby who will be on welfare. If you grant my conscientious objector position, I can do alternative service in a mental hospital or some other institution, 'working in the national interest,' while earning enough to support myself and my family." They granted his position. He had hit them, nonviolently, in the pocketbook.

To do my alternative service I chose to be a tester for Dairy Herd Improvement Association (DHIA). I took a two-week course at Penn

State to familiarize myself with the work I was to do. I was assigned twenty-seven farms where I was to take milk samples from each dairy cow at the evening and morning milking. After the morning milking I would determine how much feed each cow consumed daily, weigh the milk produced per day, test the butterfat content (using my portable centrifuge), and calculate how much it cost the farmer to keep her each day and how much her production was paying. Providing this information to the farmer would make his production more efficient and was, therefore, in the national interest.

Three of the farms to which I made monthly visits were operated by Amish families. I well remember the one family who had eleven children. At the supper table all conversation was between the father and me; the children did not speak unless spoken to. That night in bed I had to wonder where the two or three boys were sleeping since I was in their bed. Since there was no electricity used in the barn or house, it was interesting for me to see the innovative ways in which the Amish adapted to remain true to their faith. While working on these Amish farms we had interesting discussions about how our Anabaptist heritage led us to different and common views in the twentieth century.

## BRETHREN VOLUNTEER SERVICE AS A HUMAN GUINEA PIG

In August 1954 I took a week's vacation to attend the first National Youth Conference of our denomination in Anderson, Indiana. There I heard about Brethren Volunteer Service (BVS). After returning to my duties, I submitted my resignation as a DHIA tester, and on December 1, 1954, I joined the twenty-fifth BVS unit as we began training at the Brethren Service Center in New Windsor, Maryland.

Each morning and many evenings were devoted to lectures and study of a significant subject; afternoons were devoted to processing clothing for relief shipment to needy people overseas. During the eight weeks of training we concentrated one week on Bible study and Christian beliefs; another week highlighted Brethren heritage and beliefs; other weeks concentrated on social problems, history and philosophy of Brethren Service, pacifism and nonviolence, crafts, worship and music leadership, and intercultural relations.

Asked to list our first, second, and third choices for assignment, I requested an assignment in Europe, or the project on a Mexican vocational farm in Falfurrias, Texas, or a project in California. We were then informed that only those who had attended or graduated from college qualified for European assignment. I looked at my colleagues who bagged the coveted European assignments and thought, "They're no smarter than I am," but it made no difference. I was assigned to be a normal control patient—a human guinea pig—at the National Institutes of Health at Bethesda, Maryland. After a few weeks I was transferred to the Metabolic Research Unit of the University of Michigan Hospital in Ann Arbor.

A condensed account of my main assignment in the "hot room," where I barely won a wager that I would not pass out the first day (as had previous volunteers) is included in my book, *A Cup of Cold Water: The Story of Brethren Service*.[1] I was on a strict diet. I ate the very same food, weighed out to the gram, every meal, every day. I could drink only distilled water as tap water has some minerals; I could not even chew chewing gum. They wanted to know the exact weight and chemical/mineral content of everything I consumed so that they could have a constant baseline—and any change in my blood count was caused by something they had done or injected into me.

One day a physician came into the hot room to draw blood for my GTT (glucose tolerance test). He sensed my unease and extreme discomfort and said, "Ken, I just returned from my tour of duty in Korea and I never had to experience anything near what you are experiencing. You realize, don't you, that you are a volunteer, and you can walk out of here anytime you choose." I told him that I had not even considered quitting the assignment. One day I was injected with what the physicians informed me was one-fourth of the entire world's supply of that medication, and it cost them $9,000. I think it was an early steroid, but I was never informed precisely of the nature of that experiment. I learned later that this test had something to do with research on Addison's Disease and Conn's Syndrome.

## BRETHREN VOLUNTEER SERVICE IN EUROPE

Enroute to the Church of the Brethren annual conference in Grand Rapids in late June 1955, Ora Huston stopped in to visit me in the hospital. After a discussion of the life of a human guinea pig, Ora dropped a bombshell. "Would you like to go to Europe?" he asked.

I knew that those who went to Europe went for a two-year stint to justify the cost of transportation. I stammered that I had already served over half a year and had lined up my next position to work with John Eberly in New Windsor, and . . . and . . . and then I came to my senses. Of course I wanted to go to Europe. I had done everything in my power to get such an assignment—and failed. I then accepted domestic assignments and European dreams were banished from my mind. But now that I had completely abandoned the idea, it appeared! The phrase, "Let go and let God," popped into my thoughts.

Responsible for volunteer placement, Ora notified university officials that my placement at the hospital would terminate at the end of the particular test in which I was then engaged. Having been on the same diet every day for months, I ordered my first meal at termination: a ham and cheese sandwich and a half-gallon of ice cream.

Since I was not assigned to Europe with a regular volunteer unit, I was to travel alone on the SS Maasdam of the Holland-America Line. Imagine my surprise and delight to find on board with me about three dozen Mennonite Central Committee (MCC) Pax men, along with their chaperones, Pastor and Mrs. Dirksen of Hesston College. The Pax men were going to construction projects in western Germany. I appreciated the opportunity of visiting with them and participating in their worship services on board ship.

During the following two years, I was able to visit some of them (including Al Keim who would become a renowned professor at EMU) and their projects at Hamburg, Altona, and Kaiserslautern. Arriving at Brethren Haus in Kassel, Germany, I learned why they brought a young man with a farm background to Germany. There was need in the Heifer Project office for a visitation representative. But I had to learn the German language and learn to type to qualify.

A German family accepted me as their guest for a few weeks. I did cleaning and maintenance of our headquarters and studied German during the day. I would then ride the streetcar for about half an hour to my German home on the outskirts of the city. I ate the evening meal, slept in a bedroom with my eleven-year old "brother," and had breakfast with the family before returning to Brethren Haus for the day.

My "brother" and I would play chess by the window and the sisters would read a book holding the book at an angle to catch the last beams of natural daylight. When it was dark we went to bed. Electric lights were seldom turned on. Toilet paper was strips of newspaper. They lived sparingly and with environmental concern. Each day as I rode the streetcar, I would see another sign or advertisement and realize, "I can understand that; I know what that means." I learned how to type from a four-page book of instructions on where to place my fingers on the typewriter—and from there, it was just practice.

Within a couple of weeks I was on the road, visiting families that had received heifers from the United States. I recorded the addresses of dozens of families in a designated part of Germany and went there for a week. The visits were to monitor the effects of heifer donations and to establish a personal contact with the recipients. In conversation I learned where their homes were in Eastern Europe, some details of how they had lost their home, livestock, furniture, belongings, farm equipment—and some family members who died along the road as they fled ahead of the Red Army—and how they were trying to begin a new phase in their lives. They were extremely grateful for the gift of a heifer, which many of them credited with keeping their children alive. One expression of appreciation was the statement, "It surely takes a lot of love to give a cow away."

For most of these people, it was the first time they had ever had a conversation with an American. They not only could hardly believe that someone would give them a cow free of charge but also that an American actually cared about them and was willing to listen to them. As a family would learn that I represented the donor of their heifer, they would instinctively reach up to that top shelf where the most precious bottle was kept—and used only for special occasions, such as Christmas, Easter, and Grandma's birthday. When I politely demurred, saying that I did not drink alcoholic beverages, they were extremely frustrated. How can we show you our appreciation for our cow? I explained that this was not my only visit today; that if I drank even "only a little" with perhaps ten families, I would not be fit to drive. Inasmuch as DUI is seen as a far more serious issue in Europe than in the United States, they understood, but were still extremely frustrated.

"Oh, you drink milk, don't you?" Yes, I do drink cold milk, chocolate milk, even hot cocoa, but I don't like hot white milk. But, so soon after the end of the war, they had no refrigerators and certainly no cocoa. Therefore milk was brought to a boil before being served. As I sat there conversing with them with my cup of hot white milk—pushing back the skin which gathers at the top of hot milk—I looked up on that high shelf and thought, "That stuff cannot possibly taste as bad as this."

After a week on the road I would return to Brethren Haus and write letters to all the donors of the heifers whose new owners I had visited. To establish a connection between donor and recipient, I would relate to the family, Sunday school class, Rotary club, or other donor, the details of the recipient family of their donation. I was always conscious of the fact that the money I was spending for food and lodging was put into the offering plate as a gift to the Lord—to carry on the work of the Lord. I did not stay at fancy hotels. One night my hotel room cost twelve-and-a-half United States cents. One week my entire expense account for room and meals was under twenty dollars.

I could give many more stories about the ministry of Heifer Project, but I'll have to refer you to my book.[2] For over thirty years after returning home from Europe I was hoping that someone would write the history of Brethren Service. In 1988 Brethren Press asked me to do what I thought was beyond my capability. But then I remembered that my hero, M. R. Zigler from Broadway, Virginia, said that Brethren Service assigned naïve and inexperienced young people to do a job they were unqualified to do, and, not realizing they couldn't do it, they did it. I accepted the challenge, and with the assistance of a sabbatical leave from Elizabethtown College, where I was teaching, I researched and wrote *A Cup of Cold Water: the History of Brethren Service*. My goal was to get these stories of service on the record so that generations to come would know a little of what happened.

## HOLY LAND TOUR

I must digress here to mention the fantastic opportunity given to me when the Mennonites invited a few of us Brethren to accompany them on a tour to the Holy Land in 1956. I wrote home to inform my family of this opportunity, and as my father said he would, he sent the $250 from my savings account that paid for my tour to Greece and the Holy Land.

What a vacation! We traveled by train from Germany through Austria and Yugoslavia to Salonika (Thessaloniki), Greece. While visiting the Mennonite projects in the Macedonian villages of Paniyitsa and Tsakones in northern Greece, we marveled at the work of the Mennonite teams as they taught the villagers efficient agricultural and food preservation procedures. Although it was completely understandable, I was disappointed that we could not visit the Brethren projects on the other side of the mountains. It was awesome, almost unbelievable, for me to realize that we were in Macedonia, the city to which St. Paul addressed his letter to the Thessalonians. The biblical call to "come over to Macedonia" resounded through my mind.

After riding the train all night (saving a hotel charge) our next visit was Athens. While the Parthenon is indeed impressive, my most awesome impression was standing on Mars Hill while reading from Acts 17:22-32 (RSV) what St. Paul said to the Athenians as he stood at that very place: He observed that they were very religious, as they had many idols, including one which was dedicated to "an unknown god." "What therefore you worship as unknown, this I proclaim to you," said Paul.

> The God who made the world and everything in it, being Lord of heaven and earth, does not live in shrines made by man, nor is he served by human hands, as though he needed anything, since he himself gives to all men life and breath and everything. And he made from one every nation of men to live on all the face of the earth....

We then had, what was for many of us, our first commercial airline flight—to Beirut, Lebanon. From there we drove through the Beqaa Valley (the northeastern extension of the Great Rift Valley which stretches down through Syria into Africa—Kenya, Tanzania, Mozambique) to Damascus, the oldest continually inhabited city in the world, where we visited the great mosque of Umayyad. I received my first lesson in the understanding of Islam by observing the Jesus minaret (I did not know that Muslims revere Jesus—as a prophet) and seeing the reverence shown by Muslims to the area where tradition holds that the head of John the Baptist is buried.

Standing on Mt. Nebo, from which Moses looked over the Promised Land, we saw two refugee camps where 62,000 Palestinian refugees were living after having lost their homes in areas grabbed by the Israelis during events in 1948. I learned for the first time what the word *Zionist* really means, and my personal views began to change. Because the Jews had gotten such a raw deal over the centuries—the pogroms of Russia, the horrors of the Holocaust in Germany, the perennial anti-Semitic discrimination in many parts of the world, I felt they deserved their "homeland" in newly formed Israel. And I do want to continue to take seriously that the depth of persecution Jews have suffered over millennia requires justice and makes understandable the determination of many that Israel be a haven from such violations. At the same time, somehow I had assumed that this area was empty, that no one lived there before surviving Jews arrived. I had never thought to question what happened to people already living there. I had never heard or read anything about anyone living there.

When we were up on Mt. Nebo, a young man took me aside and pointed to a stand of trees far off in the distance—beyond the Jordan River. He asked if I noticed that heap of rubble to the left. "That was the house where my grandfather, my father, and I were all born. My mother and sisters were raped and then killed by Israeli soldiers there. I was a little shaver and ran into the woods. My family and home were stolen from me," he said.

I later learned that countless families lost homes, olive orchards, and farmlands that had been in their family for generations. I was told about a book illegal to possess in Israel, written by an American Jew. I eventually bought the book, *What Price Israel*, by Alfred Lilienthal.[3] Influenced by conversations with Palestinians and Israelis, seeing the situation for myself, and reading that book and many others since, caused my views on the Arab-Israeli situation to change 180 degrees. I credit the Mennonites with providing me the opportunity to vastly expand my education and understanding.

I was upset for various reasons. Not only because of the indescribable injustice and brutality—even outright thievery and death—suffered by Arab people, but also because I had considered myself fairly well read and informed. I came to realize that we in the United States were receiving only partial information and only one point of view. We were totally unaware of the complete story. Many Americans remain uninformed about the range of issues behind the Arab-Israeli conflict. Palestinians have indeed inflicted violence on Jews, and this must be named. Yet many of us hear only about Palestinian provocations and little about Israeli provocations.

Though by no means rising to the level of the systematic killing of millions of Jews in the Holocaust, I came to realize that some surviving Jews and their descendants had come to Palestine and imposed on the Palestinians aspects of what the Nazis had inflicted on them—imprisonment, racism, discrimination, confiscation of property, and even killings. This continues to this day. Hundreds of acres of farmland, olive orchards, and family homes are bulldozed by Israelis as they steal the land to make more settlements. Then comes retaliation from the Arabs, followed by additional and greater violence by the Israelis. This continues to be one of the most distressing problems for me today.

I have become sensitized to the situation and realize that Israel's annexation of East Jerusalem in 1967 has never been recognized internationally. Although about 260,000 Arabs live in Jerusalem (about 35 percent of the city's population), every year for decades the Israelis have been revoking the right of 100 to 200 Arabs to continue to live in their ancestral homes. This has been accelerated. In 2008 they revoked the rights of 4,500 Palestinians to continue to live in their homeland, Jerusalem. The United States denounces such actions, but the Israelis know that, for political reasons, they can ignore suggestions to change policy. But, getting back to 1956. . . .

When it came time to transfer over to the Israeli side of Jerusalem, we all carried our own suitcase and walked single file along an open-air passageway through no-man's-land. Above and behind us were Arab militia with automatic rifles pointed at us; ahead of us on top of the wall we could see Israeli soldiers with automatic rifles pointed at us. It was a sobering taste of reality and a bit tense; no one tried to pull anything out of line.

Visits to Bethlehem, Nazareth, Sea of Galilee, Mount Caramel, and many other significant places—including Rome on the way back to Germany—were most meaningful. Words cannot describe how this trip was indeed life-changing for me.

## BACK TO BVS IN EUROPE

Returning to Germany, I settled down to my duties as visitation

*Hungarian refugee camp distribution, 1956.*

representative for Heifer Project. Shortly after the Hungarian Revolution broke out in late 1956, I was transferred to our headquarters in Linz, Austria, where I coordinated the work of Brethren Service workers in the various refugee camps in Upper Austria.

In addition to supplying volunteers to register refugees for emigration to various countries and to supply food and clothing where needed, BVS placed a volunteer in each of the various refugee camps around Linz. They conducted English language classes; craft and recreational activity; shoe, clothing, and food distribution; and other services to the refugees. In the process of coordinating the activities of the BVSers, I developed a motion picture show. Once a week I broke the tedium of the refugees living day after day in a room with twenty to two hundred others by showing about two hours worth of motion pictures in each of the camps. The films were borrowed from the United States Information Service, and my choices were very popular with the refugees.

One day after the show, I saw a group of people at the far end of the room who seemed quite agitated. I learned that a girl had died of a communicable disease and was to be buried the next day. The parents were distraught and mentioned that the funeral service would be conducted by the Catholic priest, but they were Baptist. I told them that I would contact a Baptist pastor whom I knew, who would surely conduct the service. But when I informed Pastor Boltz of the situation, he quickly said he would not do it unless I obtained permission in writing from the Catholic bishop. Austria is a Catholic country; a Protestant church could not even be built along a street or road. By law there had to be a building between the church and the street. Knowing that obtaining permission would be impossible, I rushed back to the camp—only to learn that the Catholic priest had been dismissed in anticipation of the Baptist pastor's services. Suddenly, as a result of my rash promise, I had a terrifying vision of having to conduct a funeral service myself—in Hungarian—and I am not even a minister, nor do I speak Hungarian.

In desperation I telephoned the World Council of Churches headquarters in Vienna and was told that a Baptist professor at the seminary in Budapest had been sent by the small Hungarian Baptist denomination to serve the Baptist refugees who had fled to Austria. He was a minister and would come to Linz. At 6:00 the next morning I met him at the train station and drove him to the refugee camp where he conducted the funeral service later that day. He did not have any means of transportation and I did not speak Hungarian, but during the week before Christmas we drove from camp to camp conducting Christmas services (he and I conversed in German). Years later, while watching a television broadcast of Billy Graham's first evangelistic service behind the Iron Curtain, I was amazed to see my friend, Dr. Sandor Harazsti, translating for Billy Graham.

Individuals and congregations sent money to me to "use as needed" in the refugee camps. Realizing that many of the children had no fruit in their diet, one day I bought various fruits—apples, pears, grapes, and bananas. As I entered the camp the children crowded around me, and I distributed one piece of fruit (or bunch of grapes) per child. I was amazed to see a young boy bite into the banana without peeling it. He had understood that it was fruit and so he bit into it as one would an apple. He had never seen a banana, and that was the only way he knew to eat fruit.

One night I received a phone call from M. R. Zigler, asking me to transfer to Rome. Within twelve hours I had transferred to someone else my various assignments, including the adoption case on which I was working for an Indiana couple to adopt a Hungarian orphan.

Soon I was on the train to Rome, via Geneva, where M. R. Zigler briefed me on the expectation of my new job. In Rome I met the movie actor Don Murray, who a few years earlier had been a BVSer working with boys clubs in the slums of Naples and with refugees from World War II in two camps outside of Naples. When he returned home, he promised them that he would not forget them. His first film upon returning home was "Bus Stop," co-starring with Marilyn Monroe.

With money earned from this and other films, Don provided financing for the project of resettling "hard core" refugees still remaining in Italian refugee camps from World War II. Don returned to Hollywood and sent money for me to purchase land on the island of Sardinia—between Italy and Africa.

From Camp Aversa, I picked up three refugees whom he had recommended: Roubal from Russia, Nyc from Bohemia in Czechoslovakia, and Tony from Spain. The four of us sailed to Sardinia and set up housekeeping in a two-room cement-block house. With no furniture or electricity, we went to bed at dusk. Three of us slept on the cement floor of the ten-by-ten-foot room. Tony insisted on sleeping by himself in the "kitchen" or outside. I slept between Roubal and Nyc.

One night as we were lying there in the dark I kept pushing Nyc verbally about his past. Finally, he said, "Yes, I was in Hitler's Gestapo." That raised the small hairs on the back of my neck, but after hearing details of the reasons, I had to ask myself whether I would have done anything differently had I been in his situation.

We worked to clear and level the land in preparation for irrigation for raising crops. Additional refugees arrived and the goal was to help them purchase their own land. Later years would bring orchards, a cement block manufacturing plant, poultry enterprises, and a cabinet-making shop operated by the refugees. Observing that "the project in Sardinia was the only refugee resettlement program of its kind that really worked," the United Nations became a contributor—along with other international agencies.[4]

## STUDYING AND TEACHING AT ELIZABETHTOWN COLLEGE

After almost three years in BVS, I returned home and two days later entered Elizabethtown College as a freshman.[5] I had joined BVS thinking that I was going to contribute two years of service to others.

Actually, I had received far more than I contributed. When I graduated from high school, I had no thought of attending college. My experiences stirred in me a desire for additional education and made my courses interesting and exciting. I got far more out of my schooling than I would have, had I gone to college directly from high school. Upon graduation, I immediately began graduate studies and subsequently took a master's degree in history at Penn State. Following an additional two years of study, I accepted a position as instructor in history at Elizabethtown College in 1964. During the early years of teaching I also did extensive research on my dissertation in the Library of Congress and other places, finally receiving my PhD in history in 1969.

By this time, I had married the woman I met in college math class, and we had two daughters. My wife Carroll earned her master's in business education while we lived at Penn State. After serving as chair of the business department at the local high school, she accepted an offer to teach in the business department of Elizabethtown College. For the next thirty years, we were both members of the faculty at the college.

The mid-Sixties were tumultuous years because of the Vietnam War. In 1965, during my third semester as a beginning professor, I was asked to speak at the college's weekly assembly/convocation. My subject was "Vietnam from the Vietnamese Point of View." I began by saying that we all knew why we were fighting them, but why were they fighting us? Why were people with no airplanes, helicopters, or tanks, fighting the most powerful country in the world as its helicopters and tanks, not to mention airplanes flying so high they could not be seen or heard, dropped bombs on them? I also mentioned how counter-productive the American policy was and how we could improve.

This was before Walter Cronkite and others came out against the war; my speech caused quite an uproar. My department chair said only the first five minutes of the speech had any validity; a petition was circulated among faculty calling for my dismissal from the faculty. As we drove onto the campus the next morning we saw a figure swinging from a tree limb near Alpha Hall with a sign, "Prof Kreider."

To this day I have the distinction of being the only student or faculty member in the history of Elizabethtown College to have been hanged—fortunately, in effigy. In preparing that speech I had taken pains not to include anything that could not be supported and proven accurate. I knew that if even one fact was in error, this would be used to discredit the entire speech. I just hoped that my speech would drive people to the library—if for no other reason than to prove me wrong. I knew that in so doing they would learn a lot.

I have always seen teaching at the college as a service and missionary endeavor. Although instructors have no right to impose their personal views on students, I believe they should present various options. Likewise students have the right to know where, after years of study and experience, the professor stands.

For instance, when teaching European history and discussing the conquests and significance of Napoleon on French and European events and history, I mention that I consider Napoleon one of the archcriminals of history. Ruling over the most powerful country in Europe, Napoleon and the French had nothing to fear from any neighbor or enemy. Yet Napoleon, not being content with peace and prosperity, attacked and invaded his neighbors, not once, but numerous times. After the loss of tens of thousands of lives and uncounted treasure, he forced his neighbors to form coalitions to oppose the Napoleonic French aggression. After Napoleon's disastrous invasion of Russia and subsequent retreat, someone mentioned to him that if he had not betrayed his ally, broken his treaty, and invaded Russia, over 500,000 people would not have died and tens of thousands would not have suffered terrible agony and injury. "What's half a million men to a man like me," was the retort of the defeated French emperor. I'm afraid that very few other professors use this or similar examples to illustrate the realities of warfare and politics.

One day, while I was teaching a course on the history of the Soviet Union, a young woman from New Jersey put up her hand and said she knew why our country had so many economic problems. "The government pays preachers too much," she said.

"Wait a minute," I responded, "in Sweden, Denmark, and other European countries, the government does pay the preachers, but not in the United States."

"Well," she responded, "then from where do American preachers get their income?" Since she found it difficult to believe my claim that American churches are operated from free-will offerings of their congregations, I surely hope that she did some real research to discover the truth.

Many of my students were also biblically illiterate. Often, after making a biblical comparison, I would realize that I needed to explain the biblical reference and how it compared to the issue at hand.

In another Soviet history class a student was so upset with information he was hearing that he stood up in class, called me a communist, and offered me a one-way ticket to Moscow. I thanked him and told him I had been in Moscow and much preferred to live in the United States. Furthermore, I told him about our male guide in Moscow. I gave my students examples of how the young man in Moscow had only ever heard one point of view—the view of his government. I told this student and the class that they should be thankful that they had an opportunity to see things from various points of view.

The most rewarding course which I taught during my thirty-five-year tenure at Elizabethtown College was on the history of nonviolence. Inspired by Coleman McCarthy of the *Washington Post,* this course was first offered in 1989 with eight students. The last three years before my retirement in 1999 saw enrollments of thirty-five students in each of two sections. Beginning with the biblical vision of beating swords into plowshares, the course included readings and class discussion on the teachings of Jesus, the early church fathers, St. Frances of Assisi, the Anabaptists, Tolstoy, Gandhi, Sojourner Truth, Jane Austin, Martin Luther King Jr., Khan Abdul Ghaffar Khan (1890-1988; Muslim pacifist who preached nonviolence to his Pashtun tribesmen in Afghanistan), Caesar Chavez, Dorothy Day, Father Oscar Romero, the Berrigan brothers, and others.

One day after class a student asked me, "Are you sure Dorothy Day and the Berrigan brothers were Catholic?" When I assured him that they were, he exclaimed, "Wait until I get home; I'm going to ask my priest why I have never heard of them."

I discovered that motion pictures get a point across in ways a lecture or a book cannot. Many of my classes have seen the film *The Radicals*, which graphically illustrates the teachings of the Anabaptists—focusing on the life of Michael Sattler. Likewise, my classes saw the Oscar-winning film *Gandhi*. Students of the late twentieth century had heard the name *Gandhi*, but until seeing that film they had no idea what his life and philosophy really meant. In the same manner the film *Romero* interprets the realities and interactions of religion and government, plus the effects of American foreign policy in a non-forgettable way. Since retirement I have been attempting to get my grandchildren to enhance their education by viewing these significant films.

As most teachers can attest, it is humbling and gratifying to hear testimonies from former students at Homecoming, or some other encounter with them, how significant a certain course was for them and how it influenced their lives.

### Tour Guide to the World

Wanting to get back to Europe to visit friends, I considered offering my talents to large tour companies. Before sending any letters, however, I realized that no tour company in New York or elsewhere was going to hire some yokel from the hills of Pennsylvania to be a guide in Europe. If I were going to be a guide I would have to build my own tour. Since the two-hundred-fiftieth anniversary of the founding of our church was approaching, I decided I would offer a tour to show our people the work that the church was doing in postwar Europe and to give them opportunity to attend anniversary services in Kassel, Germany, seat of our German service work, and in Schwarzenau, where our church had originated. Beginning in 1958, I led many tours to Europe—interpreting the work of our church. I considered it to be a service to the church and to the people who would otherwise not have had such an opportunity.

But then I realized that conducting tours to other areas of the world would enable me to visit some exotic places that I otherwise could not afford to visit. How could I rationalize encouraging and abetting people to spend that amount of money merely for pleasure and an educational experience—not associated with service?

That was a job, but I could give you stories of inspirational experiences in Pakistan, China, Egypt, Israel/Palestine, Iran, Iraq, and the mission fields in India. I took a group to Egypt and followed in the footsteps of Moses to Mt. Sinai and Mt. Nebo. It was an awesome experience to take a tour group to Jerusalem, walking in some of the same places Jesus walked. Likewise, making it possible for people to experience the Oberammergau Passion Play has been a service to hundreds of people who would not have gone had I not taken them. However, conducting tours to Hawaii, Alaska, Kenya, South Africa, Russia, Antarctica, Galapagos Islands, Machu Picchu, Australia, New Zealand, and Fiji, sometimes left me with a guilty conscience—ameliorated only by the rationalization that if they had not gone with me they would have gone with someone else.

## Opportunities for Service at Home

For years I have chaired the Germantown Trust, which is responsible for preservation and maintenance of our "Mother Church" (congregation formed in 1723) just a few blocks down Germantown Avenue from the mother church of the Mennonites, built after their arrival in 1683. As an active member of our local church, I was elected chair of the Witness Commission various times and also served various terms as chair of our Resources Commission (Stewardship).

Among many local opportunities for service was to chair the committee to resettle refugees, primarily from Vietnam. We sponsored sixty-five refugees and assisted them to begin a new life in a land that was foreign to them—finding and furnishing an apartment; applying for and finding a job; registering for a social security number, social and medical services, school for the children, and English lessons; opening a checking account; providing transportation; signing up for driving lessons; and purchasing a car are only some of the duties we did in service to people in need.

Since the 1970s our church has also sponsored refugees from Guatemala, San Salvador, Cuba, Haiti, Iran, and Armenia. As a sanctuary church, we even provided housing for Central American refugees in the church itself—behind the baptistery. Some of our members were uneasy with breaking national law, but others reminded them that our Lord was once a refugee.

For a farm boy, milking cows twice a day and weary from the back-breaking work of picking tomatoes every summer, to have had the opportunity to help people in need, to introduce thousands of students to ideas they had not heard of or thought about, to guide over 6,000 clients as we visited all fifty states and 106 foreign countries—on all seven continents—has been an awesome journey.

It would not have happened had I not been influenced by my Christian religious training to decide to work in alternative service rather than join the military. I thought that I was going to give service to others for two years, but I have just told you how I received so much more than I could ever have given. It was truly a life-changing experience. For that I will be ever thankful for my Anabaptist heritage and forbearers—the Mennonites and Brethren.

January 2010
Revised August 2012

## Notes

1. J. Kenneth Kreider, *A Cup of Cold Water: The Story of Brethren Service* (Elgin, Ill.: Brethren Press, 2001), 438-440.

2. Ibid., 131-149.

3. Alfred M. Lilienthal, *What Price Israel* (Chicago: Henry Regnery Company, 1953).

4. Kreider, *Cup of Cold Water*, 299-311.

5. One day while visiting Heifer recipient families in northern Germany, I pulled off the road to read the historical marker remembering and honoring the death of ten million refugees who died while fleeing from their homes during World War II. I knew of the death of millions of soldiers and civilians and was amazed to learn of the death of so many people who were merely trying to flee to safety. I decided that I would like to go to college to discover what caused World War II. Germany was one of the most culturally and educationally advanced countries in Europe—to say nothing of being a nation of Christians. How did an evil person called Adolph Hitler come to power legally in such a civilized country?

Upon returning to Kassel, I began reading college bulletins but was mystified by much of what I read: grade point average, degrees, etc. I went to my director, Wilbur Mullen, and said, "I come from a farm. I know all about B.S., but what is a B.A.?" Writing home to my mother, I announced that instead of coming home to the farm, I had decided to attend college for a year to discover what caused the war. She responded, "We would be proud to have a college graduate in the family." I thought, "Who said anything about graduating? I'm just going for a year to learn about the origins of the war." She was a far better prophet than I.

*Dale V. Ulrich*

---

**Administrator, Professor, Editor, and Conscience of Peace**

*A Student Christian Movement gathering in the late 1950s brought Dale Ulrich and six La Verne College students to Bridgewater College in the Shenandoah Valley. The rest is history? No, there are too many historically significant twists and turns, both from a spiritual/religious perspective and academically. Providential? Dale did alternative service then got a master's and a PhD before his long tenure at Bridgewater College as chemistry prof, dean, and provost. After retirement, he served seven years on the ACRS steering committee and continues a major role in recapturing the Brethren peace witness.*

# DALE V. ULRICH

## *One Life, Many Educational Roles in Service*

### BACKGROUND AND YOUTH

I was born in 1932 in the depth of the Great Depression and raised on a small fruit ranch in Wenatchee, Washington. In my early years my family had little money, but on the farm we had plenty to eat. I have one sister who is three years younger than I am. My grandfather was a farmer-minister in the Church of the Brethren, so my father grew up in that denomination. My mother was raised in a large family on a Kansas farm and in a conservative Baptist tradition.

On our farm in Wenatchee, apples were the main crop and cherries the second largest. The workers at the apple processing plant always looked forward to my father's fruit coming across the grader because his crop would typically be around 95 percent extra fancy grade. Most of the year, our family did the orchard work with additional help employed for harvest and occasionally at other times as well. As a boy, my help was needed, and in that environment I learned to apply myself.

I will always be glad for the privilege of learning to work in the orchard. Typically, during the growing season we would finish a fifty-nine-hour work week by stopping at five p.m. on Saturday instead of at the usual six p.m. As a teenager I learned to do routine work efficiently. In those days making apple boxes was a good summer job for a young fellow. Boxes were made by hand with eight nails each on two sides and the bottom. My standard output was a box a minute, 600 per day. I enjoyed that routine work because I could do it while thinking about anything that I chose.

As a boy, I was fascinated with the mechanical equipment on the ranch—the tractor and the sprayer being of particular interest. In high school, my studies included vocational agriculture in my sophomore year, physics in my junior year, and vocational auto mechanics in my senior year. As a project in the auto mechanics course, I completely overhauled the engine of my 1936 Ford car, and afterward it ran for tens of thousands of miles. The idea of going to college was not part of my thinking as a child. That developed gradually because of my experiences in the Church of the Brethren.

From my third-grade year until I finished high school, we lived about one mile from the Wenatchee Valley Church of the Brethren. At that time, the congregation celebrated harvest each year with a week-long series of meetings with outstanding speakers. As a young teenager, I was very impressed with two of the speakers—Dr. Jesse Zigler, a professor at Bethany Theological Seminary, and Dr. Desmond Bittinger, president of McPherson College. They made such an impression on me that at Easter time, when I was fourteen, I committed myself to being a Christian and to serving the church, and I was baptized and became a member of the Church of the Brethren.

In 1948, the Church of the Brethren Annual Conference was held in Colorado Springs. During the business session, Ted Chambers, one of the youth, came forward carrying an orange crate. He was only four feet and ten inches tall and needed to stand on the crate to speak into the microphone. He proposed to the conference delegates that they implement Brethren Volunteer Service, a program to enable young people to serve under the auspices of the church. The youth had short-circuited the accepted procedure at Annual Conference to introduce this item of business. The moderator was Calvert Ellis, president of Juniata College, and the conference secretary was Paul H. Bowman, president of Bridgewater College.

When Chambers finished making his proposal, the officers called a recess during which Paul Bowman advised Calvert Ellis that he should make an exception and permit action on this item of business. The motion passed, and the first Brethren Volunteer Service (BVS) unit began training two months later at the Brethren Service Center in

New Windsor, Maryland. The impact of that action on me as a sixteen-year-old sitting in the balcony observing the proceedings was that I resolved that someday I would participate in BVS. The remaining question was, "When?"

In those years, *The Gospel Messenger,* a weekly publication of the Church of the Brethren, carried an article in each issue reporting on Brethren Service work somewhere in the world. When our family issue arrived in the mail, I quickly read that article first. I was very interested in the church-in-action carrying out its mission of service and peacemaking. Rufus Bowman's book *The Church of the Brethren and War* was also a favorite of mine at that time.

In my sophomore year of high school, I enrolled in vocational agriculture. Our chapter of Future Farmers of America formed a parliamentary procedure team on which I was secretary. The team was scheduled to enter state-wide competition at Washington State University on a day that conflicted with a West Coast Regional Conference of the Church of the Brethren in Seattle. My decision to attend the conference was a direction-changer. Our parliamentary procedure team won first place without me, and my life became increasingly involved in the church.

In my senior year of high school, I was president of the District of Washington Church of the Brethren Youth Fellowship. The primary responsibility was to plan a youth conference and to work with the cabinet to plan the youth program of the District Summer Assembly. In those days, the District of Washington held a family camp with all ages participating. We benefited from leadership of La Verne College faculty and students and from the church at large. It was through those interactions and my own thinking that my commitment deepened to serve the church. By this time, I knew that I needed to pursue more education after high school.

At age eighteen, I registered for the military draft and sought IV-E classification as a conscientious objector to military service. The chair of the draft board, an attorney, responded by scheduling an appointment for me to come to the courthouse where he asked appropriate questions to determine that I was sincere and honest and that my application as a conscientious objector was based on Scripture and the beliefs of the Church of the Brethren. My answers to his questions convinced him, and I carried IV-E classification and II-S student classification through my four years of college and two years of graduate school.

## HIGHER EDUCATION

At La Verne College, a Church of the Brethren-related school in southern California, I pursued a liberal arts curriculum with a major in physical science. Since La Verne was a tiny college, with about 300 students at that time, it did not offer a physics major. But because it was affiliated with nearby Claremont colleges, I was permitted to enroll in upper division physics courses at Pomona College. My goal was to teach physics and math in secondary school. Gradually, however, my dream of teaching developed in ways I could not have anticipated at that time.

In the fall of my freshman year at La Verne College, I was privileged to participate in a Brethren Student Movement Conference at Thanksgiving time at Bridgewater College. I was one of six La Verne students who drove a car to McPherson College in Kansas, where we joined McPherson students in their chartered bus. The conference was held for students on Brethren college campuses as well as for Brethren students on non-Brethren campuses. It was a very meaningful experience for me to meet Brethren students from across the country.

On the night before we were to begin our journey home, it snowed and all roads were closed except the one leading to Washington, D.C. Of course, we students wanted to go to Washington. There we slept on the floor and the pews of the Washington City Church of the Brethren. The next morning, a Kansas senator phoned and invited us out to breakfast. Since we students had already bought food and were preparing it in the church kitchen, our advisor invited the senator to come have breakfast with us, and he and two of his aids accepted our invitation. From that time until the roads to the west opened, we were guests of the senator with a police escort for our bus and lunch at the Capitol building. It was an unforgettable experience.

At La Verne College I took special notice of Claire Gilbert. She was an outstanding student, and we shared ideals and common outlooks on life. We dated for two and one-half years and were married right after her college graduation in 1953 in her home church, the

Pasadena Church of the Brethren. That summer we visited Church of the Brethren congregations and camps in Washington and Oregon to represent La Verne College and, of course, to recruit students.

During my senior year at La Verne, I was president of the Student Christian Association. We students decided that we would like to raise some money to contribute to Heifer Project. Harold Rowe, executive of the Brethren Service Commission, visited La Verne, so we talked with him about our idea. He responded that giving to Heifer Project would be a fine goal, but a better project for an educational institution would be to arrange for an international student exchange. So we students began procedures to select a student to exchange with a German student at the Teachers College at Goettingen University in Germany. It happened that my sister Shirley was chosen to represent La Verne College in that exchange.

At the Teachers College in Goettingen, a student named Gerda Hitzemann was chosen to exchange with my sister. The girls exchanged families, roommates, and other friends. This was how Gerda became a member of our family. She arrived in Wenatchee on the train and stayed with us for two weeks, during which time we took a trip to Yellowstone National Park. As she sharpened her English and adjusted to life in the U.S., this was a delightful period. Our friendship with this wonderful family in Germany continues to this day, and exchanges between our family members are now in the third generation.

Because I wanted to be an exceptionally well-prepared teacher, I applied for and received a graduate assistantship at the University of Oregon, where in 1954 I began studies toward a master's degree in physics. Graduate studies went well, and in the winter quarter of my second year the schedule was right for me to enroll in eleven units. The university registrar's office informed my draft board that I was a part-time student and no longer qualified for a student deferment. That was fine with me because, by that time, I was ready to enter BVS and begin alternative service. Following completion of my master's degree that August, Claire and I traveled from Oregon to Maryland to enter Brethren Volunteer Service.

## Brethren Volunteer Service

Brethren Volunteer Service training in 1958 consisted of spending two months with a training unit at the Brethren Service Center in New Windsor, Maryland. Because our unit had fifty-four volunteers, it was divided into two groups. Half of each day was spent in processing used clothing for overseas relief; the other half was devoted to classes with a different instructor each week. It was a wonderful opportunity to interact with leaders of the Church of the Brethren, to develop camaraderie with fellow volunteers, and to think about the meaning of Christian living. At the conclusion of training, we were assigned to projects. Those assigned overseas needed to be committed to at least two years of service, while those engaged in projects in the United States served for ten months or for twenty-two months if they were performing alternative service with a I-W classification. Claire and I were ready to start a family and chose to remain in the U.S., but many members of our unit went to Europe, Africa, and Asia.

In 2006 I organized a fifty-year reunion of members of our training unit. As the members reported on their BVS projects, it was obvious that they had done amazing things working in refugee camps in Europe, distributing heifers, doing construction projects—the list goes on and on. Rebuilding the Karlsschule in Vienna was one project at which Brethren and Mennonites worked together. At the reunion event, it was amazing how naturally and easily the volunteers interacted with each other after having been apart for fifty years. For each one, the experiences of BVS had been very significant—even life changing.

The assignment for Claire and me was to be directors of the Brethren Volunteer Service project in the inner city of Baltimore. This project had actually begun in 1950 when Baltimore's Health Department had initiated a slum rehabilitation program. The department had declared a twenty-seven square block area on the east side just north of Johns Hopkins Hospital as the first rehabilitation area. The run-down conditions there had already been described in the *Baltimore Sun* in shocking terms.

One evening, Frank Rittenhouse took an issue of the *Sun* with him to a men's meeting at the Baltimore First Church of the Brethren and declared, "In a city where we live, we must not have children in their cribs being bitten by rats." The men formed a committee that met with Yates Cook, head of the Health Department, and asked him, "How can we help?" Cook replied that a center was needed in the Pilot Rehabilitation Area to work with the people living there. Men's Work responded by forming a nonprofit organization called Brotherhood Service, Inc., which bought a deserted run-down row house and fixed it up as a model of what could be done with such dwellings. This house became known as the "Pilot House" and was staffed by young volunteers from Brethren Volunteer Service.

By January 1957, when Claire and I arrived in Baltimore, work in the original pilot area was essentially complete. The government had designated a fifty-square-block area for renewal on the west side of the city. Accordingly, Brotherhood Service sold the first pilot house on the east side, bought a rundown house at the edge of the Harlem Park Urban Renewal area on the west side, and fixed it up to serve as a second pilot house.

During our eighteen months directing the work of the Baltimore BVS Unit at the second pilot house, anywhere from four to thirteen full-time volunteers lived there. Claire assumed the job of managing the house, during which time she also gave birth to our first son, Vernon, in June 1957; she had plenty to keep herself busy. Our main project was to help poor homeowners, often widows, fix up their homes to meet the minimum standards set by the Health Department. Much of the work was rat proofing with cement, carpentry work, leaky roof repair, painting, and other much needed odd jobs.

We conducted clean-up campaigns one city block at a time with the residents who lived there. It was a wonderful community project in which the children also enjoyed working. The city sanitation department cooperated by providing dump-trucks to haul away the trash—five or six loads per block. This service was particularly important because weekly trash collections were limited in size to what would fit in a trash can. Also, trash would collect in the inner block walkways, and no one would take responsibility for cleaning it up. After a block cleanup, we volunteers would poison all the rat holes that we could find. On one occasion, we counted at least twenty-seven dead rats on the surface the next day. Given that most of the rats died underground in their runways, the infestations were impressive.

The volunteers also supervised play lots for children, and on a hot summer day we would block off a city street and, with permission of the police and fire departments, hook up a sprinkler to a fire hydrant so that the children could play in the water. They loved it. Behind the pilot house there was vacant space that collected trash. We worked with the city government to have that lot cleared, paved, and play equipment installed. One lovely Sunday afternoon, the new play lot was dedicated. Even Mayor Thomas D'Alesandro Jr. participated in the ceremony.

On the east side of the city, some of the volunteers worked closely with Knox Presbyterian Church to staff its daycare program for small children. On the west side, we assisted the St. James Episcopal Church to establish and run a recreational program for the young people of the neighborhood. This work supplemented significant community projects which the local churches were already doing.

Ninety-nine percent of the population in the neighborhoods where we worked were black. The northwest section of Baltimore, where the pilot house was located, had the highest crime rate in the city, but we were fortunate to have no incidence of violence against volunteers. I feel certain that our neighbors around the pilot house looked out for us and protected us.

In the 1950s, blatant racial prejudice existed in the United States. The Baltimore BVS Unit participated with the NAACP to call attention to the problem of segregation. Despite the overwhelming percentage of blacks, there was only one small restaurant chain in downtown Baltimore that would serve black people. Ironically, it was called "White Tower." One time we participated with NAACP in a demonstration outside the only restaurant in the new Mondawmin Shopping Center located on the edge of the black community. Since we were an interracial group, the management of the restaurant would not allow us to enter. As we were peacefully standing outside the restaurant one evening, a man and his large, shaggy, black dog entered the restaurant with no problem at all. We laughed out loud that a big, black dog could enter the restaurant, and we could not.

Later we participated in a walk from Baltimore to Washington to call attention to the problem of racial segregation. Quite frankly, I was so disappointed in the way the march was managed that I concluded that if the people handling that march ever got control of the government, the nation would be in very serious trouble. As a result, I have not participated in a public protest demonstration since then.

## BRIDGEWATER COLLEGE

While we were engaged in Brethren Volunteer Service in Baltimore, Dr. Warren Bowman, president of Bridgewater College, wrote a letter asking if I would have an interest in teaching physics at Bridgewater. Claire and I visited Bridgewater with the result that I was employed. Dr. Bowman wanted me to teach there for two years, return to graduate school to earn a doctorate, and, if Bridgewater liked me and I the college, then to return. His plan was to develop a physics department with two full-time faculty members, which over the years materialized.

During my first year at Bridgewater, I taught physics and mathematics, was a men's residence hall director, and coached men's tennis. One day, as the tennis team was traveling to play American University, the fellows wanted to stop in Warrenton for refreshments. When I stopped the car at a restaurant, I noticed a sign in the window that stated, "Whites only." I told the fellows that they could go in if they wanted to, but I would wait for them in the car. Years later, one of those players, who became head of the physical education department at Georgia Tech, told me that my witness that day in Warrenton was very meaningful for him.

After three years of teaching at Bridgewater, I pursued doctoral studies in physics at the University of Virginia, where I was privileged to study under Dr. Jesse W. Beams. After the first year, I received a public health pre-doctoral fellowship to continue development of a method of very precise determination of the density of a tiny one-milliliter sample. I did that, and in the process, helped to determine the molecular weight of macromolecules such as viruses, proteins, and synthetic polymers. One summer I worked at the National Bureau of Standards building a Beams Magnetic Densitometer for them. It was there that I acquired interest in applying that instrument to study the density of simple fluids near the critical point. With the aid of a grant from the National Science Foundation, we did that study at Bridgewater College.

Teaching physics was a thrill for me. I felt that I was teaching about God's creation and a scientific approach to acquiring knowledge. I have never felt that gaining scientific knowledge precludes having faith in God and believing in the Scriptures. I am pleased that many of our students enrolled in graduate school in science or engineering and are contributing to their professions today. One of them, Dr. Moses Chan, is the Evan Pugh Professor of Physics at Penn State University, and I could name numerous others.

After Dr. John W. Bointnott retired as the dean of Bridgewater College in 1967, I accepted that responsibility and continued to teach one physics or math course most years. I served as dean from 1967-1982. While in the dean's office, I enjoyed working with the faculty and applying my analytical skills to college data and making projections. Particularly attractive to me was the opportunity to work with the president and faculty committees on the hiring of new faculty members. However, I missed the classroom; in 1982 an opportunity opened for me to return to full-time teaching. I taught for three years and then accepted an appointment as provost. After nine years as provost, I returned to teaching physics for five years before retirement in 1999.

While serving as dean, one of my most valuable experiences was participation for two months in a seminar in India for U. S. college deans, funded by a Fulbright Grant and conducted by the U.S. Office of Education in India. Twenty deans spent two weeks at the University of Poona and followed with travel and lectures around the country. I will never forget a wonderful evening with Mother Teresa in Calcutta. The seminar concluded with viewing of the Republic Day Parade in New Delhi on January 26, 1973. After the seminar, I was privileged to visit Anklesvar, in Gujarat State, north of Bombay, where the Church of the Brethren did missionary work.

While serving as dean and as provost, I chaired the college self-study for the Southern Association of Colleges and Schools and was privileged to serve on several re-accreditation committees of the Southern Association and on teacher education accrediting committees of the Virginia State Department of Education.

An assignment by the State Department to chair the visiting committee at Liberty University in 1982 proved to be especially interesting. In view of the creationism-versus-science controversy that was raging in the nation at that time, the review of Liberty's teacher education program developed into a high profile case. As past-president of the Virginia Academy of Science at that time, I was also in contact with Virginia's scientific community. The conclusion was that the State Board of Education gave temporary approval to Liberty University's teacher education program, which was in line with our committee's recommendation that the science program be reviewed again in one year by a team of scientists.

For many years, I enjoyed working with scientists through the Virginia Academy of Science. It was my privilege to serve as a member of the long-range planning committee, as director of the Visiting Scientists Program, treasurer, president-elect, and president. In 1982, I was elected a fellow of the academy.

## FAMILY

As I mentioned before, Claire and I were married in 1953. After graduating as a sociology major, she studied teacher education courses for one semester and then, during the second semester of my senior year at La Verne College, she commuted to East Los Angeles to teach elementary school. She continued to teach in Eugene, Oregon, while I studied. Claire was a constant companion and help to me.

In BVS in Baltimore, she managed the pilot house while caring for our first son, Vernon. Later, after our children were older, she studied accounting, passed the CPA examination, worked in an accounting firm, and then served as the financial officer for Harrisonburg Medical Associates. She finished her career at Mountainside Software, training the staff in physicians' offices to use Mountainside's medical billing system. In addition to her paid employment, Claire did a great deal of church work, including being the first woman moderator of the Bridgewater Church of the Brethren. For many years, she served as the financial records assistant for Brethren Encyclopedia, Inc. In retirement she also worked diligently at learning Spanish and taught English to Spanish speakers in the Harrisonburg area. I could not have had a more capable and thoughtful companion throughout our years together.

We have three children and six grandchildren. In 1959, during our first year in Bridgewater, Daniel, our second son, was born. In 1966, after we had lived in Charlottesville for three years and were back again in Bridgewater, our daughter Sharon was born. We have always been pleased with Bridgewater as a place to raise children. The combination of a thoughtful, committed church, good schools, and a supportive community contributed to rearing children who are now raising their own families and actively involved in their careers and churches.

After graduation from Bridgewater College, our first son Vernon earned a master's degree in mechanical engineering at the University of Virginia, engineered for Xerox and Lexmark corporations, and earned a doctorate in engineering physics. He now teaches mechanical engineering at Grove City College in Pennsylvania.

Our other two children were involved in international education. During his junior year in college, Daniel studied in Barcelona, Spain, through Brethren Colleges Abroad. There he had an opportunity to study Hebrew among other subjects and do research for his honors paper on "The Churches in Spain." At the conclusion of his year in Spain, he was invited to spend a week living with the monks at Publet Monastery. Now a seminary professor of New Testament studies at Bethany Theological Seminary in Indiana, Dan has used his Spanish fluency to lead several workshops for pastors and laymen in both Puerto Rico and the Dominican Republic.

Upon graduation from Turner Ashby High School, our daughter Sharon participated in a year-long program in Switzerland through International Christian Youth Exchange. There she developed some lasting friendships that have resulted in additional exchanges. As a French major in college, Sharon studied at the University of Strasburg in France through Brethren Colleges Aboard. Once again, the opportunity to study abroad was a life-changing experience for her. Sharon is now a professor of French at Simpson College in Iowa.

Over the years, we have hosted several international students for periods of at least six months. The first one occurred when our children were young. At the time, I was chair of the Brethren Service Committee at the Bridgewater Church of the Brethren which undertook the project of hosting an international student from Egypt. It turned out that a situation changed suddenly in the family that was planning to host her, so she lived with us for the year. This student, Lucy Alfi, had planned to come to the U.S. the previous year, but the Six Day War in 1967 between Israel and Egypt prevented any students from coming from Egypt that year.

Lucy attended the University of Cairo and came in 1968. Because she was more advanced when she arrived in the United States, we arranged for her to attend Bridgewater College rather than high school, as is typical with exchangees under International Christian Youth Exchange. Lucy's year of study went well, and in the summer before she flew home, our family took her by car (camping all the way) to southern California, Washington state, and back east again. Today, Lucy is a physician in New York City, where she and her husband have raised two children. In 2006, Lucy and her husband invited Claire and me to accompany them on a wonderful trip to Egypt.

Following our retirements in 1999, Claire and I spent two months at Bethany Theological Seminary. We served as host and hostess at the Brethren House. That experience enabled us to become more intimately acquainted with the Church of the Brethren seminary and its partnership with Earlham School of Religion.

Soon after, I was asked to become interim director of the Brethren Colleges Abroad (BCA) program at Cochin University of Science and Technology, often called CUSAT, in Kerala, India. The director there had become ill and was in the hospital. Two weeks after I was invited to help, I arrived in Kerala. Claire was able to join me a month later. Because CUSAT is a graduate school of science and technology, with undergraduate programs limited to engineering and computer science, BCA classes were arranged using adjunct professors.

The living and instructional facilities at CUSAT were very good for the BCA program. One of the really outstanding professors was Dr. Mani, head of the School of Gandhian Thought and Village Development at Mahatma Gandhi University. Four of the BCA students were from Eastern Mennonite University: Nate Horst, Nick Hurst, Lorendia Schmidt, and Wes Strickler. In fact, Nate, Lorendia, and Wes remained for the second semester with Lorendia doing an internship and Nate and Wes spending the semester at Mahatma Gandhi University studying under Dr. Mani's direction.

At Cochin we became acquainted with a psychology professor by the name of Sarada Sreedeviamma who taught a required BCA course on Indian culture. She took a special interest in introducing our American students to Indian culture. For example, Republic Day (January 26) is a holiday all over India. In the community where CUSAT is located, a program, which consists mostly of children performing music or dance, was held at an outdoor amphitheater seating about 1,000 people. In preparation, Sarada taught Indian freedom songs in Malayalam, the local language, to the BCA students and to some Indian students living in a youth hostel in the community. She outfitted the BCA women students with saris; the men also wore appropriate Indian attire. When these American students and the students from the hostel performed Indian freedom songs in the native Malayalam language before the crowd of Indian people from the community, they were the hit of the evening!

## ON EARTH PEACE AND BRETHREN ENCYCLOPEDIA, INC.

There are two ongoing organizations related to the Church of the Brethren to which I have devoted a great deal of time and energy. They are On Earth Peace and Brethren Encyclopedia, Inc. This is how they came to be.

Wayne Geisert, president of Bridgewater College, served as moderator of the Church of the Brethren in 1973-74. In June 1973 he received an invitation from M. R. Zigler, a leader in the Church of the Brethren, to attend a meeting at Tunker House in Broadway, Virginia. Zigler invited moderators, editors, and writers from five Brethren bodies to come together "just to shake hands." Geisert brought his invitation to my office, said that he had a conflict at that time, and asked if I would like to attend. I answered that I would be pleased to do so.

To appreciate the meaning of this meeting, one needs to know a bit of Brethren history. The Brethren movement began in 1708 in Schwarzenau, Germany. Count Henrich Albert was tolerant of Radical Pietists and permitted them to gather in Schwarzenau from other parts of Germany and central Europe. Many Radical Pietists believed that no organized Christian church was needed. They argued that Christianity was in the heart of the individual.

As they studied the Bible, one group of Pietists concluded that to fulfill the teachings of Jesus a visibly structured church was needed. So, one morning in August 1708, five men and three women went to the Eder River where one baptized Alexander Mack and he in turn baptized the others—thus committing an act illegal at the time. In this way, another Anabaptist church was founded. Because of the threat of persecution, they migrated to Surhuisterveen, Netherlands where they were received warmly by Mennonites. After nine years there, they migrated to Pennsylvania. Over the years divisions resulted in six separate denominations which we now refer to as Brethren bodies.

M. R. Zigler was the executive of the Brethren Service Commission during World War II and until 1948, at which time he went to Europe to head Brethren Service work there and to represent the Church of the Brethren at the newly formed World Council of Churches in Geneva. Readers of this narrative are probably aware that Zigler and Orie Miller, then executive secretary for the Mennonite Central Committee, worked closely together during the Second World War and were the best of friends.

One time when Zigler and General Hershey were conferring, Hershey asked Zigler, "How many divisions are there among the Brethren?" Zigler responded, and General Hershey said to him, "You Brethren have some peacemaking of your own to do." Zigler never forgot that, and many years later when he was thinking about establishing On Earth Peace, he told this story to a small group of friends. One of them gave him $1,000 to bring the Brethren together.

Zigler contacted persons in the different Brethren bodies to ask them to attend a meeting with the other Brethren. After two years, four of the main Brethren bodies were committed to attend, but the Old German Baptist Brethren would not give an answer—yes or no. So, Zigler scheduled the meeting in June 1973 at the Tunker House in Broadway, Virginia, immediately following their annual meeting in Franklin County, Virginia. The Tunker House was attractive because from 1825 until 1848 it was the home of Peter Nead. Nead had moved to Ohio and become the leader of the Old German Baptist Brethren when they divided from the main group in 1881. Tunker House was also the birthplace and childhood home of M. R. Zigler. It was not until they arrived in three cars that Zigler knew for sure that the Old German Baptist Brethren would come.

While I worked with M. R. Zigler on the Brethren Encyclopedia project, he invited me to participate in On Earth Peace, a program he was starting at the Brethren Service Center in New Windsor, Maryland. One of Zigler's friends, W. Newton Long, challenged him to develop an intellectual program for peace at New Windsor that would be equivalent to the material aid program for peace that was conducted there. Zigler later said that he woke up in the middle of the night thinking of the angels proclaiming to the shepherds: "Glory to God in the highest, and on earth peace among men in whom he is well pleased!" (Luke 2: 14, *New Oxford Annotated Bible*). Thus originated the name "On Earth Peace." Zigler tested the idea by traveling by bus to meet with friends in several states. He was pleased that from these first contacts, pledges totaling $30,000 were committed to support the program.

I attended a couple of meetings of On Earth Peace. Soon the organization was forming a Central Committee, and I was elected to serve as president. Working with the Central Committee, we developed a Brethren World Peace Academy program designed for youth at age sixteen to come to New Windsor to study creative citizenship for world peace. We also initiated a Brethren World Peace Bookstore at New Windsor to make peace literature available to the hundreds of visitors each year to the Brethren Service Center. We conducted a number of On Earth Peace Assemblies open to anyone who wanted to participate, and we developed assemblies that focused on vocational groups for peace. Doctors, lawyers, and farmers were the first three groups. One emotionally charged assembly focused on veterans for peace.

The second project, development of Brethren Encyclopedia, Inc., was related to On Earth Peace. The first meeting of the Brethren bodies at Tunker House led to more meetings that resulted in a decision in 1977 to produce *The Brethren Encyclopedia*. Incorporation papers were signed in December that year creating a board of directors with members of the Church of the Brethren, the Old German Baptist Brethren Church, the Brethren Church, the Dunkard Brethren Church, and the Fellowship of Grace Brethren Churches agreeing to cooperate in producing the Encyclopedia. Donald F. Durnbaugh, professor of church history at Bethany Theological Seminary, was the unanimous choice to be the editor. I was asked to be secretary of the board, and I have served in that capacity since then.

M. R. Zigler had wanted a Brethren encyclopedia for a long time. In the 1930s, as president of the Illinois Council of Churches, he invited Toyohiko Kagawa to speak to the conference. To describe the Church of the Brethren to Kagawa, Zigler gathered some pamphlets that had been published by the church. Kagawa looked at them and asked Zigler, "Is that the best you can do?"

I am aware that at the beginning of the work on the encyclopedia, Don Durnbaugh conferred with appropriate persons about the greatly appreciated *Mennonite Encyclopedia*, and he received advice to set limits on the length of articles before asking writers to prepare them and then to stay by those limits.

The *Brethren Encyclopedia* project has been effective in promoting understanding and cooperation among the Brethren bodies. When representatives of the Brethren bodies were ready to launch *The Brethren Encyclopedia* project, Zigler recommended to the group that they form a board of directors with the understanding that no action would be taken unless the board unanimously decided to do so. When I heard him make that recommendation, I thought to myself, "This organization will go nowhere."

Over the years, however, the opposite has been true. The board has published a number of books and has conducted four Brethren World Assemblies. The quality of fellowship and understanding among the groups has also grown tremendously. Of course, the board limits what it attempts to do, and it certainly does not seek to bring about a merger of any of the groups.

Volumes 1, 2, and 3 of *The Brethren Encyclopedia* were published in 1983-84. A Monograph Series was then established with William Eberly, a biology professor at Manchester College, as editor. The Monograph Series now has seven volumes. The newest one, published in July 2008, is based on a doctoral dissertation by Marcus Meier at Philipps University in Marburg, Germany, entitled *The Origin of the Schwarzenau Brethren*. Don Durnbaugh served on Meier's doctoral committee and felt strongly that his dissertation should be published in English. Board of directors proceeded to have Meier's German dissertation translated and published.

In 1998, the board decided to produce volume 4 of *The Brethren Encyclopedia* with Donald F. Durnbaugh and Carl F. Bowman as co-editors. However, in 2000, Bowman received an outstanding offer from the University to Virginia to engage in a research project there, which meant that he would not have time to continue working on volume 4. Claire and I had just returned from three months in India, and I was available to begin working with Durnbaugh.

After nearly five years, when we were in the final stage of completing volume 4, Durnbaugh, died unexpectedly; I worked full time for the next six months to finish the publication. It contains new and updated articles related to the time period 1980 to 2000, as well as a comprehensive index of all four volumes. Those of us involved in the

*Dale working on The Brethren Encylopedia.*

project have been rewarded by seeing knowledge of Brethren history increasing and wholesome relationships growing among Brethren bodies. Contributing significantly to that growth have been Brethren World Assemblies planned and conducted by the board of directors. The first was held at Elizabethtown College in 1992, the second at Bridgewater College in 1998, and the third at Grace College in 2003. These assemblies have involved presentations of scholarly papers. Thus, only about 200 have registered for each of those assemblies with many more attending the general sessions.

The fourth Brethren World Assembly in August 2008 coincided with the 300th anniversary of the beginning of the Brethren movement in Schwarzenau, Germany. Each of the Brethren bodies celebrated the 300th anniversary in its own way, but the celebration in Schwarzenau was planned and conducted by the Brethren Encyclopedia, Inc. board of directors because it includes representatives of all of the Brethren bodies. Don Durnbaugh had begun discussions with the people of Schwarzenau about the 300th Anniversary Celebration.

After Don died in 2005, the planning was assumed by a committee composed of Dale R. Stoffer, dean of Ashland Theological Seminary, as chair, and myself as coordinator.

A fine committee of Schwarzenau villagers, viewing this event as a celebration of their own local history as well, were as eager for it to succeed as as the Brethren were. I relied on help from Johannes Haese, a retired German pastor and widower of Gerda Hitzeman Haese (mentioned earlier), for assistance in working with the Schwarzenau Planning Committee. I made trips to Schwarzenau in May 2007 and March 2008 to meet with the Schwarzenau Committee in preparation for the anniversary event to be held on August 2-3, 2008. The 300th Anniversary Celebration (also the 2008 Brethren World Assembly) at the Eder River in Schwarzenau was a very meaningful experience with about 1,000 attendees from eighteen countries.

While the Schwarzenau event allowed the Brethren to celebrate their past, another project I more recently initiated has potential significance for the future of the church. The Brethren Student Movement in the central Shenandoah Valley is a program of the Bridgewater Church of the Brethren to bring together Brethren students attending Bridgewater College, Eastern Mennonite University, James Madison University, and Blue Ridge Community College. The students have held retreats at the beginning of recent school years and have met weekly during the year. Participation so far has been primarily by Bridgewater College students. This program is especially significant in maintaining a Brethren connection with these students as they leave their home churches for the first time.

## Conclusion

Throughout my life I have been blessed with wonderful associations. I firmly believe the way to peace has been revealed to Mennonites, Quakers, and Brethren, and that we need to continue to seek ways to involve the world in such peace, which is at the heart of Christ's message for us and humankind. Many aspects of Scripture I do not understand, but how Jesus wants followers to live is clear. That is the faith and insight we are called to live and to proclaim.

October 12, 2008
Revised November 2014

*Emmert F. Bittinger*

---

**Sociologist and Historian with a Vision**

*Deeply committed to peace and the work of the church, Emmert has a phenomenally broad and rich grasp of Brethren and Mennonite history in the Shenandoah Valley of Virginia. He helped shape the development of the Valley Brethren-Mennonite Heritage Center. He has written a host of essays ranging from family histories to his introductions and editorial work in the recently published volumes on Unionists and the Civil War Experiences in the Shenandoah Valley. In 1963, he brought his writing, pastoring, and teaching skills to Bridgewater College, where he taught until his retirement in the early '90s.*

**EMMERT F. BITTINGER**

# Heritage and Promise: Strands of an Eighty-Three-Year Journey

## A Common Heritage

In preparing my personal life story, I became more fully aware of the fallacy that all individuals are self-made and a product of their own creation. Rather, each of us is inevitably and markedly shaped by our heritage: our environments, our family backgrounds, and a vast complex of socio-cultural and religious influences. This understanding shapes the writing of this narrative. My belief is that our lives are part of the flowing stream of history and that we are impacted in remarkable ways by the innumerable movements of that current.

The request to share my story in a public setting was a surprise and at first seemed unwarranted. I had at one time considered sharing it with my immediate family but not beyond those rather restrained limits. However, after reading the previous Monday Morning Breakfast stories, I began to appreciate the effort that has been been made to gather the life histories of leaders in the Mennonite faith. Those stories were both interesting and inspiring. I was challenged by the idea of adding some of the Brethren stories. And what more suitable audience could there be than one made up of Brethren and Mennonites, spiritual descendants of Alexander Mack and Anabaptists, persecuted and martyred, of Europe in centuries preceding.

Personally, I feel a tremendous empathy with our Mennonite brothers and sisters in the faith. It has always been my belief that we as Brethren owe an unsatisfied debt of gratitude to the Mennonites of Germany and Holland for their hospitality and for the haven of safety which they generously provided to us in our time of vulnerability in our beginning years between 1708 and 1729. Had it not been for the hospitality of the Kreyfeld and Friesland Mennonites, the Brethren movement might not have survived and prospered during this time of deprivation and suffering. Even in the year of this writing, in which the Brethren have celebrated their 300th anniversary, the Mennonites in Surhuistervien, Friesland, hosted the Brethren pilgrims in one of their churches; again the Brethren had the privilege of expressing gratitude to them for the kindness and generosity they extended to us three hundred years ago.

Both my wife Esther and I have strong genealogical connections to our persecuted Anabaptist ancestors. We believe she is a descendant of the 1614 martyr, Hans Landis, whose place of persecution and death we visited this past summer along the Limmat River in Zurich. And through my Fike ancestry, I am a descendant of the Anabaptist Arnold family, some of whom were burned at the stake in the twelfth and thirteenth centuries. The sufferings and persecutions of both of our ancestral families are vividly described in the *Martyrs Mirror*, the Mennonite book of martyrs. Esther's Landis ancestors have continued in the Mennonite faith until her father was orphaned and placed with a Brethren family in early childhood. Her Landis grandfather and great grandparents are buried in the Reiff's Mennonite Church Cemetery in Washington County, Maryland. Her widowed grandmother was remarried to David Kurtz and remained a Mennonite.

## GLIMPSES OF THE BITTINGER BACKGROUND

The present is always shaped by the past. The most characteristic of those influences, of course, are those transmitted through our parents, our extended families, our churches, and the surrounding cultural environment in which we have been nourished. Unraveling that story is both a challenge and a mystery. I can only hope to get it about correct, though certainly not complete.

My branch of the family shares equally in the genetic heritage of the Bittinger and Fike families of Somerset County, Pennsylvania. On the Fike side, Peter Fike had married a daughter of Peter Livengood, a generous-hearted and wealthy Amish man who left his Amish community and joined the Dunkers who chose him as a minister. Livengood was part of that rather general movement of Amish families into the Dunker faith, which occurred in the late 1700s under somewhat obscure circumstances.

Since then, the Bittinger-Fike branch has been associated with the Church of the Brethren, formerly known as the German Baptist Brethren or Dunkers, for nearly 150 years. Bittingers had earlier been Lutheran in Somerset County. By 1812 Henry, the founder of our branch of the family, had migrated southward into Garrett County, Maryland, to the vicinity of Grantsville. There Henry's son, Joseph, was called into the ministry of the Maple Grove Church of the Brethren in the latter half of the nineteenth century.[1] Jacob Brown, a contemporary, wrote about him, "If he ever done any harm, the world never knew it. In his later years he became a 'Dunkard' preacher, not a learned one, but sincere, a shade superstitious, but a little of it helps the faith."[2] The older generation is buried in the yard of the Henry Bittinger homestead near Durst Lane, but later generations are buried in the community cemetery in the small village of Bittinger.

The Bittinger Road connects this community to Grantsville in the north and to Swanton in the south and dissects Garrett County from north to south, dividing the county into east and west. Today there are thousands of Bittingers scattered across the country. Locally their involvements have placed them in widely disparate positions ranging from the local jailhouse to the state house at Annapolis and internationally from the coal mining industry to missionary activity in Asia and Africa.

Foster Bittinger, my father, was born in 1901 into the conservative Dunker farm family of Jonas and Etta Fike Bittinger. Theirs was a typical Dunker home. Deeply religious and firmly integrated into a solid Dunker community, they were devoted and active members of the Maple Spring Church of the Brethren.

Their prosperity allowed them to purchase one of the fine farms in the area, along with additional land. Their success was gained by virtue, wise decision-making, frugality, and the Protestant work ethic. Their lifestyle was simple and temperate. Jonas was bearded and somewhat tradition bound. Both he and Etta were plain dressed and stayed well within the dress code of the church, except that once before her marriage, Etta was called before the church council and admonished to remove the extra "frills" from her newly made blouse and to dress more simply and modestly in the future.

These admonishments must have born good spiritual fruit, for by mid-life, the Maple Spring Church saw fit to elect Jonas and Etta as deacon and wife, an office in which they faithfully served the remainder of their active life. True pillars of the church, they surely fit the description of what have been called the "salt of the earth people."

Grandfather and Grandmother did not always agree on family goals. Being a superb farmer, Grandfather's goal was to buy a farm for each of his sons. Less materialistic minded, Grandmother Etta, an avid reader of the denominational magazine, the *Gospel Messenger*, wanted her children to go to college and become ministers and missionaries. Three of them did exactly that. One of the three was Foster, my father, who became a pastor. Grandmother often commented, with no little pride, that there were more than a hundred ministers and missionaries among her Bittinger and Fike relatives. As a young child, I spent several summers with them on the family farm where my love and respect for the Dunker heritage was strengthened. I still vividly remember the bearded preachers and the stern messages they delivered in the Maple Spring church in the 1930s.

Unfortunately my great grandfather, Moses Fike, who lived into his nineties, had already died, and I never had the privilege of hearing him preach. Many stories of his generation of missionary-minded Fike preachers survive. Tales of their horseback-riding missionary trips through the northern half of West Virginia were passed down to younger generations, most of whom had never ridden a horse. The accounts of these peripatetic missionary pastors never failed to interest us as they were told at the various family gatherings and picnics.

### THE FAMILY IN WHICH I GREW UP

My father had hoped to become a missionary, but some early decisions foreclosed that option. To avoid building up a college debt, he interrupted his education at Elizabethtown College to take a short pastorate at a mission post at Jordan Run, near Maysville, West Virginia, thus beginning his career as a pastor. That then became his calling.

This brief interlude between his college years was to encompass another important event in his life trajectory. While at Elizabethtown College, Foster was introduced to a young Brethren woman, Esther Sellers Bair, a niece of Elder Noah Sellers, a minister and one of the trustees of Elizabethtown College. James Sellers, her ancestor, was one of the founders of the venerable Black Rock church in York County and the first person to be buried in that church cemetery.

They were married in 1924 and began housekeeping in a log cabin provided by the Jordan Run church, near Maysville, West Virginia. In September the following year, I was born into this humble abode.

Meanwhile, Father had not abandoned the goal of completing his college education, which he achieved after transferring credits from Elizabethtown to Bridgewater College around 1929. Following this, he accepted a home mission pastorate at Browntown, Virginia, where he served a Blue Ridge mountain church, supplementing his family income by teaching and serving as principal of the elementary school in Browntown. During these years, my three sisters were born. After several years of service, Father accepted the pastorate of the Brightwood and Syria churches in Madison County, east of the Blue Ridge Mountains. The cultural and social settings of these years were crucially formative for the Bittinger children.

My mother, a devout Christian woman, had a quiet and somewhat retiring disposition. She was reared in a family that spoke only Pennsylvania Dutch. She was not one to venture very far afield in trying new ideas or methods. Her natural bent toward conservatism had a positive influence on me. It was natural for her to attempt to teach and guide rather than order and command. She needed, of course, to exercise restraint on a young boy's natural impulses and tendencies toward adventurism. She was patient and kind. I never saw her lose her cool. I recall only one verbal expression of frustration. She could say with convincing sincerity, "*Ach, nicht noch einmal*" (Oh, not again).

Although more reserved, she supported Father in his progressive ideas. They respected each other, talked things over, shared decision-making, and never had open conflict in my memory. My father's ability to patiently work things through was a trait that extended into his pastoral ministry. As a result he came to be known as a reconciler in his pastoral and district work. Also, it was an important learning experience for a young lad who admired and sought to imitate those traits and use them during his own lifetime.

As a child, people would ask me, "What do you want to be when you grow up?" My answer was always, "Be a preacher like my daddy." And I began practicing at a very young age! When I was around three, I remember playing in the chicken yard. It was shortly after Father had baptized a number of people in a stream near the church. A mother hen had recently hatched a batch of baby chicks; they were so fuzzy and tempting to play with. I caught one of them and seeing the watering trough nearby, I decided to baptize it. Then I took the poor dead or dying chick to show Mother, saying, "I did baptize it!"

As she took it from me, her face showed surprise and regret, but she did not shout at or punish me. She explained that chickens don't need baptizing, and besides they can't breathe under water and might even die! That seemed quite informative to me, and I never baptized any more chicks.

My own childhood commitment and baptism remains a vivid memory. Father was preaching at a Sunday evening service in the Browntown church and had given an altar call. I was seven years old and sitting with my two younger sisters on the front bench. The invitation had a compelling effect upon me, and I went to the altar to "give my heart to the Lord." My sisters and I were inseparable, and when they saw me go forward, they followed. Their ages were five and six. Brethren, of course, do not believe in "infant" baptism, and the question arose in the minds of the deacons and congregation as to whether we were old enough to comprehend the meaning of our decision. Consequently, Father had several sessions of teaching with us and decided that we understood well enough. We were then baptized with the other applicants in the nearby mountain stream between the church and our log cabin home in July 1933. This commitment was reaffirmed in my teenage years.

While living in the more secular environment of Madison County in the 1930s, the setting was different and challenging. We were strangers and outsiders. I was nicknamed "Preach" because my father was a minister. The schoolyard bully began to pester me. I wanted to fight back and give him a lesson, but my nonviolent teachings restrained me. Finally one day, bullyboy again began to pick on me. I was sick and tired of it, so I went over to him and quickly flipped him over my hip onto the ground. He landed on the flat of his back, and his breath was knocked out. I was ready and waiting for an attack, but he decided not to engage. I never had any more trouble with him.

This story may not be a very good illustration of the pacifist approach, and I must leave it to you to decide how badly it violates the doctrine of nonviolence! At least he was not injured. It certainly restored my self-respect and secured my standing in the group.

## BACK TO THE HOME COMMUNITY AND BEYOND

At the death of Grandfather Jonas in 1938, Father was called home to the family farm at Eglon, Preston County, West Virginia, to settle the family estate. Those three years of life on the home farm were a great contrast to the sense of strangeness and isolation that characterized our childhood in Madison County, Virginia. Here we were established in a strong Brethren community where the Bittinger family was well known. This was an ideal setting in which to absorb traditional values of church, family, and community. There I, along with my sisters, learned the ethic of hard work, how to handle responsibility, the proper care for farm animals, and the value of being trustworthy. There also, I finished elementary school under a Brethren teacher and began the first two years of high school.

Father's first love was pastoral work; therefore, during the settlement of the Bittinger estate, my father became pastor of the Terra Alta congregation and served as executive of the First District of West Virginia. In early spring 1941, my parents accepted a yoked parish at Westernport and Frostburg, Maryland. The parsonage was at Westernport, an urban community along the Potomac River, whose economic anchors were the West Virginia Pulp and Paper Mill and two railroads, the Baltimore and Ohio and the Western Maryland.

The people, the schools, and the occupations were quite a contrast from the rural and relatively isolated setting of the Eglon community. During summers while in high school, I worked at the paper mill and on weekends at the local grocery store. These experiences increased my understanding of some of the issues of employee-supervisor relations and of the values and attitudes of working class people of other faiths. Also I gained the satisfaction of receiving a paycheck for my labors, although the hourly pay at the grocery store was only thirty-three and a third cents an hour. While at Westernport, I finished high school and began college at Potomac State at nearby Keyser.

These were years of crisis for the nation. In December 1941, the Japanese struck Pearl Harbor, stirring a massive U.S. war effort. It was also a time of testing for the Historic Peace Churches and their doctrine of nonresistance. True to his beliefs, Father did not ignore the issue of war in his sermons. Somehow he was able to continue to uphold the gospel of peace without alienating his congregation. Two young men of the church stood firm and registered as COs (conscientious cbjectors to war). Those that registered for the military draft were still welcomed and would attend church when on leave. His example of courage and principle taught me to understand the power of a quiet and tactful witness in the face of a community with quite different values.

Father would often engage guest speakers on peace issues at the Westernport church. During the war years, we often hosted speakers from the Fellowship of Reconciliation and other peace organizations. These exposures helped to deepen and strengthen my understandings of the peace churches and their stance on war.

In 1943, just before I left for college, the Brethren church called me to the ministry by a vote of the congregation. At that stage of my development I had never considered a different vocation. Later that same year, I became of draft age and took the conscientious objector position and was deferred. Following the year at Potomac State College, I entered Bridgewater College in 1944 and graduated on an accelerated program in summer 1945 at age nineteen.

The year at Bridgewater College was life changing in several ways. It was here that I met Esther Landis, my future wife, and where we began a life-long friendship. Living on a Brethren college campus provided a view of wider horizons and many opportunities. My exposure to broader fields of learning, along with the formation of many lasting friendships, challenged and exposed me to new activities and involvements.

Of course, being a student on a ministerial trajectory put me in association with other ministerial students and a greater variety of students from a larger geographic region. I became president of the "Clericus Club" of ministerial students and formed new relationships on campus, at the local Brethren congregation, and at nearby churches where I, along with other ministerial students, were frequently called on to preach. Dr. Charles C. Wright, the college dean, challenged me to consider graduate school and a college teaching career. I did not consider it seriously at the time. Instead, that fall I began my first year at Bethany Seminary.

Esther was a daughter of Rev. Harvey Landis, a teacher near Tampa, Florida. He was also a devoted free minister. He had been released from his public school teaching contract because of his refusal to register young men into military service at his school. This was a time of intense patriotism at the beginning of World War II, and his refusal to perform what was defined as a "patriotic service to the nation," was deemed a sufficient cause for his dismissal. He then secured employment at Ferrum College in Virginia.

Esther was a sophomore at Bridgewater College when I entered Bethany Seminary fall 1945. At the end of my first year at seminary, I accepted a yoked pastorate of five churches in West Virginia. Our courtship continued that year, and in June 1947 we were married. The following fall, we both enrolled in courses at the seminary in Chicago.

## SOCIAL AND THEOLOGICAL ORIENTATION IMBIBED FROM MY FAMILY

My father's influence on me was profound. Although he was a product of his time, his liberal education at a Brethren college had greatly modified his outlook and created in him a thirst for knowledge. He was well-read and built up a fine library. *The Christian Century* was one of several progressive magazines that helped to shape his thought and ministry.

As a farmer-preacher during the depression years, he subscribed to the *Progressive Farmer* magazine and sought to put into practice suggestions that seemed appropriate to his needs. In the 1930s he was the first in his rural community to plant soybeans because they fixed nitrogen in the soil. I can remember the disparaging comments of some of the neighbor farmers in Madison County to his use of a newfangled cattle guard to avoid the need to stop and open a gate. Neighbors thought his cows would fall in and break their legs. His willingness to change with new knowledge and adopt new methods was a good example to his children and church members and conditioned us to assume a similar attitude.

In race relations Father was far ahead of his neighbors and community, sometimes to the point of surprising them. When Father was pastor of the Jordan Run church, he visited the black community and cultivated relationships with its members. Once while living at Browntown, he asked me to accompany him on a visit to a black man who was dying from cancer. Such interracial contacts were unheard of in this segregated community. The fact that this white minister would visit and pray with him brought the black man to tears.

Father also was willing to exchange labor with our black farmer neighbor in Madison County, something none of the other white farmers was willing to do. When Mr. Humes would work with Father on our farm, Father would insist that he share the family meal and sit at the same table with our family. At first Mr. Humes consented to this cautiously, but over time he felt more comfortable doing so.

This did not work, however, when white neighbors were also helping with the threshing. He well knew that his white neighbors would refuse to sit at the same table with Mr. Humes. Consequently, on those occasions Mr. Humes ate in the kitchen with my mother who waited on the table.

I distinctly remember the disgust I felt when several counties in southeastern Virginia closed their schools rather then integrate them in the early 1960s and when the Brethren Camp Bethel in southern Virginia was disrupted by upset parents who had learned that two young black people were attending. This latter experience caused my father to organize interracial camps at Storer College, a school for blacks, at Harpers Ferry. My father also pioneered in implementing interracial camps at Camp Galilee in the 1940s. These experiences taught me to respect and value interracial experiences and accept the notion of the common humanity of all peoples.

Father's progressivism was notable in other areas as well. For example, when he would travel mountain roads on his pastoral visits, he sometimes met moonshiners on horseback carrying their illegal product. Most of the illegal whiskey in our area was made by isolated poor families living high in mountain valleys. They had no real source of money for essential needs of their home and family. Some of these families he knew. Others he wished to visit. In these occasional encounters, Father would offer a friendly greeting to which they cautiously responded, but he never reported them. His interest was in creating trust, with the hope that he would be able to minister to them. And indeed, several members of these families did attend church and become members.

His generous and tolerant demeanor was recognized and greatly appreciated by his family, church, and community. It enabled him to gain entry into many mountain homes which otherwise would have been closed. It also had a memorable effect on our own attitudes as we children grew up in the home.

In a contrasting style, another minister, whose origins also go back to the Maple Spring congregation, preached so strongly and bombastically against the moonshiners that they tried to intimidate the minister and shut down the services. They came one night during church services and set off dynamite which blew out the windows. Another night, they came with guns to the church door and made open threats. Since these did not close down the evangelistic services, they came late one night and burned down the church, effectively shutting down the Brethren presence in that immediate area. Ironically, this isolated community had originally been Quaker, and the nearby Miller family had been one of its leading families. But in the 150 years since their settlement there, they had lost their Quaker heritage and had absorbed the secular values of the mountain community in which they lived.

Father's preaching style also influenced me. In his ministry, he was able to identify the many ways people, and sometimes their ministers, would select from among the Scriptures what they were willing to observe while other obviously relevant Scriptures would be ignored or even subjected to perverse or prejudiced interpretations. In this, he was willing to take the risk of applying his own insights as well as the doctrines of the church in his preaching. He often called attention to positions locally or nationally in which scriptural teachings were being ignored or violated. During my own fifteen years of pastoral ministry, I too often followed this pattern and was quite comfortable in assuming a progressive stance.

One example of this was his attitude and interpretation of Scripture in regard to warfare. His ministry at Westernport coincided with World War II. Some ministers of other denominations in town used their pulpits to drum up support for war and heap praise and honor on their young men going to war. In contrast, Father spoke against the evils and consequences of war, stressing the need to try other more peaceful ways of engaging in international relations. He didn't hesitate to call attention, though tactfully, to policies that sharply contradicted New Testament teachings. He was somehow able to present these inconsistencies not with a condemning approach but in a reasoned and logical manner that did not alienate the congregation.

I accepted these experiences and activities as worthy, right, and good, and they became a part of my being. More importantly, perhaps, I also accepted the rightness of calculated activism as a method of expressing progressive ideas and promoting social change.

### FACING THE TENSIONS BETWEEN SCIENCE AND RELIGION

Out of this background, I was able to realize that the worldview of the biblical writers was based in a pre-scientific and superstitious era, a time in which people believed in spirits and devils, and the laws of science and natural "cause and effect" were little known. I had no difficulty in accepting the established findings of science, such as the evolution of life and the ways the planets and stars were formed over eons of time. My interest shifted to focus more on how the facts and knowledge of science could be integrated into, or harmonized with, scriptural and theological truth.

I became convinced that the scientifically established facts pertaining to the physical world could not truly be in contradiction with a valid religious worldview. I chose to believe that the increase of knowledge on both sides of this troublesome issue would ultimately reveal a natural compatibility and harmony with each other.

This approach led me into the belief that both religious thought as well as scientific thought are continuing endeavors. Though these two modes of thought seem contradictory to many today, I am inclined to believe that they will move on converging trajectories toward a common understanding and a harmonious view of the universe in which we live. Obviously our folk conceptions and pre-scientific views of creation and evolution will need to change. I believe there is progress in this direction, but I recognize that this goal may not soon be achieved. The average fundamentalist Christian, especially in our southern states, still appears to be far from achieving a reconciliation of attitudes and views about science and religion.

To me, these ideas never implied a necessity to reject belief in God and his creative and redemptive activity. This approach does not need to deny that God is the Creator and Lord of the universe. Rather, it implies to me that God, in his great wisdom and power, has worked in even more mysterious ways than we have yet been able or willing to understand. It also seems to be true that as "earthen vessels" we often fail to accurately hear and interpret the light that God reveals to us.

Perhaps human knowledge can never fully encompass the wonders of the universe, the way in which it was created, and how it all evolved. Scientists who study the "big bang," the supposed beginning of the universe, are not able, and perhaps never will be able, to see fully what came before or where all that energy and mass came from. There is plenty of mystery out there, and the solution of each mystery leads only to new and wondrous surprises!

Perhaps at this point, I need to pause to make clear my aim in this narrative. I am sure that the worldview and the religious orientation in my home setting contributed greatly to the formation of my worldview. As I look back, I also realize that the mental process of reconstructing the meaning of these events, now more than a half century past, may contribute to the error of reading back in time meanings or intentions that have developed in my mind years later, one of the typical problems often seen in *ex post facto* analysis.

Nevertheless, the facts seem accurate to me. Certainly they are infused with insights I was not capable of having for many years. But it seems obvious to me that these experiences and educational exposures in my childhood and youth have contributed in major ways to the formation of my own character and outlook. They became the basis on which I was able to make sense of my experience in college, university, in the world of work, and in the construction of my own worldview. My background enabled me to reconcile to my own mind's reasonable satisfaction the seemingly contradictory approaches of science and religion and of our intellectual and physical relations with perceived reality. Of course, this worldview necessitated the rejection of religious fundamentalism. To me, such an approach seems to imply that the religious view is necessarily in conflict with science, or that one cancels out the other.

In my own thinking, to set religion against science and its methods of understanding the material world is to inevitably alienate a great portion of the educated and informed population of the planet. Religious thought needs to accommodate to the scientific method and the generally accepted findings of science. To fail in accomplishing this difficult task will strengthen the secular view of religion as an invalid and backward endeavor. Religion should never allow itself to be seen as an impediment to knowledge. Were this to happen, educated and well-informed persons would not be able to take religion seriously without bracketing out the contradictions.

## The Years of Pastoral Ministry

My second pastorate was a part-time one at the Flower Hill church within commuting distance to the University of Maryland. This allowed me the opportunity to obtain a master's degree in sociology. At the end of that period we returned to Bethany Seminary, where I completed degree requirements.

In 1951, we accepted a call to serve a parish in Frederick County, Maryland, that consisted of the Pleasant View church in a rural setting and the Sharpsburg church located in a small town at the edge of the famed Antietam Battlefield. This ministry continued for seven years. The Sharpsburg congregation originally met in the now famous Dunker church on the Battlefield, until the congregation outgrew the building in 1898 and built a new one in the town. Also during this period the rebuilding of the Dunker church took place, and I participated in the dedication service.

These churches of my pastorate were old and stable. They treated the pastor's family with great love and respect, which in turn was much reciprocated. Consequently, these were happy years for us. It was in Maryland that our three daughters were born and where the eldest began school. The beloved and aging elder in charge of the congregation was always supportive and never critical of the efforts of their youthful pastor.

My ministry tended to focus then on meeting the needs of the families at their own level as they passed through life stages from birth, youth, family life, aging and death. While I sought to broaden and enlarge their interpretations of Scripture as it related to their world, I mostly avoided the complex issues which had so interested me in college and seminary yet were alien to the members. The sermons I preached tended to focus on the New Testament and on living as Christ taught and modeled. While in this pastorate, I was ordained into the full ministry, which at that time was called the Eldership.

Following the war, the church sponsored an intercultural student exchange program to foster a better understanding between nations. Consequently we applied to host a German exchange student for a year. This experience was wholesome for our young daughters and also for the local church. We have kept up our contacts with Maria and her family and have visited them in Germany on multiple occasions. The exchange continued into the next generation with her daughters visiting our home many years later.

Our church in Maryland also supported the denomination's program of refugee resettlement. Sponsoring two families was a broadening experience for the congregation as well as the community. (Incidentally, our support of the refugee resettlement program continued in Bridgewater, where we provided shelter for two Kurdish brothers who a year or two later moved to California. Over the years, the Bridgewater congregation has helped resettle more than thirty families. The congregation now owns a special house reserved for housing refugee families during their transition into American society.)

In Maryland I also served on the district board, on the still functioning elders body, and on several committees. I was elected three times to serve as district moderator and twice as a member of the annual conference standing committee. Our ties and relations with these "salt of the earth people" have continued through the years, and we have enjoyed the homecomings and special events to which we were invited since we moved to Virginia.

In 1957 I returned to the University of Maryland for further graduate study. Following that, I accepted the pastorate at the Long-Meadow church near Hagerstown, Maryland, where we spent a pleasant and satisfying three years. Then in 1963, President Warren D. Bowman called me to teach at Bridgewater College, a position I held until my retirement in 1988.

## Reflections on Teaching

In my twenty-five year teaching career in sociology and anthropology, both at the University of Maryland and at Bridgewater College I never hesitated to emphasize the importance of the methods and findings of science, while suggesting to my students that they needed to be fully exposed to discoveries in all fields of knowledge, including the liberal arts.

At the same time, I stressed that they should have an inquisitive mind, that they should read, learn, and discover, even though they might not at this early point in their lives feel able to fully understand or accept all they were learning. I tried to help them to see that it was important to come to grips with the issues that their liberal education posed for them, and that in so doing they would become more fully human and more fully engaged with the world in which they were living.

One of the significant goals of this approach for students was that it would enhance their ability to be comfortable in two worlds, the religious and the scientific, or the sacred and the secular; and to have a deep appreciation for both, while understanding that both are works in progress.

During the early years of my teaching career, I was fortunate to benefit from two summer school experiences at the University of Virginia. When the college desired to expand the cultural anthropology curriculum, I was able to strengthen the course offerings by taking courses on the cultures of India and of China at the University of Virginia in 1965 and 1966. Again in 1967 I was fortunate to obtain a place in the Summer Institute in Anthropology at the Boulder Campus of the University of Colorado supported by the National Science Foundation. These postdoctoral programs further enhanced my understanding of the rich diversity among the many cultures and societies of the world.

## The Focus on Writing

In 1968, while I was still teaching, the denomination, anticipating the impending anniversary year of the founding of the nation, saw a need to emphasize the history and heritage of the church. I was requested to write a book to meet that need. *Heritage and Promise* was published in 1970, and a second revised edition was published thirteen years later. It has been kept in print until recent times.

The year 1986 brought new opportunities and a challenge. The West Marva District[3] of the Church of the Brethren asked me to write a history of the churches of that large region. My father, in 1945, had published the first history of one part of that region, and it seemed a natural choice for them to turn to me for this task.

Quite aware that more than a dozen district histories had been written, and that they had sold poorly with large numbers remaining unsold, a different approach seemed desirable. I decided to strike a new note by including the stories of the founding families as well as the history of each church. I realized, however, this would require the identification of these families in their previous locations in Pennsylvania and Maryland along with the tracing of their migration into the mountain state. Because the geographic area to be included had once been divided into three separate districts with around seventy-five churches, the task was enormous. The project took the better part of five years. District officials began to wonder if the work would ever be completed. A local, well-published church historian told me he could easily have accomplished that job in a single summer! I did not share my feeling with him that this might represent a typical prejudice against the mountain state and that they deserved a thoroughly written history.

Titled *Allegheny Passage: Churches and Families, West Marva District, Church of the Brethren, 1752-1990*, the 875-page book was finally published in 1990. It was sold out in about a year. A second edition came out a year later, and it also sold out within twelve months. It was again reprinted and the supply was exhausted in a year. Requests for this book continue to the present time, although it has been out of print for nearly fifteen years. By the year 2010, the churches of the district were populated by a new generation, and the need for reprinting *Allegheny Passage* was evident. The volume will soon be out in a new edition.

The years since its publication have kept me busy responding to queries from family descendants all over the United States seeking additional information about their ancestral connections. The family history research has continued, and it is satisfying to help people in the discovery of the mysteries of their family's wanderings. In addition, I have expanded my interest to include families that settled in the Shenandoah Valley and other places. These include the families of Arnold, Bowman, Bittinger, Fike, Landis, and many others. My research collection now comprises several hundred Brethren and Mennonite family folders in which families are traced from the port of entry in Philadelphia to their places of settlement in Pennsylvania, Maryland, Virginia, and some of the western states. Some of these studies have been published in *Pennsylvania Mennonite Heritage* and *Mennonite Family History* magazines as well as in *Brethren Life and Thought*.

As one of the original members of the Forum for Religious Studies at Bridgewater College, I was involved in the planning of their periodic scholarly conferences and in editing several of their publications. One of the major events of the forum was the planning and implementing of a *Festschrift* in honor of the late Brethren historian and scholar Donald F. Durnbaugh. Although he carried a major role in planning the 300th anniversary events of the denomination, his premature death prevented him from seeing the fulfillment of his efforts. I served on this college committee for twenty years after my retirement.

My most recent project has been in partnership with two other Anabaptist historians, David Rodes and Norman Wenger. This was a ten-year project that involved the collecting, compiling, editing, and preparation of six lengthy volumes about the *Unionists and the Civil War Experience in the Shenandoah Valley*. The final volume, dealing with the loyal Unionist citizens of the city of Harrisonburg and vicinity, was published in 2012.

These volumes tell the stories of Brethren and Mennonite families and their peace witness and loyalist stance during the Civil War. Their struggles to be faithful to the nonviolent interpretations of the Scriptures as they understood them and to survive the horrible tragedies of the fratricidal War Between the States are gripping and inspiring. Union loyalists of other faiths are also included and tell of their similar struggles and persecutions as they tried to survive in a hostile and aggressive pro-Confederate environment.

These little known experiences deserve wider recognition. The Valley Research Associates, consisting of David Rodes, Norman Wenger, and me, have labored sacrificially at our own expense to get these stories into print. Once these books are fully discovered, they will significantly alter and expand the story of the Civil War in the Shenandoah Valley. These half dozen years of co-laboring with these devoted men have been rewarding and satisfying, and they have enlarged the appreciation of our respective Brethren and Mennonite heritages here in this southern setting.

## SPECIAL ACTIVITIES AND INTERESTS

The years that I have served on the Brethren-Mennonite Heritage Center board have been a blessing. It was a great pleasure and privilege to work on the planning and development of this place of witness on Garber Church Road in Harrisonburg, Virginia. Not the least of these joys has been the opportunity to observe and participate in a major collaboration between Brethren and Mennonites on telling our similar and related Anabaptist stories. It has been a long-lasting and mutually beneficial effort whose result will be a great step forward in our shared task of witness bearing. I believe that our extended and successful period of close collaboration in a common project is unique and unprecedented.

Growing up in a pastor-historian family contributed to my early interest in Elder Kline of Broadway, Virginia—the famed Civil War martyr-minister, the peripatetic, horse-back-riding servant of the Brethren Church. Although not widely recognized, Elder Kline in the early 1850s attempted to persuade the Brethren Annual Conference to support teams of traveling missionaries by paying the costs of their travel expenses. In these efforts he failed due to opposition from conservatives who believed paying preachers would compromise the integrity of preaching the gospel. He was the first to call for such support. Many favored his proposal, but the Civil War and his own assassination in 1864 interrupted this effort. In the end, however, his proposal prevailed, and financially supported missions among the Brethren were organized in the 1870s.

The Bittinger home church, Maple Spring at Eglon, West Virginia, was founded by Elder Kline in 1855 in the home of my great-great-grandfather, Peter Fike. Kline had been on one of his numerous missionary trips into the mountain state. His diary recorded not only dozens of trips into the mountains but also the number of miles traveled each year. In his most active years, he would travel four or five thousand miles on horseback. His renown is derived not only from his missionary endeavors. Among other leadership roles, he also served four times as moderator of the General Conference of the Brethren. For many years I had dreamed of organizing a riding group and replicating some of his missionary journeys.

The opportunity came in 1997 when Kline's home church, Linville Creek, at Broadway, Virginia, held a celebration of the two-hundredth anniversary of his birth. That year I led an eight-day horseback riding trek across the mountains and valleys of West Virginia to the Beaver Run and Knobley churches which Kline had visited a dozen and a half times. We established a pattern each year thereafter of visiting churches whose origins reach back to early visits by Elder Kline between the years of 1835 and 1864.

In these churches we provide an evening program in exchange for lodging for our tired bodies and horses. Our riders share stories of Kline's dual medical and pastoral ministry and his adventures on his horse, Nell. These visits bring to life the long forgotten past in which Elder Kline visited their ancestral families and held services in their homes. A goodly number of churches in this area owe their existence to his sacrificial efforts in providing spiritual nurture to their families in earlier years. The leadership of the riding group is now being assumed with enthusiasm by younger members and assures that this Kline Riders ministry will continue.

Collecting and reading old books have always been of great interest to me, especially those related to Brethren history. In the 1950s, I began to collect books published by and about Brethren. By means of advertising for used books in various periodicals, I was able to collect most of the several hundred books of this genre, including some quite valuable books from the Saur and Ephrata Cloister printing establishments, dating back to the early 1700s. The collection is fascinating in its variety and consists of books published during the time when Brethren were discovering their history and defending their doctrines by holding debates with leaders of other denominations. Great crowds of people would gather for such debates in the latter half of the 1800s, some lasting as long as a week. One of these debates attracted a crowd of 11,000 people. Usually they were reported in great detail in the daily press and then published. I was able to collect most of the books ever published by our denomination.

The late 1800s was also a time when Brethren became awakened to the larger world beyond our country's borders. Missionaries would return home and tell stories of their experiences in foreign lands and exotic cultures. One of the most intrepid of these travelers was D. L. Miller, who repeatedly traveled to foreign lands and circled the globe. His highly illustrated travel books make a quite unique collection of pictures and travel experiences during the late 1800s. These and other books on doctrine and church life document how the Brethren lived and believed one hundred fifty years ago.

I am now in the process of donating my book collections. Around seventy-five of the rare and precious German Language imprints from the Saur and Ephrata presses in Pennsylvania have gone to the Young Center at Elizabethtown College. This organization is focused on general Anabaptist history and culture. Some miscellaneous items have gone to the Brethren Heritage Center at Brookville, Ohio.

In recent years I have indulged my long-term special interest in physics and astronomy by purchasing and reading a few of the latest books in those fields. The nature of the universe both at the atomic and the astronomic levels have always filled me with amazement and wonder. The universe in all its vast dimensions surpasses the ability of the human mind to fully comprehend God's work of creation.

Keeping up with the changing world and new technology is a challenge. My wife and I try to stay abreast by attending Elderhostels. Travel remains on our priority list, especially when integrated with Anabaptist history or family connections. Joining those who in summer 2008 celebrated the 300th Anniversary of the Brethren beginnings at Schwarzenau, Germany, was an inspiring experience.

Hiking and tennis are a couple of our favorite activities. Some of my interests are gradually being passed to our children as they take interest in family history and stories. I have now given up my beekeeping hobby, but one daughter is continuing the two-hundred-year-old family tradition.

This story would be incomplete and deficient without recognizing the sixty-eight years of faithful and loving support my wife Esther has given my various endeavors. She has endured many trips to courthouses, libraries, and isolated and neglected cemeteries in three states, plus the never-ending task of proofreading. Likewise, I have supported her successful career of public school teaching as a reading specialist. She also has tutored refugees, served as a Disaster Child Care volunteer, organized exercise groups and blood pressure clinics for our congregation, and sponsored an older adult work camp at Brethren Woods. Recently she has been serving on the Curator Committee for the Valley Brethren-Mennonite Heritage Center.

Not the least of our joys has been the satisfaction of observing our three daughters and their husbands as they create their own roles in family, church, and community life as teachers and professionals. Daughter Marion worked as project manager for endangered languages at Rosetta Stone and traveled the continent recording and preserving disappearing Indian languages. Daughter Lori Lineweaver carries an active role as webmaster for the Valley Brethren-Mennonite Heritage Center and local church, and her husband David is treasurer of the Heritage Center. Daughter Millie Arnett is a librarian in the Pennsylvania school system. Our family circle has now enlarged to include six grandchildren and four great-grandchildren.

As we approach our tenth decade, Esther and I continually give thanks to our heavenly Father for many years of life, good health, and the blessings granted through family, church, and community. So long as we are able, we will continue to serve him who gives life and hope to all his children here on this beautiful and bountiful earth.

November 2008<br>Revised April 2015

## Notes

1. Wayne Bittinger, *The Bittinger, Bittner, Biddinger, and Bidinger Families and their Kin of Garrett County, Maryland* (Parsons, W.Va.: McClain Printing Company, 1986), 3-18.

2. Ibid., 3ff.

3. This district comprises western Maryland and the northern half of West Virginia.

*Carl S. Keener*

### A Botanist-Theologian, Man of Faith

*A campus provocateur during his undergraduate years at Eastern Mennonite College, Carl Keener's incisive and curious mind continued to ask the tough questions about evolution, human sexuality, the nature of God, and God's relationship to (the rest of) the universe. Here is a biologist whose love for God is inseparable from his care for plants and animals. Carl is as concerned about the church as the world of academia and as passionate about how we live our lives (ethics) as about what we believe (theology).*

## CARL S. KEENER

# *The Evolution of My Years: A Stream of Life in Process*

### EARLY YEARS

The late Yale philosopher Brand Blanshard recorded in his autobiography, "Wordsworth was able to write, 'The thought of our past years in me doth breed perpetual benediction.' The thought of mine does not" (Schilpp 1980, 3). In some respects my early years parallel Blanshard's—rough going in the Keener household, eking out an existence on a severely run-down farm, and finding my way in life as a foster child, later as an adoptee.

I was certainly not born with a silver spoon in my mouth; in fact, I was born without any spoon. Like Tania in Boris Pasternak's *Dr. Zhivago*, I was a *besprizornaia*, a rootless, neglected infant. I was born to an unmarried mother on April 12, 1931, and four months later I was "given" to what was then the Mennonite Children's Home near Millersville, Pennsylvania. I remained there for a few weeks before being "chosen" as a foster child to live with Amos and Dorothy Keener, who were childless at the time.

Through no fault of their own, my foster parents had to leave the family farm near Lititz, Pennsylvania, for a small farm just south of Brickerville, a move that meant going from a house with central heat-ing, electricity, indoor plumbing, and a bathroom, to a house that had none of these amenities. It meant going from a consolidated school (Rothsville High, from which my dad graduated) to Speedwell School, a one-room schoolhouse in Elizabeth Township. So there I was, not knowing my roots, living in a strange place, and putting up with really cold nights in an unheated bedroom. But there were woods nearby, a pasture to roam in, and books to read.

Thus I became, even at an early age, an independent person without close playmates. In a sense, my life has been like a river with many small tributaries feeding into the main stream whose course over the years has helped shape me into the person I was to become. The streams feeding into my main river included many decisions made by other persons, and these channels were quite beyond my control.

In any case, I remained a foster child until the age of twelve, when I was legally adopted by Amos and Dorothy Keener. But by that time they had a biological daughter, Edna, who eventually became a nurse. They were poor and gentle folk with traditional values, although unfortunately they both suffered greatly from depression. As they aged, they did not become bitter, a lesson I hope to have learned. My dad had a well-worn Bible that was falling apart when he died at age ninety-three. What should be done with the Bible? One doesn't throw it into the trash bin, and burning it seemed quite out of the question. So as a last rite, before the coffin lid was closed for the last time, Chad Scott, his oldest great-grandson, placed the Bible in the coffin, there to be buried along with his great-granddad. Thus my dad with his Bible—his Bread of Life—rests in peace in the Hess Cemetery near Lititz, Pennsylvania.

I made a formal declaration to follow Christ when evangelist John Hiestand conducted a series of revival meetings at the Hammer Creek church in 1941. Catechism classes followed based on Daniel Kauffman's *One Thousand Questions and Answers* (Kauffman 1941). This instruction steered me on the straight and narrow way, and I grew up as a rather good boy, at least for a while. I enjoyed going to special congregational meetings and hearing the better speakers in Lancaster Conference orate. And as a youth, I read and followed Lancaster Conference's *Rules and Discipline*. The less said about some of my teen years, the better; somehow I muddled through. For one year in my early teens, I attended Lancaster Mennonite High School. The alternative was studying various texts at home and then passing selected tests issued by the Pennsylvania Department of Public Instruction. I chose this route, which earned me a high school equivalent diploma from the Commonwealth of Pennsylvania.

In the fall of 1949, I wound up at Eastern Mennonite College (EMC, now EMU) as an eighteen-year-old. The library there was my haven. I read what I wanted to and took the required courses as a sideline. But what windows were opened! Existentialism was in the air, and for a while I breathed those heady fumes. I soaked up Professor D. Ralph Hostetter's biology classes and delved into the mysteries of botany and plant life. I even tried dating a couple of girls, but that pursuit went nowhere.

As I intimated above, a number of rivulets fed into my river of life; hence, as an interlude, let me single out several that had been an influence by the time I started college. As a lad, one of my favorite uncles was Martin Metzler, who seemed to know a lot. I asked him one day how far the sun was from the earth. His reply is as clear to me as yesterday: 93,000,000 miles. Uncle Martin had a small telescope that he lent me, and I spent many fascinating nights stargazing.

Speaking of stars, EMC's late Professor M. T. Brackbill contributed articles on stars for the *Youth's Christian Companion* during the years 1943-44. I avidly read these and wrote him a letter in appreciation, to which he replied that he would be sending me an "Astra Guide" with his compliments. This was heady stuff for a thirteen year-old, and I followed the initial exchange with several more letters.

Although I didn't go into astronomy for an academic career, my interest in astronomy was certainly catalyzed by Brackbill's friendship. He was one of my early mentors, and his responses to my letters of inquiry set a standard I always hope to emulate. In one of his replies, Brackbill wrote, "I am wondering what book or books you have been reading that have stirred up in your mind these questions in modern or atomic physics.... Perhaps you can be content with partial knowledge on these topics until you can study advanced physics and astrophysics. But I do not want to discourage you in your reading. It won't hurt you to read things to make your mind stretch" (postcard dated September 5, 1945).

Another pursuit of natural history was studying wild flowers, an interest bolstered by a teacher in elementary school but especially by my mother. In my mid-teens, I bought Robinson and Fernald's *Gray's New Manual of Botany* (Robinson and Fernald 1908) and began the study of the flora of the northeastern United States. As it turned out, Asa Gray, the author of the first five editions of the *Manual*, was my academic great-great-great-grandfather. Moreover, as a staunch Christian, he had an indelible impact on my life. Although trained as a physician, Gray saw his work in plant science as a Christian calling (Dupree 1959:45-46). One of America's finest systematic botanists and a friend and defender of Darwin set a standard for all later work on floras of the United States. I am proud to own him as an academic ancestor. Thus it was that, in my teens, wild flowers became my friends—violets, spring beauties, hepaticas, bloodroots, meadowsedges. I can still recall my excitement at having identified the Jagged Chickweed (*Holosteum umbellatum* L.), at one time known only from New Jersey and the hills around Lancaster, Pennsylvania.

A key influence—certainly more than a rivulet—were the communities I experienced as a boy and later as a youth. The extended Keener and Hershey families and my church communities, especially gifted Sunday school teachers, all accepted me as a person despite my being biologically an outsider. As I sat with Grandpa Henry Hershey on the "amen" benches in the Lititz Mennonite Church, he would press pink candies into my hand. This was a real bonding experience for a five-year-old foster grandchild. In those moments I was one of them, and I never forgot the lesson.

Howard Charles, then pastor of the Lititz Mennonite Church, was also a mentor who took time to answer my questions. He taught a winter Bible course on Jeremiah that still sticks in my mind. One time I asked him what the difference was between a PhD and a ThD. Howard, a consummate scholar, would eventually feel the call to teach Bible at Goshen Biblical Seminary. There were those who thought he should remain at Lititz, but my Grandpa Hershey believed that such calls should be taken seriously. In my mid-teens I read Guy Hershberger's *War, Peace, and Nonresistance* (Hershberger 1944), which influenced me to follow a path of nonviolence.

Some of my peers wondered about the value of an education. Several of us corralled Richard Danner, a conservative Lancaster Conference bishop, to ask him about the issue. He replied that we should get as much schooling as we needed. I resolved that I needed a lot!

As a youth, I was one of the song leaders in our congregation (Hammer Creek, in northern Lancaster County). In those days, song leaders stood up front for the Sunday school hour but sat down for the worship service that followed. We really wanted to lead the hymns standing up front for both services, so one day we approached one of the pastors about it, and he said we would have to consult the deacon who seemed to have the final say in such matters. The deacon, as it turned out, didn't like the song leaders parading from the back of the sanctuary to lead the songs, whereupon we said we would be willing to sit in the front pews. Deal closed—we could stand up to lead the hymns. In this instance, I learned that compromises can work!

I am a Mennonite Christian today largely because of the caring communities that nurtured and accepted me. As UC-Berkeley philosopher John Searle stated, "one overriding question in contemporary philosophy [is:] How do we fit in?" (Searle 2007:4). Although Searle's statement covers a broad front dealing primarily with the emergence of mind, for purposes of this essay certainly one important question has to do with our self-conception, our self-identity. There can be no doubt that my various communities helped me "fit in," to discover who I was. In summarizing my life to this point, three aspects stand out as irretrievably shaping the stream of my life: the importance of a caring and nurturing family and church communities, the role of mentors, and the opportunities to learn first-hand about natural history.

## THE MID-TWENTIES

The next phase of my life includes my first two years of college at EMC, I-W service (an alternative to the military), and teaching in two Christian day schools. I began my collegiate experience at EMC in fall 1949. Two years later I was short of funds, so I decided to teach in a Christian day school to earn enough money to go to summer school and to eventually graduate with my class. Graduating with the class of 1953 didn't happen. After beginning my second year of teaching at Myerstown Mennonite Christian Day School, I was drafted and wound up as a janitor, later orderly, at the South Mountain TB Sanitarium, located east of Chambersburg, Pennsylvania. This was a very different world from my more or less closeted experiences within Mennonite communities.

During my two years of alternative service, I experienced a failed engagement and then fell in love with Gladys Swartz. Following my release from I-W service, I resumed teaching in the Hess Christian Day School near Lititz, Pennsylvania. On September 3, 1955, Gladys and I got married and together set off to EMC so I could finish my college education. (I should say here that my marriage to Gladys was a revelation in what love can mean in a relationship. By accepting me as a person without known roots, she taught me that life is a journey in love, faith, and an unrelenting courage to face an unknown future. Whatever I have become, I owe an immense debt of gratitude to Gladys.)

In those days, I was absorbing the thought of a number of evangelical thinkers such as Edward J. Carnell, Carl F. H. Henry, Bernard Ramm, and Wilbur Smith. Their emphasis on apologetically defended propositional truths of the Christian faith appealed to me at the time, but over the years, this way of "defending the faith" had increasingly less appeal.

As a student at EMC, one of the intellectual challenges was evolution. We were encouraged to read carefully those authors who accepted evolution. Indeed, for many years, evolution was a censured subject within Mennonite circles. Daniel Kauffman's *Doctrines of the Bible* (Kauffman 1952) clearly stated that "no naturalist has ever been able to prove that since [the time of the original creation] any form of life has developed from lower into higher species" (38). More specifically, "God created the different species or kinds of flesh (1 Cor. 15:29), and the theory of evolution from one species to another is both unscriptural and unscientific" (41). Even worse, evolution "is but a waystation on the road to atheism" (42). Darwin even came in for a critical comment: "Although Darwin is still held in high esteem by evolutionists generally, his fondest theories, like the 'survival of the fittest' and 'natural selection,' have already been discredited" (44).

Another book that greatly influenced me in my late teen years was Chester K. Lehman's *The Inadequacy of Evolution as a World View* (Lehman 1933). I had bought a copy when I was seventeen and absorbed its contents by the time I was a freshman in college. Lehman carefully discussed the meaning of evolution and wrote at length concerning the alleged evidences for evolution. Evidences counted, and Lehman bluntly stated that the person "who alleges a fact must prove it" (25).

Moreover, Lehman persistently argued for the "fixity" of species. In reviewing the Genesis creation accounts, Lehman maintained that "after their kind" is taken to mean that at "creation the species of animals and plants were fixed. Life is not in a state of flux" (240). Lehman closed his book with these words:

> I would fain repeat that the theory of evolution stands diametrically opposed to the Christian world view. The two are absolutely incompatible and mutually exclusive. True science, sound philosophy, and the Christian religion unite in condemnation of this mistaken view of the world. (246ff.)

It is not my intention to denigrate the work and spirit of these writers. They were determined to defend a world view they believed best represented the outlook of the biblical writers, and thus they outlined a way to integrate what they thought was the best synthesis of science and Scripture. My regret is that I never took a class with Lehman. During the early 1960s, he had asked me for a book on evolution, and I was able to give him a small booklet containing some evidences for evolution. Unfortunately, I did not pursue the matter further with him. Chester K. Lehman was a thorough scholar, and I think eventually he would have moved beyond certain statements in his 1933 book. In any case, this was the world view with its anti-evolutionary beliefs that I accepted as a young college student.

## Two Major World Views

Based on their writings, Kauffman and Lehman lived within a world view known as "essentialism." As seen by essentialists, reality consists of substances reflecting permanently ordered essences or archetypes. Hence, Nature consists of harmonious balances among various objects whose apparent affinities reflect an underlying plan or design of creation. The natural world (cosmos) therefore is perfect *Naturae* or *Scale of Nature*, brilliantly discussed in A. O. Lovejoy's *The Great Chain of Being*, immutable, and hierarchical as suggested by the *Scala* (Lovejoy 1936).

It should be pointed out also that Kauffman and Lehman wrote in an era (roughly 1900-1936) that was marked by a deep divide between the naturalists, with their emphasis on small but gradual incremental changes within populations, and the rising science of experimental genetics, which held that evolution could proceed only by means of new mutations ("saltations"—big jumps).

However, the function of natural selection was largely to eliminate deleterious mutations (see Mayr 1982: 548ff. for an interpretative history). It was only with major books and papers by Theodosius Dobzhansky, Sir Ronald Fisher, Ernst Mayr, George Gaylord Simpson, Ledyard Stebbins, and others, that genetics and Darwinian natural selection were united to form a powerful new paradigm, the so-called neo-Darwinian synthesis. Thus mutations (i.e., new variations) plus natural selection implied a differential transfer of genes from one generation to the next (see Mayr 1982: 566ff. for a history of this synthesis).

In addition to this synthesis, key transitional fossils were eventually discovered, plate tectonics revealed that continents were not fixed, and biogeographical studies showed that even within one species there could be significant changes from one region to another. Evolutionary thought showed a growth and was increasingly placed on a solid empirical foundation (Mayr 1982: 566ff.). We now know a lot more about how living things evolve than we did only a few decades ago.

But back to when I was an EMC junior: One day the windows were opened, and I saw another way of understanding the six-day creation of all the species. I happened to buy a slim book of 135 pages by J. Heslop-Harrison, *New Concepts in Flowering-Plant Taxonomy*, in which he described polyploidy, a process whereby two different species can hybridize and produce a third species with a full chromosome compliment of the parental species. Heslop-Harrison wrote,

> From the large sample of species that has already been investigated it is estimated that perhaps half of the entire north temperate flora of the world consists of polyploids, and that of these rather more than half are likely to be allopolyploids [i.e., a hybridization involving the chromosomes of two different species]. (Heslop-Harrison 1956: 93)

Heslop-Harrison blew apart my firm view that all species were fixed and actually generated during the six days of creation. I wrote the following in my book:

> How would the creationist answer this [polyploid emergence of new species]? Apparently God did *not* create all species of plants during the days of Adam! At least, this would be a *telling* blow against fiat creationism covering the space of a few days.

I remember leaving the EMC library, running down the steps to the basement, encountering John Hershey, and telling him that at least some parts of evolution must be true—species weren't all created in the six days of creation. That was the beginning of what many Mennonite leaders feared: a slippery slope. I cannot doubt that, for me, this was an immense cognitive shift, one of the most instantaneous I have ever experienced.

The world view of evolution ("emergentism") was thus diametrically different from that of the essentialists. In this view, reality consists of "events" participating in asymmetrically changing but in orderly relationships, with space and time inextricably linked to all emergents (i.e., evolved structures). Hence, living things consist of structured adaptations with possibilities for change, whose apparent affinities reflect proximity of descent. The natural biological world therefore is an inclusively "branched tree of life" with a history. Human nature itself is dynamic, open to novelty, to transcendence. Thus living things are to be seen as unfinished, incomplete, boundless, in flux, and interrelated in various complex ways.

Following graduation from EMC, I attended the University of Pennsylvania, earned an MS in botany, and returned to EMC as an assistant professor of biology. These experiences, plus a young family of three children (Carl D., Dorothy, and Joyce), greatly enlarged my intellectual stream of thought. Moreover, during the late 1950s a number of young Mennonite academics, accompanied by older church leaders, met several times under the auspices of the budding Mennonite Graduate Fellowship. This fellowship had its gestation during the Christmas holidays in 1957 when Merle Jacobs, John Ruth, and Stanwyn Shetler met at the Jacobs' house near Johnstown, Pennsylvania, for a social event. Out of their conversations, the fellowship began as a formal meeting at Cornell University, later at Columbus,

Ohio, Chicago, and Philadelphia. Many of the early discussions centered on the self-identity of Mennonite graduate students, but at least at the Columbus and Chicago meetings, evolution was given a thorough review.

I recall that at the Columbus meeting, following my off-the-cuff oral comments concerning current biological evolutionary thought, Paul Erb, then editor of the *Gospel Herald*, remarked that were he to publish my remarks, he would get all sorts of negative letters. It is clear that from my review of the papers read at the Chicago meeting, evolution could be accepted as a biological thesis, but we were less clear about the philosophical and theological aspects of evolution. Toward the close of my unpublished paper, I wrote,

> I have dealt with evolution from an empirical standpoint only. . . . [I]t is more important to be clear about the biblical explanations regarding why we are here, why God created the earth, and what our goals in life should be, than to argue endlessly from the Bible HOW God created the living plants and animals. I believe that most of the scientific questions God has left for us to work out. . . . I am glad to say that I believe in a transcendent God who controls and directs the creative process. . . . God's revelationary breakthrough into time is not evolutionary. Furthermore, the current synthesis of evolutionary theory does not demand that revelation be an evolutionary process. (Keener 1959)

Evolution now once more made its way into the minds of Mennonite academics and church leaders. The horse was out of the barn.

There can be no question that Charles Darwin's *On the Origin of Species by Means of Natural Selection, or the Preservation of Favoured Races in the Struggle for Life* (Darwin 1967) was the crippling blow to the old concept that the natural world consisted of a series of graded forms from lower to higher forming a fixed scale of nature with no "missing links." The impact of the Darwinian revolution was immense in that Darwin's thought led to a replacement of essentialism by "population thinking" (Mayr 1982: 501ff.). Essentialism (typological thinking) implied a descent with a perpetuation of the *type* in that a species did not change over time, except possibly accidentally.

Population thinking, on the other hand, implied that successive generations within a population change over time—there is thus a descent with modification. In brief, if there is variation among individuals of a species, if the variations are inherited, if the variant organisms differ in reproductive success (e.g., have different numbers of grandchildren) there will be evolutionary changes within the population over time.

I should point out that evolution in the broad sense simply means change with modifications. For this to happen, antecedent structured events precede the emergent new structures. With respect to organic systems, this implies several causes, among which are genetic changes acted on by various factors, including reproductive capabilities and successes. Extended to philosophy and theology, evolution can be a world view. The question then is, instead of evolution being inadequate for a world view, can it be an adequate basis for a world view?

## BIOLOGY PROFESSOR AT EASTERN MENNONITE COLLEGE AND FURTHER GRADUATE STUDIES

During the years from 1960-1963, I taught biology at EMC and took four courses during two summers at the Mountain Lake Biological Station in Giles County, Virginia. In the fall of 1963, I began doctoral work at North Carolina State University at Raleigh. My academic work and copious reading further strengthened my view that an evolutionary process was absolutely essential if one were to understand the origin of species now extant on the earth. Moreover, Sir Karl Popper's writings greatly influenced me at this time. Science, Popper argued, proceeded by means of conjectures co-joined with empirically refutable tests, the result of which gradually increases our knowledge. Thus if a statement was not empirically refutable or falsifiable, it was not a statement that science could deal with.

Sir Alfred J. Ayer said much the same thing, and his notion of empirically verifiable scientific statements (as opposed to metaphysical statements) gave me much to think about. In simple terms, Ayer claimed that "For a statement of fact to be genuine some possible observations must be relevant to the determination of its truth or falsehood" (Ayer 1946: 27). These authors helped me work through some important aspects of the philosophy of science. Meanwhile, I firmly accepted the Mennonite communitarian spirit and nonviolence toward others, although my nonconformist dress and similar views gradually eroded. In any case, the next important shift in my thought was theistic: my vision of God.

When I took my doctoral written exams, Professor Ernest O. Beal asked me to write on one topic only: "Why Am I Here?" It is clear from what I wrote in 1965 that I believed then that the best vision of God was the classical theistic one: God is omnipotent, omniscient, impassible, transcendent, perfect, and the like. In my exam paper I wrote: "I believe that God is in control of operations [within the universe] although God may be inscrutable. I think that he has revealed himself to man (prophets, Christ, mystical revelations) and we're free to choose whether or not this revelation makes sense to us" (exam paper 1965). This was my vision of God when I joined the Penn State faculty in botany in 1966.

## PENN STATE UNIVERSITY AND PROCESS THOUGHT

Following completion of my doctoral studies at North Carolina State, I was offered a position as assistant professor of botany at Penn State. In looking back on this move, I could have returned to EMC; had I done so, I am sure my life would have been quite different. I admit, however, that my rather blunt announcement to President Augsburger of my change in plans could have been handled with

*Carl identifying plants by Sixmile Run, five miles northeast of Philipsburgh, Center County, Pennsylvania, 2006.*

considerably more finesse. As I recall, I merely phoned him and stated that I had accepted a position at Penn State and was therefore going there. It would have been more in the spirit of community had I traveled to Harrisonburg and talked things over with President Augsburger, Dean Miller, and some of my good friends. Fortunately, my crude departure has not irretrievably damaged our relationships.

As one can imagine, jumping into a round of teaching, research, and departmental responsibilities ate up a lot of time. E. O. Wilson once made the remark that if one wishes to advance in the academic world, an eighty-hour week is imperative (Wilson 1998: 56). Although a large university can be an exhilarating place to work, it can also be a real challenge to one's research potential, for it is on this that young, nontenured professors are principally judged.

My interest was to work on the distribution and evolutionary history of the mid-Appalachian shale barren endemics, as well as the systematics of the Buttercup Family, especially those species occurring in southeastern United States. As my major professor, Jim Hardin, once told me, it's always wise to become identified with a taxonomic group—this establishes one's identity as a professional. I tried to follow his advice. As a teacher, I gradually evolved three teaching styles: evangelist for the non-majors, drill sergeant for the majors in lower level courses, and coach for upper level and graduate courses.

In those early years at Penn State, my family and I became identified with a group of Mennonites who met regularly for worship on Sunday mornings in one of the classrooms on campus. Victor Stoltzfus entered graduate studies in sociology the same year we came to State College. His leadership certainly helped our young congregation to reach out to a number of students. How to bridge one's academic pursuits and ideas with those of our Mennonite faith was an ever-present challenge. Retired university professor Harold Schilling would occasionally preach for us and opened new vistas of thought based on process theology. What was this line of thought, and why did it influence me beyond measure?

In 1968, I bought John Cobb's *A Christian Natural Theology* (Cobb 1965) and Charles Hartshorne's *Beyond Humanism* (Hartshorne 1968). At the time, both books stood unread. I simply couldn't follow the arguments of Cobb and Hartshorne. That all changed one day in 1972 when Gladys and I were in Scottdale, Pennsylvania, and I happened to stop at the Mennonite bookstore in town. The bookstore carried a paperback edited by Ewert Cousins (1971) titled *Process Theology*, which contained "basic writings by the key thinkers of a major modern movement." I snapped up the $4.95 copy, went home, and began to read.

Later that year I also bought *Process Philosophy and Christian Thought*, ably edited by Delwin Brown, et al (1971). One of the writers was Lewis Ford, who was listed as a professor at Penn State. I looked up Lewis and, from that time on, we became good friends. I sat in several of his classes, including his lectures on Alfred North Whitehead, a leading exponent of process philosophy. All this marked an important shift in my thought, especially with respect to a neoclassical, theistic conceptuality of God, and a more rational way of thinking about the problem of evil. Suffice it to say, these are huge topics which have occupied my thinking and life for the last forty years.

In brief, although process thought has ancient roots, its modern exposition is chiefly the work of Whitehead, Charles Hartshorne, and their many followers. Process thought is thoroughly evolutionary in that the cosmos is suffused with change—the entire universe is not static from the Big Bang to the present time. Process thinkers, seeking to find the generic traits of existence, believe that events (not invariant substances) are primary. They consider reality as social—that is, all events are related in some fashion to all other events. The future is open, even to God. In their vision of God, both Whitehead and Hartshorne believed that the classical (orthodox) view of God had insuperable difficulties with design in nature, evil, and freedom.

Near the close of his Gifford Lectures, Whitehead suggested four major visions of God: *Ruthless Moralist* (the "personification of moral energy"); *Divine Caesar* (an "image of an imperial ruler"); *Philosophical Absolute* (an "ultimate philosophical principle," that is, the *Unmoved Mover* of Aristotle (Whitehead 1978: 342ff.). But there was in the Galilean vision, Whitehead believed, a fourth view that

> does not emphasize the ruling Caesar, or the ruthless moralist, or the unmoved mover. It dwells upon the tender elements in the world, which slowly and in quietness operate by love; and it finds purpose in the present immediacy of a kingdom not of this world. Love neither rules, nor is it unmoved; it is also a little

oblivious as to morals. It does not look to the future; for it finds its own reward in the immediate present. (1978: 343).

God is the ultimate mystery, and we live and think, as Gordon Kaufman (1993) stated in the title of his magnum opus, "in face of mystery." For myself, the vision of God in Christ is the best revelation of the nature and agency of God. God persuades, does not coerce; God furnishes possibilities to the created order, but the evolutionary advances are partly determined by the various entities prehending, i.e., "grasping" God's lures, as Norman Pittenger phrased it (Pittenger 1979). When we claim that God is love, we mean to suggest that there are possibilities for a creative enrichment in the lives of the creatures. Suffice it to say, process thought has been a major influence in my thinking and living.

## ADDITIONAL STREAMS

During the last thirty years of my life, a number of subsidiary streams have fed into my life's stream, although it's difficult to sort out with any precision how they have influenced my life. I am a person of simple tastes: I dress conservatively, don't do much traveling, own only one car at a time, and refuse to have all the amenities that moderns think they must have to enrich their frantic lives. I have also resisted the temptation to sprout facial hair.

I was, as you recall, raised on a farm that lacked even the bare necessities of twentieth-century living. Two mules and a horse were our power to plow and disc our stony acres. We husked corn by hand. But there were always books to be read, and in that sense, my world could range far and wide. As an adoptee, not knowing my biological roots, I felt different, and yet the Beloved Community (Royce's term) helped me to understand the nature of salvation and acceptance within a community.

According to the Myers-Briggs Type Indicator, my personality type is INTJ (Introvert-iNtuitive-Thinking- Judging), and as such, I seem to be tone deaf to the world of the mystics and charismatics. Yet I am drawn to classical romantic music such as Rachmaninoff's *Piano Concerto No. 3 in D Minor*, to Dostoevsky's *The Brothers Karamazov*, to the landscape paintings of the Hudson River School, and to the poetry of Tennyson ("Enoch Arden") and Longfellow ("Evangeline").

The little wildflower garden in our back yard brings me great joy each spring. Gladys' bird feeders provide an endless stream of many feathered friends.

I also rejoice in the abiding friendships Gladys and I have had, particularly with three other couples with whom we have met for several days on an annual basis for many years. Our deep discussions have greatly expanded my horizons—friends will do that, you know. I also rejoice in the skills of modern physicians—a quadruple bypass operation in 2006 undoubtedly saved my life.

I am thankful that the genetic recombination of meiosis has generated three very different children, four grandchildren, plus two step-grandchildren, and now five great-grandchildren, plus two step-great-grandchildren. Yet the stream of DNA that carried instructions for making me a unique individual goes all the way back some billions of years to when the first eukaryotic cells emerged and meiosis evolved. We are all part of this "living stream," to use Sir Alister Hardy's felicitous phrase (Hardy 1965).

One important tributary that impacted my thought was a lecture at Penn State given by Bishop John A. T. Robinson in September 1980. Robinson maintained that too many Christians want high, tight fences with nothing getting in and nothing getting out (cf. Mennonite colleges in their earlier days). Such Christians spend lots of time in fence repair and making sure their faith is securely enclosed. However, if one asked these Christians what's at the core of their faith, they really have no certain answer. Later that evening at a dinner, I asked the bishop what was at the core of his faith, and he replied, the cross of Christ. Unfortunately, we didn't have time to unpack what all that meant, but his answer set me to thinking about the necessity of a clear core that can guide us in these uncertain times. High, tight fences aren't the answer, I think, and yet sadly, one can trace numerous splits within the Mennonite community of faith that resulted from fence building and repair.

In 1983 I took a sabbatical to work on the Buttercup Family of the southeastern United States at the Gray Herbarium of Harvard University. The Gray Herbarium has lots of rare books and one in particular was kept in a locked safe. When I learned that the book was a copy of the first edition of Darwin's *Origin* sent to Asa Gray, I asked the librarian whether I could see it. She graciously gave me the book to examine. So there I was, touching a book written and handled by Darwin (autographed "from the author") with annotations by Gray. This was a real "ark of the covenant" moment for me!

One day when Gladys and I visited the Mount Auburn Cemetery, I was moved to see that Gray's tombstone, shaped like a coffin lid, had a concrete cross on top. Since the Divinity School was a stone's throw from the Gray Herbarium, I sat in on Gordon Kaufman's lectures on constructing a concept of God. Gordon maintained that our vision of God must see God as the relativizer and humanizer of all other such visions, or else our concept of God makes God into an idol. I appreciated Gordon's interest in natural history and his willingness to continue working at his theological projects. For Gordon, theology was an ongoing project involving imaginative constructions based on experience, reason, and insight. This, I thought, is exactly what scientists do!

And then there was *the* search! Spurred by some of my daughter Dottie's questions, I began a search for my roots in the early 1980s. I had always known I was a foster/adopted child, but until I reached my 50s, I really didn't do much searching for my biological ancestors. Fortunately, I had original supporting documentation (birth certificate, adoption papers—Pennsylvania hadn't yet "closed" the books) that were grim reminders of earlier tragic circumstances.

During my time in Cambridge, I recall sitting at the table in the apartment I was renting and opening a letter from a friend. The letter contained the funeral service in 1974 for my biological mother. The letter that cold February evening in 1983 effectively closed the books on ever meeting my biological mother. To this day, the identity of my biological father remains uncertain. Although one should not live too much in the past, nor harbor too many regrets, I have often wished that I could have talked with my mother. It would have connected me biologically to the past. It was a strange feeling indeed to meet my first child (a son) in 1956 and to realize that he was the closest living relative I had up to then ever seen!

Other important tributaries to my life's river include David Griffin's syntheses of science and religion and his careful treatments of the problem of evil. There can be no question that this problem is one of the most intractable problems for classical theists. If this is the best of all possible worlds with a God-ordained balance and harmony, yet one in which children can be tortured, I'll join Ivan Karamazov in returning the ticket. How can an all-powerful God also be good and loving if God could have made the world a little bit better than it is?

The process theologians think they have an answer, but then one can never be sure if human freedom will be sufficiently curtailed to prevent future horrific evils. Brand Blanshard's rationalistic idealism has taught me the nature of thought, that ethics can be objective and teleological, that one must always adjust one's beliefs to the evidence, i.e., follow the evidence where it leads. For Blanshard, the highest virtue is reasonableness reflecting a "settled disposition to guide one's belief and conduct by the evidence," and "to make reflective judgment the compass of one's belief and action" (1984: 247).

Although there are a number of theories regarding the nature of truth, John Searle (1998) helped me to see the value in the correspondence nature of truth and how to distinguish between brute realities independent of human existence (e.g., the moon, trees in a forest) and the construction of social realities dependent on human creativity (e.g., printing money, building houses, writing memoirs). His defense of external realism helped me steer away from social constructivism, postmodernism, deconstruction, etc., and to regard the universe as "completely intelligible and that we [are] capable of a systematic understanding of its nature," key elements in what Searle calls the "Enlightenment vision" (1998: 2). Gary Dorrien's trilogy on American liberal theology and his two books on social ethics helped organize some of my thinking about American theological currents.

One of the important recent changes in my thinking occurred one day when several members of the University Mennonite Congregation met over lunch and one of the persons told us that he is gay. Up to this point, I had not given much thought to human sexual orientation. What were the causes of sexual preferences? What about same-sex relationships? Could such people remain members of our congregation? Should we accept them into membership?

And so in the last decade of the twentieth century, I became involved with other Mennonite writers to forge a path toward a greater understanding of the biological aspects of same-sex orientation. This meant considerable reading and eventually co-authoring and writing three chapters that were included in Mennonite publications (Keener and Swartzendruber 2001a, 2001b, Keener 2004). As one can imagine, human sexuality is an immense topic, which unfortunately has led to bitter and acrimonious debates within church circles, the shunning of individuals, and the disenfranchisement of congregations. As a biologist, it is my belief that one's sexual orientation is largely fixed at birth and that neither one's choice nor bad parenting results in a homosexual orientation. Sadly, both views are current within the Mennonite church, and I can only plead that persons with this mindset do some serious reading and reflection.

## Closing Remarks: Credo

This brings me to some final comments about my world view—how I "see" the way the world works. I remain an Anabaptist Mennonite Christian. As an aside, while worshiping with a tour group in the Anabaptist Cave in northeastern Switzerland one day in May 1990, we were reminded of our roots going back to the brave Anabaptists who had gathered many years ago in this cave in secret. As I see it, the Anabaptist stream of the Christian faith is a communitarian, non-creedal group which has, over the years, derived wisdom and ethical directives from discussions of the Word within communities. Confessions of faith are modeled on the Sermon on the Mount, and the ways of peace and nonviolence are central to our faith. To walk with Jesus implies, among other acts, being sensitive to the needs of other persons around us. It also requires being acutely aware of one's environment. As I see it, Anabaptism is a pragmatic type of faith that requires action. Salvation has indeed both a personal and communitarian-mediated transformation of one's character.

There is no doubt that as I age, the world seems more mysterious. Who God is remains for me shrouded in mystery, for the simple reason that as we understand more about how the world (cosmos) works, our vision of God becomes that much more complex and harder to systematize. The old dichotomy of pantheism/God as Wholly Other (i.e., transcendent) appears too simple. Throw into the mix the dipolar theism of the process theologians, various deistic views, God as Creativity (Gordon Kaufman), or God as a Divine Force (along with the other four fundamental forces within this cosmic epoch), and a narrow view of God becomes increasingly problematic.

To be sure, one's faith enters into this picture; that said, I'm not sure how to parse out the meaning of faith in this context. Does it mean trust in some negative formulation of God, a rigid acceptance of certain creedal formulas, one of Whitehead's four visions of God, or what? Moreover, if as Brian Greene (2011) suggests—"Sometimes [science] challenges us to examine our view of science itself"—does this also apply to our vision of God? As I see it, when science and theology continue their work of integration, are we not then impelled to reexamine our current vision of God, one based largely on ancient cosmologies and philosophies?

So at this point in my life, one big question for me is how best to integrate the vision of God, as best seen in Christ, with the current views of the cosmos. If one accepts the notion that there is one world, with one complex history governed by certain basic operations (evolution, particle interactions, fields of force, etc.), the question then for me is how the God we envision interacts with this type of universe. I grew up with a certain vision of God that was more or less taken for granted, as spelled out by classical theism (e.g., views of God as omniscient, omnipotent, impassible, simple, unchanging, perfect, etc.). That vision fell apart when I studied biology (evolution, not instantaneous creation), and later wrestled with the problem of evil (a good vs. powerful God). Adjustments in thought had to be made and, for the most part process theism seemed then, and still does, to make the most sense. This shift certainly meant revising the vision of God I was taught as a child.

Meanwhile, in bald summary fashion, here is my credo: The cosmos (i.e., our universe of several hundred billion galaxies) has had a single complex history beginning roughly 13.7 bya (billion years ago). In this cosmic epoch, there are a number of fundamental particles (>100) acted on by four fundamental forces (weak and strong nuclear, electromagnetic, and gravitational), processive evolutionary patterns, and complex neurological bases of mental operations. Truth has objective components and one test for truth includes a correspondence of our propositions with reality. I agree with G. E. Moore that, axiomatically, we have a moral obligation to make the world a little better than when we found it.

As a written witness of God's acts in community, the Bible shows the life of Jesus as best revealing God's nature and agency. Although this can answer certain existential questions regarding God, it doesn't answer important cosmological and ontological questions such as the location and activity of God at the time of the Big Bang. My core of faith requires walking as Jesus walked, and this means carrying one's cross, a symbol of vulnerability to other persons (1 John 3:16 is clearly linked with John 3:16). Walking with Jesus also implies growth. Reaching the final stage of love requires a number of intermediate steps, as the second book of Peter clearly indicates (I1 Peter 1:5ff.).

One aspect of love, thus, requires a creative enrichment in the lives of interactive persons, but if this love is not mutual, love is, to a degree at least, fractionated, i.e., incomplete. Suffice it to say, love in this context means something entirely different from the word *love* when used to describe my "love" of ice-cream. For this and other reasons, what a person means by love must be clearly spelled out. For me, the church is to be seen as a body (1 Cor. 12) with Christ as its head (Eph. 1:22), not as a kingdom, which for me smacks too much of hierarchy, paternalism, control, and identity with secular political structures.

So in my quest for understanding ourselves and our location within our societies, I begin with certain starting points: religiously, I begin with the cross of Christ, and scientifically, I begin with the claim that we live in a huge and old cosmos that had a single complex history understood in terms of process and change. Both aspects are marked by relationships whose quality is to be judged in aesthetic terms.

But BIG questions will always remain. Here are several:

1. Cosmological problems: What is the origin, age, history, structure, and future state of our particular universe of several hundred billion galaxies? Are there many other universes, like ours with its several billion galaxies, as Brian Greene (2011) suggests?

2. Vision of God: Given our current views of the cosmos, how might we best envision God, whether as Creativity or Divine Power, along with the four basic forces within our universe, or some Deistic God who rolled the dice once at the beginning of the Big Bang, or a transcendent Wholly Other God with all the "omni" aspects, etc.?

3. Origin and transmission of human evil (known as original sin): Why do people "sin"?

4. Nature of salvation: What is Jesus' role in this process?

5. Origins of human morality: Can natural selection account for altruism toward outsiders?

6. Ethical ambiguities: How might nonviolent groups deal with the bullies of our time? What does it mean to "love a bully"?

7. Origins of consciousness: What are the most compelling current theories?

8. How do I "fit in"?

Indeed, we live within a mysterious universe. We also live within loving families and communities that are an integral part of that stream that helped "create" me, now an octogenarian. Sisters and brothers, I rest my case.

## Acknowledgments

Special thanks are due to Gladys Keener, Carl D. Keener, Dorothy Keener, and Joyce Thompson, who offered comments on an earlier draft of this essay, and also to the editors of this volume for their skill in smoothing some of the rough edges.

March 14, 2011
Revised September 2014

## References

Ayer, A. J. 1946. *Language, Truth and Logic*. New York: Dover Publications.

Blanshard, B. 1984. *Four Reasonable Men*. Middletown, Conn.: Wesley University Press.

Brown, D., R. E. James Jr. and G. Reeves (eds.). 1971. *Process Theology and Christian Thought*. Indianapolis: The Bobbs-Merrill Co., Inc.

Cobb, J. B. Jr. 1965. *A Christian Natural Theology Based on the Thought of Alfred North Whitehead*. Philadelphia: The Westminster Press.

Cousins, E. (ed.). 1971. *Process Theology: Basic Writings*. New York: Newman Press.

Darwin, C. 1967. *On the Origin of Species* (A facsimile of the first edition with an introduction by Ernst Mayr). New York: Atheneum.

Dupree, A. H. 1959. *Asa Gray*. Cambridge, Mass.: Belknap Press of Harvard University Press.

Greene, B. 2011. *The Hidden Reality: Parallel Universes and the Deep Laws of the Cosmos*. New York: Alfred A. Knopf.

Hardy, A. 1965. *The Living Stream: Evolution and Man*. Cleveland: Meridian Books of the World Publishing Co.

Hartshorne, C. 1968. *Beyond Humanism: Essays in the Philosophy of Nature.* Lincoln: University of Nebraska Press.
Hershberger, G. F. 1944. *War, Peace, and Nonresistance.* Scottdale, Pa.: Herald Press.
Heslop-Harrison, J. 1956. *New Concepts in Flowering-Plant Taxonomy.* Cambridge, Mass.: Harvard University Press.
Kauffman, D. 1941. *One Thousand Questions and Answers on Points of Christian Doctrine.* Scottdale, Pa.: Mennonite Publishing House.
Kauffman, D. (ed.). 1952. *Doctrines of the Bible.* Scottdale, Pa.: Mennonite Publishing House.
Kaufman, G. D. 1993. *In Face of Mystery: A Constructive Theology.* Cambridge, Mass.: Harvard University Press.
Keener, C. S. 1959. "Regarding Certain Evolutionary Concepts as Formulated by Christian Biologists." Unpublished paper.
———. 2004. The Biology of Homosexuality Updated, 43-54. *In* Ruth Conrad Liechty (ed.), *These, Too, are Voices from God's Table.* "Welcome to Dialogue Series," Booklet #7. Goshen, Ind.: Economy Offset Printers, Inc.
Keener, C. S. and D. E. Swartzendruber. 2001a. "The Biological Basis of Homosexuality," 148-173. In C. Norman Kraus (ed.), *To Continue the Dialogue: Biblical Interpretation and Homosexuality.* Telford, Pa.: Pandora Press U.S.
———. 2001b. Does Homosexuality Have a Biological Basis? 17-48. In Ruth Conrad Liechty (ed.), "Welcome to Dialogue Series," Booklet #5: *Biological and Psychological Perspectives.* Goshen, Ind.: Economy Offset Printers, Inc.
Lehman, C. K. 1933. *The Inadequacy of Evolution as a World View.* Scottdale, Pa.: Mennonite Publishing House.
Lovejoy, A. O. 1936. *The Great Chain of Being: A Study of the History of an Idea.* Harvard University Press: Harper Torchbooks, 1960.
Mayr, E. 1980. Prologue: "Some Thoughts on the History of the Evolutionary Synthesis," 1-48. In E. Mayr and W. B. Provine (eds.), *The Evolutionary Synthesis: Perspectives on the Unification of Biology.* Cambridge, Mass.: Harvard University Press.
———. 1982. *The Growth of Biological Thought.* Cambridge, Mass.: Belknap Press of Harvard University Press.
Pittenger, N. 1979. *The Lure of Divine Love: Human Experience and Christian Faith in a Process Perspective.* New York: The Pilgrim Press.
Robinson, B. L. and M. L. Fernald. 1908. *Gray's New Manual of Botany,* 7th. ed. Cincinnati, Ohio: American Book Co.
Schilpp, P. A. (ed.). 1980. *The Philosophy of Brand Blanshard.* La Salle, Ill.: Open Court.
Searle, J. R. 2007. *Freedom and Neurobiology: Reflections on Free Will, Language, and Political Power.* New York: Columbia University Press.

———. 1998. *Mind, Language and Society: Philosophy in the Real World.* New York: Basic Books.
Whitehead, A. N. 1978. *Process and Reality: An Essay in Cosmology.* Corrected edition ed. D. R. Griffin and D. W. Sherburne, 1978. New York: Free Press.
Wilson, E. O. 1998. *Consilience: The Unity of Knowledge.* New York: Alfred A. Knopf.

**PART II**

# Re-Envisioning Service
# . . . as Writers and Publishers

*Margaret Jantzi Foth*

---

**Voice of Feminist, Mother, Writer, Mediator, Friend**

*Some of us know Margaret Foth simply by the tone of her melodic, soft-spoken, encouraging voice. Others know her as community relations coordinator for the Center for Justice and Peacebuilding and for the Summer Peacebuilding Institute. Some, however, might remember her from earlier years when you tuned in to hear her on your favorite radio program,* Your Time. *Margaret comes to us via the path of service—Mennonite Central Committee, Mennonite Media Ministries, and Mennonite Board of Missions. In the process of giving, she has discovered that "Life is too short . . . to miss today."*

## MARGARET JANTZI FOTH

# *The Road Taken*

Robert Frost's poem "The Road Not Taken" begins,

> *Two roads diverged in a yellow wood,*
> *And sorry I could not travel both*
> *And be one traveler, long I stood*
> *And looked down one as far as I could*
> *To where it bent in the undergrowth;*
> *Then took the other.*

Frost concludes with the reflection,

> *And that has made all the difference.*[1]

As I reflect on my life, I recognize that the road I took "has made all the difference," including times when I experienced with Frost that "way leads on to way." From this vantage point, those unexpected "ways" were a special gift from God.

### FROM THE BEGINNING

My father, Peter Jantzi, was born in Wellesley, Ontario, Canada, the oldest of nine children in an Amish Mennonite family. He was fourteen when his mother died of tuberculosis (after making sure that her baby would be cared for by giving her to an Amish family for adoption). When his oldest sister died of tuberculosis a year later, the family was split up, with the two youngest children going to live with their maternal grandmother and the middle children to families looking for farm help. My father moved with his father into a rented room, and they worked together in a cheese factory. At age eighteen my father moved to Alden, New York, southwest of Buffalo, where a number of other Ontario families had located and where there was a small Conservative Amish Mennonite Church.

My mother, Elizabeth Helmuth, grew up in Kansas and Indiana. She was the youngest of five children in an Amish family. When her father lost his Indiana farm, the Amish community there took their home and belongings to pay off the debts, and my mother and her family became homeless. They traveled eastward staying with relatives along the way. When they reached Buffalo, they began attending a small church in Alden. My mother found work as a maid in a wealthy home in Buffalo, so when her parents moved to Ohio, she chose to stay in New York.

My parents met at the youth gatherings of the church in Alden. In 1928 at the end of a regular Sunday morning service, they were married. Although there was no special service or reception, my mother wore the new gray silk cape dress she had made. They rented a small upper apartment in the town of Alden, and my father continued working in a local machine shop.

My parents were typical of the families in this church, established in the early 1900's by the Conservative Amish Mennonite Conference. Each family had moved to this area looking for cheap farm land and jobs. They had come from eastern New York State, Kansas, Michigan, and Ontario. In this congregation there were no large farms, inherited resources, or even extended family. It was led by a bishop and a minister who had no formal training and who took turns preaching while earning their own livelihood.

### 1930-1948: The Beginning of the Road for Me

I was born in 1930, the beginning of the era known as the Great Depression. Two brothers, a sister, and another brother followed in six years. Although my father's dream was to own a farm, he worked at various jobs—a few years as a farmhand, sometimes in a factory, and once driving a long-distance truck. We moved from one rented house to another. While my father was working for subsistence wages, my mother was responsible for feeding and clothing our growing family. She worked very hard raising chickens as well as gardening, baking bread, canning food for the winter, and keeping a house without modern appliances. She also made all our clothes from donated castaways.

Wherever we lived, we always attended church: Sunday morning and evening services and often Wednesday evening as well. My parents participated in the Sunday school classes and conversations. We children learned to sit still while waiting to play with our friends afterward. Often families invited each other to come and share a simple Sunday dinner. On Thanksgiving Day we went to church for a day-long service with a potluck meal at noon.

As we were growing up, our home was a place for my father's brothers and sisters to visit. My mother always welcomed them, made room for them to sleep, and served their favorite meals. His sisters came to help my mother after the birth of each baby. His brothers came when they could find a ride. They played with us, and we thrived on their attention and love. Later, we traveled to Ontario, where we also met aunts, uncles, and cousins.

I was eager to start school, but my mother wanted me to wait until I was almost seven. That summer we moved to a small farm in an immigrant Polish community outside of Alden. The one-room school was a two-mile walk. The first mile I walked alone, but at the corner I met two other students, and we walked the second mile together.

In this one-room school we listened to the lessons of all eight grades. After the first two weeks the teacher told my parents that I was now in the second grade. I loved school and learning to read. There was a small bookcase with books we could borrow. Since we had only a Bible storybook at home, this was a treasure chest and I read every book.

Growing up I often helped my mother with the housework, but it was going to school and learning that I loved. Since my classmates were almost all from homes where their parents spoke Polish, I had an advantage in language skills. But I was very aware that I looked different than the other girls with my long hair in braids, cotton stockings, and homemade dresses.

When I was in fifth grade, our family moved back to Alden, and we children transferred to the Alden public school. Here I found a different room for each grade, a more diverse community, and stiffer competition to get the best grades. And I discovered another big gift. This town had an unusually fine public library at which I often stopped on my way home from school.

We did not have a radio at home, but when I arrived at school on the morning of December 7, 1941, I learned of the Japanese attack on Pearl Harbor and the U.S. declaration of war against Japan. Life changed for us all as the news of war headlined daily newspapers and filled radio broadcasts, as the young men in the senior high school class enlisted in the armed forces, as sugar and gas were rationed, and as the U.S. economy shifted toward producing armaments.

When I was baptized and joined the church at fourteen, being "different" took on yet another dimension. I knew that our church did not believe in going to war. Although I still loved school, I could not dress like my classmates and was never invited to parties. In addition, my family did not buy war savings bonds or join the patriotic clubs. Thinking of the complexities ahead, my parents decided that I should go to Eastern Mennonite School (EMS) in Harrisonburg, Virginia, for my high school. Although that meant leaving home and living in a dorm, I was very excited. I expected that there I would finally fit in.

Arriving in this Virginia Mennonite high school, I learned almost immediately that I still did not fit in. My plain dresses and covering were not quite the same cut as those worn by students from Lancaster and Virginia. However, I did make friends, including many who have become lifelong friends, and I had a wealth of learning opportunities. I had some exceptional teachers, including A. Grace Wenger, Ruth Brackbill, and C. Norman Kraus. I also enjoyed the opportunities to sing in choruses and participate in public speaking in the literary societies.

Traveling to and from Virginia required either my parents making a round-trip by car or me taking a train and bus—at least twelve hours each way. We stayed in touch by letters. When I was sixteen, my mother gave birth to my fourth brother, ten years behind his last sibling. I returned home each summer and attended the Conservative Mennonite church where I was still a member.

EMS belonged to the Virginia Mennonite Conference, a conference with a proud history of conservatism. There were strict rules for women's clothing, which included a certain length for one's skirt from hem to floor and wearing coverings all the time—even in gym class. There was an emphasis on private devotions as well as mandatory attendance at daily chapel, weekly Sunday services, plus weeklong fall and spring revival meetings. Each student was expected to take one Bible class a year. For our senior year President J. L. Stauffer taught Bible doctrine, and I along with my classmates had to memorize the verses Paul wrote to Timothy: beginning with "All Scripture is given by inspiration of God..." (2 Tim. 3: 16-17 KJV). The emphasis was on literal acceptance of the words, verse by verse, of the King James Version.

During my four years at EMS, I had received an excellent education, had experienced genuine friendships, and was recognized for my gifts in writing and speaking. But I had also lived through too many revival meetings and had succumbed to too many rules, which I thought unfair to women. By the time I graduated in 1948, I thought I could not continue to be a Mennonite.

## 1949-1957: THE EDUCATIONAL CHALLENGE

I returned home to New York, hoping to find work and save money to go to college. Job hunting revealed that there were not many opportunities for a high school grad without specific work experience. Then a friend wrote to say that the Mennonite Publishing House (MPH) in Scottdale, Pennsylvania, was looking for a typist—my one marketable skill! I applied, was accepted, and moved again. At MPH the editors all recorded their letters and sent the discs to the central typing pool. We picked up the discs, typed the letters, and returned them for signatures. Manual typewriters, multiple copies, struggles to understand correctly the dictated words, recognizing sentences and paragraphs—it was a challenge!

However, the most meaningful change in my life in Scottdale was being welcomed into a group of professional women—Ethel (Yake) Metzler, Lois (Yake) Kenagy, Beulah (Stauffer) Hostetler, Gerry (Gross) Harder, and Alice (Buckwalter) Hershberger. They were college graduates, still single, and active in the local Mennonite church. Since our wages were low, we shared living spaces, cooked together, walked (no one had a car), sang, and talked a lot. We also taught Sunday school classes, planned and directed summer Bible school, and directed summer programs at the new Laurelville Camp Center—in effect declaring active roles for ourselves in the Mennonite church.

By September 1950 I had saved enough to accept the offer of Nancy (Burkholder) Lee, who invited me to live in her home while beginning college at Eastern Mennonite School. Back in Harrisonburg as a college freshman, I was greeted with more options and enjoyed the challenge of new studies. However, during that year I faced the reality that although my father supported my dreams of further education, my family could *not* help me with college tuition. I had also decided that I wanted to transfer to Goshen College (GC). I moved back to Scottdale to work in the publishing house again. Over the next years, my college and work times at MPH alternated until I graduated from GC in May 1955.

When I began my final two years at Goshen, I expected to enter the education department so that I could become a teacher. But in the first week of classes I recognized that I really wanted to study in other disciplines, and I switched to an English major. With my first speech class, Dr. Roy Umble, professor of drama, debate, and public speaking, became my mentor and friend, as well as professor. Besides classes, I joined the debate teams, competing in the Indiana/Michigan tourneys with all the major universities: Notre Dame, Purdue, Northwestern, Indiana University, Ball State, Manchester, and Earlham. Our teams were respected, and we won tournaments. I always chose the affirmative side, which meant arguing for an alternative to the status quo. I participated in the public speaking and peace oratorical contests. In drama I directed a production of *Everyman* and played the part of Portia in *The Merchant of Venice*. I also joined a choir each year.

Besides developing abilities, I gained a new world view. Dr. Umble had participated in Civilian Public Service during World War II, and from that experience he had a new vision for the role of the Mennonite church. We were to be change agents, "salt" and "light." Many other conversations and classes added to this perspective, including having as best friend a young woman from India.

At Goshen we also had regular chapel services, and I attended the College Mennonite Church. By this time, I had learned more about the historic roots of the Mennonite church and had grown to appreciate this faith as a vision for living. In my senior year I audited a course Professor Howard Charles taught in the Bible department. Using the Gospel of John, he led us through a book study, similar to the way we studied literature, and I was surprised at the new perspectives on Jesus' life and teachings.

As graduation drew near, and I had no funds for graduate school, I applied to the Mennonite Central Committee (MCC) requesting a service position in a foreign country. MCC had no overseas assignments to offer, but they did invite me to a two-year position as director of communications, located in their headquarters in Akron, Pennsylvania. Following graduation in June1955, I moved to Akron.

As director of communications for MCC, I was responsible for the preparation of weekly news notes, which were mailed to Mennonite magazines and newspapers in the U.S. and Canada. An interesting side note: although William Snyder was the executive secretary of MCC at that time, Orie O. Miller, the founding executive secretary of MCC, was still living in his home across the street. One week Bill Snyder told me that Orie was "inviting me to bring the news notes for him to review before I send them!" I actually appreciated this opportunity to learn from Orie that "MCC is not looking for headlines. We don't highlight individual persons. These news notes are to be informative and focus on the work rather than personalities."

Besides the news notes, I edited various monthly newsletters and was responsible for developing program marketing materials. This position was challenging and gave me invaluable experience in organizing and scheduling production. Our department included another writer, a secretary, and an artist. Besides the routine of news notes, I particularly enjoyed working with the artist and the printer to produce marketing brochures for the various departments of MCC.

The staff at MCC included a number of other recent graduates from various Mennonite schools. In the second year of my term, I began dating Don Foth, a Mennonite Brethren from Hillsboro, Kansas, who was doing his I-W service (civilian public service performed by conscientious objectors in lieu of military service) as assistant accountant in the business office. Since we lived and worked in this small community, we knew each other as friends. I already knew that Don's parents and a younger sister had been killed in an auto accident when he was sixteen, and that he had graduated from Friends University of Wichita, Kansas, where he had lived with an uncle.

When he proposed marriage that spring, he assured me that he did not expect me to give up my professional dreams, as his mother, a nurse, had worked professionally. I was sad that I could never know his parents, but I did meet his surviving brother and sister as well as other relatives when my parents joined us on a visit to Hillsboro.

We both completed our MCC terms in June 1957. Two weeks later we married on a very warm day at what had become my parents' home church, the Clarence Center (N.Y.) Mennonite Church. We had a double wedding! My sister Annamae and her fiancé Tom Hostetler planned this service with us, saving wedding expenses for us and one trip for out-of-town relatives!

Don and I then moved to Hillsboro, Kansas, where Don had been offered an accounting position in the local Ford Motor Company. That summer in Hillsboro was painfully hot and dry. I found the isolation of Hillsboro difficult, and there were no professional opportunities for me. The Mennonite Brethren churches seemed like a throwback to my earlier church experiences of rigid rules and limited roles for women. I missed both the climate and the life in the east. When Don's job was terminated the next year, we decided to move to my home community in New York state. My parents found us an apartment a couple of miles from their home, and Don secured a position in Buffalo, in the public accounting firm Ernst & Ernst.

## 1958-1968: A Decade of Parenting

I was pregnant when we moved to New York, so I did not look for a professional position. When our son Robert was born in July 1958, I was not prepared for the new joy I found. I was amazed at the love I felt. I had not dreamed of having children nor thought I would be happy without a profession, but my dreams of graduate study and a professional career disappeared. Watching and nurturing the development and growth of this baby was challenging and very satisfying, and I did not want to miss a bit of it.

Two years later, during my second pregnancy, I learned another lesson. One morning while I was showering, I suddenly began crying. What will I do? I certainly can never love another child as much as I loved this first child! Of course, I learned that was far from reality. When I held Ellen, and then Mary, and then our fourth child Janice, I always marveled at love—it is not a limited commodity!

For almost ten years, being a mother was my full-time work. From both reading and experience I learned so much about child development, about working out loving relationships in daily living, and about organizing time to meet the requirements of a family of six.

Since I loved books and reading, this was an opportunity to fill our house with lots of wonderful children's books with beautiful illustrations, and I read aloud every night—beginning with singing and counting books, then A. A. Milne's Pooh books, the Laura Ingalls Wilder series, Narnia, *Anne of Green Gables*, and all the other stories that opened a world of imagination as well as history and diverse cultures. Our family Christmas shopping trips were to a well-stocked bookstore where the children bought books for each other. When a child was ill, I read more stories. One time Mary came home from college with the flu and begged, "Read to me, Mom. Read *Winnie the Pooh* again."

My parents continued to be a supportive and loving presence during these years. We all thrived in this extended family—and it was a new experience. My parents had not had relatives nearby through their parenting years, so we all made our way without old patterns to either guide or restrict us. Even when we bought a home five miles away, we could share meals at Grandma's table and ride with Grandpa on the tractor. Grandma and Grandpa could be counted on to provide fun, as well as a helping hand.

Don and I joined the church my parents then attended, Clarence Center Mennonite. Although the church was about twenty-five miles east of Buffalo, it was started by and was still affiliated with the Ontario Mennonite Conference. This congregation of about 150 members welcomed us and our children in the usual activities connected to congregational life. Like the Alden church of my youth, this congregation was also made up of first- or second-generation members, but there was no longer the emphasis on specific clothing for women or men.

The pastor of the church was Edward Diener. He and his wife Esther were educated and given partial support by the church. With Esther's talents, a cappella music was an integral part of every service, but women were not invited to teach or even read Scripture aloud. I enjoyed teaching Sunday school classes for women or children, and we all enjoyed potluck dinners and other gatherings.

I found a new friend and reopened a dormant interest when Lila and Gerry Miller, Bluffton College grads, moved to Buffalo and began attending our church. Lila was a drama and music major in college. She soon began directing musicals and dramas for the church youth group and invited me to assist. Together we also decided to audition for and join the Schola Cantorum, a semi-professional chorus in Buffalo, which performed with the Buffalo Philharmonic Orchestra. This meant weekly rehearsals in Buffalo as well as wonderful concerts. Three years later, when the Millers moved back to Ohio, I continued to work with the youth dramas and invited others to join me in the chorus.

Those Wednesday evening rehearsals became my weekly re-creation. The music, the rehearsals, and the concerts continued to be a spiritual well-spring for me through the next ten years. We prepared the usual choral works for concerts—Bach's *B Minor Mass*, the Brahms *German Requiem*, Bruckner, Beethoven, Vivaldi, Dvorak, and many others. A highlight was the annual performance of Handel's *Messiah* with artists from New York City as soloists. I remember especially the soprano soloist Adele Addison from New York City. She sang all the solos so beautifully that she was immediately engaged to return for the following year. During that summer she learned that she had cancer, but she did return to Buffalo for *The Messiah* concert. When she began singing "I know that my redeemer liveth . . ." it was magical—not a sound except for this soaring faith, mystery beyond words.

Our children developed their own talents and interests which we enjoyed and encouraged. They were good students in schools, which offered creative classes as well as required studies. Along with enjoying their special interests, I looked for opportunities to expand our world. We invited international guests to our home: a Japanese doctor's family who had moved to Buffalo, two young men from India attending the University of Buffalo, and some visiting Chinese and

Japanese scholars. I wanted our family to be part of a world community.

## 1968-1976: A Decade of Re-Entry

When Jan, our youngest child, was old enough to attend preschool, I saw an opportunity to reenter the professional field. As part of President Lyndon Johnson's War on Poverty, one entitlement program targeted the inner city schools of the nation. Persons with bachelor degrees but no education certification were invited to join this program to be trained as tutors in either reading or mathematics. I took the two weeks of training and received my assignment to be a reading tutor in one of Buffalo's elementary schools.

I soon learned that Buffalo's inner city schools were generally either black or predominantly another recent immigrant group—reflecting the makeup of the city's communities. The building where I would teach was in the black community and old, with dark hallways lined with old calendar art of white children in country scenes. The teachers were overstressed and underpaid. When I walked by the kindergarten class, I could hear the teacher screaming at the fifty kindergarteners in front of her. She would have a second group of fifty for her afternoon class. The principal and most of the teachers were white. You could hear them shouting at their classes as they tried in vain to maintain some order and teach. I was stunned and sickened at what I saw and heard.

My role was to take a group of six who had been identified by their teachers as reading at least two years below grade level. I followed a scripted pattern of teaching from materials designed to accelerate their learning. Of course, the most important thing these children received was individual attention. One teacher told me later that the biggest gift I gave my students was the way I talked to them.

I was totally unprepared for this reality. The school system in Clarence Center where we had chosen to live was rated one of the top school systems in New York state. The class sizes were limited and teachers well paid. Students scored high in the state administered tests called the Regents. Besides their classes, students had extraordinary opportunities in music and art. Although the school taxes were higher than in some other places, we had chosen to live where our children could have these opportunities.

During my time in Buffalo's inner city schools, I had to face my ignorance and mistaken assumptions. Our schools did not offer all children equal opportunities. How could I continue to support our children in their education, and at the same time advocate for these children who, with their parents, were caught in the web of failure? For these children, education was a daily dose of defeat, disheartening messages, and a hopeless future.

This experience resurrected my long-ago dream of teaching, and I decided to begin a master's program in secondary education. In 1970 I enrolled at Canisius College, a private Catholic school in Buffalo, with a schedule that would allow me to complete the MA in five years while continuing the part-time tutoring. I found, however, that teaching in a public high school did not work for me, so I taught for two years in a private school and completed my MA in 1975.

Frost says in his poem, "way leads to way." At a Goshen Homecoming weekend in 1972, I met Urie Bender from Ontario. He invited me to join his team producing a pageant to celebrate the 150th anniversary of the coming of the Amish Mennonites to Ontario. He had written the script, and the production team had hired Loretta Yoder, an Indianapolis professional director. The actors would be from that large Amish Mennonite community, non-professionals chosen by try-out. It would be staged at the Avon Theater in Stratford, Ontario. Urie needed an assistant director who could take over the rehearsals between Loretta's monthly trips. I couldn't say "yes" fast enough! Getting back into drama was a dream I didn't even know I had.

Urie opened the pageant with scenes from Anabaptist beginnings in Zurich, Switzerland. Each scene continued the story across the hundreds of years of martyrdom and persecution in Europe until the first settlers were granted land in what was now Ontario. The climax was "the present" very large and thriving community. I was particularly moved by the concluding scene—a parade of all those historical persons reappearing across the stage. Loretta had designed sets and costumed each scene beautifully and with historical authenticity. When the production was actually staged in September 1973, the Avon Theater in Stratford was sold out for every scheduled performance, and more were added.

The following year our local New York church community—the Alden Conservative Mennonite and the Clarence Center Mennonite churches—decided that our community should do a dramatic history production and asked me to direct it. The actors would again be volunteers from our church community. Myron Augsburger, president of Eastern Mennonite College (EMC), had hired a scriptwriter to produce a drama from his book about the sixteenth-century, martyred leader, Michael Sattler. Myron gave us permission to use that script and to adapt it to our needs. The Mennonite community in western New York was reenergized as they learned of their Anabaptist history. After staging the drama in our area, we were invited to take it to the larger eastern New York Mennonite community and eventually, at the invitation of Myron, to EMC. We hired a bus to take our large cast to Harrisonburg, Virginia, for a performance in Lehman Auditorium.

In 1975, as I was settling back into completing my degree, teaching, and being a mother, I received a surprise letter that was about to change our lives significantly. Ken Weaver, director of Mennonite Broadcasts Inc. (MBI) in Harrisonburg, wrote that they were looking for someone to replace Ella May Miller, who was retiring as speaker of the radio program, *Heart to Heart,* and wondered about adding my name to the list. Don and I actually laughed, since I never listened to the radio. (I always treasured silence when I was at home.) I had no idea how this program sounded! But since I knew I'd never be chosen, I figured it was okay to let my name stand.

Then a second letter arrived offering more details. The person being considered must be willing to move to Harrisonburg as a full-time employee of Mennonite Broadcasts. As we considered this, Don offered that he could get accounting work wherever we lived, but creative opportunities for me were not as probable. Besides, it would never happen! So we said "yes" a second time. The third round came with a request to write a sample script and go to a Buffalo religious radio station to record a tape. I wrote a script, set out for Buffalo twenty-five miles away, and realized that I had forgotten to pick up the script. So I went into the studio and told a story of our surprise weekend guests, two young women from Vietnam who had been denied entrance to Canada.

## 1977-1988: A Decade of Professional Ministry

I never asked questions about how the decision was made, but I did receive a phone call and a letter with the invitation for me to take the Heart to Heart position. Now we had to really examine this option. I agreed to try it for one year. From August 1976 to July 1977, I made monthly trips to Harrisonburg, staying for a week to write four weeks of programs and then to record these twenty programs. After being transferred to tape, the tapes were mailed to stations in the U.S. and Canada, which had been airing *Heart to Heart*.

I stayed in Doris Rosenberger's home during my weeks in Harrisonburg and went with her to Park View Mennonite Church. Although I could see that the college had changed greatly from my student years, I also wanted to be sure that our family could be at home in this Virginia Mennonite church.

In August 1977, Don and I bought a house just over the hill from the college and moved our family to Harrisonburg. Our two older daughters would attend Eastern Mennonite High School, and Jan would attend the public school for seventh grade. Our son Bob had entered college in New York and did not move with us until a year later when he transferred to the College of William and Mary in Williamsburg, Virginia.

*Margaret in the studio at Mennonite Broadcasts, Inc. recording for* Heart to Heart.

I was hired by Mennonite Broadcasts, Inc., a ministry of the Mennonite Board of Missions. The work was totally new to me and I had many questions. How does one write a script for a daily five-minute radio program? How would I find ideas week after week? Who was my audience on these 190 stations in the U.S. and Canada? Most important, however, was deciding what I wanted to do with these programs.

Heart to Heart had been focused on programming for Christian women who were full-time mothers and homemakers, to encourage them to live faithfully in those roles. In the broader religious community, this was also the era of *The Total Woman*, a book written to promote the idea that a woman's role and responsibility was primarily to maintain a happy marriage. I didn't find my sole purpose in any of these roles.

An advisory board was formed to help me in developing a platform statement with purpose and objectives for a different kind of program. Together we talked about enlarging the scope of interests and roles available to women from the perspective of a Christian woman—a Mennonite Christian woman. I discovered that my years of pursuing varied interests and experiences were useful: How do children learn? What education happens in our segregated schools? How can we welcome the international students who come to our universities? How can women contribute to caring for needs in our communities? Our nation? Our world?

All my interests and the books, music, and drama, as well as my family experiences, were relevant resources for my programs. Additionally, I would interview women and men with other varied experiences to broaden the scope of the programming. When Ron Byler joined our team as producer, he added his media expertise, and we decided to change the name from *Heart to Heart* to *Your Time*, with an original music introduction. Each program concluded with "*Your Time* is brought to you by the Mennonite Church."

The task of writing each week's scripts was daunting, but I received help from Evelyn Sauder, secretary, and Melodie Davis, a recent EMU graduate also hired by MBI as a writer. Melodie began writing the scripts for one week per month and later wrote more to cover vacation times. Over the course of my programming, our team included three different engineers.

It is fun to look back over the list of programs. As early as the first month, I interviewed Nancy Williams of Mennonite Central Committee (MCC), a specialist in caring for developmentally disabled persons. Over the years my list of interviewees included Omar Eby, an EMC professor with international experience, who talked about the lessons he learned from being a father. Alta Mae Erb, an early childhood educator, talked about the wonderful mind of the child. Mike Garde, a student from Ireland, told of his hope to establish a Christian peace community in Northern Ireland. A victim and offender who met in the Elkhart VORP (Victim Offender Reconciliation Program) told their story of reconciliation. Alice Parker, the musical arranger working with Robert Shaw, described returning to her work after the sudden death of her musician husband.

Earl and Pat Hostetter Martin, just returned from Vietnam, shared some of their stories of working amid the devastation of war. Miriam Krantz, a nutritionist sent to Nepal by Mennonite Board of Missions, described the cereal she developed to save the lives of babies in rural Nepal. Two different recovering alcoholics told their stories. Ben Weir, a Presbyterian minister who had been held hostage in Lebanon, talked of forgiveness for his captors. A number of interviewees were musicians, such as Chuck Neufeldt and Tom Hunter. We also made Christmas and Easter programs with some of my favorite seasonal music.

All these interviews and many more were interspersed with more traditional programs exploring the development of family goals, discipline which is nurturing and respectful, the care of aging parents, social service agencies in the community, hospitality toward international guests, and books which I found to address current issues.

Besides writing and producing the radio programs, another major part of my work involved speaking engagements and attending conferences. I regularly attended the Mennonite Church assemblies and the Mennonite World Conference in Strasburg, France, and Wichita, Kansas. I also participated in the annual Mennonite Women in Ministry Conferences and the Evangelical Women's Caucus. Besides invitations to speak in Mennonite churches, I was invited to many Church of the Brethren, United Methodist, and Quaker groups. Various social service agencies and educational groups also invited me as a resource person. I enjoyed meeting people from such diverse places and welcomed these interactions as an opportunity to learn.

The changes in the radio program, including the name shift from *Heart to Heart* to *Your Time*, did not go unnoticed by listeners and radio stations. Predictably the reactions went both ways. A number of religious stations and country and western formats dropped my program. A few of the women's church groups also dropped sponsorship. Fortunately, other stations and other women's groups picked up the *Your Time* program when we had marketing drives. I think the number of stations carrying the program ranged between 120 and 190.

At a five-year evaluation, stations were asked whether *Your Time* was a public affairs program or a religious program. Twenty religious stations responded: thirteen considered it public affairs and six considered it religious. Of the thirty-five secular stations that answered, eighteen said Your Time was a public affairs program, six categorized it as religious, and twelve said it was both.

Listeners were also across the spectrum. Each week we received mail with comments and questions. Most were welcoming and strongly positive. Some were highly critical. I didn't save particularly negative responses, but I did save an early and very heartening note, which came on the letterhead of a Congregational church in Connecticut. This pastor wrote, "I have *Your Time* on the radio when I go to pick up children from nursery school. The program is uniformly excellent: clear, pointed, faithful and gracious. When so much of the media's religious offering ignores the Christian's responsibility to the world in which we live, I'm much encouraged by the simple but clear response to the gospel's imperative that you proclaim." I was gratified that my program had carried this clear sense of what I wished to convey.

Besides the taped radio programs, each week's script was edited into a leaflet. By this time our daughter Ellen was an art major in college, and I enjoyed having her draw the artwork for the cover of each leaflet printed and offered to listeners as an invitation to respond. Over the span of eleven years, there were always interesting letters in the mail: some with questions, others with grateful words and thanks. Since the short-wave station HCJB carried my program, I sometimes heard from listeners in South America or Alaska.

Another expectation was that I would write a book. I found this daunting, but when I discovered a poem by Doris Janzen Longacre, "Reflections on Things That Life Is too Short for," I used it as the basis for one week's programs. We received an unusually high number of requests for this leaflet. With adapting and expanding, I used these programs as the foundation for a book which was published by Zondervan Press under the title, *Life Is Too Short—to Miss Today*.

One special opportunity came in September 1984. My daughter Jan went with me to Washington, D.C., for the National Women's Conference to Prevent Nuclear War. Joanne Woodward chaired the conference. Speakers included Helen Caldicott, who organized Physicians for Social Responsibility; Congresswomen Bella Abzug and Patricia Schroeder; Elise Boulding; and Coretta Scott King, whom I later interviewed. The conference culminated with a women's march against nuclear weapons. Women knew that nuclear war was unthinkable and that stockpiling weapons was a terrible threat to the world. They challenged the current U.S. policy! It was exhilarating to hear women speak with knowledge and power.

By the mid-1980s, radio formats were changing, and our producers decided that we should cut the length of each program from four and one-half minutes to two and one-half minutes. The final two years of *Your Time* were the short programs, and I found it more difficult to make this format carry a thoughtful presentation. There was also a growing interest at Media Ministries to begin video production. The last *Your Time* program aired during the first week of October 1987.

For me, the decision was bittersweet. The short format had become increasingly frustrating for me, and I was running out of ideas. I was also aware that my chances of finding full-time employment were slim. For the next two years I taught freshman communication and Bible courses part-time at EMC. My MA degree was enough to allow the part-time work, but it was not adequate for a full-time position.

## 1989-1999: A DECADE WITH A NEW DISCIPLINE

On one *Your Time* program, I had interviewed Barry Hart, at that time director of the new Community Mediation Center in Harrisonburg. As he described mediation, it had immediately seemed a wonderful "aha" for me—here was a framework, a process for resolving conflicts that was workable, a new tool kit. I did not anticipate that I would find a new direction for my life in this discipline, but in summer 1989 the Community Mediation Center advertised the position of executive director. I applied and was given the job.

It was an exciting time in the development of mediation activity, not only in Harrisonburg but also in the state of Virginia. The Community Mediation Center had established itself in the local community and had been operating with part-time staff for three years. Moving to full-time staff, the first priority was making the center self-supporting. Our three-person staff developed training modules for businesses, started peer mediation programs for schools, and built up a case-load of mediations, many of them court referred. We sought support from the United Way and other grant agencies to supplement fees. The staff also participated in statewide efforts to incorporate dispute resolution into the Virginia judicial system as well as to help other communities in beginning mediation programs.

After four years I again faced termination. Trying to keep a new and unusual service solvent and moving ahead was very challenging, and in the process I alienated a few. I also learned that mediators do not necessarily use the processes they teach to resolve their own issues.

However, by now I was certified as a mediator and trainer by the Office of Executive Secretary of the Virginia Supreme Court. I began to work with a mediator and trainer in Charlottesville to develop a training manual and workshop certified by the state office. In the next five years we worked with a new mediation center in Charlottesville, supporting the director and training their mediators. As a private consultant, I also provided mediation and training for businesses, churches, and other organizations as opportunities arose, but it did not bring in consistent income.

## 2000-2010: A WORLD BEYOND

A new path opened up in 1999 when I audited a mediation course taught by John Paul Lederach in the new Conflict Transformation Program (CTP) at Eastern Mennonite University (EMU). The two-year MA in the Conflict Transformation program graduated its first class in 1997. The more I learned about this education for peace and reconciliation, the more I wanted to be involved. I volunteered to help with news writing and producing marketing materials. In 1998 I accepted a part-time position as coordinator for the Partners in Peacebuilding development program. This job gave me the opportunity to learn to know students as well as staff as we worked to enlarge the support base. In 2000 when the Summer Peacebuilding Institute (SPI) needed a community relations coordinator, I picked up that work as well. In each task, students worked with me, visiting churches and speaking to civic groups.

Following the attacks of September 11, 2001, CTP (now CJP, the Center for Justice and Peacebuilding) and Church World Service worked together to develop and offer monthly Strategies for Trauma Awareness and Recovery (STAR) seminars. Carolyn Yoder directed these seminars and invited me to work with her as a co-facilitator.

Besides my work assignments in these ten years, I also developed relationships with students from areas of conflict—from Africa and the Middle East, from countries of Southeast Asia, even Europe. Since I worked part-time, I always had time for conversations. I listened to their stories and their hopes for peace, and I learned about life amid trauma. Along with other CTP staff, Don and I hosted potluck dinners in our home and took students on shopping trips and rides to airports.

In the past decade, this last new path has been an introduction to the richest experiences of my life. My world has expanded beyond the familiar borders of my family, my community, and my church. My circles now include friends from every continent but Antarctica, people of color and different religions, many with histories of pain and suffering I could never have imagined. Their stories of faith and courage and their dreams for peace have grown out of forgiveness that I can only humbly bless. With email and phone I continue to hear from graduates as they begin to work out their vocations in peacebuilding.

## THE PATH TAKEN

I began this memoir with lines from Frost's poem, "The Road Not Taken." But my reflections are on The Road Taken. From my earliest memories I saw myself as a Mennonite, a part of a local church; and I have lived my life (taken this road) within the Mennonite church as my community of faith.

When I was a small child, I observed my parents and the members of the churches we attended, and I considered myself as belonging in that small group which had rules. I remember one time when my parents invited a couple to our home who did not attend our church. They ended their evening together with prayer, but that woman did not wear a covering. "Is she a Christian?" I asked my mother. "Of course," she said. But I wondered how she could be a Christian if she didn't follow the rules.

Through my years in school, the specifics of these rules sometimes varied, but they were always, from my perspective, directed specifically at women. Although other Christians did not follow these rules, if I wanted to be a Christian, I had to follow these Mennonite rules. We were taught from stories and verses in the King James Version of the Bible, which were interpreted by the conservative religious teachers and leaders.

How did my vision of God—a God requiring that we live by a specific set of rules—grow to be a vision of a God loving and welcoming me and all the peoples of the world?

As I described earlier, in my move to Scottdale and then to Goshen College, I met new models. They were Mennonites, but they were educated and their focus was on living joyfully. In conversations as well as in classes, I learned from professors like Roy Umble and Atlee Beechy, Mennonites who saw Jesus as teacher, as the one to be followed in daily life. In the class with Howard Charles, I realized that I could study the Gospel of John, just as I had learned to read and look for meaning in other books. When I began working with MCC, I joined an organization in which the words "In the name of Christ" told the world that we were offering our service as well as our giving out of this vision. And I learned that Mennonites were not all alike!

A major turning point in my life was choosing to marry and have a family. I had grown up expecting that I would have a professional career and remain single. But I took the "other road" when I married Don, and it has made all the difference. My life changed from its focus on myself to caring for others. Of course, it is only in retrospect that I can say this. In the experiences of being a wife and mother, I changed. And my vision of a loving God kept growing, changing colors, and changing edges. Watching the daily new and individual steps of each of our children was miracle every day. And I often thought about Jesus' words, "God so loved the world."

Throughout my life I experienced singing and music as worship. My mother had sung as she worked, and I learned from her. During my years of attending Mennonite churches and singing in college choirs, music was the most meaningful expression of worship for me. My years of singing in the professional chorus, while my children were young, continued to be an experience of both worship and learning. The choral works of Bach, Brahms, and Mozart were from other times and other church traditions but were expressions of worship of the same God. The music made me sing inside as well as with my voice. And the people I sang with, as well as those who came to the concerts, opened a new and much wider vision of a church, a multinational church, past and present. I was singing an affirmation of God's glory, with great joy, and with my whole self.

During this period of my life, I taught Sunday school classes in which I used the principles I had learned in college to do my own Bible study. Again and again, I read a whole chapter, looking for the purpose and organization that gave meaning to the parts. Since I was a reader, I also found many books that offered other perspectives, including history and background on cultures of the biblical eras.

The second major turning point in my life was moving from New York to Virginia when I accepted the MBM position to produce and write a daily radio program. It was clear to me that my purpose in this programming would be to share my perspective on living as a Christian woman in this time and place. I thought I could be a friend who walked alongside, who often brought new possibilities to a conversation, and who celebrated the work of women in our society. I also believed that this was a ministry growing out of my faith, a faith shaped by the Mennonite church, a faith which was a vision for peace.

In that period, the 1970s, a major issue within the Mennonite church was whether women could be ordained as ministers. Since my work was recognized as "ministry," I was involved with this issue in Virginia Mennonite Conference just by living here and being a member of Park View Mennonite Church.

As was my usual habit, I did a study of biblical materials related to this issue, beginning with specific times when Jesus interacted with women, then studying Paul's letter to the Ephesians, and then reading some scholarly works. My personal convictions grew—Jesus treated women, as well as men, with respect, responding to their needs, offering healing, forgiveness, and hope. In Paul's writings, the cultural settings for each new church dictated some of the restrictions which were now being used to justify limiting Mennonite women's participation in worship in twentieth-century America.

I participated in conversations during this time, especially in support of the Women in Ministry Conferences being held annually in Mennonite communities. At one point I helped to plan such a conference in Harrisonburg. These were always welcome times of learning and celebrating God's calling and leading of women within the Mennonite Church.

In my own understanding, this issue—refusing to honor God's calling of women to ministry—connected with when I first realized how people of color had been oppressed by Christians. From the period of slavery to the present, they continue to suffer social, economic, and political oppression.

Although much less restrictive, I have also known oppression as a woman in the Mennonite church. My study on the issue of whether or not women could be ordained in the church became a major development in the faith path I took. Whether the issue swirls around same-sex relationships, or women, or persons of color, I start from a deep knowing that I am loved and accepted by God. I will not participate in the construction of walls or rules meant to shut others out. My vision of God is now the One who created all, who welcomes all, who loves all.

During my years of working with the Center for Justice and Peacebuilding, many of our students were Muslim, a few were Buddhist or Hindu, others were "none." Now the questions are changed. Do we worship the same God? Can we find ways to live out the vision of peace, accepting differences? Can we pray together? And the answer again is "yes."

My road continues to be an exploration of a God of mystery, a God I experience in the "good news" of Jesus. As I walk with friends of many cultures and religions, their experiences continue to challenge me to live without violence, honoring and respecting all of God's people.

I also feel grateful that my family members continue to be my friends. Our three grandsons continue the task of teaching me more about love. They are now my companions on this road.

October 12, 2009<br>Revised March 2015

## Notes

1. Robert Frost, "The Road Not Taken," *The Pocket Book of Robert Frost's Poems* (Rockefeller Center, N.Y.: Cardinal Edition, 1953), 223.

2. Margaret Foth, *Life Is too Short—to Miss Today* (Grand Rapids, Mich.: Zondervan Publishing House, 1985).

*Paul M. Schrock*

### Moses of the Mennonite Publishing House

*As a prelude to the fuller story, let me list a few categories of intrigue in the life of Paul Schrock: How does a high school run-away kid from the "wild" West end up at Eastern Mennonite College? And become an editor of the* Weather Vane *for two years—which is four times longer than most WV editors hold out nowadays? How did college newspaper editing prepare him to become a book editor, whose name for almost forty years was a near-synonym of "Mennonite Publishing House?" But like Moses, he didn't end up in the Promised Land!*

## PAUL M. SCHROCK

# *From Reluctant Farmer to Passionate Book Editor*

### EARLY EDUCATION OF A CURIOUS FARM BOY

I was the firstborn of eight children to a young Mennonite farmer (Melvin Schrock) and his bride of two years (Anna Roth) in the fertile Willamette Valley of western Oregon seventy years ago. My parents scratched out a living on 200 acres for me and my five sisters and two brothers, who arrived at two- and later four-year intervals over a period of nineteen years. In addition to ryegrass, we sometimes made hay and grew oats, wheat, or barley for animal feed. We kept a few cows and chickens and pigs (which we occasionally butchered) and tended a large garden for our own use. We ate lots of berries, cherries, and nuts in season and had a small orchard.

After harvest each year, we brought fresh fish and crabs home with us from the nearby Oregon coast. Homemade ice cream was our favorite food, prepared in hand-turned freezers when we could find an excuse to bring together various combinations of cousins, uncles, aunts, and grandparents.

Soon my father was ordained to the plural ministry, serving without salary the rural Fairview Mennonite Church. This congregation of several hundred members was surrounded by ryegrass farmers raising seed for lawns and pastures. My family and the Fairview congregation were intensely loyal to the Mennonite church and to all of the publications offered by the Mennonite Publishing House from a place some 2,500 miles away called Scottdale, Pennsylvania.

Most of the walls in our home were covered with plaster of Paris mottoes and with Bible verses and other inspirational and motivational quotations. My mother and other women from neighboring churches made a social event out of pouring the raw mixture of mysterious ingredients into molds, later removing the mottoes and letting them cure, before painting them many bright colors. One smaller wooden motto, hung above the doorway between our dining room and kitchen for all of my growing up years, intrigued me. It said simply, "Aim high. There is plenty of room."

In 1939, when I was four years old, our family headed for Detroit, Michigan (by train, I think), to pick up a new Plymouth car at the factory. We then drove to Big Valley, Pennsylvania, where the Allensville congregation had erected a large tent and was hosting what was then known as the General Conference Mennonite Church. On our return trip to Oregon, we stopped at Hesston College, where my father had studied for one year. Someone snapped my picture standing on the front steps of one of the campus buildings. Back in Oregon, my family was delighted to see me on the cover of C. F. Yake's *Youth's Christian Companion*, known affectionately as YCC. This issue about Mennonite schools is dated August 4, 1940, my fifth birthday.

At Fairview church we used the colorful little Bible picture memory cards that came from Scottdale, as well as the big teaching pictures, the various Sunday school quarterlies for all ages, vacation Bible school curriculum, and missionary banks shaped like little world globes with a slot in the top for our coins.

At home, from my earliest years, I was surrounded by periodicals from Scottdale: *Words of Cheer, Youth's Christian Companion, Gospel Herald, Christian Monitor,* and *Mennonite Community*. We read them faithfully when they came. Then we stacked them in the attic to reread on rainy days, especially the Christmas Carol Kauffman "continued stories."

When I was seven, I wrote a letter to *Words of Cheer*, where the refrain often appeared, "If I have a twin or someone near my age, please write and I will gladly answer." Ellrose Zook was chief editor and Lina Ressler letters editor. She wrote a brief response to each letter, signing as Aunt Lina. Eighteen years after I wrote that letter, Ellrose invited me to become editor of *Words of Cheer*. I served in that role for nine years, producing more than 400 issues. I wrote brief responses to more than a thousand children's letters published during that time, although I never adopted a pen name such as "Uncle Paul."

Paul Erb, a church-wide statesman, became editor of the official Mennonite Church weekly, *Gospel Herald*, in January 1944. I was nine years old at the time, never dreaming in my wildest fantasies that, fifteen years later, I would be hired by Mennonite Publishing House as his assistant.

At the age of ten, I accepted Christ, along with a bench full of my friends, under some social pressure and a sense of childhood conviction for my sins, in a week-long series of revival meetings led by a traveling evangelist from the east. After six weeks of instruction during the Sunday school hour by our bishop, N. M. Birky, who led us through the historic Dordrecht Confession, we were baptized.

I completed eight years of primary education in seven years in one- and two-room public schools and four years of secondary education in five years at Western Mennonite School (WMS), with a student body of less than one hundred. Since WMS was in Salem, Oregon, forty miles from home, I stayed in their dormitory four nights a week. But I was delayed from graduating with my class because of my youthful escapades. In one of these adventures, I hitchhiked to Seattle, found bittersweet entertainment in an all-night movie theatre, and was miffed when, after showing three movies, they repeated themselves. With no cash to rent a room, I slept under a nearby bridge the rest of that cold, drizzly, foggy night.

I was twice expelled for running off to see movies so was given a year off between my high school junior and senior years to find myself. My parents, trying to harness my itch for adventure with their concern for my spiritual well-being, suggested that I attend a six-week Bible term at Eastern Mennonite College (EMC) that winter. I gladly accepted. Before leaving home, my mother said, "If I asked you not to go to any movies on this trip, would you agree?" I said yes, but on a technicality (she never asked me), I proceeded to see many movies. (Parenthetically, I am bored sitting through most movies now.) I enjoyed my time at EMC and would return there for college after graduating from WMS in 1954.

Although there were fewer than 100 students at WMS, I was thrilled to serve as editor of the mimeographed school newspaper, *Western Breezes*, and of the yearbook, *Western Pioneer*. During Senior Sneak in the fall of my senior year, our class, along with our sponsors, Clayton and Margaret Swartzentruber, happily left on an unannounced camping trip to Crescent Lake in the Cascade Mountains east of Eugene. Of the twenty-three students who went, only twenty students returned. Three drowned in a boating accident. I had been in the same small boat with five other fellows all afternoon. Riding low in the water, without life jackets, we had crossed the deepest part of the lake to arrive in time for the evening fireside meal. The three who drowned that evening were Ellen West from Oregon, Sanford Kauffman from Montana, and Wayne Snyder from Idaho. Eighteen schoolmates served as pallbearers at a funeral of perhaps a thousand people in the new WMS gym a few days later. This event had a lasting and profound effect on my life.

During my last semester at WMS, one of our teachers encouraged the seniors to write an essay that would be entered into a competition sponsored by the Peace Problems Committee of the denomination. I usually spent weekends helping around my parents' farm and attending Tangent Mennonite Church with them on Sunday. But one rainy Saturday afternoon, when it was too soggy to work outside, I went to the desk in my upstairs bedroom and wrote an essay on peace, which I handed in the next week. I never heard any more about it until after graduation.

One day I came in from combining oats for a farmer's dinner at noontime. I asked Mom what had come in the mail. (We received rural delivery at the end of our dirt lane seven miles from town.) "Not much except the *Gospel Herald*," she said. I picked up the July 20, 1954, issue and started leafing through it. At the end of an article, I noticed the location of the writer was Tangent, Oregon. "Hey," I said with excitement. "Someone from Tangent has an article in *Gospel Herald*." Then I found the beginning of the piece and could hardly get the words out: "It's me!"

There it was. "Atomic Love," by Paul M. Schrock. A blurb in small type beneath the article said, "The author, a student at Western Mennonite High School, has been awarded first place for this entry in the annual peace essay contest." A few days later, I received an official letter of notification, a $10.00 check, and a complimentary copy of *War, Peace, and Nonresistance*, by Guy F. Hershberger as my prize. Paul Erb was editor of the issue in which that essay appeared. Interestingly, my grand-daughter Grace Schrock-Hurst, as a senior at Eastern Mennonite High School, placed second in the same contest and received a check for $250.00.

## THE SCHOOL OF HARD KNOCKS

For the most part, I never enjoyed farming. At every opportunity, I read whatever I could get my hands on, even if it was the few "preacher books" owned by my father. I kept a book with me when driving the tractor pulling our combine and hoped for a breakdown so that I could read while my father solved the crisis. My mother wondered aloud how I would ever make a living if I did not take up farming. Later I reminded her that professional editors took home a paycheck, even though it was pretty meager at a church institution.

In early August, the year I graduated from WMS, I turned down my father's offer of wages, room and board, and a car if I stayed home to help him on the farm. Instead, I headed, along with four or five others, on a nonstop trip—three days and three nights across the country—in a car without air-conditioning. The outside temperature was above 100 degrees the whole way. We drove with all four windows open every night and arrived at Eastern Mennonite College (EMC) just in time for a watermelon social which I was in no shape to enjoy.

We went into a battery of freshman entrance tests and I managed, despite my fatigue, to score well into the nineteenth percentile on most of them. I was peeved, however, at one category of testing, wondering why it was even administered at a place like EMC. The test was on popular and classical culture, about which I knew practically nothing. I grew up in a home without musical instruments (even a piano), or radio, or a record player. My family never attended concerts, movies, or even high school plays. So that test was tough sledding.

Nevertheless, I was admitted to college, probably against the better judgment of some of the staff. I had no money for tuition, room, or board, but somehow things were patched together. I had no sense of direction as to what courses to take so I majored in social life. I enjoyed dormitory living in the old ad building, basketball in the cracker box gym, the Smithsonian literary society, and such traditional events as School Day Out.

By mid-year however, the glamour of college had worn off. My studies were not going well. I was in debt, discouraged, and depressed. I did not know where to turn. Swallowing my pride, I wrote a letter to my parents telling them that I had decided college was not for me. If they sent money for a bus ticket, I would return home and help on the farm. But I did not even have three cents to buy the first-class stamp to mail the letter. I could have borrowed a stamp or the money but hesitated to drop the letter in the mail slot.

One day as I procrastinated, I went to my student mailbox and found an envelope for me with a scrawled return address from Oliver Zehr. Oliver was a bit eccentric and never quite fit into the home church. I opened the envelope to find a check for several hundred dollars, nearly enough in those days to cover tuition, room, and board for the next semester. Oliver included a handwritten note that read something like this: "Dear Paul. I believe in Christian education. I believe in you. Here's a little gift to help you along. If you can ever pay it back, pass it along to someone else struggling with their school expenses."

I stayed at EMC. (Later I did pass the money along.) Second semester I was asked to help with the student paper, the purple ditto *Weather Vane*. A year later, I became the founding editor of Volume 1, Number 1 of the *Weather Vane* in its newspaper format. All of this boosted my morale considerably.

Between our sophomore and junior years, my roommate Lowell Herr and I drove vehicles and helped Myron Augsburger in his evangelistic tent campaigns. At the Williamsville, New York location (near Buffalo and Alden), I took a liking to a petite identical twin, June Bontrager, who was coming to EMC in the fall. After courting on campus, we were married on September 7, 1957, just before my senior year at EMC. I graduated in 1958 with a BA degree in secondary education with a teaching field in English. I spent summer 1958 at the Mennonite Publishing House (MPH) working on the retail sales catalog and then moved to June's home community of Alden, where I taught grades five through nine in the Christian day school, drove school bus every morning and afternoon, and worked in Richard Bender's small Christian bookstore one evening a week and on Saturdays.

## Cutting Teeth on Magazine Editing

By September 1959, June, baby Carmen, and I were settled back at Scottdale, where I had been offered a full-time editorial job. I saw my name in print in an official capacity for the first time in the September 1, 1959, issue of the *Gospel Herald*. I was hired as assistant *Gospel Herald* editor and assistant to the book editor, Paul Erb. I also edited the Sunday evening program section of *Builder* magazine. It was in my capacity as assistant editor of the *Gospel Herald* that I came across a poem by a fourteen-year-old boy from Lancaster, Pennsylvania, which I felt was worthy of publication. I sent the author, I. Merle Good, a check for $2.50. He says it was the first acceptance he ever received and helped to launch his writing and publishing career.

Two years later, in the July 2, 1961, issue of *Words of Cheer*, Ellrose Zook introduced me as the new editor to thousands of nine-to-fourteen-year-old readers of this story paper. As executive editor of MPH, Zook carried leadership responsibilities for periodicals, curriculum, and books. No sooner had he established me as editor of *Words of Cheer* than he encouraged me to leave for a year to study for my master's degree in journalism at Syracuse University. Arrangements were made for Jane Peachey Lind to edit *Words of Cheer* in my absence, and off to Syracuse I went for twelve months with my young family—June, Carmen, and now Brent. (National Democratic leader Adlai Stevenson and British novelist C. P. Snow spoke at commencement that spring of 1963.)

I've never studied as hard as I did at Syracuse. Statistics was an especially difficult challenge for me. In another class, a documented ten-page research paper was due each week of the semester or a twenty-page paper every two weeks. More than once I worked all night on class assignments. Nevertheless, I was meeting my goal of earning straight A's until a final summer class hit me broadside. Well-known American novelist Phyllis Whitney told her fiction writing class on the first day that she did not believe in grades. Therefore, she was giving everyone a B for the course and, much to my displeasure and wounded pride, she did just that.

We returned to Scottdale at the end of my studies, but the pay was low at Mennonite Publishing House. Our small family had high medical costs, including several hospitalizations. Andrea, our third child, was born in 1964 and remained in the hospital while she received blood exchanges for RH incompatibility followed by more blood transfusions.

Four years later, in 1968, June had to go to University of Pittsburgh Medical Center for intrauterine blood transfusions into the child in her womb for the same blood problem. Douglas Paul was born prematurely, given multiple blood exchanges, cared for by a group of RH specialists, but died after two days. June made more than thirty trips from Scottdale to Pittsburgh (eighty miles round trip) as the first person in Pennsylvania to contribute antibodies from her blood to develop RhoGam. This shot now routinely protects against RH disease.

I carried a strong sense of call, however, that God had led me into Christian journalism. I settled in at MPH for forty years (like Moses in the wilderness), in a part of Appalachia extending into southwestern Pennsylvania, but I needed to find a way to make additional money. MPH editors received packets of black and white, eight-by-ten photos from freelance photographers from which selections were made for our magazines. Payment was often $10.00 or $15.00 for non-exclusive use of a photograph. I decided that maybe I could supplement our family income by taking photos. I bought MPH Treasurer Joe Buzzard's third-hand Rollicord camera after he returned from a trip to Africa. He agreed to accept my offer of $5.00 per two-week pay period to purchase it. Harold Beachy, a designer colleague, and I rented a small, dark corner of the MPH basement for our darkroom at $5.00 a month. Later I always had a darkroom of some sort built into my home.

I sold my first $10,000 worth of photos, seldom at a price of more than $20.00 each, from that camera before buying somewhat better, but never top-of-the-line, equipment. I made up eight-by-ten black and white prints, always in my own darkroom, on evenings and Saturdays. My most frequent models were my family. I mailed the photos every Saturday morning in packets of sixty to as many places as I could manage. For several decades, my photos appeared on the cover of *Christian Century* and in the magazines and curricula of most Christian denominations. I became better known in many quarters as a photographer than as a Mennonite editor and administrator.

Before I became book editor, I was a member of an interdenominational group of periodical editors who met once a year for fellowship and professional stimulation. In September 1971, Ken Taylor, founder of Tyndale House Publishers, met with us. He brought with him autographed copies of the just completed first edition of *The Living Bible*, which he translated, and presented one to each of us.

While *The Living Bible* is a paraphrase and not recommended as a standard text for public worship or for serious Bible study, I found it an excellent tool for devotional use. I decided that I would ponder this paraphrase for fresh language to make the Bible more understandable, especially those parts which had been less clear to me as a young boy growing up. I had read the Bible through once or twice in my youth, but I decided I would do it again with *The Living Bible*.

Further, believing that all of the Bible should speak to me to some degree, I decided to read with red pen and ruler in hand, looking for something to underline which I found meaningful in each chapter. I knew the hazard of getting bogged down somewhere in Leviticus, so I decided not to read the Bible straight through. I would pick books pretty much at random and record them on the back flyleaf as I finished each one until my objective was completed. I still enjoy looking at this *Living Bible* with Ken Taylor's autograph, the red underlining, and my reading record inside the back flyleaf. The first book I finished was Job in October 1971, and the last one was Proverbs in July 1974, almost three years later.

## THE DISCIPLINE OF BOOK EDITING

Gradually, during the seven years following my studies at Syracuse, I became restless. I did not see much prospect of advancement beyond editing for children, even though in July 1968 I became the founding editor of *Purpose* magazine, the successor of *Youth's Christian Companion*. Editing *Words of Cheer* and *Purpose* simultaneously, each with weekly schedules, was no small feat. I think I was growing weary.

I decided to resign from MPH. Myron Augsburger, president of EMC, heard of my intention and invited me to join the EMC staff as his assistant. I accepted. Shortly thereafter, an offer arrived from an independent Christian publisher, the David C. Cook Publishing Company, to move to Elgin, Illinois, and edit one of their magazines. In seeking God's leading, I felt my call and experience were more suited to editing than to college administration. I asked Myron if he would release me from my decision to join him in Harrisonburg. Myron graciously relented. "I am not the Holy Spirit," he said. "Go where God leads you." By the time I sorted this out with Myron, D. C. Cook withdrew the offer, having hired another editor.

I remember thinking, "What in the world is the Lord's leading for me in this confusing situation." There I sat at Scottdale, having resigned from MPH, but now without a job. Paul Lederach, then president of the Mennonite Board of Education, said, "MPH should not lose a man like Paul Schrock." General Manager Ben Cutrell asked if there was anything at MPH that would interest me. I said that I had always loved books and would consider an offer to become book editor, a job then held by retiring editor and former administrator, Ellrose Zook. Publisher Ben Cutrell and Director of Trade Books Maynard Shetler took June and me to dinner and formally offered me the job of Herald Press book editor, if I would withdraw my resignation. I agreed, if MPH would give me a two-year leave of absence to refresh my spirit and to gain some additional professional experience before continuing my tenure at MPH. My request was granted.

And so, June and I packed up our family again, with Carmen, Brent, and Andrea this time, and headed for our rented home at 1235 Upland Drive in Harrisonburg, Virginia. From 1971 to 1973, I spent part-time teaching linguistics and rhetoric, short story writing, and photojournalism at EMC. I also did some staff assignments for Mennonite Broadcasts, Inc. (now Mennonite Media). I was editor of their *Alive* magazine and was producer of the Mennonite Hour and the Way to Life radio programs. During the first year in the Valley, I also continued as editor of *Purpose* magazine, working from my bedroom office on Upland Drive. From 1968 until I turned *Purpose* over to my successor, David Hostetler, I had edited 170 weekly issues.

Following my return to Scottdale from Harrisonburg, I settled into the all-consuming job of Herald Press Trade Books editor. This involved sorting through about 1,000 book proposals and manuscripts a year, helping select about 100 a year for serious committee consideration, from which about thirty books a year were then scheduled for publication. I set the agenda for the monthly Book Approving Group and was a voting member of that committee, along with the publisher, the director of the trade books division and its marketing manager, the director of congregational literature, and the director of Provident Bookstores. Following approval, I managed each book project, interacting with the author, church committees, illustrators, designers, copy editors, proofreaders, the printer, marketing people, reviewers, and the like.

One of the perks of my job was to attend professional meetings, church-wide conventions, and writers' conferences. Many of these were a mixture of work and fun, but mostly work. Over the years, I represented Herald Press books at more than thirty consecutive week-long July meetings of Christian Booksellers Convention International. These began to blur together until I literally did not know if I was in Minneapolis, Los Angeles, New Orleans, Denver, or Washington, D.C. Herald Press was a small player in the huge religious publishing arena, but we built a loyal constituency who appreciated the distinctive emphases of our books.

Meanwhile, to make a life for herself after our youngest child was a teenager and to supplement our income, June became a partner in the Scottdale Fabric Shop. She then studied for three years at the Youngwood Community College and obtained her RN degree. She worked in a number of area hospitals, followed by several years as a state health nurse.

Despite the demands of my job at MPH, I was also active in the church and community. At one time or another I was chair of the congregation, chair of the elders, chair of the Christian education committee, and Sunday school teacher at Kingview Mennonite Church. As the first lay secretary of Allegheny Mennonite Conference, I also ended up sitting on their executive committee.

Through a bit of a fluke, I was president of the Scottdale Merchants Association and president of the Southmoreland Parent Teachers Association. I was also board chair of the Mennonite Federal Credit Union and a board member of both Frick Community Hospital at Mt. Pleasant and of the larger Westmoreland Health System at Greensburg.

In 1988, after sixteen years as book editor, I was promoted to director of Herald Press Books, a role in which I continued until I turned sixty-five in 2000. In addition to administering the Herald Press book publishing program, this placed me on the five-person management team of Mennonite Publishing House, Inc. The other team members were the director of curriculum and magazines (at first Laurence Martin, then Levi Miller), the head of the Provident Bookstore chain (Jack Scott), the head of job printing, operations, and information services (Reuben Savanick), and CEO Robert Ramer.

The first book editor responsible to me was Loren Johns, who went on to become dean of the Associated Mennonite Biblical Seminary in Elkhart, Indiana. When he left, I hired Michael A. King from Telford, Pennsylvania, who eventually founded Cascadia Publishing House LLC and *DreamSeeker Magazine*. In a reversal of roles with Michael, I later served on the editorial council of his enterprises.

I was always awed by the way a limited number of dedicated persons at MPH with minimal resources were able to produce so much material that impacted the Mennonite church and far beyond. I remember a delegate standing in a business session of our denomination's general assembly making an impassioned plea that our Anabaptist understandings of following Jesus should be spread more widely around the world. I know that this does happen in many ways in various church programs and by many individuals. However, my mind went immediately to my Scottdale desk where I saw evidence nearly every day that the printed message in our books was intersecting in powerful ways in unexpected places.

One of the first manuscripts I helped to shape as book editor in the late 1980s was John M. Drescher's *Seven Things Children Need*. This book has sold tens of thousands of copies in at least seventeen languages. *The Upside-Down Kingdom*, by Donald Kraybill, won the National Religious Book award the year it was published and became a classic on the Herald Press list for decades to come. The phrase *upside-down kingdom* entered firmly into the vocabulary of Mennonites and other Christians.

The *More-with-Less Cookbook*, by Doris Janzen Longacre, sponsored by Mennonite Central Committee (MCC), was published in 1976. Released at Scottdale, New York, and Toronto, it became an instant best-seller, even by New York standards. We printed 15,000 copies month after month with total sales eventually exceeding 600,000 copies. Hundreds of thousands of dollars in royalty have gone to MCC, and the phrase *More-with-Less* has entered into the lexicon of Mennonites and other Christians around the world. Along with its companion book, *Living More with Less* (which itself sold more

# From Reluctant Farmer to Passionate Book Editor

*Valerie Weaver-Zercher and Paul Schrock with Paul Longacre at a book signing for the thirtieth anniversary edition of* Living More with Less.

than 100,000 copies), these books have affected the worldview and lifestyles of countless persons.

During his Soviet Union Crusade before the breakup of the USSR, Billy Graham carried for reference inside his suit coat some pages from Walter Sawatsky's book, *Soviet Evangelicals Since World War II*. Herald Press books have been a prominent part of MCC's peace library which is made available throughout the world. The books in this collection helped temper the thinking of persons in South Africa who achieved regime change without a bloody revolution. The Peace Shelf was carried to Vietnam during the war, was at the core of a new Anabaptist center in South Korea, and is seminal in many other countries.

Herald Press peace books were also among the resources consulted by the U.S. Conference of Catholic bishops when they drafted a peace statement for their churches. A Catholic scholar from Buenos Aires informed Herald Press that Millard Lind's *Yahweh is a Warrior* had profoundly altered his understandings of war in the Old Testament. He referred to Lind's work as being of Copernican proportions. A Lutheran graduate student mentioned to me at an annual meeting of the American Academy of Religion/Society of Biblical Literature that his mind was reeling, having just discovered the writings of John Howard Yoder. I encouraged him to continue his search with an open mind.

One of the significant projects during my time as book editor, and then as director of Herald Press, was to help launch and give guidance to the *Believers Church Bible Commentary* series. I helped develop the prototype for the series in 1986 with the *Jeremiah* volume by Elmer Martens. To date, after twenty years, nineteen volumes have been released with many more in process. I worked with the editorial council on that series. Most of my years, this included representatives from the Mennonite Church, the General Conference Mennonite Church, the Church of the Brethren, the Mennonite Brethren Church, the Brethren in Christ Church, and the Brethren Church (Ashland, Ohio).

Throughout my years at Herald Press books, I maintained a professional relationship with the Institute of Mennonite Studies (IMS) at Elkhart, Indiana. I worked closely with C. J. Dyck on *Mennonite Encyclopedia* (vol. 5), and many other IMS projects. I interfaced with C. J., Theron Schlabach, Leonard Gross, and others on the scholarly Studies in Anabaptist and Mennonite History (SAMH) series. A sampling of some EMC/EMU (Eastern Mennonite University), Harrisonburg persons whose works appeared in Herald Press books during my tenure at Scottdale includes C. Norman Kraus, Samuel Horst, Harold Lehman, Omar Eby, Calvin Redekop, Myron Augsburger, Al Keim, Calvin Shenk, John Martin, Ervin Stutzman, Howard Zehr, and Earl and Pat Hostetter Martin.

I like books! Always have. Always will. Burned in my memory as I left MPH was a special bookcase almost filling one wall from floor to ceiling. Marked off by year were single copies of books officially released by MPH in Scottdale beginning about 1908 and continuing through the century. Most bear the imprint of Herald Press.

As assistant to book editor Paul Erb, I helped on some twenty books in 1959-61. I was more deeply involved with about 520 books during my years as trade book editor, 1972-88. As director of Herald Press from 1988-2000 I was responsible for the selection, editing, design, production, and marketing of some additional 230 books with the help of an overworked but capable staff.

To paraphrase the apostle Paul, I do not think it wise to boast about one's own work. But if I am to do so, let it be in the area of book publishing. I reflect with satisfaction on participating personally in helping bring to birth about 770 of the 1,140 books shaped at MPH during those ninety years. It has been a privilege to work with so many book authors: John Howard Yoder, Willard Swartley, John Ruth, Jan Gleysteen, Alan and Eleanor Kreider, Merle Good, Nelson Kraybill, Helen Good Brenneman, John Driver, Lowell Detweiler. Also with Katie Funk Wiebe, Dave and Neta Jackson, and Walter Klaassen. Other authors were David Augsburger, John W. Miller, Ruth Nulton Moore, Nancey Murphy, Eugene Roop, Theron Schlabach, Mary Swartley, Joetta Handrich Schlabach, Wilbert Shenk, Barbara Smucker, C. Arnold Snyder, Erland Waltner, Paul Zehr, and many more.

In 2000 Peter Dyck wrote a note to me that I will always treasure: "I thank God, Paul, and my computer, in that order for enabling me to write six books since my retirement. Paul has always encouraged me—except when he informed Elfrieda and me that Herald Press liked our manuscript, *Up from the Rubble*, and that they were going to publish it but that it needed condensing. 'Just take out 100 pages, but don't take out any of the stories,' was the message. I appreciate Paul as editor and publisher, as friend, and as a brother in the Lord."

Among my favorite responsibilities as director of Herald Press Books was to manage the foreign rights for our titles. When I retired, several large notebooks in the MPH fire vault contained more than 100 contracts with foreign publishers licensed to issue Herald Press books in foreign languages or in English editions for certain parts of the world. These languages included Afrikaans, Arabic, two dialects of Chinese, Creole, Croatian, Danish, Dutch, Finnish, French, German, Hindi, Indonesian, Italian, Japanese, Korean, Norwegian, Polish, Portuguese, Romanian, Russian, Spanish, Swedish, Tagalog (in the Philippines), Thai, and Vietnamese. Additionally, special English editions of Herald Press books were published in Australia, England, India, Nigeria, the Philippines, and Sudan. And many of our books were recorded for the visually impaired or issued in Braille.

One of the last projects on which I worked was the highly illustrated and carefully researched coffee table book for Mennonite Disaster Service, *The Hammer Rings Hope*. James Lee Witt, director of the Federal Emergency Management Agency (FEMA) at the time, attended the fiftieth anniversary celebration of MDS at Hesston, Kansas. According to Witt, "This book is a national treasure, the story of caring people helping others with devastating losses in a spirit of selflessness, joy, and sacrifice. The oral histories," Witt continues, "disaster case studies, and colorful photographs, present the rich history of Mennonite Disaster Service (MDS) in a lively way. We value our opportunity to work alongside MDS."

Well into my tenure as book editor, I was not computer literate. I loved the feel of pencil on paper and edited whole books that way. I did a line edit of all but the scholarly books which we published. One of the first of these in the early 1980s was the already mentioned book on child rearing by John M. Drescher. In 2000, Jack Scott, director of Provident Bookstores at the time, wrote, "Paul, on one of our first trips together, I recall you sitting in our motel room with chapters of the *Seven Things Children Need* manuscript covering the bed. I watched as you brilliantly reshaped the book. From that point on, I've been in awe of your ability to produce a wonderfully crafted sentence and to help any writer (including me) to achieve clarity, order, and conciseness. I've appreciated that you have been willing to speak the truth in love!"

In addition to needing to sharpen a dozen editing pencils at a time, I wore out more than one electric typewriter for other office tasks. But gradually, in a steep learning curve, I became dependent on my computer for word processing, e-mail, and other electronic programs that became standard tools. I came to recognize electronics as my servant, not my master. Computers help at every point, from the idea for a book in the mind of an author, through the printing and publishing processes, to the mind of the reader.

By 1999 we had taken our first baby steps into eBooks (electronic books). In one of our electronic contracts we joined forces with netLibrary, headquartered at Boulder, Colorado. Here's how it worked. They initially offered 240 Herald Press titles as eBooks to libraries, organizations, and individuals around the world. Each netLibrary book retained all the content of the printed volumes, including the cover color and design, page-for-page reproduction of the body, and any photos, charts, or other graphic material.

Essentially, netLibrary functioned as a jobber for Herald Press. They received a normal jobber's discount for eBooks they sold, setting terms with their electronic customers based on our retail prices. They provided a stream of royalties to Herald Press, which in turn was shared with our authors according to the terms of each contract. Purchasers of netLibrary books were allowed to buy as many copies as they wished. In a library, only one copy could be "checked out" at a time. The library could buy multiple copies if demand warranted.

## RETIRED BUT STILL LEARNING

After spending forty years of my professional life at MPH, I regret to report that the overall business was falling apart by the time I retired on August 17, 2000. Many factors contributed to its downfall. At the risk of over-simplification, I will mention five:

1. The debt load was greater than the business could sustain.

2. A longtime system of financing with personal debenture notes was no longer recognized by banks as a valid asset.

3. Inventories were higher than sales justified.

4. Our printing and computer abilities did not keep pace with the rapid technological developments in these fields.

5. We tried to serve a relatively small denomination, mostly without the benefit of denominational subsidies. MPH, as the official Mennonite church publisher, was expected to publish unprofitable materials (books and other items). Mennonite churches, in turn, often bought the products of other publishers, with non-Anabaptist presuppositions, rather than supporting our MPH publications.

While our curricula received high marks in other denominations for innovative approaches to Christian education, we were often bypassed by our own churches for being theologically out of synch. For instance, some Mennonite churches used vacation Bible school material that featured patriotic themes and that prominently displayed the American flag, and any mention of Mennonite peace understandings was missing.

The publishing house as such, physically located at Scottdale since 1908, virtually imploded in a messy process. The jobs of many long-term employees were terminated rather abruptly with loss of a promised portion of their retirement benefits. The old MPH building gradually became an empty shell as various parts of the business were closed down or moved elsewhere. As of this writing about two dozen persons remained in the old MPH building compared to perhaps 120 before the cuts began. Less than half of these were Mennonites.

In the coming together of the Mennonite Church and the General Conference Mennonite Church, a new entity emerged called the Mennonite Publishing Network. It was brought formally into the denominational structure under a new board of control and new management. It sought ways to retire long-term debt and to provide core faith material for Mennonites before eventually being folded into what was to become MennoMedia.

Despite the trauma, the Herald Press book program continues. Provident Bookstores kept going for a significant period before finally being sold. MPH curriculum has been decentralized to several places in North America. The job printing business closed down.

As I was phasing into retirement, June and I operated Inn the Woods Bed and Breakfast at Scottdale. This was a delightful three-year chapter of our lives and provided June with an opportunity to put her decorating, cooking, and hostessing skills to good use.

Eventually we moved to Harrisonburg in semi-retirement. June works part-time as an RN in the Family Birth Place at Rockingham Memorial Hospital. I manage a publishing consulting business from our home under the name Schrock Media Enterprises. Two of our children and their families live nearby. My favorite activity, apart from playing Scrabble, is volunteering half a day a week at Book Savers of Virginia, one of the businesses associated with the Gift and Thrift Shop on Mt. Clinton Pike in Harrisonburg.

My daughter, Andrea, says my life may be summarized with eight Loves—Love of Roots, Love of Learning, Love of Family, Love of Words, Love of Pictures, Love of Church, Love of Community, and Love of Laughter.

I am grateful to the Lord for my rich heritage of faith in the Mennonite tradition, for several generations of a wonderful family, and for my wife who has journeyed with me for the past forty-eight years.

March 2006<br>Revised July 2015

*On April 18, 2011, Paul M. Schrock died as a result of head injuries sustained in a fall at the Hartzler Library at Eastern Mennonite University. He had just finished a shift of volunteer work at the Menno Simons Historical Library among the books he so loved.*

*Earle W. Fike Jr.*

---

### "Dean of Brethren Pastors" and Seminary Prof

*When he was just eight years old, Earle Fike's mother died; yet hers was the hand that held his destiny. As Earle tells it, "My mother read the story of Samuel to me, then said, 'I want you to know that I commissioned you for service to the Lord, just like Samuel's mother.'" Neither his mother nor the Lord were let down! Earle has dedicated his life to the ministry of the Church of the Brethren. A colleague of Earle unequivocally calls him "the dean of Brethren pastors." While teaching at both Elizabethtown and Juniata College for a total of twenty years, the pulpit and pastoral work remained his passion.*

EARLE W. FIKE JR.

# Flock Chefing

## THE COMMISSION

Donald Durnbaugh, a fellow faculty member at Bethany Theological Seminary, delivered the commencement address to the graduating class of 1978. Known by many for his serious scholarship, his precise and careful historical research, and his knowledge and articulation of Pietist and Anabaptist themes, he was known by those who worked with him as a warm friend with a sneaky sense of humor. He let that less visible side come to the fore in his commencement address titled "Flockfood," subtitled, "A Consumer's Guide to Better Sermons."[1] I'd like to share some bits and pieces of his challenging message as an invitation into the beginning of my pilgrimage.

Don told the graduating class, "I am reminded of Jesus' admonition to his followers to care for the sheep. As it happens," he said, "I find the imagery objectionable. I have never quite forgiven Jesus for coming down so hard on the flock and sheep language. Granted, it was a natural metaphor for Palestine. But sheep? They look stupid, they sound stupid, and they are in fact stupid. You know that if one sheep jumps over a cliff to destruction, the rest will follow—a clear case of the 'blind leading the blind,'"

Don went on. "The problem is that being one of the flock makes us feel sheepish; in fact we tend to be wooly headed, bleat a lot, huddle together, and are generally not too smart. We do come in handy, however, once a year when we line up to be fleeced during the stewardship enlistment program."

After allowing that Jesus also referred to us as fish who are easily fooled and hooked, an analogy Don didn't feel any better about than sheep, he summarized his introduction by saying, "I want to speak about preaching from the point of view of the flock. Here is what consumers want from you ministers in a sermon. Think about us—the sheep of your flock. We need your 'flockfood.' Make it nutritious, timely, in good English, earthy, candid, short, and specific. Care enough about us to give us the right food. Do it if you must by hook or by crook, but do it. Feed your sheep."

I share this material from Don because, from the time I heard it, its theme has been a watchword for my work, whether in local churches, in teaching, or in administration. Flock Chefing, the act of providing healthy and inviting spiritual food, is a primary responsibility for those of us who respond to the call of the ordained ministry. And since it is my assignment to share my life pilgrimage, I need to begin with some thoughts on preaching and what it means to be a preacher.

What are some of the practical realities of doing the work of preaching which the average person seldom realizes? Sermons may take various forms. Those of us who grew up in the free ministry, with modestly trained preachers, most likely experienced expository sermons. We likely heard sermons that took the text verse by verse and expounded on the meaning.

More recently, courses in preaching have emphasized two other major sermon forms. The *deductive method* begins with a general truth that the minister comes to by study or revelation. The sermon's purpose is to find ways to convince the listener of that truth and seek appropriate responses. The *inductive method* reverses the process. The pastor, in study of Scripture, discovers something new; what one writer calls "an itch that needs to be scratched" which pushes the minister to search for deeper meaning. There is an "aha" moment, a revelation of truth. The sermon then becomes a faithful telling of that revelation, an experiential journey which takes the listener along in the discovery process.

Much of the preaching in the early New Testament church was deductive. The apostles knew and spoke the truth, gave evidence to support it, and expected appropriate responses to their revelation.

Much of the gospel preaching done by Jesus exemplified inductive preaching. Jesus began with human experiences like sowing, tending sheep, and fishing; and, from those experiences, he induced that "... the kingdom of Heaven is like this." In so doing, he invited listeners to experience the truth and to live accordingly.

And what of the use of simple stories? Whether as a complete sermon or a single illustration, stories are an important style of biblical preaching. Stories are experiential. Listeners not only understand words with their mind, they emotionally feel the truth. I've used different styles in preaching, but I suspect that some of the most effective have been story sermons, or those using significant illustrations that speak to the heart.

A second reality about the preaching task has to do with time investment. Consider first of all the investment of congregational time. If perchance, as a preacher, you are preaching to a congregation of 150 persons, and you preach for twenty minutes, that equates to 3,000 minutes of person-time. That means that your parishioners commit fifty person hours into your care each Sunday message. Fifty person-hours is nothing to sneeze at. It is worth careful and dedicated work. One wonders if it is symptomatic that in our day the pastor's work place in our churches is referred to more often as an office than as a study.

And what work time does a sermon take? Ministers work differently. In my experience, it takes about twenty-five to thirty hours to prepare a twenty-minute sermon. One of the books I've written is entitled, *A Month of Sundays: Making Sense of Things*.[2] It is 256 pages long and contains thirty-two sermons which, in actual time, is less than one year's work. My pulpit ministry stretches across twenty-seven years. One way to look at where a significant block of my time was spent is to suggest that the Flock Chefing time I spent to prepare for preaching is somewhat equivalent to the production of more than thirty books.

More than that, I take praying in the morning worship seriously. In five to seven minutes, parishioners need words that fit the theme of the worship and their experiences as they live before God. Getting ready for that important privilege takes me, on average, sixty minutes, which means that the book, *Pray With Me: Prayers for People at Worship*,[3] consisting of slightly over a hundred pages and fifty-eight prayers, represents slightly over one year of my twenty-seven years of praying with people in public worship.

Add to those two specific functions various special request meetings, non-congregational presentations for special events, weddings, funerals, and pieces prepared for denominational publications. You begin to see how writing, preparation, and presentation have constituted a major portion of my life. I share this not for accolades but with the belief that most persons do not really take time to think about what goes into agreeing to the vocation of being a Flock Chef. Since very early in my ministry, I've worked under the conviction that inspiration welcomed in the sweat of preparation to say some meaningful Word from the Lord is far more dependable than relying on the Spirit for instantaneous inspiration while extemporaneously shooting from the hip. Responding to and living in this kind of call has constituted a major part of my life.

That's enough about the labor of Flock Chefing. For some minutes now, let's take a pilgrimage to see how the commission was developed and exercised.

### THE FIRST PERIOD: BIRTH TO EIGHT YEARS OF AGE

It was a proud moment when at the age of two I went forward in the Sunday school hour of the little Brick Church of the Brethren and put my two pennies in the small light house that blinked and rang a bell for each year. It was an early age crisis two months later when my sister was born, and I was no longer the only attraction in our Maysville, West Virginia, parsonage. The pain of that demotion was only assuaged when my father built me my first "ride in" pedal car. I like to blame my lifelong fascination with autos on that gift. We moved from Maysville to Petersburg, West Virginia, and several years later to Roanoke, Virginia, where my dad, Earle Senior, began a ministry in what was for the Brethren a sizeable city congregation. The pains and joys of being a "PK" (Preacher's Kid) came to memorable reality in that location.

PKs are the recipient of all kinds of supportive "Oohs" and "Aahs." But we also endure our more than fair share of, "You're a preacher's son! What would your dad say if he knew?" It was a warning worth heeding in my case. My dad, a better-than-average preacher because of the content, emotion, and energy he exhibited in sharing the good news, was also a firm disciplinarian to be feared when angry.

My dad's normal reaction to what he would have termed irresponsible behavior was sorely tested during the singing of the hymn, "Just As I Am," at the conclusion of a revival sermon by pastor M. Guy West. Much to my dad and mother's surprise, what did their wondering eyes behold but their seven-year-old son marching down the isle to demonstrate his desire to give his life to Jesus. It was a tearful moment I did not plan, but one in which I did what my heart felt I should do. Careful discussion among older persons and a private session between me and Brother West ended in my baptism. Although a PK, at seven I could hardly understand the Anabaptist Pietistic commitment to adult baptism.

On the other hand, my mother, Hannah Myers Fike, daughter of J. W. Myers of Edom, Virginia, was one of the gentlest, most patient persons, and much loved by all, including me. It was she who early in my life told me the story of the biblical Hannah and how she dedicated her son Samuel to God. After my baptism, she gave me a full-size bear hug and a kiss, informing me that she had also dedicated me to God and wanted me always to remember that.

A year later, on an early October morning in 1938, I was awakened from sleep by the sounds of sirens and loud voices. My mother, in pain from a broken back, had risen early to heat water for her hot water bottle. When she later returned to the kitchen to get the hot water, she was overcome by gas because of a faulty pilot light on the stove. Her death radically changed the course of my life.

Sitting in the parsonage parlor with family after the funeral service, I listened as older persons shared their grief and their statements about their faith in the love and care of God at such times. Finally I could stand it no longer, and in a loud and angry voice, I shouted, "Stop it. Stop it! If God is love, then why did he allow my mother to die?"

There was a stunned silence, and then my Grandmother Myers reached out to me. She put her arms around me and held me to her breast. I felt her shaking as we both wept. And softly between sobs, this wonderful woman, who had just lost her daughter, whispered in my ear, "I don't know, Earle Jr., I don't know. But I do believe that all things work together for good for those who love the Lord." It was important to hear this affirmation then, and it still is an influence in my life.

My mother must have had some premonition, because months before as she struggled with her painful condition, she had told family members that if anything happened to her and if my sister and I needed a home, she hoped that we would be given to Joseph and Dove Miller, my father's half sister and brother in law who were unable to have children of their own. Later in a family discussion, my Grandfather Ezra, the only person from whom my father easily took counsel, determined that Dad would have trouble raising us children and having the necessary time to truly fulfill his pastoral work. So it was decided that my sister and I would go to live with Joseph and Dove Miller in Broadway, Virginia. As it turned out, moving to their home was an unbelievable blessing.

### THE SECOND PERIOD: ELEMENTARY AND HIGH SCHOOL

Life in Broadway was an exercise in learning what love and responsibility is all about. My Uncle Joe was an ordained free minister, a gifted musician, and a kind man with whom people of all ages shared problems. He knew how to listen and be genuinely interested and helpful. From him I learned the importance of honesty and how love and trust are based on listening and understanding. He was for me the living example of the prodigal's father love.

He encouraged me in sports, something he never participated in and had little skill in doing. He attached a basketball rim to the back side of the house. Across the street, where his aging mother lived, was a small barn that had, of all things, a second story haymow with a hard wood floor. A small space, but if for your son's sake, you only filled it half way with hay, there was enough room to encourage a young boy to learn to dribble and shoot hoops in all kinds of weather. He also encouraged me in music, helping me to learn to sing parts and play the piano.

There was no television, so I read books and more books: Edgar Allen Poe, Nathanial Hawthorne, and all the Hardy Boy books and Tarzan episodes I could find. I read anything that was deemed acceptable for a young Brethren boy to read and some classics, which would not have made that list. I also listened to programs on the radio: dramas like "The Shadow Knows," soap operas like "Ma Perkins," and pop music like the "Saturday Night Hit Parade." But mostly, I played sports.

From my Aunt Dove, I learned that anger in itself is not evil, that the way one takes responsibility for it and responds to it is the important thing. I came to understand later that the disagreements she and I had were a shared responsibility. My share of our disagreements was due to my desire to have my wishes honored, regardless of their merit. Her share was due to her residual feelings about how my dad imposed his will on her as a sister. But I grew to love and honor her dearly. She became indeed my second mother.

Whatever family differences arose and whatever actions needed attention were ironed out in a weekly family counsel meeting in which all four of us, the two parents and my sister and I, shared our concerns. In those meetings we were required to listen to one another and to own our feelings and to come to an agreement on solutions. The learnings from those family sessions have served me well across the years in my personal and pastoral relationships with others. In the love and care of Joe and Dove Miller, I learned and experienced at a human level what the love of God is like.

Life in Broadway was filled with a myriad of normal early school experiences. I confess that for me academics seemed secondary to the joys of athletics, music, and drama. For four years I played on the Broadway High School basketball and baseball teams. The coach and principal, J. Frank Hillyard, was a no-nonsense but fair-minded man from whom I learned much. One day during my sophomore year, he called me out of class. "I have a job for you today," he said. "The Junior Class play, scheduled for tonight, is in trouble. One of the characters is ill and unable to be present. Miss Lester and I don't want to cancel the program, so we agreed that if you are willing, you may have the day off from school to memorize and practice with the members of the cast to be a substitute in the performance this evening. Are you willing?"

His confidence in me was hard to refuse. I agreed. Besides, a day off from school looked good! The play came off without whispered aside prompts. So you begin to see that early on, being before the public in speaking and singing provided helpful training for ministry.

My early years in school also intersected with World War II. Being a young, pacifist Brethren was not as hard as it might have been due to the large number of Mennonites in the area. People were accustomed to antiwar neighbors. Nevertheless, it was tough to be the person who kept your class from winning contests for buying savings stamps.

In summer 1946, three teenage friends and I signed up to be seagoing cowboys. Under chaperone guidance of a good-natured, middle-age farmer, the five of us were members of a crew who took 700 horses across the Atlantic and down the Weser River to Bremen, Germany. For a sixteen-year-old boy with limited life experiences, it was a sobering experience to walk through the total destruction of that bombed out city, to see women and children scraping mortar from piles of brick rubble which were then neatly stacked to be reused in the future, to have a small boy offer, in broken English, a night's lodging with his sister for the price of a single cigarette, and to notice the almost total absence of men at work or present in public anywhere.

During this period, other experiences also contributed to my commission to preach. Every year preachers came to the Massanetta Springs Bible Conference, south of Harrisonburg. My uncle Joe took me to hear some of the greatest preachers of that day—Bishop Arthur Moore, Clovis Chapel, and others. It may come as a surprise that someone whom many would have called a teen-age jock enjoyed listening to sermons. There is no question in my mind that many of my activities during these years contributed to my ability to write sentences and paragraphs that passed as acceptable English and to be somewhat comfortable in public appearances. Unbeknownst to me at the time, these influences also set standards and styles for preaching that would later impact my life's calling.

## THE THIRD PERIOD: BRIDGEWATER COLLEGE

Grandfather Ezra, ahead of his time in support of higher education in a denomination where it was viewed with suspicion, put all seven of his children through Bridgewater College. And he provided a fund to partly support any of his grandchildren who chose to attend Bridgewater. It gives new meaning to the term preordained, doesn't it? I had little choice but to attend Bridgewater College.

A most significant part of my college experience began on a freshman progressive hike. That experience introduced me to Jean Kiser, a freshman girl from Dayton High School, Broadway High School's arch enemy. As we walked and talked, I couldn't remember what it was about Dayton that I didn't like. That meeting resulted in a date the next day for a freshman event and steady dates and time together for two years. At the end of our sophomore year, we were married and attended our junior and senior years while living together in a campus trailer court provided for veterans returning to complete education on the GI Bill. Since there were no veterans who wanted the space, and it was available at the cost of eleven dollars a month, we gladly lived there for two years.

Jean's interest in sports and music matched well with my interests. We both sang in the Glee Club, both spent four years on respective basketball teams, and both found it easier to study being married than being single. In addition to basketball, in which I lettered four years, I earned letters in tennis and track. But after two years it became clear that sports and music did not constitute a good mixture, so I graduated with a major in English literature and a minor in music.

I grew up in the Linville Creek Church of the Brethren, home congregation to Brethren heroes such as John Kline and M. R. Ziegler. The congregation licensed me to ministry in 1947, although early on I felt no real calling to full-time ministry. But as it was for many young Brethren men, the draft and its demands had to be met. As a licensed minister pre-enrolled in Bethany Seminary, my exemption from the draft was legal, a fact not celebrated by the Rockingham County Draft Board. While I had hoped to take a year before seminary to teach, try out coaching, and seriously consider my calling to ministry, the draft board officer informed me that if I wasn't in school at Bethany when their year started in fall 1951, he would have my butt (not the word he used) in I-A before I knew what happened. So off we went to Chicago for seminary training.

## THE FOURTH PERIOD: SEMINARY

Bethany Seminary was located on the near west side of Chicago, 3435 W. Van Buren Street, to be precise. Other Brethren institutions nearby included Bethany Hospital across the street and, two blocks further west, First Church of the Brethren. Inner city life was an adjustment. We began our life there in September, and the following January our first child, a daughter, was born in the hospital across the street.

Life included studies and employment to earn additional money to support our educational pursuits and growing family. As soon as daughter Dwynn was old enough to be in the school sponsored nursery, Jean went to work at Sears & Roebuck, the most logical place for students to work. I found employment selling and delivering home orders for Bud Meyer, owner of the Fifth Avenue grocery store.

At the death of President Rufus Bowman in fall 1951, there was a rapid turnover in the administration of Bethany Seminary. By the beginning of my third year, President Paul Robinson was installed. During that same period, an educational relationship began with the Mennonite seminary in south Chicago. Every school day, they journeyed to our campus, teachers and students alike. Classes were held jointly, with graduation requirements that included courses with teachers in both schools. I had classes with Mennonite students and teachers. My favorite Mennonite teacher was Donovan Smucker, an excellent ethics scholar with a keen sense of humor.

My favorite story involving a Mennonite student happened in Floyd Mallot's course in Old Testament. The student, whose name I've forgotten, was severely sight handicapped, enough to be recognized as legally blind. He was a good student, who sat in the front of the class right next to Dr. Mallot's desk. On many occasions, in an effort to help the student understand certain Old Testament practices, Mallot would demonstrate physically what he was talking about, as when he demonstrated the manner of a patriarchal blessing by laying his hand on the student's head. When he talked about the Old Testament suspicion of left-handed people, he demonstrated by shaking the student's right hand and pointing out that in that symbol of friendship, the left handed person was free to strike a killing blow with a knife in the free left hand.

One morning when Mallot came into the classroom, he discovered during roll call that the student was sitting in the back row of the class. Mallot looked up from his roll book and asked him why he had changed his accustomed place beside his desk. The student replied, "I remembered that today you would be discussing circumcision."

While I learned much in all my classes, my favorite courses were in preaching, pastoral care, and counseling. At the beginning of the introduction to preaching course, Professor Alvin Brightbill, one of the co-teachers, focused on having us preach one-minute radio sermons. It was an extremely beneficial exercise. In a one-minute radio sermon, you have basically twelve lines of material to make the point, which means that the first sentence is critical in attracting attention and interest, and you can't really tarry in making the point and coming to a conclusion. Professor Brightbill introduced the concept to us by turning on a recorded sample. We heard this opening sentence: "Roses are red, violets are blue, but they don't get around like the dandelions do." That beginning was followed by fifty seconds on the nature and character of true evangelism. The discipline necessary to do one-minute sermons was important training for my later focus on the preaching ministry.

As graduation approached in 1954, it became clear that the decision as to whether or not to enter the pastoral ministry needed to be made. Two persons greatly influenced that decision: Dr. Jesse Ziegler and President Paul Robinson. Separately, they both said, "Being a PK doesn't give a fair picture of pastoral work. Find a good parish that will challenge you and give it a try. You are still young enough that if you don't like it, you can go on to graduate education if you wish." And so, after some negotiating, Jean and I moved to Meyersdale, Pennsylvania.

## THE FIFTH PERIOD: EARLY PASTORATES

The Meyersdale Church of the Brethren was a large congregation with a sizeable facility when compared to most of our churches in that district. The sanctuary could comfortably seat 200, and there was a second-story balcony in the rear.

I remember arriving at the church, going into the empty sanctuary, and being overcome by the enormity of what was ahead. I stretched out, face down in the middle of the open chancel. The prayer, as I remember it, was simple, tearful, and heartfelt: "Lord, you know I'm not sure this is where I want to be. I'm not sure I know what I'm doing here. But I ask that you give me words to say to these people which will help them in their understanding of you and your importance in their lives, and I pray that you will give me a caring pastoral heart that will be sensitive to their needs."

My first sermon there was an important learning experience. One of the women who served on the search committee, a retired English teacher, shook my hand at the door, thanked me for the sermon, and then moved closer to whisper in my ear, "Earle, Jesus did not die for you and I. A person with a graduate degree should know better how to use the objective case." Every pastor needs that kind of honesty and support.

Two early pastoral experiences were particularly memorable. Meyersdale had never had a public baptismal service in the sanctuary. With approval from the church board, we planned a baptismal service as part of a morning worship service. My sermon was short because we had eleven persons to baptize. The final candidate was a fifty-year-old lady who was deathly afraid of the water. I had spent major time preparing her for what we would do, giving lessons on how I'd hold her nose and mouth to prevent her from swallowing water as I dipped her.

The lessons proved ineffective. We struggled mightily there in the water—she literally scared stiff and I wondering what persons would say if I didn't get her bent over enough to be sufficiently covered with water to make the baptism stick. Finally it was finished. I solemnly put hands on her head and began the prayer, "Lord Jesus, as you were baptized...."

But that was as far as I got, because a four-year-old girl, sitting in the front row of the balcony, spoke her mind about this first baptism she had ever seen. Loud enough for all to hear, her strong little voice drifted out across the congregation: "I'm never going to let that man try to drown me."

The second experience involved my continued interest in sports. I received an official visit from the elders of western Pennsylvania about my unacceptable playing of tennis on Sunday afternoon. I was astounded. The congregation did not have evening services and no church member had raised the matter with me; in fact some came to watch and were appreciative that their pastor was investing that kind of visible time in the community. I agreed, however, with the elders that I would cease and desist. The church board chairman later shared with me the name of the man who had raised the objection.

Less than a month had gone by when an older man in the church, who loved baseball and the Pirates and had seen me play softball with the church team, asked if I would be willing to play baseball with the Meyersdale town team, which he patronized regularly. This team, incidentally, also played on Sunday afternoon. You know what's coming don't you? It was the same man who reported me for playing tennis.

When I told him that the elders had forbidden me to play tennis on Sunday afternoon, he said, without batting an eye, "Oh, this is different. That was tennis and this is baseball." Even though I had no interest in playing baseball with the town team, my response was simple. "Brother, I do not wish to offend members of the congregation, so I'll not be able to play baseball on Sunday." It was, in my estimation, one of my finer moments in exercising pastoral care.

After only three years at Meyersdale, a call arrived to become the pastor of First Church in Chicago. It came as a complete surprise. People in First Church knew me but not in a pastoral role. The church, located two blocks from the seminary, was in a community rapidly changing from white to black residents. The congregation wanted to remain in the community and continue to minister to the mixed-race community. Ministerial candidates interested in such a challenge were scarce. The opportunities of that ministry, along with the proximity to the seminary community which had meant so much to us as we lived there, influenced our decision to move.

Despite common concerns about race, to the members' credit, the congregation supported our efforts at community ministry with finances, attendance, and a welcoming presence to persons of all races. The congregation already supported a Chinese fellowship, which met in the afternoon and had their own pastor. By supporting a part-time Spanish-speaking minister, we also began a Spanish-speaking ministry for those moving into the community. We hired a seminary graduate to help with a community and church youth ministry.

However, as we continued the ministry among the black families, we soon discovered that African Americans were not as interested in becoming a part of us as we were in welcoming them. So we made a decision to hire a full-time black minister, Tom Wilson, a graduate of nearby Northern Baptist Seminary, who had also taken courses at Bethany. There were four of us, all wearing blue work shirts with white clerical collars and busy doing community work. The collars granted us freedom to move about in the community with relative safety to us and those we sought to visit.

Preaching and worship remained central in my pastoral work at First Church. Preaching was a challenge that included ways to present the gospel which would be interesting and meaningful to both those in the seminary with PhDs and families in the community struggling to make ends meet. Sermons took major blocks of preparation time, sometimes twenty-five to thirty hours a week. In addition, during my tenure there, I did some one-minute radio spots and participated in late-night television meditations, both as part of the Chicago Federation of Churches ministry.

My first real efforts at using a narrative story sermon were tried at First Church. I believed stories were a good way to share important truths in a different way. The sermon, "The Year Easter Got Lost," which appears in my book, *A Month of Sundays: Making Sense of Things*,[4] was first preached there. But there is an old adage about best laid plans. One of the good old deacons, a salt-of-the-earth layperson, shook my hand at the door and said, "Earle, I'm sorry, but I don't think this is the kind of thing people want to hear on Easter Sunday." It took me back, but with genuine truthfulness, I replied, "I'm really sorry it was not meaningful to you. I had hoped it would help persons really celebrate Easter."

A month or so later, I was in his place of business, and out of the blue, he turned to me and said, "You know Earle, I can't get that crazy sermon out of my mind. I don't think I'll ever celebrate Easter again without being thankful for it." I thanked him for his words. And was glad that at least one person got the message.

As the program at First Church moved along, we decided that for the first year of Tom's service, he would serve as my assistant, the second year we would be co-pastors, and the third year I would be his assistant. During the following year, I would seek part-time employment and move on to some other ministry. That plan to phase out my part in the developing ministry at First Church in Chicago provided the opportunity to say yes to a call for me to join the faculty of Bethany Seminary, specifically to teach courses in preaching and worship and to direct the field ministry program.

## THE SIXTH PERIOD: BETHANY SEMINARY

In accepting the invitation at Bethany Seminary, I joined not only a remarkable faculty and staff deep in the throes of adjusting to a new location on Butterfield Road in Oak Brook, Illinois, I entered a community already filled with great friends. Two faculty were former seminary classmates, two were former teachers, and the others were well known. We had hoped that the Mennonite seminary would continue our joined relationship at the Oak Brook location, but they decided to remain in south Chicago.

Teaching involved a different kind of preparation and function. There was the necessary intense study in the history and disciplines of preaching and worship. Bethany was one of only two seminaries nationwide that had excellent TV equipment to use in preaching instruction. It was my privilege to co-teach this course with long-term friend and former teacher, Alvin Brightbill. He had exceptional skills in vocal training. The worship courses, which required a deeper investment in the history and purpose of worship, were aided by my participation as a member of the committee which prepared the new *Book of Worship*[5] for the Church of the Brethren. My involvement provided a background in established and changing worship practices throughout the denomination.

Life changed radically for both Jean and me and our family during those five plus years on the Bethany faculty. We moved into the first home we ever owned. Our children, now three in number, were in suburban school settings. Jean, who had begun her vocation of teaching in a Greek Orthodox school in Chicago, settled into a regular teaching position in the Lombard public school system. The opportunity to be a professional in her own right, rather than just a pastor's wife, was a wonderful opportunity for Jean to develop her own special skills appreciated by those around her. And taking my turn in regular chapel appearances under the scrutiny of faculty and friends, along with invitations to continue periodic preaching assignments in local parishes, allowed me the opportunity to continue to grow in sermon preparation and delivery.

Athletics? Yes! Aside from golf and coaching the seminary basketball team, there was a weekly three-person faculty handball match involving close faculty friends, Graydon Snyder, New Testament professor who later became dean at both Bethany and Chicago Theological Seminary; and Robert Neff, Old Testament professor at Bethany, eventually to become the general secretary of the General Board and, still later, president of Juniata College. Handball games were fierce contests, but to this day we are best friends and close confidants. I've been blessed in my preaching ministry to have live biblical experts as near as the phone.

At this point, I need to back up slightly in chronology. Just before and during my teaching at Bethany, my sojourn into denominational organization began. Having written a major criticism of our church bureaucracy under the pen name of "Pathfinder," it was almost as if the church said, "Okay, young upstart with large mouth, take your best shot," because they elected me to the General Board of the Church of the Brethren, where I served the better part of ten years. It immersed me in the working structure of the denomination, including major program emphases such as the emerging interest in group processes, whose chief proponent was Dan West, and the congregational training program known as "Mission Twelve." That program has been credited as having saved many younger church members for continued important involvement in the Church of the Brethren.

Growing concerns about the working structure of the General Board also emerged during this time, culminating in the reorganization of the board in 1967 and my being approached by the new general secretary of the board, S. Loren Bowman, to consider a call to the position of associate general secretary of the General Board as executive of the Parish Ministries Commission. The acceptance of that call meant giving up my teaching career and a partly completed doctoral program at Garret and Northwestern University.

### THE SEVENTH PERIOD: GENERAL BOARD SERVICE

My eight prior years of service as a member of the General Board provided experiences that made the transition to administration somewhat easier. But being in on the ground floor of helping to fulfill a new design and perspective for denominational work required not only a complete change in operation but also the need to improve my administrative and personnel skills. Specialized training in administration included an early four-day retreat in organizational development which included all the staff and a full-scale course under the auspices of the American Management Association. The camaraderie of the five-member administrative council, the skill and competence of General Secretary Loren Bowman, the close friendship of colleague Joel Thompson, and General Board member Dr. Paul Hersch provided the support base for my ministry in Elgin.

My almost ten years in denominational work was a growing experience and enabled me, I believe, to offer significant service. The Parish Ministries Commission included oversight for materials and training for lay leadership in the local church. The first efforts at joint curriculum publication between Mennonites and Brethren occurred during these years. Social action, often considered the prerogative of the World Ministry Commission, also had its day in some of our efforts. We hired the first woman staff person with the explicit task of supporting the rising concern for equal opportunity for women, including the right of women to be ordained and serve local churches. We hired the first official husband and wife team to fill one staff position in family life. We developed the first social action initiative to provide assistance for the development of business and employment opportunities for poor and underprivileged persons in this county.

During these ten years, my writing and speaking included sermons and program interpretation. Near the end of this time, my first book, *A Raspberry Seed Under God's Denture: The Wisdom and Wit of William McKinley Beahm, Missionary, Preacher, Educator*[6] was published. It was a labor of love about Dr. William Beahm, first my teacher, then my parishioner, and then colleague and friend. The book used one of his definitions of sin as the title and consisted of a collection of letters and remembered sayings. Also during this time, sixty-five one-minute radio messages for the Church of the Brethren Radio Ministry were completed. The recording of those messages took place at the Mennonite Media facility in Harrisonburg, Virginia.

## THE EIGHTH PERIOD:
## ELIZABETHTOWN AND HUNTINGDON, PENNSYLVANIA

And then I was invited back into parish ministry at the Elizabethtown Church of the Brethren (COB). I walked into the empty sanctuary of the Elizabethtown church and, remembering Meyersdale, I stretched out in the open chancel much as I had done years before in that first parish assignment. I clearly remember my prayer. "Thank you Lord for bringing me here. It feels like I'm home where I belong. Re-gird me for the task of bringing your Word to and caring for your people in this place."

The Elizabethtown COB was a large congregation located adjacent to the campus of Elizabethtown College. The membership included all ages, and the church had a significant history of support for the denomination's involvement in social issues. The youth advisors were a mixed-race couple, remarkable in their ability and commitment. On one occasion, parents of one of the youth came to me and said that they could not continue to allow their daughter to come to the youth group unless the advisors were dismissed.

I expressed my sorrow at their decision but affirmed the excellent character and work of the couple. We lost that family. But there were, in the congregation, other families with adopted children of mixed-race backgrounds. And there were families with gay and lesbian children who had not yet come out. The fellowship events were warm and friendly. During my time there, we helped to settle refugees by providing sanctuary for them and assisting them in finding employment. We also supported a Spanish-speaking family and helped them find lodging and employment.

It was an exciting congregation to be serving. All the ingredients for good worship were present: a fine pipe organ, an exceptional choir, and a congregation that enjoyed singing. The task of preaching to this congregation, which averaged close to 400 per Sunday, was challenging. My first introduction to the computer came through the helpfulness of a member of the church; this allowed me to write and prepare material with a different methodology. Writing long hand, scratching out changes, and then typing was replaced by that wonderful creation called word processing.

Several significant events outside of regular parish work happened during my tenure at Elizabethtown. I was elected by Annual Conference to serve as moderator of the Church of the Brethren Annual Conference. The congregation graciously allowed me the time necessary to serve. That experience constituted a period of two years, one as moderator elect and the second as moderator. During that period, I visited most of the twenty-plus districts in the Church of the Brethren, preaching and meeting with district boards. The conference theme for the year was taken from Luke 19:42—"Would that you knew the things that make for peace." While it is dated in illustrative material, I consider my moderator's sermon titled, "The Wish That Still Waits," one of my better efforts.

The decade in Elizabethtown included the Three Mile Island meltdown, which significantly increased the preaching and pastoral load. Also, I suffered a heart attack which resulted in damage to my heart but did not require surgery. Of necessity, my lifestyle changed radically. The nine-plus years of ministry at Elizabethtown, living in a church-owned parsonage without opportunity for gaining financial equity, multiple staff requirements, and health and energy issues all combined to lead to some personal re-evaluation of my capabilities for continued work at Elizabethtown.

With strong encouragement from several friends at the Stone Church in Huntingdon, also a college-related congregation, I accepted the call to minister there. While smaller, the congregation had many characteristics similar to Elizabethtown. The church was recovering from a ministerial crisis related to an accusation of pedophilia against the pastor. The congregation had been ably helped through the early throes of this experience by an excellent interim pastor, but the scars were still apparent. There was only one couple with children in the congregation, a very small choir, and a strained budget.

The preaching and worship ministry was important in rebuilding church membership, and the hiring of an excellent director of Christ-

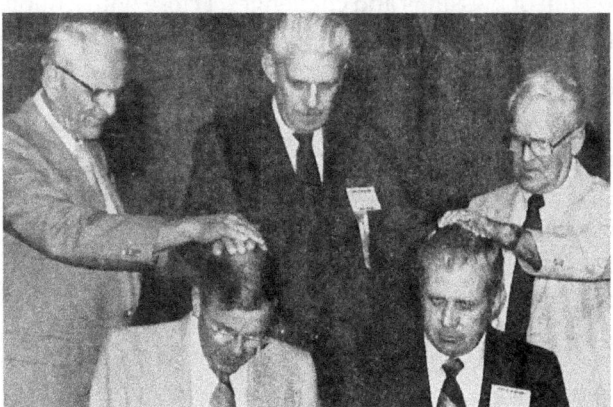

*Earle Fike (l. front) and Paul Hoffman are consecrated 1982 Church of the Brethren moderator and moderator-elect.*

ian education began a process of nurturing families with children. Early in my ministry there, I suffered a second heart condition that required bypass surgery. Due to the depressed economic situation in Huntingdon County, the beginning of the 1990s Desert Storm, the first war in Iraq, and several major illnesses in the congregation, there was ample opportunity for pastoral care and preaching that dealt with faith and life.

Dr. Esther Doyle, retired professor of speech and drama at Juniata College, found my pastoral prayers helpful. She pressed me to publish some in book form, yielding *Please Pray With Me: Prayers for People at Worship*[7] in 1990. As I reached age sixty-two, it seemed wise to retire. Resignation and movement to Virginia, back to our family roots, phased us into our present lifestyle.

It has been great to be back in the beautiful Shenandoah Valley. Retirement has included three interim experiences: the publishing of *A Month of Sundays: Making Sense of Things*,[8] and working for and contributing to the Church of the Brethren pastor's manual, *For all Who Minister*. The most recent writing project was *The Something Else Lady*,[9] a children's story about Sister Anna Mow, a sister of William Beahm. Anna was also my teacher, my parishioner, and a dear friend. Few lives have exhibited a more generous presence of the Holy Spirit. This story too was a labor of love, the more special because her great-granddaughter, Yolanda, age eight and living with her family in the Bruderhof, did the wonderful artwork. The book was published as part of Bethany Seminary's Centennial Anniversary.

My pilgrimage in being a Flock Chef, called by Jesus to "Feed my Sheep," has been full of blessings and challenges. I close with a quote from Robert Farrar Capon in *The Parables of Grace*:

> After all the years the church has suffered under forceful preachers and winning orators, under compelling pulpiteers and clerical big mouths with egos to match, how nice to hear that Jesus expects preachers in their congregations to be nothing more than faithful household cooks. Not gourmet chefs, not banquet managers, not caterers to thousands, just Gospel pot rattlers who can turn out a decent nourishing meal once a week.[10]

March 2009

## NOTES

1. Durnbaugh, Donald, *Flockfood* (Elgin, Ill.: Brethren Press) 1980.
2. Scottdale, Pa.: Herald Press, 2001.
3. Elgin, Ill.: Brethren Press, 1990.
4. Scottdale, Pa.: Herald Press, 2001.
5. Elgin, Ill.: Brethren Press, 1964.
6. Elgin, Ill.: Brethren Press, 1979.
7. Elgin, Ill.: Brethren Press, 1990.
8. Ibid.
9. Oak Park, Ill.: Bethany Theological Seminary, ca. 2004.
10. (Grand Rapids, Mich.: William B. Eerdmans Publishing Co., 1988), 91-2.

*Daniel Hertzler*

## A Populist Intellectual

*A populist intellectual, Dan Hertzler is widely read and knowledgeable in many disciplines, including theology. (Don't let his populist style fool you; he holds several master's degrees and a PhD.) In his writings he practices the art of clearly stating where he stands, without being dogmatic and without letting you feel there's no room for a counter-argument. Dan doesn't just let you think; he sparks your imagination and elicits your thoughts, which is why whenever I got a new issue of* Gospel Herald *in my hands, I turned to the back-cover editorial first thing.*

DANIEL HERTZLER

# Coming to Terms with Our Heritage

Where should I begin in telling my story? Basic logic calls for beginning in the farmhouse where I was born in Berks County, Pennsylvania, at the end of the first quarter of the twentieth century. My father Melvin grew up in Tennessee, but after he married my mother Susan Shenk, daughter of a minister in the Warwick River Mennonite Church, Denbigh, Virginia, they moved to a double house in southern Berks County on the edge of the Conestoga Valley in Pennsylvania.

Our family attended Rock Mennonite Church near Elverson, Pennsylvania, a "plant" of the Conestoga Mennonite Church west of Morgantown. Conestoga was one of a group of Amish communities which had innovated in the nineteenth century by building meetinghouses. They organized the Eastern Amish Mennonite Conference that merged in 1927 with the Ohio Mennonites.[1]

But my story must wait as it connects with a larger story that must be alluded to first.

## A Church Without Creed or Ritual or Emperor

One might rehearse that larger story beginning with creation; or one might begin with the exodus; or with the exile; or with the life and death of Jesus and the earliest years of the Christian church. But let me somewhat arbitrarily begin with the fourth century (CE). By this time the church had become a force to be reckoned with, and Emperor Constantine had made a deal with the church. The resulting relations with government became a millstone that would hamper the church for more than 1,000 years. Then came the Anabaptists who said this would not do. Christians should find their standards in the Bible, not in the actions of a town council. For this, many were executed beginning with Eberli Bolt in 1525 and ending with Hans Landis in 1614. The total number of the Anabaptist martyrs is estimated at around 4,000.[2]

A lot of other killing went on during these times. Diarmaid MacCulloch observes that "The Reformation might indeed be viewed simply as two centuries of warfare. The sixteenth century witnessed fewer than ten years of complete peace and there were less than a couple years during the first half of the seventeenth." Regarding the issues, he suggests that "it might seem to symbolize a Reformation that was a story of two bald men fighting over a comb: an ultimately futile struggle over issues that now seen trivial or irrelevant.[3]

Anabaptists had neither formal creed nor formalized ritual, although we have developed occasional confessions of faith beginning with the "Schleitheim Confession" in 1527;[4] throughout our history we have mainly relied on the Scriptures and a gathered community determined to follow the teaching of Jesus and the apostles. However, the Bible needs to be interpreted and the community is not always faithful. Disagreements in the interpretation and implementation of Scripture have pursued us throughout our history.

An early disagreement in Switzerland in 1693-97 resulted in an Amish schism soon after Mennonites first arrived in Pennsylvania in 1683. My mother's Mennonite ancestor, Melchior Brenneman, arrived in Pennsylvania early in the 1700s.[5] My father's Amish ancestor, Jacob Hertzler, arrived in 1749.[6] No doubt they hoped that the harassment they endured in Europe would be left behind when they came to Pennsylvania. But John Ruth reports in his book, *'Twas Seeding Time*, that the controversy followed them.

First were the delicate relations with the Native Americans. As Ruth recounts it,

There had been no real trouble with the Indians on land the Mennonites had bought. Penn had "paid" their chiefs or "sachems" as they called them by various gifts.... In the Lancaster settlements to the West it was much the same story. There the Mennonite children played with their red counterparts racing and wrestling while chiefs watched gleefully.[7]

"But," as Ruth continues, "by the 1750s the Delaware Indians' trust of the white man had grown sour. Penn had gone the way of all flesh, and his sons and their agents were motivated by commercial interests."[8] Other settlers who did not favor peace with the Indians complicated their relationships.

Then came the American Revolution, and a Quaker peace position, which had for a time prevailed in Pennsylvania politics, became marginalized. The pressure was on to sign up for military service. Having settled in Pennsylvania on a tract of land given by King George I to the Quaker leader, William Penn, Mennonites, Church of the Brethren, and Moravians were reluctant to join the fray. Ruth describes scene after scene of harassment because of Mennonite failure to support the violent rebellion. It was difficult to be a Mennonite during the Revolution. Some made it worse by selling food to the British who had hard currency. One hapless Mennonite was taking eggs to the British when the rebels caught him and plastered him with his own eggs.

With evident sadness Ruth recounts how divergent responses to the war resulted in conflicts among the Franconia Mennonites. When Bishop Christian Funk

> suggested that people who use the Continental money to do business might as well pay taxes and fines imposed by the government that issued the money, he was considered by his Mennonite neighbors to be reflecting an attitude deriving from "the world" not the brotherhood of the church.[9]

This difference of opinion would ultimately result in a division in the Franconia Conference.

The effort to maintain and pass on a minority position through an emphasis on Scripture and the support of community has continued throughout our experience in North America. Like the Jews after the exile, Anabaptists have pressed ahead despite opposition. There has been an ebb and flow of insight and activity, at times strengthened by opposition during warfare. C. J. Dyck once remarked that Mennonites do not believe in war, but it takes a war to bring the best out of us.

## A Modest Legacy

Mennonites and Amish were moving about the country during the nineteenth and early twentieth centuries. When my parents came to Pennsylvania in the 1920s, they came back to the area where their ancestors had first lived in North America. For my father, Melvin Hertzler, it was by way of Maryland, Tennessee, and Virginia. For my mother Susan Shenk, the road led through Ohio and Virginia.

Dad was a great-grandson of John Stoltzfus, who led a family group from Gap, Pennsylvania, to Concord, Tennessee, in 1872. This move is described by Paton Yoder in the book, *Eine Wurzel: Tennessee John Stoltzfus*. This family story makes me pensive as one who respects our heritage. We read that three of John's four sons joined the Plymouth Brethren in Tennessee. The less than imaginative Amish emphasis on Scripture and behavior evidently did not satisfy their need for more of a feeling kind of faith.[10]

In 2007, the *Mennonite Church USA Directory* listed Concord Mennonite Church as a member of Virginia Mennonite Conference with fifteen members. My wife Mary and I visited there years ago and saw the special gravestone for John Stoltzfus and his wife Catherine. It seemed like a modest legacy. However, there is one chapter in the history of this congregation that is of particular interest to me. William Jennings, an illegitimate son of one Elijah Jennings, was harassed by his stepmother and half-siblings. Finally in March 1893, he walked away from home to look for work. The family of Henry H. Good, pastor of the Concord Mennonite Church, took him into their house, employed him, and started him on a road to personal development.

Although he had a very limited educational background, William was highly intelligent and resourceful. He would marry Anna, one of the Good girls, raise a large family, and eventually be ordained as a Mennonite minister. He became a traveling revivalist, and I remember him speaking in the Rock Mennonite Church where I grew up. In 1962 Will and Anna moved to the Virginia Mennonite Retirement Home where she died in 1965 and he in 1972 at ninety-seven. His experience is chronicled in a biography prepared by Merrill and Boots Raber.[11] Perhaps not surprisingly, this congregation has recently been engaged in inter-denominational peace efforts.

The family of my grandmother, Katherine Stoltzfus, stayed with the church, and my grandfather, Levi Hertzler, found her in Tennessee. My father Melvin grew up in Tennessee, but when his parents moved to Denbigh, Virginia, and later to Elverson, Pennsylvania, he and his younger brother Milford went along to operate the farm their parents bought. Dad could have been a good high school science teacher had he not become burdened with the farm. But he enjoyed farming, worked hard, and left a modest farm operation when he died. Two of my nephews operate a dairy on this farm today.

## APPOINTED AS AN EDITOR

And now I pick up my own story again. As ancestors of Anabaptists who took Scripture and community life seriously, our family incorporated Bible study into our everyday lives. The Bible was read regularly at home. At church there were the usual preaching, Sunday school, Sunday evening Bible interpretation meetings, and vacation Bible school, which began when I was in fourth grade. We had visiting revivalists, and at a young age I raised my hand timidly to indicate my intention to follow Jesus. We did not celebrate the church year as such but did take note of Christmas and Easter. A couple of specific details included fasting at breakfast on Good Friday and observing Ascension Day with an all-day preaching event.

When I was growing up it was understood that I would one day go to college. I do not recall that any reason was articulated for this assumption. Of course, my parents had both been "school" people—my father attended Goshen College and my mother graduated from high school at Eastern Mennonite School. World War II delayed my entry into college.

In 1942 my father's hired man was drafted and Dad announced that I would need to drop out of high school after the sophomore year to work for him on the farm. He paid modest wages so I was able to save money in preparation for college. In 1946, at age twenty, I explored the world on a cattle boat sponsored by the United Nations Relief and Rehabilitation Administration. We left from Baltimore for

Poland with a load of heifers and horses and returned after six weeks to Houston, Texas. UNRRA arranged the transportation and the Church of the Brethren at New Windsor, Maryland, recruited the cattlemen. Finally in 1947, when I was just short of twenty-two, the way was open and I entered Eastern Mennonite College.

*Dan (left) with the late Elam Petersheim on a cattle boat headed for Poland, 1946.*

My father said nothing about what I should study. English or history would have interested me, but with the five-year integrated Bible program just beginning, one could receive a BA in four years with a major in Bible and a ThB after the fifth year. It seemed a reasonable program and some of my friends were entering it, so I signed up. This program called for a course in science or mathematics. I elected biology since I had missed high school physics and chemistry, and high school math had taken extra effort. As a college sophomore I was enrolled in biology at the same time I was studying New Testament Greek. Daniel Suter, well pleased with my work in biology, invited me to change my major and become a laboratory assistant. It was a potential fork in the road, but I was already well into New Testament Greek, and it did not seem an appropriate time to change my major.

I did a little writing for college publications now and then and participated in Scriblerus, the extracurricular writing club. But I did not do much writing of a literary nature. As a senior I served on the staff of the college yearbook, the *Shenandoah*, but the next year my brother-in-law, Willis Hallman, was appointed as editor. However, there was also an election for the president of the YPCA. He and I turned up on the ballot, and he was elected. Since there was a college regulation against a student having more than one major extracurricular assignment, I was appointed editor of the *Shenandoah* for 1952.

As I review it now, the 1952 *Shenandoah* does not appear to be a literary masterpiece. Yet I think it basically served its purpose as a record to which graduates can go back and say "Oh yes, there is old so and so. I remember him well." By today's standards, it looks too solemn, but we did what we could. The yearbook was printed at Mennonite Publishing House (MPH), and it would appear that it impressed someone at MPH enough to call me, sometime later, when they needed an office editor for the *Mennonite Community* magazine.

After graduation I went to work on a farm in Ohio. In July I married Mary Yoder (Junior College Bible, 1949), the daughter of Eugene Yoder, a minister in the Ohio and Eastern Mennonite Conference. Her picture appeared on the cover of an issue of *Crossroads* magazine along with Pauline Peachey Lehman. They were holding bows and arrows. Mary has said that this was the first and the last time she held a bow and arrow. The photo is part of a permanent exhibit at EMU tracing the development of athletics at the university.

### THE FLOW AND EBB OF PUBLISHING

By early September we moved to Scottdale, where I became an office editor at the Mennonite Publishing House and Mary began working in the MPH bookstore, an assignment she would terminate before the birth of our first son. The *Mennonite Community* had first been published in 1947 with Grant Stoltzfus as editor. It was a remarkable journalistic achievement for its time, with extensive documentation in pictures, but it never received enough circulation to cover its expenses.

By the time I arrived Grant Stoltzfus had left and the magazine was being edited by a committee. As office editor I was expected to prepare for publication articles which committee members supplied me. However, within a year *Mennonite Community* was to be merged with *Christian Monitor*, a monthly magazine which had been published at Scottdale since 1909 and seemed to be ready for regeneration. The editor of the new publication was to be Millard Lind, who was also writer of the adult Sunday school lessons. The name chosen for the new magazine was *Christian Living*. It began as a forty-eight page monthly magazine for home and community. The first issue was dated January 1954, and I was identified as assistant editor with a function similar to what I had been doing for *Mennonite Community*. *Christian Living* was to last forty-eight years, ending with the December 2002 issue.

*The Mennonite Community* magazine had begun as a project of the Mennonite Community Association, an organization promoted by Mennonite sociologist Guy F. Hershberger. Leadership for this effort also emerged from Civilian Public Service, a pacifist alternative to military service in World War II. H. Ralph Hernley, chair of the committee I first worked for at Scottdale, was a leader in this movement. In addition to seeking to influence *Christian Living* as a consulting editor, Hershberger fostered community relations conferences held throughout the church. These conferences were remarkable in their ability to bring together academic types along with farmers, small-business leaders, and workers to consider how to follow Christ in their work. As assistant editor I would attend these conferences and write reports for the magazine.

In July 1958, I reported on the conference held in March that year in Kalona, Iowa. My report is titled "Witness While You Work." I noted that "this conference has been meeting in various communities throughout the church where Mennonites have gathered together to search for answers to the problems of making religion practical in everyday life."[12]

Hershberger would consolidate his thinking on ethical questions in the book, *The Way of the Cross in Human Relations* (Herald Press, 1958). His ethical stance is summarized by his biographer Theron Schlabach in a chapter on Hershberger's encounter with Reinhold Niebuhr's thought. He observes that "Hershberger insisted on beginning with the ethical teachings of Jesus and the New Testament. From these premises he developed a strategy, not of political power but of a faithful church giving its corporate witness."[13]

The Mennonite Community Association eventually declined, although some of its concerns are carried on by Mennonite Economic Development Associates. But as Calvin Redekop was to write in *Mennonite Encyclopedia*, "Clearly the traditional rural church knew how to integrate the farming occupation with its faith, but the Mennonite church community has yet to learn how to relate to the burgeoning commercial and business membership."[14]

Mennonite Publishing House in the 1950s and 1960s was a vigorous institution. It had survived the Depression of the 1930s and the paper shortages of the war years. Now it was responding to the church's need for literature in the postwar expansionary period. I recall that A. J. Metzler, who had been its leader since 1935, once remarked that the gross income for one of these years had been $1 million. During this era, MPH was not only Mennonite church publishing headquarters, it would also become part of a church-related network. The executive secretary of Mennonite General Conference was to have an office there and the secretary of the Mennonite Commission for Christian Education would be there along with a churchwide youth worker.

I have proposed that our tradition is maintained particularly by the twin supports of Scripture and a worshiping and practicing community since we have no sharply worded creed, precise ritual, or sophisticated organization. With these frail supports we have sought to maintain a point of view our culture does not support. My MPH assignments were to involve one or the other of these support systems: biblical interpretation and community maintenance.

Several significant changes were made during these years in how we developed biblical study materials for Sunday schools. When I first arrived, the Sunday school lessons were developed from the Uniform Series outlines. The assumption was that everyone in the family and every Sunday school in the larger Christian church should consider the same Bible text on a given Sunday. The local weekly newspaper supported this with a column on the weekly text written by a recognized Bible scholar. These lessons were developed and distributed on a short schedule. Christian education theory came to the conclusion that children would be better served by "graded" lessons outlined and developed especially for them. For MPH this called for longer-range investment of capital and more warehousing.

A similar issue emerged with the expansion of book publishing. Whereas books had been edited on marginal time, beginning in the 1950s, there was a book editor; when the book supply built up, there would be a promotion manager, warehouse space, and a division manager. This kind of expansion had long-term significance for MPH.

In the meantime, instead of an on-location adult lesson writer, there was an editor—myself—and writers would be engaged from around the church, particularly from church institutions. On occasion this would cause tension when the lesson writers interpreted Scripture in a manner that some Sunday school students were not ready to follow, and I was not always alert enough to forestall controversy.

The Revised Standard Version (RSV) of the Bible appeared soon after I arrived in Scottdale. It was to become an issue of controversy. A committee made up of H. S. Bender, C. K. Lehman, and Millard Lind examined the new version and gave it qualified approval. They wrote, "We see no ground for condemning anyone who wishes to add . . . for the study of Scripture any of the new translations which are offered in our day, including the R.S.V."[15] For many this was not enough criticism.

In 1965 we began to print the RSV beside the King James Version (KJV) in *Herald Adult Bible Studies.* Some were not comfortable with this and so an edition was provided with a blank space where the RSV would have been. I was not able to find a copy of the KJV-only edition, but in bound volumes I found the twin texts from 1965 until August 1972. Then RSV was replaced by the New English Bible (NEB). On the back cover of the first quarterly of 1983, I found this statement: "Beginning in March, 1983 the New International Version (NIV) will replace the NEB text in the Uniform Series. . . . It is thought that eventually the NIV will be the only text printed."

My own developing view of the Bible was that it was compiled to meet specific needs. My experience as an editor suggested to me that somebody somewhere had been responsible for writing and/or editing any published material, the Bible as well as anything else.

As suggested in my opening comments in identifying my story with that of the Anabaptists, I view the Bible as our story, the background of our tradition. I do not find words such as "inerrancy" useful in our study of the Bible. Higher criticism and lower criticism have had their day, the Jesus Seminar and radical archaeologists will challenge the Bible's integrity, but we keep finding our story in the Scriptures. If we decide to go with it, we should try to understand and practice its teaching. Some of those who are strongest on inerrancy seem to waffle when they come to the Bible's most radical teaching.

In 1960 Millard Lind resigned as editor of *Christian Living* to teach at Goshen College Biblical Seminary. I was assigned this responsibility along with my work as an editor of curriculum material. A leadership magazine named *Builder* began in 1959, and in 1964 the publisher asked me to edit this also. There was also an occasional Christian service-training manual. In a 1966 issue of *Mennonite Yearbook* I am identified as editor of four different publications: two monthlies, one quarterly and one yearly.[16] MPH, of course, was a small operation as publishing went, and multi-tasking was seen as necessary.

Along the way I completed work for a PhD in religious education by commuting to the University of Pittsburgh. My adviser insisted that doctoral students do a study involving hard data—not historical or philosophical studies. So I devised a test to measure the comprehension of theological language in our curriculum material by sampling adult Mennonite Sunday school students. Analysis of the data was done with help from the university computer. I was to find that one of the most difficult items in the fifty-item questionnaire involved the definition of the word *righteous*. The easiest was *heaven*. I was interested to see that the random sample included the congregation where I had grown up, and when the scores were separated by congregation, this one had the highest mean score. However, the differences among congregational scores were not found to be statistically significant. I must confess that I have not had much ongoing use for the statistical tests used.

Ben Cutrell had become publisher of MPH in 1960, and in 1970 he reorganized the institution. Instead of editorial and sales functions being separate, these would be done within the division. There would be a book division, a periodical division, a Christian education division, and a bookstore division. There were also production, finance, and personnel divisions. I was asked to lead the periodical division, and my education-related projects were moved to the Christian education division. I continued as editor of *Christian Living*. And I saw myself as a group leader of the division more than as a top-down manager. Whether the other editors perceived me in this way would be for them to say.[17]

It is of some interest to note that of the six periodicals in the division I directed, only one is still published. This is *Purpose*, and it was a "reinforcement" publication rather than one to raise issues. We were all aware that we could not match the sort of literary material which was available to our readers on a newsstand. Yet we did try to advocate for good writing. Given the limitations of our resources, we hoped to be visually and intellectually appealing to our Mennonite audience.

In 1971 a cloud the size of an office building appeared on the MPH horizon. With the reorganization of the Mennonite Church, the new general secretary worked from an office in Rosemont, Illinois, instead of in Scottdale. Also the new Board of Congregational Ministries was set up in Elkhart, Indiana. Perhaps there was a kind of historical justice in this. In 1908 Scottdale had wrested publication headquarters away from Elkhart. Now important church related activities would go back there.

Another significant change with the 1971 reorganization was a different makeup of the publication board. From its beginning in 1908 the board had been made up of representatives elected by the Mennonite district conferences, with the number of representatives based on the conference membership. Larger conferences had more than one member. The full board met once a year while an executive committee did the "heavy lifting" by meeting oftener. The new board, however, would be elected by the general assembly and not all of the district conferences had their own representatives on the board. This change probably had long-term significance for the publishing house.

In 1973 John Drescher resigned as editor of *Gospel Herald* after serving for eleven years. I was asked to succeed him. The rhythm of editing a weekly publication was new to me compared with the monthly, quarterly, and yearly deadlines I had faced before. The *Gospel Herald* was intended as an advocate for the whole church. Of course the church institutions were better able to provide news of their activities than the average Mennonite congregation. But whereas with curriculum material the scholar's interpretation might make Sunday school people restless, reporting on the work of church agencies at times alarmed the agency people.

It seemed to us important not just to be a mouthpiece for church organizations. However, I was well aware that a church organization is a delicate thing, and we needed to recognize that we were all in it together. As reporters, we "covered" every meeting of Mennonite Church General Board and the biennial general assemblies. We also aimed to attend at least one meeting a year of the other boards. We felt that we could write these reports more objectively since we were responsible to Mennonite Publication Board, separate from the other boards. (Of course we were not in the position to do objective reporting on the publication board.) The distinction was not clear to everyone. At one point Paul Kraybill, general board secretary, suggested that the other half time of the news editor be assigned as information officer for the general board. I declined this proposal.

I did at times in my mind compare us unfavorably with the secular media who seemed to be more able to do objective reporting. On reflection, I am less inclined to emphasize this difference because I now perceive them as also being restricted by the powers that control them. Even the PBS Washington Week includes a representative of the military industrial complex among its sponsors.

It was assumed that the editor of the *Gospel Herald* would comment on issues faced by the church. I tended to view this assignment cautiously. I do not recall that I ever commented on the issue of homosexuality, but viewing the experience of those who did, this was probably wise. I did take up the issue of the ministry of women and advocated for them.

On April 4, 1989, I published "Keeping Women Quiet" in response to 1 Corinthians 14:35. Using the book, *What Paul Really Said About Women,* by John Bristow,[18] I indicated that we need to recognize a variety of Greek words for "speak" and that Paul was calling for order. I wrote that "as Bristow points out, he did not forbid them to preach, teach, pray or prophesy as long as it was done in decency and in order."[19] Reviewing the issues of the *Herald* following this I found only one objection, from a woman no less.[20] Recently I reviewed the comments on this text by Richard B. Hays. He suggests that "All things considered, this passage is best explained as a gloss introduced into the text by the second or third generation Pauline interpreters who compiled the Pastoral Epistles."[21] It appears that Bristow and I did not dig deeply enough. On the other hand, suggesting a gloss could have unnecessarily alarmed some readers.

All of our six periodicals depended on the work of writers both within and without the church. We saw ourselves as liaisons between writers and readers. It was our intention to present an article in a manner that would get readers' attention. Often we felt an article could be improved by a little tinkering. I would sometimes find that a writer really got down to business by the second or third paragraph and so would start there. If I made major revisions it was my practice to share a copy of the edited version with the writer. On occasion this copy may have startled the writer. (Sometimes now when I am subject to the work of an editor I wonder why a word which I thought I had carefully composed was eliminated.)

What I was glad to do was to give aspiring church leaders the opportunity to address the church on subjects they considered important. I perceive that I was able to help them find their voices in articulation of a vision for the church.

Periodical publications came and went. At the end of the year they would be bound for future reference. On occasion I aspired to publish something more permanent, such as a book. The first opportunity came when I was called upon as chair of a Philosophy of Christian Education Research Committee to prepare for publication a report on behalf of the committee. It appeared as *Mennonite Education: Why and How?* (Herald Press, 1971). It was intended mainly for Mennonite Church educational institutions but later it went into a second printing because of wider interest.

A second effort was *From Germantown to Steinbach* (Herald Press, 1980). I researched and wrote this in connection with a 1979-80 sabbatical. After visiting the Germantown and Diamond Street Mennonite churches in Philadelphia during summer 1979, Mary and I made a sixteen-week trip early in 1980 along the border of the U.S. and southern Canada as far as Steinbach, Manitoba, visiting Mennonite congregations. I wrote a draft of the book week by week in motel rooms after we had visited congregations on the weekends. Mary wanted to call the book *A Mennonite Odyssey*, and I should have followed her suggestion instead of using it only as a sub-title. Germantown and Steinbach suggested an ethnic survey, something I had deliberately avoided.

To celebrate the seventy-fifth anniversary of the *Gospel Herald*, I edited *Not by Might* (Herald Press, 1983). We identified it as "A *Gospel Herald* Sampler with profiles of the editors and selected writings from 1908 to 1983." After retiring I wrote *A Little Left of Center* (Dream-Seeker Books, 2000). As of this writing, the book is still in print. In addition to my personal story, the book includes some history of Mennonite Publishing House from the time when it appeared to be a viable institution. In 2013 Cascadia Publishing House published my second memoir, *On My Way: The View From the Ninth Decade*.

When I retired in 1990 I could not have imagined that MPH would go down as it did. The full history of this episode needs to be written by someone several generations later than mine.[22] I do observe that a church institution is a frail thing. It appears that a complex of factors conspired against MPH. Changing technology, the merger of two denominations, and changing governmental regulations, combined with loss of market share provided a set of challenges which management was not able to meet. One or two of these might have been dealt with, but there were evidently too many of them.

After the debacle, I was assigned by Allegheny Mennonite Conference to interview persons who had been "let go." One of these was Jack Scott, whose last assignment had been church relations representative. He made a comment that seemed prescient. He said that "some organizations have stability with their boards. The board serves as the source of the corporate culture. Members of the Mennonite Publication Board were not permitted long-term service. So it became the responsibility of the staff to interpret the culture." He implied that with longer terms and more stability, the board might have given more astute counsel to the staff. Perhaps before 1971 this would have been more possible.

I could only wish that some other method might have been discovered to close the institution rather than employing a professional "closer downer" to fire people. Michael A. King, who as a book editor had been downsized earlier, reports,

> I'll never forget the e-mail of anguish I received from my former secretary the day she was told at 9:00 am that she had been downsized and should have her desk cleared by 4:00 p.m. and

not return to the building. She felt told that, "We took from you as long as we needed you, then the moment we didn't want you we threw you out the door."

In contrast, I read in a local newspaper of a downsizing process in a company some miles away. Three persons were told one must go. They negotiated among themselves, seeking to favor the one who had the most family responsibilities. I clipped the article and kept it in a folder along with a record of the interviews.[23] I find it ironic that after employing Kurt Horst half-time to close the Scottdale operation, the church discovered that what was being done there could not be done elsewhere more cheaply. So they hired Russ Eanes full time and the work went on. For a time it was possible to rent space on the roof of the building to cell phone companies. Then even such measures proved inadequate and all publishing operations shut down in Scottdale as the remnants of MPH merged to become part of MennoMedia in Harrisonburg, Virginia. Even there, however, former MPH employees keep the MPH spirit alive in the communication business.

## DOES THE MENNONITE CHURCH HAVE A HORN?

In the end I come back to the theme with which I began. As advocates for the Anabaptist tradition, we Mennonites are a little people with limited resources who insist that the Lord is not a tribal god but has adherents over the whole world and we all belong together. The logic of the Lord as leader of the whole world and creator of the universe appears sensible to many. But when our security is threatened, we tend to retreat to a view of God as a tribal god with a special concern for America.

With our minority point of view, we need to be particularly vigilant to keep our support systems functional. Since the middle of the twentieth century we have had professional Bible training for an increasing number of pastors. But Sunday school teaching for adults is not as vigorously done as formerly. This calls for vigilance. The Bible is a complex book. Before it can be interpreted adequately we need to be familiar with it.

I am aware as I reflect on what I have written that I have outlined carefully my ethnic identity. This does not mean that I consider *Mennonite* by definition an ethnic church. I agree with the point of view expressed by Everett Thomas in *The Mennonite*. He emphasized that of course a family line is important and worth noting, but for us Mennonites, what counts is faith in the God of our Lord Jesus Christ.[24]

Shane Hipps, former pastor of the Trinity Mennonite Church in Phoenix, Arizona, addressed the Mennonite assembly in San Jose, California, in 2007. I seem to remember that he joked that in one hundred years Hipps would be a "Mennonite" name. He also reported that when his wife had an accident and was incapacitated, members of the Pasadena Mennonite Church brought in food. People in the office where she worked were astounded. But any Mennonite knows when there is an emergency you bring in food. It is something we do. Such a practice needs to be continued and cherished. I am sure that Guy F. Hershberger would be pleased to know that "community" can be practiced in an urban setting as well as on farms and in small towns.

And it is in the context of community that Mary and I raised our family. As our life in Scottdale developed, Mary chose to work at home until our four sons had mostly left home. Although she had skills that MPH could have used and numbers of her peers worked outside the home, she chose homemaking. She also taught Sunday school and vacation Bible school and pioneered in several church roles. She was the first female elder in Kingview Mennonite Church and the first female editor of Allegheny Mennonite *Conference News*.

Because I was expected to travel as an editor, Mary adapted to my absences by planning a variety of creative activities within and without our home. One of the things she accomplished was to teach our boys how to cook. There were, of course, family crises which called for heroic actions on her part. Our family physician Dr. Gilbert was available as needed. On one occasion Mary helped him set a broken arm right in his office.

Over the past number of years, it became obvious that Mary was having trouble with memory and related functions, but she was able to continue reasonably well until 2012. In January she began to walk with a cane, and on February 20, she fell down the basement steps and was in a Pittsburgh hospital for five days. By spring she was in skilled nursing care.

Nothing in our experience had prepared us for this. But our siblings, our sons, and our church family have all been supportive. Although Mary protests often, people whose judgment I respect say she is where she needs to be. I visit her every day and take flowers. She was an artist and considered a flower the ultimate work of art. I take her to church in a wheel chair and get her out at various other times to relieve the boredom of life in a nursing home. I was comforted recently when Mary remarked that she had no regrets about her life. I could have thought of some situations she might have remembered otherwise.

At the end of Psalm 148 the psalmist avers that the Lord "has raised up a horn for his people."[25] What was this horn? James Waltner writes that "Raising up a horn means bestowing dignity, honor and strength. . . . The Psalm proclaims that God has helped Israel again to attain a place among the nations that commands respect."[26]

Does the Mennonite church have a horn? This little scattered people, less than two million strong but with membership in eighty countries of the world? I think we should take heart from the increased interest in Anabaptism around the country and around the world. As a symbol of this, I suggest the occasion when Nancy Heisey as president of Mennonite World Conference met the pope. Her gift to him was an artistic representation of Dirk Willems, the Anabaptist who rescued his pursuer from drowning and was subsequently executed. She made our point.

February 2012<br>Revised June 2015

## Notes

1. Grant M. Stoltzfus, *Mennonites of the Ohio and Eastern Conference* (Scottdale, Pa.: Herald Press, 1960), 201.

2. Paul Showalter, "Martyrs," *Mennonite Encyclopedia*, vol. 3 (Scottdale, Pa.: Herald Press, 1957), 521-525.

3. Diarmaid MacCulloch, *The Reformation* (New York: Viking, 2003), 648, 646.

4. J. C. Wenger, "Brüderlich Vereinigung," *Mennonite Encyclopedia*, vol. 1 (Scottdale, Pa.: Herald Press, 1955), 447-8.

5. Albert H. Gerberich, *The Brenneman History* (Scottdale, Pa.: Mennonite Publishing House, 1938), 4.

6. Silas Hertzler, *The Hertzler-Hartzler Family History* (Berne, Ind.: Economy Printing Concern, 1952), 11.

7. John L. Ruth, *'Twas Seeding Time* (Scottdale, Pa.: Herald Press, 1976), 15.

8. Ibid., 16.

9. Ibid, 100.

10. Paton Yoder, *Eine Wurzel. Tennessee John Stoltzfus* (Lititz, Pa.: Sutter House, 1974).

11. Merrill and Boots Raber, *The Life and Times of William Jennings 1874-1972: A Biography* (Newton, Kan.: Graphic Images, 2000).

12. *Christian Living*, July, 1958, 27-29, 40.

13. Theron Schlabach, *War, Peace, and Social Conscience* (Scottdale, Pa.: Herald Press, 2009), 214.

14. Calvin R. Redekop, "Mennonite Economic Development Associates," *Mennonite Encyclopedia*, vol. 5 (Scottdale, Pa.: Herald Press, 1990), 570.

15. *Gospel Herald*, January 6, 1953, 21.

16. *Mennonite Yearbook and Directory*, (Scottdale, Pa.: Mennonite Publishing House, 1966), 23.

17. For an account of this division, see "To Look at and to Touch," Daniel Hertzler, *A Little Left of Center* (Telford, Pa.: DreamSeeker Books, 2000), 114-130.

18. John Bristow, *What Paul Really Said About Women* (New York: Harper & Row, 1988).

19. *Gospel Herald*, April 4, 1989, 248.

20. *Gospel Herald*, May 16, 1989, 347.

21. Richard B. Hays, "First Corinthians," *Interpretation* (Louisville, Ky.: Westminster John Knox Press, 1997), 247.

22. John E. Sharp has begun the telling the story in "A Century of Publishing Ends at Scottdale, Pa.," *The Mennonite*, June 1, 2011, https://themennonite.org/feature/end-era/

23. Barry Michaels, "Heroism and Hope on the Job," *Focus Magazine* in Greensburg (Pa.) *Tribune-Review*, July 14, 2002.

24. *The Mennonite*, February 2010, 64.

25. Psalm 148:14a.

26. James Waltner, "Psalms," *Believers Church Bible Commentary* (Scottdale, Pa.: Herald Press, 2006), 706.

**PART III**

# Re-Envisioning Service
# ... as International, Relief, and Development Workers

R. Jan Thompson

**Disaster Response Man**

*He was called "The Little Dutchman" when he started school because few could understand his speech; however, Jan Thompson overcame many hurdles in his life. Those struggles only served to sensitize him to others for whom life was not easy. He and his wife, Roma Jo, served in Africa for eight years. Later, he headed up the Disaster Response Program for the Church of the Brethren. And for many years he was administrator of the Child Disaster Center operating out of New Windsor, Maryland. Until his death in 2015, Jan continued to be on call, responding to disasters near home and across the globe.*

## R. JAN THOMPSON

# *From Small Town to an Extended World View*

### EARLY DAYS: BRETHREN ROOTS

Seventy-five years ago in September on Friday the thirteenth, on my father's birthday, I was born, the second of five children, to George and Lois Thompson. They had graduated from high school during the Great Depression, and although both had dreams of going on to college, it was not to be. My father worked in a factory all of his life, and my mother worked at odd jobs and tended the house, raising four boys and one girl.

My little town of Ludlow Falls, Ohio, had a population of 350 or so. The community lived by the saying, "It takes a village to raise a child." Whenever we misbehaved anywhere in the town, one of the neighbors would open the door and say, "George and Lois Thompson would not want you to do that." We knew that before we arrived home, a phone call would have been made, and we would hear about our misdeeds.

I was called "the little Dutchman," so I have been told. When I first started to talk, my older brother translated for me, since he was the only one who could understand my speech. Luckily, when I entered first grade I was assigned to a teacher who had some training in speech therapy. But even as a senior in high school I was not able to achieve an A in speech class since, according to the teacher, I did not clearly enunciate my words.

My mother was from a third-generation Church of the Brethren family. My father, however, grew up in the Friends tradition. I remember witnessing his baptism into the Church of the Brethren when I was nine. My folks were youth advisors, and Dad felt he could not discourage the young men from joining the military if he was not a member of the church. So he asked to become an official member through baptism, even though he had been an active participant since their marriage.

One strong memory from my childhood is coming home from church and, following dinner, seeing my dad in the living room crying. There had been a call for men to serve as "Seagoing Cowboys," to attend to cows and horses being sent to Europe. He wanted to volunteer, but he knew that as a factory worker he could not get a leave of absence and, without his income, his family of five children could not survive. That made an impression on me as a twelve-year-old boy.

True to my status as a "city boy," I entered the workforce early. One of the members of our church raised potatoes. When I was in fourth or fifth grade, I, along with other boys from our community, would ride in the back of a pickup truck to the farm to pick up potatoes. My older brother Joel and I and two other boys worked two or three summers for this farmer. We spent the early summer months pulling weeds and moving the metal irrigation pipes every two hours. We had to carry the pipes over twenty-four rows of potatoes. The first twelve rows were very muddy, and the next twelve were hard, dry dirt, too hard for our bare feet, so we had wet shoes and wet pants all day long.

During my teen-age years, I was what might be described as a sort of humdrum, middle class guy. When I turned twelve I joined the local Boy Scout troop where I was active until I achieved the rank of Eagle Scout. In junior high I had a monopoly in our community of the newspaper business. I delivered the morning paper before breakfast and the afternoon paper after school. Entering high school, I played football and was elected to serve as co-captain my senior year. That honor came not because of my athletic ability but out of respect for me as a person. At my twenty-fifth class reunion, one of the players told Roma Jo that he had never heard me say a curse word.

When it came time for me to consider a college, I would have preferred going to almost any college other than Manchester. I was tired of simply being identified as Joel's little brother. However, Manchester gave a one-third discount of all college expenses to family members. Since we both were paying our own way, that discount left me with little choice. Joel was "famous" and I became "infamous," although, in my freshman year I played football which kept me out of some trouble. Nevertheless, I spent lots of time in the office of the dean of men for mischief in which I was involved.

I registered for the draft as a CO and was given that classification without any problems. I was told that the FBI spent time interviewing people where I went to school and in the larger community. My reputation in the community must have spoken well for my beliefs. Since I was not ready to be a serious student, I decided I would leave college and do my service obligation. But by fall I returned to Manchester College to serve as co-chairman of freshmen days and to play a second season of football. I was "drafted" in December 1954 and joined the Brethren Volunteer Service (BVS) workers which met at New Windsor, Maryland. There were thirty-eight persons in that unit. One young gal, Roma Jo, caught my attention, and we have been friends ever since. She served here in the United States, while I served my two years overseas. When my term of service ended, we married and have been together for fifty-three years.

## BRETHREN VOLUNTEER SERVICE

I served as a human guinea pig or normal control patient at National Institute of Health in Bethesda, Maryland, for a month while waiting for my passport to be issued and for transportation to Europe. I was told when the assignments were made that I would be the Heifer Project representative in Germany.

But when I arrived in Germany and started the German language lessons, I was informed that I was being sent to Austria to work with the *Evangelishe Hilfswerk*, where I was to help with the food and assistance program for refugees living in Austria. I helped to assemble food packages and bundle clothing and other supplies that were delivered to refugee camps or sent via mail to refugees who were living in low-income apartments. I also drove an old army surplus truck to and from the railroad depot, moving relief supplies to a warehouse before distribution.

The Church of the Brethren had also placed four BVSers in Vienna in 1954 to help with the rebuilding of the *Evangelische Karls-Schule*, commonly known as Karls School. This school, located in the heart of Vienna, had been designed by a famous Danish architect. Following World War II, the building was declared a national heritage building and had to be rebuilt with an outside appearance the same as before the war. The Lutheran Church did not have the money to pay for the reconstruction, so they were quite happy to have an offer from the American and Canadian Pax volunteers do the work.

An agreement was made with the Mennonite Pax organization in 1955 for the Mennonites to join with the Church of the Brethren to work at the remodeling of the Karls School. Bob Steiner from the Mennonites was to serve as the construction leader. I was transferred from my assignment with Evangelishe Hilfswerk to serve as the unit leader of this combined Brethren-Mennonite unit.

Every three months or so, I would go to the Pax unit leaders meeting in Frankfort, Germany, where I learned to know Dwight Wiebe and others in the leadership of the Mennonite Pax organization. When the Church of the Brethren had their annual conference for the European workers, the Mennonite Pax fellows were included. And when the Pax organization had their annual conference, we Church of the Brethren volunteers were also included. Thus I had the opportunity to get to know many fine young men and a bit about the Mennonite Church.

On one of my trips through Germany, I visited the concentration camp of Dachau. Seeing the cremation ovens and the small plots of ground where the ashes of 10,000 persons were buried made a lasting impression on me as a nineteen-year-old. I resolved then and there that I would spend my life trying to make the world a better place to live.

In the fall of 1956, a revolt in Hungary caused many refugees to cross the border into Austria. Since some of the refugees could speak English but not German, I was assigned to the World Council of Churches office to help with the processing. This was my first stint in assisting in refugee resettlement.

## FINDING MY WAY VOCATIONALLY

After two years in Europe, Roma Jo and I were married in June 1957. That August, I returned to Manchester College a bit more mature in my reasons for attending college. The dean of men, with whom I had become very well acquainted during my first stint at college, asked Roma Jo and me to be dorm parents for ninety-eight male students. This provided us with an apartment and a stipend of $45 a month. I completed the balance of my college education in two years. During that time our first son was born.

I felt a strong call to be in some form of ministry and asked to be licensed by the North Manchester church in spring 1958. It would be twenty-five years before I was ordained by the Union Bridge church. I had felt that being licensed served me well in my employment; however, the Mid-Atlantic District said one was not to be licensed for such a long period of time, and were I to refuse ordination, my licensed status would be revoked.

I wanted to return to Europe and work with the church in one of the many programs that were operating at the time, but I was told that no one would be sent as a director unless they had a seminary degree. Thus I enrolled in Bethany Seminary. Soon after I started seminary, a person who had graduated from college with me was sent to Europe as a director. I was surprised and, quite naturally, hurt by that action. I had, after all, enrolled in seminary to qualify for such an assignment. I did not feel a calling to be in the pastoral ministry, so after one year at the seminary we moved to La Verne, California, where I opened an insurance agency.

I ran the insurance agency for two years, during which time our second son was born. We wanted our children to know their grandparents, so although we were making ends meet, I felt ready to leave the insurance business. I contacted the school district in West Milton where I had graduated and asked if there might be a position open for a person with my skills and education. I was offered a position teaching driver's education and coaching at the junior high level. Thus we moved back to southern Ohio, where I taught for four years and our third son was born. During this time, I also obtained a master's degree in counseling.

Roma Jo and I then learned of a new position on the mission field that did not require a college degree. We applied and were accepted with the stipulation that I return to seminary for a second year. So we returned to the Bethany Seminary with three sons and a vision for working in Nigeria. In summer 1967, we arrived in Jos, Nigeria, a few weeks after a civil war had broken out in the southern part of the country. We were the last family to receive visas for almost a year due to the civil war.

My work was to be that of a "lay churchman." I served as an assistant to the local Nigerian pastor, and I was again licensed but not ordained. Thus when people would come to me and ask that I perform a wedding for them, or dedicate their baby, or do other pastoral duties, I could honestly say, "I am not ordained; Pastor Joshua is the person who will do that for you." It was the beginning of the removal of missionaries from primary leadership in all of the mission programs, thus allowing the Nigerian clergy to assume their rightful role as leaders of the church. With this change, the Church of the Brethren in Nigeria began to grow and is now larger than the "mother" church here in America.

We were the only non-Nigerians living in a village of about 1,000 compounds. I was just getting comfortable preaching in the local Bura language when we were asked to move to Hillcrest, a boarding school for missionary children, to serve as house parents for the younger students, grades one to four. The previously assigned house parents needed to return to the United States for medical reasons. We served there for two years. The first year we had thirty-five children in our care; the second year we had twenty-eight children from eight different countries.

Upon our return to the States, I was able to obtain a teaching position in a vocational field. There I worked with senior boys who were having problems completing their high school. In spring 1971, I was offered the positions of dean of men and director of housing at Manchester College. This provided Roma Jo the opportunity to resume her college studies. To some it seemed strange that a person who spent so much disciplinary time in the office of the dean of men would be offered the position a few years later. Maybe it was because I knew many of the things that students were prone to try. To me it was interesting to be on "the other side of the desk" as we talked about acceptable activities for college students. On the mission field I was seen as a liberal; at college I was the conservative dean.

President Helman felt that it was good for administrators to teach a class each semester. It gave students the opportunity to know us outside of our administrative roles. I taught in the psychology department, usually the introduction to psychology class. I appreciated this assignment since it allowed me to get to know many students whom I would not have known otherwise. They also learned to know me as someone other than the dean who was responsible for discipline and parking tickets.

Manchester had a January interim term in whicha students and professors were able to travel and study in various locations. I began to wonder what a dean and psychology professor might do for an interim term. Tornadoes came through south central Indiana and southern Ohio in spring 1974. People began to realize that persons affected by such disasters suffer psychological as well as physical damages.

When Hurricane Fifi devastated the northern portion of Honduras in fall 1974, I contacted Mac Coffman and Ken McDowell to see if I could take a group of students to Honduras during the January interim term. They contacted Church World Service, and an agreement was made that if a course were approved by the college, they would welcome such a group. I was able to get an interim course approved in four weeks—though it usually takes a full semester to do so. The course was entitled "The Psychological Aspects of Disasters." Requirements were that it must be a group of at least ten persons and that one-half of the class have the equivalent of two years of college Spanish.

I took ten students in January 1975 to a community on the outskirts of San Pedro Sula, where several thousand people had been killed in the flooding. We worked with the local community to build new houses and a community center. We lived on the construction site, cooked our own meals, used a pit latrine, and took showers with rainwater collected in an elevated fifty-gallon drum.

In 1977, I took a second group of students to Guatemala following an earthquake. Once again we lived on the construction site and interacted with the local community. Some evenings we had lectures on local affects of disasters; other evenings we had class discussions.

While the position of dean of men/assistant dean of students had many positive opportunities, eight years of being in charge of discipline began to wear on me. I applied for the alumni relations position but was told, "Some of the recent alumni do not respect you. If you had applied as someone from the outside we would hire you." To which I responded, "You are saying that because I did the job you hired me to do—enforce college rules—you will not hire me to a new position?" The president responded, "Yes, that is the situation."

When I saw an announcement about a position to expand the Disaster Response Program, I applied. For this job, my previous experience with interim term students in Central America and my interest in the psychological aspects of disaster opened a door for me far beyond anything I could have imagined.

## MY LIFE WORK IN RELIEF AND DISASTER SERVICE

On February 1, 1978, I started work as the Disaster Network development and project coordinator with headquarters located at the Brethren Service Center in New Windsor, Maryland. The family stayed in North Manchester until the end of the school year; however, I immediately moved to New Windsor, where I was a bachelor for six months. D. Miller Davis, H. McKinley Coffman, and Ken McDowell had worked with disaster response in addition to their assigned positions. They felt that the disaster program needed a full-time person to develop a better district network and to train persons to be project directors.

In the early 1970s, a movement among disaster response organizations was underway to build trust and cooperation among the various agencies. National Voluntary Organizations Active in Disasters (NVOAD) was an organization representative of this movement. It was started by Red Cross, Salvation Army, Mennonite Disaster Services (MDS), Catholic Charities, Church of the Brethren Disaster Response, Seventh-day Adventists, Christian Reform World Relief, and a few others.

Since MDS and the Church of the Brethren (COB) were both part of this new organization, we tried working together. Due to the different understandings of some of the volunteers in both organizations, however, we were not always successful. Early on there was as much competition between the COB and MDS as there was between the Red Cross and the Salvation Army. My two previous years working on a combined COB-Pax project served me well in working at some of these tensions. I could call upon some of the Pax men with whom I had worked. They were able to help open doors and bridge the differences. Serving as a keynote speaker at five of the NVOAD regional conferences was another opportunity that came my way during this time.

Another great experience in solving problems through networking with past contacts happened in fall 1979. I was on a disaster location in Jackson, Mississippi, visiting a Disaster Assistance Center (DAC) where all of the disaster relief agencies were located under one roof so the victims could fill out the necessary forms at a single location. It was a hot, humid, Mississippi day, and people, many of them with children, were standing in line. I noticed one little girl ask her mother to take her to the rest room. The mother was unable to help her child without losing her place in the line. Very soon, in a kind of chain reaction, other children had the same need. Clearly, some kind of childcare was called for.

I contacted Karen Doubt, an early childhood professional in North Manchester, who had directed the local "Day Care" at the time I served on the governing board. I challenged her to think how the children could be better cared for in this situation. With Karen's assistance, after overcoming some resistance from my boss, we organized a childcare training program with a manual specifically adapted to disaster related conditions.

The first training seminar was held at the Brethren Service Center in March 1980. Karen and I taught the first ten workshops and then began to train others to help since there was such a positive response. It soon became clear that I could not direct this growing program and continue to direct the disaster clean-up and rebuilding programs. So in January 1983, a director of the Disaster Child Care Program was hired full-time. Due to her background in early childhood training, her fund-raising abilities, and her on-site experiences as a volunteer in the program, Roma Jo was hired to fill this position, now known as director of Children's Disaster Services. That was on a Friday; by that Sunday afternoon she was off to Los Angeles responding to a disaster.

Children's Disaster Services was well received. Both the Federal Emergency Management Agency (FEMA) and the Red Cross claimed that they could process parents in about half the time with the children in our program. There is now an agreement between the Church of the Brethren and the American Red Cross that in the event of a large plane crash, train wreck, or similar disaster, Children's Disaster Service will be present as part of the Red Cross response. Each month there are six specially trained volunteers who are on-call. Volunteers agree to leave within two to four hours to respond to such disasters. Following 9-11, there were over one hundred trained Children's Disaster Services volunteers who worked with children and parents near ground zero and at a second center further up-town in Manhattan. Volunteers were there for two or three weeks at a time on a rotation basis.

Since the beginning of the program, there have been 223 training workshops; 3,725 volunteers have taken the training. From 1980 to the present, 83,290 children have been ministered to at different disaster sites. People from Canada have been trained as well, and there is now an independent training program in Canada. In 2010, four persons came from England to take the training held at East Aurora, New York. They also plan to establish a similar program in England.

In 1981, I was asked to assume the role of director of refugee resettlement and disaster response. This increased my responsibilities; it also moved me into a higher administrative level that was responsible for the Brethren Service Center. I became a full staff person under the General Board of the Church of the Brethren, which placed me on several Church World Service Committees: Executive Committee, Finance Committee, Disaster Response Committee, Refugee Resettlement Committee, and the full Church World Service Committee. Working in the ecumenical arena was a rewarding experience since I learned to know so many wonderful people from many other church organizations.

In the early 1980s, the world became aware of millions of people facing starvation in northern Somalia. Nomadic herders were restricted to one area where there was a drought and their cattle were dying from lack of grasslands. Church World Service and other humanitarian groups organized a relief effort to save the population. Church World Service initially pledged ten million dollars for the international effort. Being a member of the committee that made this commitment, I pledged one million for the Church of the Brethren to raise. People on the committee looked at me and said, "That is a lot, but knowing the Church of the Brethren, you will do it." I left the room thinking, "Now what have I gotten myself into?" That afternoon at another committee meeting, I met a Presbyterian woman from Texas. She shared how the Presbyterian women's groups in Texas were raising money by having the women donate two cents each time they ate a meal.

I presented a proposal for a Two-Cents-a-Meal Club to the World Ministries Commission at the 1983 fall General Board meeting. The proposal was approved, and many individual families and local churches started saving two cents each meal. A label was designed by Howard Royer that could be fastened to a soup can or another container and was often found on tables in individual homes or in public worship centers. Even after the goal of one million dollars was met, the donors wanted the club to continue to support other hunger projects. Another more general program against hunger was created called the Global Food Crises Fund, which used the two-cents-a-meal concept as a main source of funding. This fund supports developmental agriculture programs and responds to immediate hunger needs.

In 1983, COB Annual Conference met in Baltimore. As I was driving from home to a pre-conference meeting, I heard a public service announcement on a local radio station in which the Red Cross was asking for blood donors. It was near the Fourth of July holiday, and the blood supply was extremely low. When I arrived at the convention center, I called the Red Cross Blood Services and asked if they would bring a mobile blood unit to the convention center if I could recruit twenty-five donors. All mobile units were scheduled, but they said if I had called earlier they would have been glad to schedule a blood drive at the conference.

In preparation for the next year's conference in Carbondale, Illinois, I received permission from executive director of Annual Conference to schedule a blood donation program for the 1984 conference. I called the Red Cross Regional Blood service in St. Louis, and after a few referrals, I received a phone call from the St. Louis Blood Service. Arrangements were made to have a mobile blood unit at the Annual Conference for one day. We had so many conference attendees and students from Southern Illinois University at Carbondale sign up to donate blood that not everyone could be processed in one day. The Red Cross staff volunteered to return the next day, using their free time to draw from any donors who had not been seen the first day. The draw for that first year at Annual Conference was 306 units. (The largest blood draw to date was in Cincinnati, Ohio, in 1987 when 506 units were collected.)

Let me share one more example of leveraging people-power with the appropriate organizational tools to maximize efficiency. When I started as director, there was a loosely organized district disaster network but not many trained project directors. Since the program had no vehicles and very few tools, I was always leasing a truck from a local car dealership and asking the volunteers to bring their own tools. Soon the first tool trailer was made from an old camp trailer by three men in the Harrisonburg, Virginia area: Paul Hollinger, Elzie Morris, and Carlton Ruff. Presently the program has five trucks, three national tool trailers, five district tool trailers, four passenger vans, a shower trailer, a bunk house made from a semi trailer, two travel trailers, and an RV for housing.

During my nine-and-one-half years with the disaster response program, I was responsible for having volunteers at nearly one hundred disasters sites. These varied from floods to forest fires, tornadoes, hurricanes, and landslides. The Brethren Service Center served as a transit center for CWS. Many refugees stayed there until the church organizations could make final arrangements for their placements. As director, I was responsible for nine staff and fifteen to twenty refugees on a regular basis. Sometimes we would have over one hundred refugees at the transit center.

## CAST INTO THE OVERSEES VORTEX OF RELIEF AND DISASTER

I resigned from the Refugee Resettlement/Disaster Response Program in summer 1987 and moved to Arizona, hoping to find a climate more tolerable for Roma Jo's arthritis. I found employment with Glencroft Retirement Community, a Mennonite and Church of the Brethren sponsored organization. I started out as director of volunteers but was soon moved to the position of director of public relations and fund raising. While at Glencroft, I was asked to speak at the Annual Arizona Mennonite Disaster Service banquet.

In December 1988, we received a call from the Church of the Brethren asking if we would be available for employment with the

Presbyterian Church and the Sudan Council of Churches in Khartoum. We were anxious to return to Africa, so we gave our ninety-day notice and left Glencroft the middle of March, following the fund raising auction that was my major responsibility. We returned to our unsold home in Maryland and waited for our visas to be issued. Roma's visa was finally issued in early August, and she left for Sudan. I remained at home, volunteering at the Brethren Service Center until my visa was issued in early September.

My work was in the Disaster Response office of the Sudan Council of Churches (SCC) as a consultant to the director. I also served as a liaison between the SCC and the many relief organizations that were giving grants or supplies. Due to some neglect in the past, there was not a lot of trust from the donor organizations. Basic expectations, such as regularly reporting to donor agencies, had been neglected. With some improvements in this area, distributions were enhanced so that, for example, we were able to have CWS send 50,000 blankets to the displaced Sudanese who had fled the civil war in the south and were now living in squatter villages around Khartoum and even out in the desert.

What follows is a brief anecdotal list of "successful adventures" in relief and emergency work, the kind of events that not only bring *life* to those in need but *meaning* to those fortunate enough to be able to serve: The SCC had tried to deliver supplies to the southern community of Wau. The rebels had surrounded the city and people were slowly starving. Trucks had been prohibited from approaching the city, so the supplies were distributed in other needed places. The normal population of Wau was about 25,000, but due to the civil war and fighting in the rural areas, many people had fled to the city, and the population had grown to about 250,000. My Sudanese colleague and I were able to obtain permission from the Sudanese government to airlift 1,500 metric tons of food and other relief materials into the city. We received authorization to fly into Wau to make arrangements for the distribution of the relief supplies. As we were arriving over the town of Wau and still at 10,000 feet over the airport, the pilot did a corkscrew landing. The plane could not come in on a normal glide, as the rebels would shoot down the plane at the lower altitudes.

When we arrived in Wau, we had to report to the army garrison headquarters and show our travel permits. When I presented my papers, I was in trouble. The "Homeland Security Office" in Khartoum had listed me as being a Canadian, but I was carrying an American passport. The commanding officer said he would have to hold me in jail until this could be straightened out. My co-worker went to find the chief of the community. Upon their return, we sat and drank tea and talked. We talked and drank some more tea. Finally the officer said to the chief, "I am releasing this man into your care. If he causes any trouble, both of you will be jailed."

When we had boarded the plane in Khartoum, the pilot said, "This is our last flight into Wau." I thought he was kidding. However, when our planning with the local SCC representatives was completed and we were ready to fly back to Khartoum, the plane did not return. We waited for three extra days. It just so happened that the International Red Cross had an emergency medical evacuation and we were able to get on that plane.

The Mennonite Central Committee was able to provide most of the grain and seeds that were to be airlifted. CWS and other organizations supplied money to pay Lutheran World Relief for the cost of the air flights from Nairobi, Kenya. The first plane was loaded with fifty-gallon drums of gasoline, diesel, motor oil, and grease for the delivery trucks since nothing was available in the community.

Because Roma Jo and I had relocated to Kenya, I had CWS send money for blankets to be included in the airlift. We negotiated to have the blankets made in Kenya for $4.00 per blanket, thus saving the ocean transportation cost. The planes carried fifteen to seventeen tons on each load depending upon the temperature. They would also fly in at 10,000 feet over the airport and corkscrew down for a landing. The airlift was able to transport 700 metric tons of relief supplies before the Sudanese government withdrew the landing permission.

During the first Gulf War, Sudan supported Iraq and granted Iraq the use of Sudan's airport space. The Sudanese government was making it very difficult for relief organizations to function in the country, and many organizations began to send their personnel out of the country. Early in January 1991, leaders of the Presbyterian Church in Sudan came to us and suggested that they would feel better about our safety if we would "take a vacation" to Kenya. We were on the second to last plane that flew civilians out of Sudan before the U.S. and others invaded Iraq.

It was impossible for Sudanese citizens to transfer any of their funds out of the country, so while I was in Kenya I was able to have CWS "buy" a fairly new Toyota Land Cruiser from a Sudanese businessman by depositing funds into his American bank account. He then "donated" the vehicle to the Sudan Council of Churches. Thus SCC saved paying import duties and the businessman had funds in his foreign account.

While in Sudan, I was not able to send telexes or to make any phone calls for these arrangements. I did, however, feel safe doing it from Kenya, but I did not discuss it in public when I returned to Sudan for the final three months. When we returned home in summer 1991, it was interesting to compare the news that Americans had been told concerning the war in Iraq with what we had heard from African news sources. The understandings were remarkably different. The Africans felt that America and its allies had new weapon systems that they were waiting to test on non-white Iraqis.

## LANDING BACK HOME AGAIN AND SEEKING TO MAKE SENSE OF IT ALL

Returning to the United States was not an easy transition. I applied for three different positions within the Church of the Brethren, but nothing came of the applications. For several months, I worked the 11:00 p.m. to 7:00 a.m. shift on the assembly line at Black and Decker.

Roma Jo was, however, offered a job back in Phoenix teaching at a school for homeless children. Thus we moved back to Arizona. I finally found employment as a teacher's aide in a classroom for emotionally disturbed high school students. This was the worst employment I had ever had. The kids would swear at us and spit on us, and when they became too violent we had to physically restrain them.

Again making connections helped to move us forward: I made friends with the counselor at the school whose wife happened to be the school psychologist at a neighboring school district. When the decision was made to add counselors in the four elementary schools, I was able to secure a position due to this friendship and his recommendation. The last five years before my retirement, I served as counselor for two elementary schools.

During this time, I became active in the COB Pacific Southwest District, which included all of Arizona and California. I served as co-chair of the district board for two years and chair for two years. I also served as chair of the committee that interviewed persons seeking licensing and ordination within the district. I eventually served as moderator for the district.

In 1996 the decision had been made by the disaster office to sponsor a "Blitz Build" with Habitat for Humanity during the annual conference that was to be held in Cincinnati, Ohio. Unfortunately, the person who had agreed to be the director of this project suffered a heart attack and died in March. So I was asked to assume this responsibility, which I was glad to do. This meant flying back to Brethren Service Center for a few days and also meeting with the Habitat organization in Cincinnati.

The Church of the Brethren along with several other organizations built three houses in two weeks in Cincinnati. It took lots of good volunteers and lots of planning to accomplish this project. Millard Fuller, the prestigious head of Habitat for Humanity, was present for the dedication of the three houses. This lent a special celebrative edge to the event.

A year later, I was asked to be the project director for another "Habitat Blitz Build" for the annual conference in Long Beach, California. The plan was to build two houses in a week plus a weekend. The Long Beach Habitat organization, however, did not have the foundations poured nor the permits ready as had been promised. Thus the building went a bit more slowly. We had to make sections of prefab framing on a nearby church parking lot until the foundations were poured and set. We then had to carry the prefab framing to the site so it could be erected. We were able to have the two houses framed, the interior walls set, plumbing installed, electrical wiring pulled on both the first and second floor, and the exterior sheeting on both houses and the roofs completed, including the shingles.

At the end of the 1996-97 school year, I retired from the public school system. Since my retirement, I have served in four interim pastorate positions—three in California and one in Maryland. These have lasted from three months to eleven months. Roma Jo and I volunteered as disaster project directors in Puerto Rico, Dominican Republic (three months), and Lucedale, Mississippi, following Hurricane Katrina. I spent one week as a volunteer on rebuilding following Katrina. And so it is—activities old and new continue to occupy us. The "new" continues to expand what has already been; the "old" is not mere repetition but deepens the experience of the past.

In 2000, Roma Jo and I took a tour of western Europe. When the tour stopped for a few days in Vienna, I could not resist a visit to Karls School, where I had first worked as a Brethren volunteer. It so happened that as I approached the front door, a teacher was coming out. In my broken German, I explained that I had worked on the school in the 1950s. She gave me the name and email address of an American exchange student who had married an Austrian and who was now a teacher at the school. We had been told that there would be a plaque in the entrance of the school telling the students and all who visited the school that the rebuilding had been done by volunteers who were opposed to war. But I saw no plaque there.

When I returned home, I wrote to the "American" teacher and suggested that I would raise the money for the plaque if she could get permission from the school authorities. The school officials agreed, and with assistance from Don and Heldi Durnbaugh the wording was in both English and German. I started to raise money for the plaque from former volunteers, both Mennonite and Church of the Brethren, but was a bit shocked to learn that the cost would be $2,800.

The plaque was dedicated in May 2001. Don Willoughby and I, both former unit leaders, spoke at the dedication. Also present were two Mennonite couples who had worked on Pax projects in Germany. The inscription on the plaque reads,

> FROM 1954 TO 1961 VOLUNTEERS FROM THE CHURCH OF THE BRETHREN AND MENNONITE CHURCHES IN NORTH AMERICA, UNDER THE SUPERVISION OF ING. REINHOLD LIEBE, HELPED REBUILD THIS SCHOOL IN THE CAUSE OF PEACE AND RECONCILIATION.

Before his death, Engineer Liebe wrote,

> No war has left a monument, but from the ruins is a monument erected. This is a monument to religious freedom, to the right to object to violence, and in turn, to create something positive and eternal. It is an important and strong expression of Christian love.

April 2009 saw the release of a book, *Beyond Our Means: How the Brethren Service Center Dared to Embrace the World*. Starting in 2000, Roma Jo and I spent the summers interviewing people who had been related to the work at Brethren Service Center since 1944 and some people who had been related to the Blue Ridge College that occupied the grounds from the early 1900s. We learned that much of the oral tradition that was being communicated on tours of the center was not in fact true. After five summers of research we started recording the findings of our study. With the assistance of an editor and the Brethren Press, we became published authors. Thus we continue to seek ways to serve others in our retirement years.

September 13, 2010<br>
Edited September 2015<br>
(following the author's unanticipated death due to a brain cancer)

*H. D. Swartzendruber*

---

**Service Pioneer on an International Scale**

*The oldest child and only son of an Iowa Mennonite bishop, H. D. Swartzendruber inherited the curiosity and service orientation of his father. His heroes were people like Orie O. Miller, C. F. Klassen, and "Big Dan," his paternal grandfather. In 1950, at the age of twenty, H. D. found himself in Europe, a Mennonite Central Committee worker in the aftermath of World War II. In the intervening years, he has set foot on the ground in 105 countries and has done relief and service work in fifty-five countries across Asia, Africa, and Latin America, covering nearly all the world's hot spots.*

## H. D. SWARTZENDRUBER

# *My Life and Times*

### EARLY YEARS

Like most American Mennonites of my generation, I was born in rural America. I was born on my grandfather's farm five miles northwest of Kalona, Iowa. When I was nearing my tenth birthday, after three years of attending one-room country schools and one year of public school in Iowa City, my parents were asked by the Mennonite Board of Missions and Charities to go to Kansas City, Kansas, to assume the responsibilities of superintendent and matron of the Mennonite Children's Home.

My sister Ruby and I then acquired sixty siblings and began attending public school in a big city. However, as soon as school was out, I caught the first ride back to Iowa, where I once again became a country boy. This shifting of places and roles probably helped me to be more adaptable to changing circumstances in my later years.

My fascination with international travel began at an early age. As a boy I read *National Geographic* magazine from cover to cover. Geography and history were the school subjects I most enjoyed. My interest in overseas service came early as well. Being reared in the Mennonite church, which historically had very active overseas mission and service programs, I was naturally attracted to the idea of service.

In 1940 or early 1941, before the U.S. entered World War II, M. C. Lehman, the Mennonite Central Committee (MCC) director for Germany, came to our church in Kansas City to talk about MCC relief programs in Europe. He spoke quite eloquently about attempts to minister to suffering people while working under the eyes of the Nazi regime. I was greatly impressed by his stories.

After the war in 1947, MCC worker Peter Dyck showed a movie and gave a presentation at Hesston College to several hundred students and people from the community. His lecture and movie communicated the challenge of moving several hundred Mennonite refugees trapped in West Berlin to the port of Bremerhaven. There they were to board a ship destined for Paraguay, where they would be resettled in the Chaco. The Russians had refused permission for their train to move through the Russian Zone of East Germany.

The SS *Volendam*, a Dutch liner that had been converted into a troop carrier during the war, had been contracted by MCC to take two ship-loads of Mennonite refugees to their new homeland. The ship had already made one voyage and was partly loaded and awaiting the arrival of the Berlin contingent. Finally, as a prayer meeting was underway on board, the Russians granted the train permission to pass through the Soviet occupied zone, and it left immediately. Everyone present at the lecture found the presentation to be absolutely riveting. When an offering was taken following the lecture, we ushers had to empty the overflowing baskets halfway down the aisles.

## College Years

During my freshman year in college and upon completion of his sophomore year, a dorm friend, J. B. Shenk, volunteered to serve one year in the MCC headquarters in Akron, Pennsylvania. A year later, he wrote advising me to do the same. In the fall of 1949, instead of working on a plan for financing further studies, I inquired of MCC about a Voluntary Service (VS) assignment. I was selected for the orientation class in mid-April. Since I had a chauffeur's license and experience driving trucks, they put me to work right away. MCC was changing warehouses and had many tons of relief supplies to be moved from one warehouse to the other. I was delighted! Thus began my experience in logistics.

Toward the end of my orientation, MCC's Director of Relief, J. N. Byler, returned from a long field trip. He asked me what was in store for me. I told him that I had hoped to go to Germany, but there were to be no more VS assignments in Europe, only relief worker assignments. He suggested that I consider going as a relief worker.

I reminded him that the minimum age for MCC relief workers was twenty-four, and I was only twenty-two. He replied that there were always exceptions to the rule. He said that there was an urgent need for a maintenance man in an MCC Children's Home in Nancy, France. He was sure that someone of my background could easily handle it. I readily agreed to the France assignment. "Now H. D.," were the director's parting words to me, "I don't want you just hanging around the MCC ghetto like so many of our workers. I want you to get to know the natives."

## WITH MCC IN EUROPE

In the early morning of May 29, 1950, two of my fellow VSers and I loaded my baggage and a large chest of supplies for MCC Europe into the MCC carryall and headed for Hoboken, New Jersey. There I was to embark on Holland American Lines' SS *Volendam*, the same old former troop ship that had taken the refugees to Paraguay. She had not been retrofitted for passenger service but was being used to take students and anyone else who wanted cheap passage to Europe. As I recall, the fare was $135 for a voyage of about eight days.

Arriving in Rotterdam, I was met by Paul Ruth, the Menno Travel Service representative. After spending several days in Amsterdam to get my "land legs" back, I boarded a train to France. I had to change trains at Metz for a local to Nancy. Not speaking French and with few French people at that time speaking English, I had to resort to writing and hand signals to communicate, but somehow it all worked out.

When I arrived in Nancy, John Howard Yoder, who was using the Children's Home as his base as he worked on peace issues with the French Mennonites, met me at the station. He took me to the home, where I was able to meet the staff and take a tour of the place. The last person I met was a young secretary/monitrice named Françoise Quirin. She made a very favorable impression on me, especially her smile. Unfortunately she spoke virtually no English and I spoke even less French. I had already been motivated to learn the French language as rapidly as possible to be able to accomplish the tasks required of me. My interest in learning to know Françoise gave me an even greater incentive.

One of my jobs at the home was shopping in the market for groceries and other supplies. Within six weeks I was making myself understood with my limited French combined with sign language. French came relatively easily to me, as I became immersed in the French culture. I followed C. N. Byler's instructions and found most of my friends in the French community, particularly since my American coworkers were somewhat older than I. In due time, Françoise became one of those friends as we developed a romantic relationship.

Shortly after my arrival in Nancy, when schools had closed for the summer, we sent all of the children to summer camp and moved the home to Valdoie, a suburb of Belfort, where it continues today. I was in charge of the logistics for the move and was involved in helping to get the new building into useable shape. It was a large three-story chateau with two outbuildings, a greenhouse, and several acres of park. The main house had been the headquarters of a German military unit during the occupation and was badly in need of clean up and repair. MCC and the French Mennonite churches had bought it jointly to be the new location for the home. Eventually, the French churches bought the MCC share. Much of the cleanup, painting, weed cutting, etc., was done by several international youth work camps. Besides the hard work, we had lots of fun.

After eighteen months in France, I was transferred to an MCC refugee camp in Gronau, in northwest Germany near the Dutch border. This was the camp where Mennonite refugees were being processed for resettlement, either in West Germany or abroad. It was here that my education accelerated.

I was what today would be called the camp logistician. I was responsible for the two drivers and four vehicles of the transportation unit and for the purchasing and supply unit headed by Herr Martins, a refugee from Prussia. Our relationship was somewhat like that between a new second lieutenant and a senior sergeant. I was his manager, but he was my teacher. He taught me many life lessons, the most important having to do with material possessions. He believed that our two most important possessions were our friends and our knowledge. He said that before the Soviets took over, the Mennonites in Russia and eastern Germany had been very affluent with big farms and financial wealth. Now the survivors in his family were able to carry all their material goods in several cheap suitcases. "The powers that be," he said, "could take away all our material possessions whenever they chose, but friends and knowledge endured." I have never forgotten that lesson. He also taught me systems for inventory and distribution control, which later in my career stood me in good stead.

Working in the camp was a moving and sometimes emotional experience. We were helping Mennonite sisters and brothers who had suffered tremendous losses. For most, the loss included many family members and all their property. In fact, their only personal belongings consisted of what they could carry with them. Many had become separated from other family members during the war as they moved from east to west.

Among my fondest memories were their worship services. These camp participants, despite their present condition, were still possessed of a fervent faith in God and a hope for the future. One of the favorite hymns sung in their worship services was *So Nimm Denn Meine Hände* ("Take Thou My Hand Oh Father"). Even today, when I hear that hymn, I am often moved to tears, remembering those courageous people whom we helped to find a new and better life. And I feel gratitude that I was allowed to play a role, however miniscule, in this noble enterprise.

MCC decided to close the camp at the end of summer 1952 as most of the refugees who could easily immigrate had already done so. Only those with serious health issues remained behind to be resettled in different parts of West Germany. I was asked to extend my term of service through August to help close the camp. I agreed, provided that MCC would permit Françoise and me to marry when my regular two-year term was complete. I had continued courting her by mail and occasional visits after my transfer. MCC agreed.

We were married in the Children's Home in Valdoie by Pierre Widmer, a French Mennonite pastor. A civil marriage followed in the Town Hall. After a brief honeymoon in Switzerland, I returned to my duties in Gronau with my new bride, who was put to work in our office keeping the inventory up to date. When my tasks were finished and the last refugee had left the camp, we said our goodbyes and sailed for a new life in the United States. I believe it is safe to say (and most MCC alumni would agree) that our experiences, at whatever level and in whatever place we worked, changed our worldviews. In many cases, it also changed the direction of our life's work, and we are all the better for it.

## WITH CHURCH WORLD SERVICE IN PAKISTAN

In 1954 the U.S. was just completing a very successful program for the reconstruction of Europe, known as the Marshall Plan. It seemed that the U.S. was committed to "doing good" around the world, hopefully making it a better and safer place. The U.S. Department of Agriculture held enormous food surpluses, costing the American taxpayers an estimated $1,000,000 per day in storage costs. Recognizing these factors, a young Democratic senator from Minnesota, Hubert H. Humphrey, drafted legislation designed to reduce these surpluses by making them available to combat hunger around the world. The legislation was designated "Public Law 480" and signed into law by President Dwight D. Eisenhower, a Republican.

The Cold War was well underway, and the U.S. was providing military assistance to a number of countries loosely allied with them. As a counterpoint, this food assistance program was dubbed the "Food for Peace Program," which exists to this day. One of the provisions included in the legislation was that the organizations receiving and distributing this food had to have an American Citizen Representative to supervise and sign for the commodities in the given country of distribution. (This condition was modified many years later.)

After leaving Europe, Françoise and I had spent nearly one year in the Kalona, Iowa, area and then moved to Ft. Dodge, where I worked in sales. After five years of working in the U.S., both Françoise and I felt a desire to return to overseas service. After much discussion, I contacted MCC, who put me in touch with Church World Service (CWS). CWS was in the process of recruiting the first direct hire personnel for overseas assignment. We were told that although CWS had no openings in Europe, there were several possibilities in Asia.

Our family now included two sons, four-year-old Freddy and two-year-old Danny. As we were preparing for this move to Asia, we decided that it would be better if we all traveled on the same nationality passports. This meant that Françoise would need to apply for American citizenship. We then decided that it would be best if Françoise, who by then was known as Frances, should have her name legally changed to Frances.

Frances and I and two of our friends, who were to be our witnesses, met in a restaurant for her interview with the immigration officer. It was very cordial and nearly pro-forma. Some hours later, as we waited with dozens of new citizens-to-be, the judge announced that before we were sworn in, the court had one more detail to attend to; there had been a petition for a name change. He said, "Would Frankee-oy-zee Swartzendruber please rise." She stood, and he asked if it was still her desire to change her name to Frances. She answered in the affirmative, and he said, "So be it." And with his butchering of her name, we knew that we had made the correct decision.

Dr. Stevenson at the CWS headquarters in New York asked whether we would consider going to Pakistan for a two-year assignment for me as the country program director. We readily agreed. In 1947, at the time of British India's independence, Pakistan had been created as a Muslim majority nation. It consisted of two wings; East Pakistan made up of East Bengal Province (now the nation of Bangladesh) with its capital in Dacca, and West Pakistan, made up of the West Punjab, Baluchistan, Sind, and the Northwest Frontier Provinces with its capital in Lahore. The national capital was Karachi, a small but crucial and busy seaport with an international airport. The two wings were separated by the large expanse of the remainder of the Indian sub-continent, a distance of over 1,000 miles with no land connection. The only connections were by air and by sea.

The partition of British India resulted in widespread communal violence with entire populations moving from one country to the other. Thousands of Muslims fled to Pakistan, leaving behind their homes, businesses, and personal belongings. And the same applied to Hindus living in what became Pakistan. It is said that the number of people killed in the communal violence that followed the partition of India was in the hundreds of thousands. We heard and read stories of people from one religion hiding friends of another religion, including Christians, who sheltered people until the situation settled down. But the entire event created deep feelings of animosity and distrust between the general populations, which to some extent still exist today.

This was the situation that we found ourselves moving into, not quite ten years after independence and Pakistan's partition from India. We heard about the horror stories from actual witnesses of the events.

The West Pakistan Relief Committee consisted of about a dozen members, with the majority being western missionaries. When I attended my first meeting with the Relief Committee in Lahore, I received a warm welcome. But there were comments by the committee chairman that I was really young and totally unaware of all the complexities of Christian work in Pakistan. I assured them that I was well aware of that and would always seek their counsel and advice on issues concerning the culture and the mores of the country and its churches. However, I said that as the CWS representative, I had a responsibility to see that the program operated within the regulations laid down in Public Law 480 and the laws of Pakistan. I assured them that there would surely be much discussion in the future.

One day my assistant, Mr. Wilkinson, came in to tell me that the local Urdu paper carried an article reporting that large quantities of relief food were being sold on the black market in Multan. I immediately contacted my counterpart in Catholic Relief Services (CRS), who had received the same report from his staff. We agreed that we had to take action immediately, before the people at the United States Agency for International Development (USAID) got onto the story, as indeed they would. To insure accuracy in our findings, we agreed to each select one of our local staff members to go independently to Multan to investigate matters. When we compared the two reports, there was about an 80 percent overlap. Each one had details missing from the other. This was natural as one was checking on CRS distributions, the other on CWS outlets.

We immediately took our findings to the mission director of USAID, asking it to suspend further shipments until we could get our respective houses in order. He said that this was most unusual. Generally, he said, the United States government (USG) discovered the problems and, over the protests of the NGO's (non-governmental organizations) stopped the programs. We were to be commended for our prompt action.

It was agreed that the program could only be carried out properly if the old Pak-American agreement was augmented with new agreements between the government of Pakistan and the respective voluntary agencies: Church World Service and Catholic Relief Services. The agreement between the government of Pakistan and CARE (Cooperative Committee for Relief Everywhere) was operating with only minimal problems. This began about a year of negotiations, sometimes quite intense, between representatives of the governments of Pakistan, the United States, and the respective voluntary agencies. Finally an agreement was reached, and it continued to be honored until several years ago, when a new agreement was negotiated that included sending supplies to Afghanistan.

## WITH CHURCH WORLD SERVICE IN INDIA

In many ways, India, my next assignment, was one of the most enriching assignments of my entire career. The attitudes of the governments of Pakistan and India toward foreign assistance were quite different. Pakistan had become a member of the Southeast Asia Treaty Organization (SEATO), which had been created in 1954.

India, on the other hand, had not joined any power bloc. Prime Minister Nehru, in a 1954 speech in Colombo, Sri Lanka, had used the term, "Non-Alignment." This stressed the intention of avoiding involvement in either the North Atlantic Treaty Organization (NATO) or the Soviet bloc, and of steering a course independently of both. This resulted in considerable suspicion of any foreign involvement in Indian affairs, particularly if it was to be in a position of any line management authority.

As indicated earlier, a requirement of Public Law 480 was that NGOs distributing Food For Peace commodities must have an American citizen representative directly involved in the program, not simply there as an adviser or monitor. In the case of India, the American was the country representative of both Church World Service (CWS) and Lutheran World Relief (LWR) as well as a staff officer of the counterpart agency. The counterpart agency in India was the Committee On Relief and Gift Supplies (CORAGS) of the National Christian Council of India (NCCI).

The suspicion of foreigners who had any authority filtered down and made the life and work of persons such as myself, who had come to work within an Indian organization, somewhat sensitive, requiring considerable tact. One time I was actually told that I was only in India because of an American law requirement and that Indians knew how to handle their own affairs. We should just send the supplies and they would get along just fine. Most Indians were more tactful and had more subtle ways of delivering the same message.

Thanks to the foresight of Don Rugh, the first director of CORAGS, its program was organized on an entirely different basis than the general distribution of the Pakistan program. CORAGS ministered to the many thousands of Hindu refugees who had fled their homes during the creation of Pakistan. Rather than distributing through churches to all and sundry, as we had witnessed in Pakistan, CORAGS had decided from the outset that the program would be based on institutions, including schools, orphanages, hospital dispensaries, and other service organizations.

*H. D. Swartzendruber (far right) with staff of the Committee on Relief and Gift Supplies of the National Christian Council of India.*

The CORAGS committee was relatively small and consisted of very capable people. The chairman was Mr. Samuel Mathai, the Secretary of the University Grants Commission of the government of India. Mr. Mathai was an active member of the Mar Thoma Church and one of the highest level Christians in the government of India.

Another senior member of the committee was Methodist Bishop, S. K. Mondol. Also on the committee were the general secretaries of the YMCA and the YWCA, who frequently were at loggerheads over whatever issue was on the agenda.

Mr. Mathai's leadership as chairman was exceptional, as demonstrated by the fact that in the three years that I was in India, I never saw a vote taken at a committee meeting. When an issue was presented and a debate occurred, as it generally did, particularly between the two general secretaries, Mr. Mathai engaged the rest of the committee in discussion of the issue at hand to see where the other members stood on the issue. He then framed a position for consideration. After stating what he felt was the general sense of the meeting, he asked the members whether or not they were in agreement. Usually all answered in the affirmative, and the motion was carried by consensus.

I once asked him why he never called for a vote. He told me that face is crucial in Asia, and if you lose on a vote, you also lose face. Therefore, by taking the extra time to find consensus, everybody winds up a winner and there are no losers.

### WITH WORLD COUNCIL OF CHURCHES IN ALGERIA

During a debriefing on India at the CWS Headquarters in New York in 1962, I was told that the World Council of Churches (WCC) had requested my services as material aid director of the newly formed, international Christian Committee for Service in Algeria (CCSA). Since I spoke French, was an American citizen with experience in material aid programs and the regulations pertaining to the use of PL 480 commodities, and a staff member of CWS, they felt I was well suited for this assignment. Furthermore, they recognized that the bulk of the food shipments to Algeria would be from the U.S. government, which required an American citizen representative to supervise it. I naturally accepted and after a brief vacation, proceeded to Algiers to be joined by my family several months later.

The Algerian officials were eager for advice and assistance in planning. There were technical advisers from France who, being considered "liberal" as supporters of Algerian independence and against the war, were welcomed. They provided excellent planning assistance to the new administration. It was reassuring to know that so much planning had already been done and that CCSA, largely due to Vern Preheim, who represented both MCC and CWS, already had excellent contacts, both in the new Algerian administration and in the U.S. Consulate General.

I knew that there had been a lot of fighting in Algiers. But I was not prepared for the extent of destruction I witnessed on the drive from the airport to the guesthouse where I would be staying temporarily. I saw an apartment building of about six floors where the walls of the entire second floor were blown out and only the support columns, made of reinforced concrete, were supporting the rest of the building. There were other buildings that had less extensive damage, but there were still many broken windows and pockmarks on the walls from the street fighting.

Vern was to remain several months until his MCC assignment ended. He took me to the office of the provisional executive in Rocher Noir, a suburb of Algeria, where I was introduced to Mr. Benzerfa, the head of the Department of Social Affairs, and his staff. I was issued my *laissez passé*, a travel document allowing me to travel relatively unhindered throughout the country. This was crucial in facilitating our work.

I asked Mr. Benzerfa if the word *Chretien*, in *Comité Chrétien de Service en Algérie* (Christian Committee for Service in Algeria) created a problem, as some in Geneva had argued. He replied that the Algerians were well aware that all the agencies coming to work in Algeria under CCSA were Christian organizations. If we had not acknowledged that openly they would have suspected our motives. This confirmed that our decision to openly acknowledge that our motivation was Christian service to those in need, regardless of race, caste or creed, was the correct approach to have taken.

The Emergency Distribution Program began in earnest with the arrivals of shipments of PL 480 for LICROSS (International League of Red Cross Societies), CRS, and CCSA. We were programmed to receive about 12,000 metric tons of food per week over a six-month emergency period. This was roughly one entire shipload of food every week to feed slightly over one million needy Algerians, mostly fatherless families and other generally destitute people. By the end of the program, we had received and distributed 231,000 metric tons of food to 1,265,000 persons valued at more than $8,700,000.

As the end of the six-month emergency program neared, the representatives of CRS and LICROSS suggested an extension of the program for one or two months, as there was still need. The Ministry of Social Affairs did not agree. They argued that eventually the government of Algeria had to handle their problems. We in CCSA concurred. At this point, we learned the value of timelines in emergency programs. It is always possible to extend, if necessary. On the other hand, if no timeline is established, as long as the resources are available, there is a tendency to keep on, creating dependency as a result.

In early 1962 CCSA was assigned an abandoned farm at Henchir Toumghani, south of the city of Constantine. The farm had been abandoned for some time, and it was assigned to Mennonite Central Committee to be used as an agricultural training center for the community. As MCC workers began arriving, the first two volunteers had to thoroughly clean the house before it could be used as staff accommodation. It had been used as a stable for goats and sheep. Among the things that were taught, once the training center opened, were animal husbandry, agronomy, industrial arts, and home economics for the local girls. There was also a community medical program component.

The program continued until 1967, when it was turned over to the Algerian Ministry of Education, which turned it into an agricultural high school. When I was in Algeria on a follow-up mission in 1976, I was told that the Mennonite training had played a vital role in improving the economic well-being of the entire community.

While we were receiving the shipments for the emergency program—this included wheat that needed to be processed into *semoule* (semolina) for food-for-work—the shipments for the reforestation program were also beginning to arrive. The reforestation team had to prepare their tree nurseries from scratch, as none existed at the time. They had to import the seeds from France, as well as the small plastic bags (pots) and the pumping equipment for watering the nursery. They also had to prepare enormous quantities of potting soil to fill the bags for seeds.

They were also hiring their cadres for the nursery labor and for the planting areas. Most of the supervisors were former Algerian guerrillas, whose sole profession had been making war. They were however, temperamentally suited to be foremen on the project. They were accustomed to taking orders and giving orders. And because of their success in the fight for independence, they were highly respected by the general population.

During the ten-month dry period, while the nursery was being organized and the seeds potted, the people on the project site were busy putting in roads, terracing the hillsides to prevent further erosion, and eventually digging the holes for planting. Actual planting only occurred during the two or three months of the rainy season.

The workers were lodged in tents on the project site. A canteen was organized on each site to provide the meals. This consisted of bread made from the PL 480 flour, sardines, corned beef, and other items provided by various donors. This was not a part of the rations to be taken home but was to sustain them while they were on the project.

At the end of three years, the government of Algeria asked CCSA to continue for a further period on an expanded basis. They were told that there simply were not enough funds available but that we were generally supportive of the idea. It was finally decided to turn the entire operation over to the government of Algeria (GOA). Included was the equipment, over fifty million seedlings in the largest nursery complex in the entire Mediterranean basin, and two hundred former guerrilla fighters, now competent foresters. President Ben Bella signed a decree creating a new department called the *Chantiers Populaires de Reboisment* (Popular Reforestation Projects).

An agreement was negotiated with the United Nations World Food Program (WFP), which was then in its early days. WFP was happy for the opportunity to continue such a well-known program as one of its first projects. WFP and GOA continued the operation for another nine years, planting an additional 70 to 80 million trees, covering 12 million acres or 18,750 square miles. When I went back to Algeria in 1976, the trees were twelve to fifteen feet tall, and the forests stretched for many miles along the road. I was told that the survival rate was above 80 percent.

Recently I read a report from a missionary who had just visited the area. While admiring the trees, he was told by one of the local people that these were "Christian trees," as they had been planted by a Christian agency.

## WITH DIACONIA IN BRAZIL

The relationship between Church World Service and the Evangelical Confederation of Brazil (Confederacão Evangélica do Brasil—CEB) began at some point in the 1950s, but Food for Peace commodities were not introduced into the program until the early 1960s. The relationship was through its Department of Social Action (Departamento d'Ação Social—DAS)

By 1965 and 1966, it was clear that there were some very serious problems with the management of the food program. DAS did not have an adequate financial management system. In its eagerness to get a food program going in Brazil, USAID had issued a waiver of the Brazilian government's obligation to pay for port clearance and inland freight to the point of distribution, as in other countries. Hence Church World Service and Lutheran World Relief (LWR), who were the partners in this operation, had to provide the funds to pay the port costs.

This finally came to a head in 1966, resulting in a consultation of church leaders in Brazil with representatives of CWS and LWR to come up with a satisfactory solution. It was decided to create a new organization, independent of but sending reports to the Evangelical Confederation of Brazil. It was decided to name the new organization "Diaconia." (The letter *k* doesn't exist in Portuguese, hence the misspelling of the Greek *diakonia*.)

CWS and LWR provided a list of the support that they were prepared to give this new organization. It included personnel, funding, commodities, medicine, and other material aid. This support was contingent, however, upon CWS/LWR nominating the first executive secretary of Diaconia. I was nominated to be this person. These conditions were accepted.

Among the decisions that were made by the executive committee was to centralize the administration of the Diaconia program. In other words, the regional programs would function as regional offices of Diaconia and not autonomous bodies as they had in the past.

In the meantime, I announced that we would prepare a manual of operations so that we would all be working from the same basic document. We brought the four principal field people to Rio for a week, and they, together with the national program and shipping staff, were given the manual of operations, outlining a commodity management system that I had prepared during a study leave at the University of

Iowa the year before. They were told to develop a working manual based along these lines.

The two field men from the south, being fluent in English, were able to translate the document into Portuguese. I played no direct role in preparing the manual. Each day I would critique the previous day's production, and, if necessary, it would be amended. At the end of a week, they had prepared a very good product. Having produced it themselves, they felt an ownership; it was not something that had been foisted upon them. Consequently it was up to them to make it work, and work it did. After a year, we updated the manual based upon experience, and it continued to be the official manual of operations for Diaconia for years to come.

As had been learned in earlier country programs and was generally accepted by Food for Peace and other NGOs, there should be no more general distributions of food except in the case of emergencies. There were many activities in which food could be used, but all of them had a goal of long-term improvement of the situation of the participants. The highest priority was child assistance; this included maternal-child health, nutrition classes, school lunch programs, and other child feeding programs, such as orphanages or other such institutions.

The second category had to do with economic and community development activities. These included road building and improvement, digging irrigation and drainage ditches, digging wells, and so forth. There were also courses in adult education and training such as adult literacy, sewing, and training in sanitation activities. Assistance to institutions such as hospitals, sanatoriums, and more was also approved.

In early 1968, we were informed that USAID had money available for nutrition rehabilitation centers. Working with the local AID mission, we prepared a proposal for three centers to be located in the northeast near Recife. When the grant was approved, we received word that June Sauder, an MCC nutritionist, was available. She had just completed a term of service in Vietnam and came with strong recommendations from both MCC and CWS. After a brief orientation in Rio de Janeiro, she went to Recife. June had limited Portuguese, but with the help of a part-time interpreter, June soon had a highly rated project of three centers up and running.

We had learned in Algeria that to ensure project success, real community dialogue had to take place before commencing projects. We learned in Brazil that for a project to succeed, we had to begin with the community's felt needs. Otherwise the people would go through the exercise simply to get the food but would not feel any real ownership of the project.

A good example of this practice was a village in northeast Brazil. They had applied for food assistance but when asked what project they felt was the most important, they said that they wanted the road through town blacktopped. It was a main highway and the traffic going through town raised so much dust that it was a nuisance.

When asked where their water came from, the men replied that water was really no problem at all. There was a stream a couple of kilometers away, and in the morning the womenfolk walked to the stream, filled their water containers, and returned to their homes. This, of course, was the opinion of the men. Upon inspection, it was discovered that the stream was polluted because of people and animals drinking, bathing, and performing other bodily functions upstream. This, of course, contributed to some of the diseases prevalent in their village.

The villagers were told that if they could persuade the mayor to provide the material for blacktopping the main street and the necessary engineering work to insure a project, up to standard, we would then provide the commodities for a Food for Work project. It was a small village with municipal elections coming up; somewhere the mayor found the resources and the project was completed.

At that point, the women began to have their say and insisted that a well be dug to provide clean water for the village. It was learned that the water table was not too deep for a hand-dug well, so another project was drawn up. This time it was up to the mayor once again to provide bricks, cement, rebar, and sand to make a proper project.

When the project was completed, it was a masterpiece. The pump was powered by a small diesel engine that had been donated by a local company. It was installed in a pump house with a several-hundred-gallon tank on top. Water from this tank fed supply taps on one side to fill the water containers to take home. On the second side, there was a laundry tap and basin. And on the third side, there was a water tank for watering the livestock.

While the project was nearing completion, the village women were queried about having water piped into their homes. The women declined, saying the village well was the primary place for the village's information exchange. The well not only provided clean water and better health, it also reinforced the sense of community among the inhabitants. We learned that this attitude was prevalent in most small towns. This hearkened back to Bible stories of people gathering around the well, exchanging information and socializing.

With the revision of the manual and the field personnel having had a year of experience, things were looking up. About the same time, the USAID mission announced that there would be an audit of both the CRS and Diaconia programs. A team of auditors of the regional auditor general would do the audit. Hence there would be no influence upon the auditors by any Brazilian or American personnel based in Brazil.

Their final report was nothing short of glowing. In fact, one of the recommendations was that the Diaconia manual should be replicated and provided as a guide to all NGOs with food programs in Latin America. We had succeeded, despite the skeptical predictions of some U.S. government and a few church officials in Brazil and the U.S., that Diaconia would never be able to mount an effective and honest program. The Diaconia staff was elated. They had proven that they could exceed all expectations.

I had been elected as executive secretary for two years, but Diaconia asked me to extend six months while they looked for a replacement. CWS and LWR concurred and we agreed, but we were coming to the end of our visa extensions.

I was gratified when several of the board members asked me privately if I wouldn't consider returning for another three years at their invitation, rather than at the initiative of CWS, as had been the first time. I knew that my friends in New York were somewhat surprised that, rather than being resented by the Brazilian committee members, I was actually considered as one of them and no longer a gringo foisted upon them. I had to decline with regret. After eight years of working overseas, we felt that it was important for the family to spend more time in the U.S.

During our overseas assignments, our social life centered on the church that we regularly attended, plus friends working in the several NGOs. There were also occasional diplomatic receptions to which we were invited as representative of Church World Service. Our two oldest sons attended excellent schools: American School of New Delhi, St. Joseph Boys School in Algiers, and the American School in Rio de Janeiro.

David, our third son, was born in New Delhi. When he was a toddler, he became ill with a high fever producing episodes of severe delirium. We took him to St. Joseph Hospital for Women and Children, the best in New Delhi. But despite their best efforts, when he came home we noticed a difference. Six years later he was evaluated and determined to have mild intellectual disabilities. We were able to have him admitted to the Woodhaven Learning Center in Columbia, Missouri, before our move to Rio. My parents lived several hours away and were able to visit him and host him for the holidays. He was flown to Rio twice to spend his vacations with us.

When we moved to the U.S. he graduated from Woodhaven and moved to Pleasant View Homes in Broadway, Virginia, where he still resides and works in a local super market.

## CHURCH WORLD SERVICE DIRECTOR FOR THE EAST ASIA REGION

I asked Jim MacCracken, then an executive of CWS, if he could arrange some kind of a position for me stateside. As we were leaving Brazil in 1969, I was told I would be appointed to the post of Church World Service Director for the East Asia region. This included programs in Korea, Hong Kong, Taiwan, Okinawa, and the Philippines. My main responsibility in East Asia was to develop a strategy for nationalizing most of CWS's area programs—handing them over to the National Christian Councils. Our family would reside in one of the towns near New York City, and I would travel back and forth between the U.S. and East Asia.

The Japan Church World Service program had been autonomous for several years. The program had a very successful fundraising department, supported programs domestically, and contributed to projects through the World Council of Churches Project List. The PL 480 Food for Peace programs had already been reduced in Korea and Hong Kong. In the case of Okinawa, the program was eventually turned over to Japan Church World Service as Okinawa was transferring from U.S. military occupation back to the government of Japan. The remaining food program in Hong Kong came under the management of the local Christian Council, with CWS providing a representative and financial support rather than directorship.

When Korea Church World Service was organized soon after the Korean War, it was necessary to buy property from which to operate. Because of the circumstances, real estate was quite inexpensive at the time. By 1970, property values had increased dramatically. As we phased out, we sold the properties at a considerable profit. It was agreed by the CWS Committee that this profit should be reinvested in Korea. Consequently, we gave several grants to the National Christian Council of Korea (NCCK) and Yonsei University Department of Urban Studies. The remaining funds were turned over to the NCCK.

In the Philippines, which because of the needs, continued to have a sizable PL-408 program, the National Christian Council of the Philippines assumed responsibility for the program. The Filipino deputy director became the director, and Church World Service sent a CWS representative as the associate director. All of these developments were in process as I was leaving to assume the directorship of the Latin America and Caribbean office.

## CHURCH WORLD SERVICE DIRECTOR FOR LATIN AMERICA AND THE CARIBBEAN

At the time of my transfer in fall 1971 to the Latin America and Caribbean program, it was rather small. The denominations that made up Church World Service in the U.S. were few in Latin America and the Caribbean and were virtually nonexistent in Central America.

Church World Service only had large food programs in Brazil, Dominican Republic, and Haiti. The Peru earthquake of May 31, 1970, changed that. There had previously been a small CWS program in Peru, but suddenly there were teams of relief workers in the country, working mostly in the high Andes Mountains, where the major earthquake damage occurred.

The work was not for the fainthearted, as the only access to most of the affected areas was by horseback. The teams were primarily medical personnel and people working in reconstruction. This eventually evolved into community development projects in the affected areas. Rather than simply rebuilding houses, repairing wells and trails, and then leaving, it felt important to help the communities better themselves in the long term. Among the activities introduced was animal husbandry focusing on small animals and poultry. A very popular animal in the Andes was the guinea pig, which was raised in the kitchen and considered a delicacy.

About the time that I felt I had a reasonable handle on the program, an earthquake flattened Managua, Nicaragua, on the night of December 23, 1972. Immediately dispatching one of our most experienced field officers to Managua to see how we might help, we learned that the local evangelical churches had organized CEPAD, a committee headed by Dr. Gustavo Parajon. Gus, Nicaraguan MD and Baptist lay minister, and his American wife Joan were under American Baptist Mission Board, a member of CWS. This helped us enter a country where few other mainline U.S. denominations had representatives.

As normal communications were completely disrupted, the only contact was via ham radio. Joan Parajon was a ham radio operator, and I was able to make contact with her through different U.S. ham operators. I was not comfortable, however, with our discussions being transmitted via unknown persons who happened to have a phone patch. I learned that Dr. Gerald Brunk at Eastern Mennonite College was not only a ham operator but also had a phone patch. We arranged that on Monday, Wednesday, and Friday noons, Gerald would go to his radio, and when he had Joan on the line, he would call my office in New York and connect me directly with Joan. For several months, this is how we managed our earthquake response in Nicaragua until phone service was reestablished, and Joan was reminded by the government that ham radios were for amateur use only.

Because of the quality of leadership provided primarily by Gustavo and Joan Parajon, CEPAD continues today as a crucial development arm of the Nicaraguan evangelical churches. CWS recruited and fielded several people who had worked in the Peru disaster to work with CEPAD as advisers. It was clear from the beginning, however, that our personnel were there in support roles and not as directors. CWS funded CEPAD and provided technicians to build hundreds of small concrete houses for those whose homes had been destroyed in the earthquake. Most of these houses are still standing today and have been enlarged or otherwise modified to reflect the individual tastes of the residents.

The reconstruction in Nicaragua was followed by community development activities involving health care, education, and eventually micro-finance. This activity, similar to that of Mennonite Economic Development Associates (MEDA), developed to the extent that it became larger than the rest of CEPAD and was spun off into a separate organization, still in operation today.

Less than two years after the Managua earthquake, on September 1974, Hurricane Fifi smashed into Honduras, adding to our responsibilities. Fifi, contradicting its relatively frivolous-sounding name, did extensive damage in Honduras. CWS immediately sent personnel from the U.S. and Nicaragua. We helped to form CEDAN, an evangelical organization in Honduras. This organization functioned similarly to CEPAD in Nicaragua. Again we helped in reconstruction on a large scale, building several entire communities, and helping in community development.

While these two programs were still functioning reasonably well, in the early morning of February 4, 1976, a major earthquake struck Guatemala, destroying much of Guatemala City, killing about 23,000 people and leaving over one million homeless. We were able to send in personnel from Honduras, and CEPAD sent in several people from Nicaragua that were essential. We immediately flew in three planeloads full of medicines, blankets, and clothing to begin relief operations. And we received funding from the U.S. Office of Foreign Disaster Assistance to build thousands of small houses in several new communities to house those whose homes on the hillsides had been destroyed in the earthquake.

Meanwhile in the Caribbean, a young Jamaican pastor, Robert Cuthbert, was interested in community development. CWS provided him with a small amount of funding to begin doing some projects through the churches in several of the islands. CADEC (Caribbean Agency for Development in the Eastern Caribbean) was thus formed. However, this small program in the Caribbean rapidly expanded. When CADEC began operating, it caught the attention of the World Council of Churches, groups in the Caribbean, and churches in Europe and the United States. A consultation was held in Trinidad to discuss development in the Caribbean. Cuthbert opened an office in Kingston, Jamaica, and began getting groups together to talk about development and starting projects.

CWS funding had worked as seed money, and we were soon one of the smaller donors. But because we had supported the idea in the beginning, provided funding for their administrative costs, and were more flexible in our grants than the European donors, we were treated by the CADEC team not as a donor agency but as a partner with the West Indians. This dynamic expanded through a number of meetings and conferences leading to the formation of the Caribbean Council of Churches.

In November 1978, having worked with CWS for twenty-one years, I decided that it was time to move on. I spent the next nineteen years in consulting work, using the skills and lessons I had learned to help a number of other organizations, including the United Nations High Commissioner for Refugees, the Office of Food for Peace, World Vision International, and the Office of U.S. Foreign Disaster Assistance in several dozen countries. All in all, my life has been wonderful, though at times difficult. The entire course of my life was the direct result of my early experiences with the Mennonite Central Committee.

May 19, 2012<br>Revised April 2015

**PART IV**

# Re-Envisioning Service ... as Interreligious Presence

*Bertha Beachy*

### Ambassador of Peace in a Muslim World

*Growing up in an Amish home that was outwardly tradition-bound but ideologically progressive, Bertha Beachy absorbed enough of her intellectual introverted mother so that her curiosity for the novel and her solidarity with the marginalized could not be undone. And she inherited enough of her witty extroverted father, who was careful never to pee into the wind, to enable her to engage a conflictive world of both Mennonite and Muslim men without getting snagged in the brambles. For nearly half a century, Bertha was an engaging presence in a Somali Muslim world.*

## BERTHA BEACHY

# *The Journey of My Life: Crossing Borders, Defying Boundaries*

### THE EARLY YEARS

I was born on July 2, 1931, the eighth of ten children. My early life was always lively and full of adventure. I was number five of seven daughters. We lived on a medium-sized farm in Indiana with lots of animals, gardens, and work. I loved being outside—helping to make hay, cutting oats, going after the cows, and riding horses. But I also enjoyed going to the woods to sit and watch the birds. A tall maple tree in our yard with a long swing provided a great escape for dreaming.

Reading was a significant part of my childhood. I grew up with the German *Martyrs Mirror* (later the English version), a daily newspaper, many of the Mennonite magazines, and *Egermeier's Bible Story Book*. Library books fed my hunger for adventure, particularly the Bobbsey Twins series, the Little House series, and the Thorton Burgess books about animals and birds, but the most important was the Anne of Green Gables series. These stories caught my imagination and I knew anything was possible!

Family and community were crucial in our Amish context. My mother loved books, history, and her flower gardens. My father loved people, horses, and his registered herd of cows but read little beyond the Bible and *The Budget*, a weekly periodical published for an Amish readership. He played a harmonica and liked to sing. He would often call out when he came into the house, "Can we have a song?" We had daily family devotions in Pennsylvania Dutch German and memorized Bible verses. I still have a German New Testament that I received in Sunday school for memorizing 600 verses in German. But I also memorized 500 verses in the King James Bible for the Iowa Rural Bible Crusade at the Snake Hollow public elementary school.

At meals we were all allowed to speak but in an orderly fashion. Each of us had daily chores, but we also had time to play games like softball and "dare base." We also played the game of Authors, with bird cards from Arm and Hammer soda cards, and eventually Scrabble, among others. My mother joined us at times.

Both of my parents were deeply committed to the church and to justice issues in the community. My father grew up in Holmes County, Ohio, and seldom traveled beyond that until he followed the harvest to the Dakotas in his mid-twenties. His father was active as a mediator in the community and a great storyteller. I loved when he came to visit us. I have lovely memories of listening to my father and grandfather telling stories. My mother was born in Illinois, moved to Ohio, and to Texas in her teens, then back again to Ohio. Her father was a quiet, reflective reader of the Bible and a very principled man but also one with *Wanderlust*. My mother was very much like him. I met both of my grandmothers, only one time in their homes, but I have little memory of them. My mother and father were both working in Iowa when they met.

When I was seven years old I went to a consolidated public school with more than 300 pupils; I always rode on a school bus. But when I was nine my family moved from Indiana to Iowa, and my world turned upside down. Our first farm in Iowa was 300 acres, and instead of riding a bus, we walked one-and-one-half miles over hills and mud roads to a school with only ten students beyond the four from our family. Nine months later we moved close to a larger Amish community. Snake Hollow, the public school we then attended, had fifty-some students with eight grades plus kindergarten ("primer grade").

We moved on December, 3, 1941. The Japanese attack on Pearl Harbor took place four days later. This event affected our community because many Amish sons chose to go into Civilian Public Service

(CPS) rather than to join the military. Community people sometimes called us "yellow COs"—failing to understand that it was not for lack of courage but due to biblical convictions that we were opposed to participation in war. One of my brothers served in Puerto Rico for two years.

By the time I reached fifth grade I knew that someday I would become a teacher, but I also knew that I would not be able to go to high school. I would have to work for my parents until I was twenty-one. At sixteen I was baptized into the Old Order Amish Church. We normally had Sunday school during the summer months and often German language school in the winter months. At nineteen I attended the first Amish Mission Conference, held in Iowa. This gathering was inspired by the experiences of the CPS men, now back in their home communities but with greater awareness of the world beyond their Amish encultured people. I felt called to missions and joined more than thirty young men when the leader prayed for us. My mother's ninety-year-old Amish father was present and looked very pleased that I had responded. I had many wonderful Amish friends, but early on I knew I would follow a different path.

After we turned sixteen my parents gave each of their children a monthly allowance of twenty-five cents, which I invested in my father's hogs. By the time I was twenty-one I had a nice nest egg. During this time I also worked for my married sisters and at other local jobs. I managed to take GED tests when they were offered locally, believing that my calling to missions would somehow be connected with my earlier feeling that I would become a teacher. I worried that I might not be able to go to college, so I joined friends for an eight-week Bible school in Johnstown, Pennsylvania. I loved it. For the closing ceremonies I was asked to reflect on a topic. I had never spoken in front of a group of people before! It was a great gift to have the main speaker cross the room to express his appreciation for what I had said. After I returned to Iowa, I managed to get a job as a nurse aide at the University Hospital in Iowa City for six months.

## OFF TO COLLEGE AND SOMALIA

In summer 1953, Howard Hammer had tent revival meetings in Iowa. His next move was to Youngstown, Ohio, and he asked for volunteers to help with visitation. I was jobless at the moment, so I joined eight others from our community and went to Ohio. It was a profoundly spiritual two-week experience for me. I returned to Iowa and moved my Amish membership to a Conservative Mennonite church. I wrote to my parents, who were on a western trip, about my change, but they never chided me for changing.

Nor did my parents protest when I decided to go to college that fall. When I explained to my father why I wanted to study, he smilingly said, "I think you should be a preacher!" My mother raised no questions. Thus it was that this twenty-three-year-old Amish woman left by bus with two friends for Eastern Mennonite College (EMC) in Harrisonburg, Virginia. I was shocked by the racial segregation I saw along the way.

I enrolled for a Bachelor of Science in elementary education. Later I discovered that five of my professors were teaching for the first time. I enjoyed the study and college atmosphere—the family style eating, sports, and musical programs—but I sometimes found the strict rules for behavior in the dorms and off campus confining. That year I first met Palestinians, one Christian and the other Muslim. In my sophomore year I met my first Somali. (Some forty years later he came to my Nairobi office to see me.) I always attended chapel, prayer meetings, and missionary events. By the end of the school year my money was all gone despite my three jobs.

Before I left Virginia to return home, I applied for a job at the University of Iowa Hospital where I had worked before, but to no avail. That summer I had five jobs that ended with the season. Late in the summer I decided I could not return to EMC due to lack of money. The next morning there was an offer in the mail for a job at the hospital in Iowa City. I worked for a full year and returned to EMC the following fall. This time dorm life was more satisfying; I also had some very good Bible courses. To add to my experiences, I was an announcer at the newly formed WEMC radio station and chaired the dorm council. Certain routines were established: For the next three years I worked as a waitress and continued outside work over the weekends. Academically, I picked up as many English courses as I could which, in the end, gave me an added English minor.

For my senior year I returned early to campus because I was to be the head waitress in the college dining hall. The day before I left home

I got word that the roommate I had expected was staying in Puerto Rico for the year. The dean of women asked me to choose another roommate from among sixty some possible replacements. I chose a missionary who was home on furlough for a year. Later when I interviewed for an overseas mission assignment, the first question the mission executive asked me when I told him I was interested in Africa was whether I knew this missionary. They needed two elementary teachers in Somalia, and he wanted me to speak to her about it.

In November 1957, I wrote to my parents and to my nine siblings about my call to Africa; they were all supportive. A month later I had filled out my doctrinal papers, was duly examined by twelve bishops, and was appointed by Eastern Mennonite Board of Missions and Charities (EMBMC) for work in Somalia. The following month of May I graduated, and by the next month I attended orientation at Salunga, Pennsylvania. In those days missionaries took everything but the kitchen sink with them on their assignments, so I shopped and packed all summer.

But quite suddenly I found myself afraid. Had I understood God correctly? I began to pray earnestly that God would keep me at home if I had misunderstood. I attended a church conference in Michigan that summer and stayed at my uncle's house. I was visiting with my cousin Leona when someone turned off all the lights. I stumbled into a sixteen-step stairway in the dark and fell to the bottom. I seemed unharmed and my new glasses were lying intact. I got up and went to bed, but by the next morning I was very stiff. As soon as I got back to Iowa, I went to see my doctor. He found nothing wrong with me. In his office I met a good friend with a cast on her arm. She had put on a new pair of shoes that morning and had fallen and broken her arm. I never again doubted my calling to work with Somalis or Muslims!

On September 5, 1958, I set sail from New York City with five classmates who had graduated with me in May. My parents and youngest sister were in the east attending a reunion so they came to New York City to see me off. My parents were great supporters during my African days. They prayed for me daily. My mother wrote me weekly letters and carefully saved all that I sent home.

We African-bound travelers stopped in Gibraltar. We disembarked in Naples, crossed Italy by train, and in Brindisi boarded a new ship called *The Africa*. From there we headed for the Suez Canal and waited for sixteen ships to pass before we entered the Red Sea. We had a brief stop in Aden where an Ethiopian-bound EMBMC couple left us. Eventually we arrived in Mogadishu, a beautiful East African coastal city. Six of us with all our luggage were swung down in baskets and landed on small tenders. Because the city lacked a proper harbor, everything and everyone arrived this way. The sights, sounds, and smells were, of course, all new for me.

## THE SOMALI CONTEXT

It is thought that the Somali people migrated to the area of present-day Somalia in the ninth century. They were known as the sons of Cush because their language has a Cushitic basis. Somalis share a common camel culture with other nomadic peoples along the sandy East African coastline. Islam arrived along the coast with the Arabs in the tenth century. Thus Arabic is the religious language and many Arabic words are part of the Somali vocabulary. The population is 99.6 percent Muslim. Traditionally all children attend Qur'anic schools. The brightest often memorize the 114 chapters of the Qur'an, although they may never have attended any other school. The Qur'an, along with Shar'ia law, are the guides for daily living. Somalis follow Sunni Islam of the school of Shafi'i. A few Sufis and practitioners of mystical Islam live among them.

Somalis are a tall, handsome people of various shades of darkness who share more in common with Ethiopians than black Africans. They are intellectually curious and interested in world happenings, although many do not read or write. I once saw a nomadic house on the back of a camel with a transistor radio dangling from the frame, typifying interest in world happenings. They love poetry, honor their poets, and use many proverbs in their conversations. Many Somalis I knew had relatives who had worked on ships and eventually settled overseas. Today there are thousands of Somali expatriates around the world in such places as Toronto, London, Montreal, Chicago, and Minneapolis, to name but a few places.

While many commonalities distinguish the Somalis as a cohesive and unified people, clan consciousness exists and separates. Somali myths identify certain clans as more royal then others. Often known as the Horn of Africa, Somalia has been colonized by the British,

French, Italians, and Ethiopians. Parts of the country were given to Kenya as early as the mid-1850's and another part to Ethiopia. There were always some schools in these various languages, but no one took seriously the writing of the Somali language. Arabic became the religious language and often the second language. Much attention was given to training Somalis to work with the colonial governments. Richard Burton, an Englishman who made a pilgrimage to Mecca in disguise in 1853, was the first European to enter the capital of Somaliland in 1854. His observations are still relevant today.[1]

## BEGINNINGS OF MENNONITE MISSIONS IN SOMALIA

On a flight in East Africa in 1950, Orie Miller, founding executive secretary for Mennonite Central Committee (MCC), became aware that the General Assembly of the United Nations had just adopted a resolution recommending that Italian Somaliland be placed under an international trusteeship system for ten years with Italy as the administering authority and with independence to be granted at the end of the ten years. Miller noted that these Islamic people were to have religious freedom during this time. EMBMC had work in Tanganyika and Ethiopia. By October 1950, senior missionaries from these countries made a trip inside Somalia. Miller joined one of the missionaries for a second trip in February 1952.

Wilbert and Rhoda Lind and son Daniel arrived in Mogadishu on January 16, 1953. By March a nurse and teacher joined the Linds. Wilbert began making exploratory trips around the country. In Kismayo in the south he found a Swedish Lutheran church abandoned in 1935 under Italian occupation. He found some Swahili speaking people along the Juba River who remembered Padre Cheese, an English man who had walked among them on foot. In 1954 Lind took a trip to the north of Mogadishu with Orie Miller. Everywhere they went they received requests for English language schools and medical facilities.

A boarding school and clinic were built at the first chosen location, Mahaddey Weyn, north of Mogadishu. Later a development project was also begun near the school. Despite objections by the Italians, Somalis helped to make land available. A builder couple was recruited. They were followed by two others. Pax men (young men under MCC who worked overseas instead of going to war) did farming with oxen near the equator. Adult English classes in the capital city expanded to include bookkeeping and typing. A bit later, in Jamama to the south, adult English classes, a clinic, a day school, and a twenty-five-bed hospital with a nursing school were started. Farther south along the coast, English, bookkeeping, and typing classes were begun. An English language bookstore, begun on the compound in Mogadishu, was later moved downtown across from the Parliament building—one of the few programs not held on mission compounds. In 1972 a secondary boarding school was opened seventy-five miles north of Mogadishu.

The first Bible class was held in November 1953. Requests for Bible classes continued in all the locations—it was another way to improve English language skills. Eventually the Somali Mennonite Mission (SMM) required written requests for a class and only one person was taught at a time. At three of the locations, Sunday services were held, which Somalis could also attend. Friday services, geared to Somalis and the Islamic tradition, were soon begun in two places. Somalis helped to lead these services. Swahili services were also held in the south along the Juba with the Bantu people. Baptisms sometimes took place in bathtubs and sometimes in the Indian Ocean. Several sessions of Bible study were held during school holidays for ten-day periods. Three Somalis did their secondary education in Ethiopia before the mission built a secondary school in Somalia.

Sunday school was also begun for international children. SMM normally held a Protestant service each month for the international community. At the time of President John F. Kennedy's death in 1963, the U.S. Ambassador to Somalia asked SMM to hold a memorial service. I helped to sing "Lift Your Glad Voices" in a quartet. The next day the Catholic Cathedral in Mogadishu also held a memorial service.

## MY WORK IN SOMALIA

I settled into Mogadishu with an excellent Somali language teacher and began teaching an English language class. I loved walking in the city—to shops, markets, the post office, and the oceanfront. In March 1959 the mission moved to a new location we had bought. Suddenly I was told by the EMBMC Somali Mission Council, without any discussion about it, that I would move to Jamama 265 miles to the south where a new school was being built. In Jamama I lived with my language teacher and had no Somali helper. I began going daily to the village of some 5,000 people where I also taught an adult English class. As I walked through a graveyard, I always had some huge marabou storks watching my every move. I sometimes had three invitations in one morning to stop in homes for spicy Somali tea. It was the best language learning I would ever have. Equally important, the village learned to know and trust me.

Thus it was when the new day school opened in August 1959, people knew who I was. I had thirteen students and was pleased that two were girls. We used British textbooks written for East Africa. I had much to learn about teaching, along with the challenge of beginning in Africa. We had to charge a small fee; this had the effect of eliminating the poorest students. Later I had an Arab and a Somali helping me to teach. Both were great persons and taught me a multitude of important cultural things. By the third year we had forty-five students.

I continued to be involved in village happenings. At the first wedding I attended, I ended up in the bridal chamber when the groom came in for the bride. I sometimes carried babies outside for the mother after the forty-day cycle of seclusion and rest ended. According to Somali cultural beliefs, that child would then become like me. I sometimes helped the nurse with night-time deliveries. Other times I helped with cooking and sewing classes in one of the mission homes. We were always invited to the village for the celebrations of religious and national holidays.

Independence Day came on July 1, 1960, and religious freedom continued. Our students sang and marched proudly in the village in their new uniforms for the day. In March 1962, however, all our activities were suspended then opened again in July. On July 16, as one of our Mennonite missionaries, Merlin Grove, was registering students in Mogadishu, an imam came in with the students and assassinated Merlin at his desk. His wife, Dorothy, heard the noise and came to check; then the imam knifed her several times. Students threw stones at the imam, which caused him to flee. Dorothy survived and lived until 2011. These violent attacks seemed to be inspired by outside Muslims. By June 1963 the government ruled there could be no more proselytizing except to Islam. A year later, the government declared that all private schools must teach Islam and Arabic, and they would provide the books and teachers.

When the EMBMC executive secretary Paul Kraybill came to visit, I asked if his traveling partner, A. J. Metzler from the Mennonite Publishing House in Scottdale, Pennsylvania, had brought us a bookstore. Thus it was that I was asked on the spot to move to Mogadishu and begin one. During my next furlough, in addition to visiting my family in Iowa, I spent time at the Mennonite Publishing House. I also took one semester at Hartford Seminary in Connecticut to study Islam and Arabic.

When I returned to Somalia following my home leave, I began selling books on the mission compound. Later we moved the bookstore downtown across from the parliament building. We had to sign an agreement with the Indian owner of the building that we would not do anything counter to Islam. We sold textbooks, books written about Somalia/Somalis in English, English fiction, art done by Somalis, and books written in Somali with the Latin script. And it just so happened that sometime later the government chose the script of an author I sold in the store for the writing of the Somali language. Somalis loved books and treated them with great respect. New Africa Booksellers was the only SMM work not on a compound.

I normally walked the short distance to work. I learned many cultural things as I walked, and I always had Somali friends walking with me. As I walked past the Chinese Embassy, fifty-some people were going off to work but I heard only their footfalls—no talking. I often passed polio victims walking on all fours and talking. I learned when to smile and how freely Somalis gave alms if they had anything with them. I decided early on that I was not there to give alms on the street but always greeted them. Living in Mogadishu was a joy.

I had a stall at the Somali Fair which gave us great exposure. Many small shop owners bought textbooks from us which they resold in other parts of the city. I learned to know many of the English speaking educators, politicians, poets, writers, and Peace Corps volunteers, plus the European wives of Somali men. We even watched at the American Embassy as Neil Armstrong landed on the moon and took one small step for mankind!

Another responsibility I had was to help orient new SMM people when they arrived. I had just returned from a furlough when a new mission person came to work with Somali believers. This was a decision made by the home office in Salunga, Pennsylvania, and then announced to the Somali believers. During a week of orientation for the mission person, I found it important to have Somalis speak as often as possible. Believers were speaking more freely than usual when one believer announced, "We don't even like him!"

I invited believers to come an hour early each Friday morning before the church service began to continue the conversations that would encourage the believers to ask questions. I attended but asked one of the mission men to lead it. These conversations began in July and ended on October 20, 1964, when they chose the American to work with them whom they initially thought they didn't even like. That very night an army coup took place, which happened one week after the second president had been assassinated. The new political leaders turned toward Russia and scientific socialism. Two months later the Peace Corps was sent out. Our Friday conversations with believers about concerns and differences created much trust between us as we all adjusted to a new political reality.

Another highlight for me was meeting with the fifteen women who had finished all the English we offered for adults but who wanted to continue getting together. They came to my house for an American meal and discussions about our different customs. We attended a Somali play at the new theater. I also taught Bible courses during this time but always on a one-to-one basis.

The next year USAID ended in Somalia. The staff and aid for the College of Education at Lafoole, the teacher training school begun by the Americans, were withdrawn. The one property we owned was nationalized. Government officials took our mission vehicle and some of our furniture but were considerate of us. We moved to rented places.

In December 1972 the government requested that all foreign medical and religious teachers leave Somalia. Our builder and development couples left at this time. We offered all our remaining teachers to the Ministry of Education. Two SMM teachers with Bible degrees were asked to leave, but they kept ten of us, myself included. Some of our teachers remained in our secondary school, but the rest of us taught in various secondary schools throughout Mogadishu.

After nationalization, I taught in three secondary schools. One of the schools had been built by the Russians, and there were thirteen

Russian teachers there when we arrived to teach English. With help from a Russian and a Somali, I helped to set the final English exam for high school seniors in the whole country. Later the minister of education, whom I knew personally, asked me to transfer to Lafoole. When I arrived on campus, I was the only American, the only Christian, and the only woman on a faculty of twenty-some Pakistanis, Egyptians, East Germans, and Somalis. I loved it. I was there when South Vietnam fell—the one "common enemy" on campus. At that time, I was teaching thirty-five Islamic teachers of the Qur'an, who treated me royally.

In 1972 Somali leaders chose the Roman script to write the Somali language. They held a nationwide Somali literacy campaign. Students from grades six through twelve were sent throughout the country to teach the Somali language. In 1974 the Sudan Interior Mission (SIM) closed its schools, clinics, and hospital and withdrew from Somalia. They finished the Somali translation of the Bible, and it became available in 1977, the same year the Russians were asked to leave. In April 1976 we were informed they would now be using the Somali language in schools and we were no longer needed. On May 20, 1976, my colleagues and I all left Somalia.

I was very sad. Since I was not scheduled to leave Africa for another two years, I transferred to Nairobi, Kenya, and worked with AFRO-LIT to prepare three literacy primers in Somali, which were then translated into Swahili. Many Somalis lived in Northeastern Province, about 265 miles north of Nairobi on a rough road. I actually sent the Somali primers back to Suleiman, a man who had been my neighbor at one time. He had helped to write the Somali language and had also written the letter asking us to leave. I moved four times that first year in Kenya. It was a gift to have some of my foreign friends from Mogadishu spend time with me in Nairobi. One of them gave me a gift of money so I could, for the first time, get my driver's license. During this time I also wrote the Women's Missionary and Service Commission (WMSC) devotional book for Mennonite women in the USA.

I became the contact person for believers inside Somalia, but it was a complicated two years since Kenyans and Somalis did not like each other because of the colonial history. I ended up with an ulcer. Two weeks before I left Kenya, I was invited to speak to a group of charismatic women. I knew only one person. I found myself saying that perhaps I was there so they could pray for the healing of my ulcer. They prayed, and it was healed according to my final X-ray before I left for America!

In 1981 the Somali government requested the return of Mennonite teachers. A former secondary teacher at our mission school was now working at the Ministry of Education. In January 1990 nine Mennonite teachers went to Somalia, but they all left by the end of the year because of clan conflicts. For half a year, MCC supported an effort to bring about peace among Somali clan elders. A Somali believer who had done peace studies at Anabaptist Mennonite Biblical Seminary was seriously injured in one leg when a bomb was thrown into the house where he was staying. He miraculously managed to get to the U.S. His life was saved but his leg was not. Later two Mennonite nurses were loaned to World Concern in Mogadishu, but they too came and went rather quickly.

## RETURNING TO THE UNITED STATES

I returned to the United States feeling lost. EMBMC asked me to write the story of the Somali Mennonite Mission. They had loved everything I had written while in Somalia. I bought a car and moved to Salunga in Lancaster County, Pennsylvania, where the EMBMC offices were located. But I was in a lot of emotional pain over leaving Africa, and it seemed I could not please the committee which was to work with me. Eventually, I gave up trying to write. Omar Eby would, in time, write the story, *Fifty Years, Fifty Stories: The Mennonite Mission in Somalia, 1953-2003*.[2]

I did, however, share the Somali story in many other ways. I spoke in more than seventy-five churches. I began a monthly prayer meeting with other missionaries to pray for believers in Somalia, a group which still meets today. I helped with orientation for both EMBMC and MCC workers heading to assignments. I also helped to organize the first Mission Festival, still held today. I joined a group of Mennonite women who were working to promote leadership of women in the church. It wasn't until 2008, however, that the first woman was officially ordained in the Lancaster Conference of Mennonite Church USA. And I distinctly remember when the first woman joined the forty-five men on the Eastern Mennonite Board of Missions and Charities!

I attended the first Women in Ministry meeting held in Akron, Pennsylvania. Several of us attended an Evangelical Women's Caucus in Saratoga Springs, New York. Through my discovery of Elizabeth O'Connor's books, I spent a weekend at the Church of the Savior in D.C. I tried to get a job at the Provident Bookstore in Lancaster but ended up being invited to manage the Provident Bookstore in Goshen, Indiana. Thus began my initial fifteen years in midwest U.S. after twenty years in Africa and two years in the Lancaster area.

## THE PROVIDENT BOOKSTORE

In the fall of 1980 I moved to Goshen. I was fleeing from the harrowing experience of failing to write the Somali Mennonite Mission story to the satisfaction of EMBMC. Yet it was a move that in many ways saved my life by giving me vocational direction for the next twenty years and an enduring community of faith. Goshen was a totally new community for me, loaded with Mennonite churches but lacking in sunshine. It took me three years to discover why I felt depressed in the fall and winter months. After my years in the tropics, the lack of sun from the gloomy lake weather affected me deeply though I did not mind the cold or the snow.

This was my first experience in managing a staff. When I first arrived at the Provident Bookstore in Goshen (owned by Herald Press, Scottdale, Pennsylvania), I was startled to find the wife of the former manager working there, but she proved to be a great gift to me. From my mother I had learned to love books and from my father I had learned to love people. During my tenure as manager at the Provident Bookstore, we greatly increased the selections in children's, spirituality, peace and justice issues, Anabaptist theology, Bibles, and music cassettes. Every year we offered workshops on resources for Sunday schools, church libraries, and children. (Recently I met people who still lament the closing of the store.)

We did some renovating: I moved my office to the street level where I was less isolated from both staff and clients; the Sunday school materials (representing the most routinized and reliable purchases) went upstairs. Eventually we became computerized—not an easy move for me. When I arrived we had a single page of eight hundred numbers for ordering. By 1995 when I left we did our ordering online. We began to have regular staff meetings. One day I had three requests for material dealing with improper sexual actions. We put everything we had on one shelf and were shocked at how many people spent time with those books. It just happened that I could see them from my office.

I had much to learn about the mostly evangelical sales persons calling from different publishing companies. My having been a missionary made it easy for them to accept me, yet it was often difficult for them to understand my section of inventory and displays. I listened endlessly to things I would later challenge. I was sent a display of Oliver North books which I had not ordered (remember the days of the Nicaraguan Contras secretly supported by the Reagan administration?). That very day a company sales person arrived with a new regional person. They gladly took the books back by the time I had finished sharing my opinion!

After my first managers' meeting in which all the others brought a spouse, Provident Bookstores offered to pay for a monthly consultant for me. That was a great gift. At my hiring they had assured me that my salary would be the same as a male's salary would be. I became a member of the Association of American Publishers and the Christian Booksellers Association. I also attended national Mennonite conferences as well as the Indiana-Michigan gatherings. It was a time of great learning about the local and larger Mennonite church and about other denominations in the area.

I enjoyed being close to Goshen College and the Associated (now Anabaptist) Mennonite Biblical Seminary (AMBS) and even managed to take a course from time to time. I joined three Goshen City organizations. I became a member of Mennonite Women in Ministry and related to the MCC Women's section for some years. I was also privileged to serve eight years on the Mennonite Board of Missions (MBM). I enjoyed the challenge of learning to know a new system, missionaries, and countries. Serving on the board was very different from being a mission worker. But male biases on a variety of issues continued to be nearly ubiquitous.

In May 1981 I became a member of Assembly Mennonite Church in Goshen, changing my membership from the Conservative Mennonite Church in Iowa for the first time. Within "The Assembly" I joined a small fellowship group. I frequently led worship and on occasion preached. Eventually I served as an elder and later a spiritual resource elder. At that time The Assembly had no ordained pastors as salaried leaders, though five ordained men were members in the congregation and would serve in numerous leadership roles.

My utter failure in writing the Somali mission story became, ironically, a great gift to me. It put me on a spiritual journey which still nurtures me in special ways today. The Hermitage, a retreat center in southwest Michigan, began in the mid-1980s and offered things that blessed me greatly. I attended workshops there on the healing of memories, journaling, listening to dreams, forgiveness, and Enneagrams. I heard wonderful speakers, such as Morton Kelsey, Henry Nouwen, John Sandford, Sean Pennington, Jean Bolin, and Robert Johnson, to name a few. I went to counseling and had a spiritual director. In 1979 I began New Year's Eve reflecting and journaling, something I still do today.

## Returning to Africa

I had chosen not to return to Africa in the 1980s. The only Social Security I would have for retirement came from my fifteen years at Provident Bookstore. I retired from Provident at age sixty-four and returned to Africa in October 1995. This time I was invited to direct the Nairobi office for Somalis for both EMBMC and MCC. The last EMBMC (now Eastern Mennonite Missions) person had left Somalia in 1990, but the contacts were continuing through the Nairobi office.

In Nairobi I promptly found a spiritual director and planned a personal monthly two-day retreat at a Benedictine convent. I related to believers, refugees, and the local Somali church group. I always attended the UN Somali meetings. My greatest joy, however, was working with Somali women from many different clans who were working at peace issues. I attended a meeting in Djibouti aimed at making a new beginning over clan issues. Some women were actually chosen to be part of the new Somali government. But eventually all of these many efforts failed.

I was able to travel inside Somalia five times during my time in Kenya, but I was never able to pass the old mission compound in Mo-

*Bertha with Fatima Jibril, who had her own NGO, at a meeting in Basaso, Somalia, to discuss relief for the Horn of Africa.*

gadishu. I was only allowed to walk on my own very briefly one time. Somali soldiers were guarding the airport and keeping an eye on all foreigners. I did manage a trip to Johar and Mahaddey under guard, but it gave me no joy to see all the mission buildings destroyed. Everything was overgrown; goats were eating grass where the "mission compound"—the religious institution that so distinctively paralleled Western colonialism—had once been securely erected.

When the American Bible Society launched the Good News Bible, I was privileged to be present. I attended an Anglican church where I heard a Kenyan announcing that a Mennonite had launched the Decade to Overcome Violence at the World Council of Churches meeting in South Africa. During this special time in Nairobi, I also worshiped with a group of Somali believers who met on Saturdays. The head of the Islam in Africa Project was from Nigeria, a convert from Islam. He took a special interest in Somali believers. With him, I helped to plan a gathering in Ethiopia of Somali believers in East Africa. Successfully I insisted that a woman have devotions. I passionately wanted them to learn that women were also believers and active participants in the church. Some of the American evangelicals left the meeting when I got up to speak. However, they later came to ask for my help.

## Back to Goshen

I returned to Goshen in late 2000. At my reentry retreat in 2001, I felt a need to be anointed. When questioned why, I found myself saying it was to relate to Islam. I wept as I waited. Two weeks later, the World Trade Center was destroyed and soon America's war in Iraq commenced. The calling to work with Islam will always be with me. Thus I continue at age eighty to do all I can to bring understanding and hope in this complex period of time.

I have experienced God's direct leading through the Holy Spirit in many different ways. We were blessed in Somalia by the visit of a person who, during a conference experience, taught us the ways of the Holy Spirit. There was greater unity among us as a result of this new focus, and we prayed together in new ways.

Some of my greatest failures also became my greatest blessings. It put me on a new personal journey. I have come to a greater commitment to active nonviolence. Nurturing my spiritual life has meant different things at different times. I always got what I needed—or so it seems in retrospect. The healing of my ulcer was one of many gifts God provided. Sometimes a Scripture verse was dropped into my mind, as when I tumbled down sixteen steps ... "the gifts and the call of God are irrevocable." Into complex situations came unexpected answers through Bible study, prayer, books with spiritual insights, and even a friendship with a staunch Muslim. God has been faithful.

I had put my name in at the Greencroft Retirement Community in Goshen earlier but nothing was available. I found plenty to do as I waited. MCC asked me to come and fill in at the Akron office while a staff person was on a three-month leave to have her baby. I managed one orientation and sat in on committees. I had time to write materials on spiritual disciplines which I later used for orientations. I did a significant amount of speaking in churches about my Somali experiences. Sometimes they were actually sermons on a Sunday morning.

In April 2004, I finally received notice that in August there would be a place available in Greencroft. With the help of my church, other friends, and family, I sold my home and moved into an apartment in Greencroft, happy to no longer have responsibilities for the upkeep of a house—though I would, at times, be happy for more space. But my life continues to be full. I am part of a monthly dream group, a weekly prayer group, a peace and justice group, and a 2-percent fund group.

For the past four years, I have done monthly retreats on different topics at the Quiet Place in Milford, Indiana. Two friends made it possible for me to travel to the Mennonite World Conference (MWC) in Zimbabwe so I have attended MWCs in Amsterdam, Wichita, Winnipeg, and Zimbabwe.

Other activities since returning to Goshen—some before and some after the Nairobi interlude—include the following: I reconnected with my support circle of single women who had worked overseas. I did a missionary retreat in Guatemala and was able to visit good friends in Miami on the way. I helped with Mennonite Board of Missions missionary retreats three times and offered an elective at The Assembly congregation on Islam. The latter put me in touch with a Muslim couple in Goshen and the mosque in South Bend. I led a senior retreat at Camp Friedenswald in Michigan. I joined a local Just-Peace group and helped plan local events on Islam and later Iran. Late in 1990, during the Gulf War, I joined the first Christian Peacemaker Team to Iraq. Later, I joined a peace group for a two-week trip to Iran.

## A Few Final Reflections

It is now more than fifty-two years since I first went to Africa. I had much to learn since I had had little experience in Mennonite organizations. The Somali Mission Council, for example, consisted of all the ordained Mennonite men, whether they came to Somalia for only three years or for more. Most of the single women were used to the system and often were given no responsibility for any program. It caused me to be aware of the partnership of my parents and the way they worked together on things that affected any one of us.

I had worked hard to have the Somali Mission Council share their minutes with us in person. At a certain meeting I discovered the council had decided that I should sell the Bible in the store. Then I saw it in the minutes for first time. One of our men had been to the Catholic Bookstore and saw that they sold the Bible. But the Italians owned land. They had a huge cathedral, many schools, and people living in Somalia. We, on the other hand, had signed an agreement with the Muslim owner that we would not do anything counter to Islam. When I asked for clarification, I was met with silence. The woman who had been in Somalia the longest announced she wanted to go home first if I had to do this. All the women present agreed. Later I checked with SIM and with the believers; everyone advised against it. The members on the council changed their minds and I was greatly relieved.

On my next furlough I stated that I would not return unless I could be on the council. As I waited for their response, I cried a lot. Four nights in a row I heard the Somali call to prayer in my ears which helped me to relax and pray. Eventually, I was invited to return and manage the work with Somali women. I met with the council only one time until we were all asked to leave! But here lies a double irony: The tension as to whether or not to return to Somalia was due to a conflict among North American mission personnel; EMBMC's forced leaving of Somalia was a spill-over of the Cold War. Neither emerged from a Muslim-Christian conflict or from East African inter-tribal conflicts.

I have become aware that my Amish roots were a great gift in my work with Somalis. From the time I entered elementary public school, my lifetime adventure in cross-cultural enrichment began (though I was often unaware of it). All public experiences, excepting church, involved crossing boundaries. I spoke Pennsylvania Dutch and read the Bible in (mostly sixteenth-century) German, but I also learned English before I attended school. I was taught to speak directly to people instead of behind their backs—thus failing to master the art of "passive aggression" or so it would seem in retrospect. Somalis, too, could be direct if they trusted the person. And it was all right to be different.

My parents were deeply spiritual people and very connected to the local community and to the Amish church. This body of believers was central to their lives. They were committed to working for justice within the church but also in the community. My exposure to Africa and the wider world, with all its inequalities of colonialism, and the realities of our American warmongering cause me pain and sadness. When I reflect on the poor, whether migrants, prisoners, or the homeless, and the lack of equal opportunity, lack of food, or insufficient medical care, I weep at times. I feel accountable before God for all the refugees that we have helped to create and for the suffering of our veterans and their families. I am grateful that Assembly, still my congregation, cares about these things as well.

Amish people love children and so do Somalis. Somalis and the Amish also both respect age, which is not found in all cultures. Because of my background in an oral tradition, I never tired of the conversations, proverbs, and poetry. I believed strongly that how I lived and conducted my life among/with Somalis was more important than instantly giving a word of witness, such as "Jesus Saves" or "Jesus is the only way." I clearly knew what I believed at a deep level, but over these many years I have sought to accept Muslims for who they are and what they believe. I became a better Christian as I lived among Somalis. I never converted a Muslim—God does the converting. I have come to trust a good Muslim as I trust a good Christian. God loves Muslims as God loves this Amish woman.

When I reflect on my journey, which started as an Amish girl, I am very thankful for God's direction and care. I remember that little girl swinging and dreaming, and I realize that my background and interest in the world was a great gift. It has been crucial in my journey with Somalis and with Islam. Daily there are new challenges and opportunities. Somalis would say: *Illaheh Mahaddis*. . . . Thank God.

October 11, 2010<br>
Revised August 2012

## NOTES

1. Sir Richard F. Burton, *Personal Narrative of a Pilgrimage to Al-Madinah and Meccah*, vol. 1 (Mineola, N.Y.: Dover Publications, 1964).

2. ———, *Personal Narrative of a Pilgrimage to Al-Madinah and Meccah*, vol. 2 (Mineola, N.Y.: Dover Publications, 2011).

3. Omar Eby, *Fifty Years, Fifty Stories: The Mennonite Mission in Somalia, 1953-2003* (Telford, Pa.: Cascadia Publishing House, 2003).

*Kenneth L. Seitz Jr.*

---

### Transcultural and Interfaith Traveler

*Like so many of his generation of Mennonites, Kenneth Seitz began his life on a farm. But between that farm in Franconia and his present habitation at Virginia Mennonite Retirement Center, Ken spent three decades in and out of the Middle East. On this journey, wearing too many hats in too many places, how did he manage to get a bounce (instead of a bruise) out of every bump? How did all this transcultural exposure and interfaith praxis factor into the maturing of his faith? What changes has he observed in the church and its institutions?*

**KENNETH L. SEITZ JR.**

# *Thirty Years in and out of the Middle East and What Lies Between*

### THE CANVASS FOR SKETCHING LIFE'S LARGER PICTURE

It is mid-August 1977. Kass and I have eagerly packed our bags and rented out our house in Elkhart, Indiana. Friends are waiting at the curb to convey us to Chicago's O'Hare Airport, where we board a Scandinavian Airlines overnight flight to Copenhagen with a connecting flight the next day to Ben Gurion Airport in Tel Aviv. The journey from Elkhart to Jerusalem culminates with a taxi ride, literally *up to* Jerusalem. Just as the sun drops over the Judean hills, we approach the gleaming front doors of Tantur Ecumenical Institute, commonly known just as Tantur, midway between Jerusalem and Bethlehem. And so began what turned out to be three decades (1977-2009) in and out of the Middle East, a significant feature of my life's career.

Tantur, named for the hill on which it is located, was to be home for the academic year 1977-78. As a graduate student in biblical studies and biblical languages at Notre Dame University in Indiana, I had enthusiastically accepted the invitation to spend an academic year as a junior scholar at this international ecumenical institute for theological and pastoral studies in Jerusalem.

The impetus to establish an ecumenical center along these lines had its roots in the Second Vatican Council as a location for Catholics,

Orthodox, and Protestants from around the world to study and worship together in the Holy Land. The late Fr. Hesburgh (d. 2015), then president of Notre Dame University, had accepted responsibility to implement the project, which was dedicated and formally opened in 1972. Other Mennonite scholars and professors, including John Howard Yoder, Millard Lind, and Clarence Bauman, had preceded me at Tantur and influenced my decision to live and study there.

Many new experiences as a resident, junior scholar at Tantur lay ahead. In addition to participation in numerous seminars, lectures, and presentations given by renowned scholars and would-be scholars on a broad range of topics, Tantur organized regular guided field trips to the historic and religious sites throughout Israel and the West Bank. And I had the run of Tantur's extensive library to pursue my own studies in preparation for the upcoming comprehensive exams scheduled for the following year.

With an aptitude for language learning, I arranged to study Modern Hebrew away from Tantur. Three mornings a week I took the bus to an Israeli cultural center in West Jerusalem to a class of mostly younger Jewish students from all over the world: Canada, South America, Europe, Soviet Union, and the United States. The classes, ranging from basic to advanced, were conducted in Hebrew, designed to teach language facility, as well as to orient students to the customs, culture, and politics characteristic of the modern state of Israel.

Some of my classmates were already new immigrants (*olim*), while others were exploring the possibility of immigrating to Israel with permanent residence in mind (called "making *aliah*"). As a class we regularly went on field trips throughout the country for exposure to everything from historical sites to religious shrines, even an Israeli military encampment in the Jordan Valley, deep within the West Bank. On one such trip I learned that apartment-housing blocks constructed by Israel in the West Bank were to be called "new neighborhoods" rather than "settlements."

While I was thus engaged, my wife Kass was teaching in the English department of nearby Bethlehem University, established by the Order of Christian Brothers for post-high school Palestinian students from the West Bank. Her involvement with students there educated us to the hardships for those living under Israeli occupation. Young male students were frequently absent from class due to imprisonment and even torture by the Israeli military police. Visits to students' homes in Bethlehem, as well as other villages and towns, became occasions to hear and enter into the grim stories related by family members. I was clearly being exposed simultaneously to two worlds embodying two realities—Israeli and Palestinian—with the implications for peace and justice sinking in and taking root.

The year at Tantur included occasions to share in the Mennonite presence in Israel-Palestine since we were included in several retreats designed for Mennonite agency personnel, some serving with Mennonite Central Committee (MCC) and others with the Mennonite Board of Missions (MBM). In those gatherings it was obvious that the sharply divided geo-politics of Israel-Palestine impacted even the Mennonite presence there. MCC personnel were living the Palestinian experience while MBM personnel were living the Israeli experience. While these retreats attempted to bridge the divide, the gulf between us was real despite Christian charity and altruism.

At the close of Tantur's academic year, we prepared to return to the U.S., permanently affected by having witnessed the difficulties the Palestinians endured under occupation. Yet despite the conflicts and uncertainties endemic to life in Israel-Palestine, I was fascinated with the people, languages, history, geography, archaeology, and religions of the Middle East (lands of the Bible). As the plane lifted away from Ben Gurion Airport, my heart nourished the hope to return.

## FAMILY TALES AND EARLY RECOLLECTIONS

I am the firstborn (1938) of Kenneth Seitz and Grace Heebner, who met at Eastern Mennonite School in Harrisonburg, Virginia, in the early 1930s. They were deeply influenced by the piety and emerging mission thrust characterizing "The School" at that time. They were in admiration of several classmates going off to Tanganyika (now Tanzania) as the Eastern Mennonite Board of Missions (EMBM) was opening work in Africa about that time. They married in 1937 and set up housekeeping in Lansdale, Pennsylvania. Dad was an assistant manager in several local A&P grocery stores, earning $20 per week and raised to $22 when I was born. Meanwhile my mother—I marvel at this now—worked temporarily outside the home in a hosiery mill.

To avoid being drafted in World War II, Dad went into dairy farming while the family grew. Despite my mother's being from the Plains congregation in Hatfield, Pennsylvania, my earliest recollection of church life was attending an outreach mission church in Lansdale proper with Dad leading singing and teaching the youth Sunday school class. When Franconia Mennonite School (now Penn View Christian) opened its doors in 1944, I was enrolled there for second grade having attended public school for first grade. Even when we moved to the far edge of the Mennonite community in 1946, my parents went to great lengths to keep me in the Mennonite school. I continued at the parochial school until 1951, when as a seventh grader we moved to Harrisonburg, about which I'll say more later.

During the years following World War II my parents were struggling with vocational and lifestyle issues. For instance, Dad was thinking about a suitable car for the family so he placed an order for a Buick. But after months of waiting for one of the early postwar models, he passed when it finally became available. Rather than purchasing it for himself, he released it to my uncle. It was a beauty, I thought, but my parents worried what church people would think. In 1946 the family actually did move to a dairy farm with more acreage. The folks dreamed of developing a herd of registered Holstein milk cows, which would have been a step up in the dairy industry. Ultimately, that dream, too, was put aside.

Being the oldest child and while still a pre-adolescent, I was a candidate to help with practically every aspect of farm operations. I was quite proud when Dad claimed that he didn't need to hire outside help because he had me. At 4:45 we got out of bed for morning chores. But when my mother occasionally noticed me sleeping in church, she insisted on taking my place to help with the morning chores so I could sleep longer. Since she was helping with the chores, I was instructed to get out of bed and put breakfast on the table.

My dad and I spent hours and hours together milking the herd and dealing with the crops. Barely eleven years old, I delighted in being tasked with operating major farm equipment in the fields. I did envy, though, my schoolmates who could come home from school in the afternoons with free time until supper. Some of them even listened to Tom Mix and Roy Rogers on the radio—not permitted where I grew up, although we did have a radio.

Typical of the era, church life included annual revival meetings. We'd get the chores out of the way early to be at church every night during the week of revivals. I recall evangelists Nevin Bender Sr., Nelson Kauffman, Clarence Ramer, James Bucher, and Kenneth Good—to name a few. Each time the revivals came around, Dad would bring up the subject of my accepting Christ. At age eleven, sometime in 1949, I was baptized at the Finland Mennonite Church, a Franconia Conference congregation. Then and there, according to Dad's prescription, I was expected to begin daily Bible reading, starting with the gospel of John. I also recall memorizing all sixty-six verses comprising the core of Milo Kauffman's curriculum on personal evangelism. Later I'll address other elements of home life, such as the pattern of family worship and the family's move to Harrisonburg in 1951.

## OPTING FOR MENNONITE VOLUNTARY SERVICE

A few months before graduation from EMC in June, 1960, I decided not go on to seminary (the only graduate school consideration) but rather to take advantage of being drafted by Selective Service to enter Voluntary Service (VS) with MBM in Elkhart, Indiana. Unit leaders were needed in Mathis, Texas, we were told. Kass (Kathryn Hunsburger)—now my wife—and I had read in the church press about Mennonite Voluntary Service involvement in Hispanic communities of South Texas.

September 1960 found us living in Mathis, Texas, as VS workers; at that point I recall thinking to myself and saying aloud "This is the first time in sixteen years that I'm not in school." For sure, much important learning outside the classroom lay ahead. Where would it all lead to and how would I be shaped forever by the opportunity to live as a service worker in several homogeneous Hispanic communities?

In that era, VSers, short for voluntary service personnel, were attached to local Mennonite-sponsored efforts to establish churches in Hispanic settings in half-a-dozen locations branching out from Corpus Christi, Texas. Most of these were in rural towns, like Mathis (pop. 7,000 at the time) with a strong agricultural base. Such towns were largely Latino with a minority Anglo population that formed more or less the upper class holding the wealth and power. The Hispanics, or Mexicans as they were called then, provided the labor force to pick cotton by hand. These towns were quite segregated into homogeneous Anglo and Hispanic communities. VSers like ourselves were based in Hispanic communities by design.

Texas education did not provide kindergarten in the public schools. Consequently, children from Hispanic homes entered first grade with little or no knowledge of English. In fact, speaking Spanish in public schools was cause for school-administered discipline. Mennonite VS, along with other church-based and secular programs, stepped into this vacuum to offer private kindergartens at the request of numerous Hispanic parents who recognized the difficulties their children faced in public schools. These kindergartens provided entrees into homes and conversations with parents. Much of our own VS experience focused on operating kindergartens in Mathis and Robstown, Texas. The kindergarten efforts were supplemented with opportunities for older children and youth, such as club programs and recreational activities.

Since many in the Hispanic community spoke little English and since VSers were expected to participate in the local churches as teachers, musicians, custodians, and youth workers, we were expected to study and practice our Spanish. I thrived on this opportunity. Thus we'd gather daily for formal Spanish classes. An overarching goal was to enrich the programs of the local Mennonite church in a holistic witness that included the physical, emotional, and spiritual needs of the community

Another dimension to the VS experience was what we called "unit life." VSers were expected to live in community and to function as households. This was fertile ground for conflicts to arise. Unit leaders like ourselves were expected to help work out the rough spots and keep the team on task. What a laboratory for learning how to accept persons from a variety of backgrounds, personalities, and levels of commitment! Moreover, this laboratory exposed me to the basics of community development in a cross-cultural setting. I gained an appreciation for what the church on the cutting edge looks like and how it functions, in contrast to church back home. I recognized at the same time that it was those very home churches that were supporting us. The VS years in South Texas were life-changing for me.

In July 1963 we left Texas and any plans for settling there to move to Elkhart, Indiana, where I began an eight-year stretch in the Relief and Service Office of MBM as one of several administrators of the VS program working under the direction of Ray Horst. Simultaneously we became members at Prairie Street Mennonite Church in Elkhart.

## INFLUENCES AND IMPACTS

### Family

There were significant influences that contributed to whom I was then and am now. First, I was raised in a home where faith was lived out and where what was preached was to be practiced. My father sincerely believed that he was the spiritual head of the home and proceeded to give guidance and mete out discipline accordingly. In all likelihood, his understanding of parental roles was typical of the era, although we knew of homes that operated on a more egalitarian basis. While Dad was strict and authoritarian with us, I cannot accuse him of stressing a set of behaviors and ethics for us that he himself was unwilling or unable to practice.

Several examples illustrate the impact of family life. As noted above, family worship was part of the daily routine. This was held each evening when we didn't attend church. (In those days there were regular midweek prayer meetings and Sunday evening church services.) I recall all eight of us gathering in the living room following the evening meal, after the dishes were done. This forty-five minute family liturgy included singing of hymns, sharing of memory verses, Bible reading with commentary, and kneeling prayer time around the circle. We systematically sang through the hymnal, learning new hymns as we went along. Bible reading began at Genesis and moved on through, a chapter or two each evening, omitting the genealogies and certain other passages deemed unsuitable for young ears.

Growing older, I began to observe that not all Mennonite families blocked out such time, nor was there the leadership in the home for such a religious exercise. Although we siblings have reacted differently along the way to this exercise in family church, I cherish the memories of family worship and its positive effect on my faith development. Somehow hymns and Bible stories gripped my heart.

Another vivid recollection of home involves being in contact with needy people, mostly neighbors. I remember Dad's being gone overnight on occasions to sit with a man related marginally to the church yet struggling with alcoholic addiction. Trips to church usually included stopping to pick up people who would not get there otherwise. It meant squeezing ever more tightly in the back seat of whatever vehicle we had at the time. On several occasions my folks opened up our home to a needy person; we siblings often resented the intrusion into our family life, but I guess we learned something about the less fortunate around us.

I'll never forget getting a new 1949 Chevrolet (not a Buick, remember) station wagon. Since it was brand new, I thought we should treat it with utmost care. But Dad thought to justify the purchase by loading it down with neighborhood kids for vacation Bible school the following Monday. "Boys," he'd say, "it's only rubber and metal." I'll wager it took a while before we internalized that perspective. But the fact that I still remember it means it made an impression.

A major impact on the family came with our 1951 move from Pennsylvania to Virginia. This move resulted from my parents' spiritual awakening and recommitment growing out of revival fires stoked at our church by evangelist Kenneth Good. It was now time to pursue the call to a more specific mission endeavor, likely in a foreign country. The farm was sold—land, buildings, cattle, and machinery—and in spring the family moved to Harrisonburg to start a new life.

We arrived in March and Dad started summer school at EMC in June. As eldest, in addition to high school studies, I was responsible, along with my younger brothers, for keeping the broiler-raising business going while Dad focused on summer and winter college studies.

Subsequently, in 1953, Dad was ordained at Weaver's Mennonite Church, along with Hubert Pellman. Immediately thereafter, the family started attending church at a schoolhouse at the foot of the Blue Ridge where Dad was assigned to a pastorate. In 1955 the family moved to Harman, West Virginia, for Dad to pastor there, which freed me to be an EMC high school senior dorm student. Then in 1958, when I was a college junior and a year away from marriage, the family moved to Mexico City, where our parents spent twenty years planting churches. Dad had achieved his ultimate calling.

While it took time to come to terms with this spiritual questing, my parents' many moves impacted my life as I witnessed security and convention being sacrificed for the sake of following a vision, if not an outright call, to follow a particular path to be in ministry to others for the sake of the gospel. When I look at my own path through life, it has some of the same characteristics as my father's, while in many ways different.

To my deep satisfaction, the family's move to Virginia positioned me to attend EMC as an eighth grader in the 1951-52 school year.

## Eastern Mennonite College

I am a product of EMC of the 1950s, which I attended 1951-1960; yes, five years of high school and four of college. I fondly recall our eighth grade class sponsor and teacher, Harold Lehman, who, himself barely thirty, impressed me as one who modeled being Christian and Mennonite in new, refreshing ways. At that time he modeled for me a follower of Jesus who was not overly pious (like I considered my dad) but who took time to breathe, relax, and enjoy life.

In both high school and college I had ample opportunities to discover and develop gifts, particularly in music and a bit of drama, such as existed on campus those days. Then there was the Young Peoples Christian Association (YPCA) pointing us in the direction of off campus ministries. In my college sophomore year I was given responsibility by the YPCA for Saturday evening street meeting outreach designed to put those students who felt so called onto the street corners of surrounding towns such as Elkton with loudspeakers. I don't recall putting much effort into the street meeting endeavor, but during my junior and senior years, I was far more diligent about serving as Sunday school superintendent at Mt. Jackson Mennonite Church under the oversight of pastor Linden Wenger. I contributed my voice to several men's quartets that sang on the Mt. Jackson radio station on Sunday mornings before church.

The best part of the EMC years included singing in high school Vesper Chorus and eventually in Collegiate Chorus and the college touring choruses. Imagine the adventure of traveling to and singing in Mennonite churches with overnight lodging in Mennonite homes in Ohio, Michigan, New York, and Ontario—for those of us who had never been beyond Pennsylvania and Virginia! And there was always a men's quartet to which I could blend my voice.

Bible courses were required at EMC, but I regret now that nowhere were we introduced to any of the critical questions, although inductive Bible study received some attention—a movement in the right direction, at least. My introduction to dealing from a faith perspective with the critical questions surrounding biblical studies would have to wait another decade. It may be, however, that taking G. Irvin Lehman's Old Testament course as a college sophomore, complete with his travelogue slide lectures, did whet my appetite for the Middle East and lands of the Bible.

Thinking that someday I might go into linguistic studies, I graduated with a BA in ancient languages (Latin and Greek) and with a minor in sociology. Looking back, EMC provided a setting for deepening faith commitments, for enlarging my worldview, and for gaining a larger perspective on the church—a church called to be involved in global mission and service. The two went hand in hand. EMC was what I needed at that time to transition from my home background into the broader church and society.

### Mennonite Voluntary Service

Earlier I mentioned moving from VSer status in south Texas to that of employment in the home office of VS at Mennonite Board of Missions headquarters in Elkhart. This was a crucial period in my life and formed the major part of my decade of involvement with Mennonite Voluntary Service.

It is significant that starting at the young age of twenty-five I was part of giving direction to one of the church's major service programs. Reciprocally, while contributing a great deal of time and effort to administrative and personnel matters related to VS, I learned much about myself, the church, and society's needs.

This was the era of President Johnson's War on Poverty as well as the escalation of the Vietnam War. Poverty in general and conditions in Appalachia and the inner cities was gaining notice. Race riots erupted in Cleveland, Detroit, and Los Angeles. The government's Head Start program was coming on line. The Selective Service drafting of young men for military service was in full force.

The VS program administered by MBM in Elkhart was chiefly domestic, with projects and personnel in Puerto Rico, Mexico, and Canada. Women as well as men, single and married, entered the ranks of VS. In fact, we stressed that the motivation for Christian service went beyond what Selective Service was imposing upon us. During the peak period of my work in the VS office, some 350 volunteers were assigned to more than fifty locations as teachers, hospital aides, and youth and community development workers. VS assignments routinely began with group orientation conferences in Elkhart. At the time we were offering up to ten ten-day orientation conferences per year to prepare new personnel for their assignments.

Our duties as a team of VS administrators were to help with orientation conferences, to visit field locations (known as VS units) around the country, and to keep up with office work, which included reporting on all field visits and maintaining contact with our respective units by snail mail and landline telephone. In addition we were expected to accept speaking assignments in Mennonite churches and on college campuses as well as to attend meetings and conferences for our own education and enrichment.

Travel demands were heavy as we attempted to get around to our assigned VS units anywhere from Florida to Oregon, California to New Hampshire. I could count on being away from home 50 percent of the time. Unit visits, lasting several days, were demanding since it was necessary to evaluate service assignments, deal with personnel matters (read "conflicts"), and support the leadership. These service units often included as many as a dozen young adults.

By then in my early thirties, having given myself to the job for nearly a decade, I began to consider other options. I am grateful, though, for the opportunity Mennonite Voluntary Service afforded me to nurture the flame of Christian service in a generation of youth. Contact with hundreds of young people as well as dozens of fellow staff persons in the several departments of MBM enriched me.

### Associated Mennonite Biblical Seminary

In the early 1970s I spent more than a year between MBM employment and becoming a full time student at Associated Mennonite Biblical Seminary (AMBS). I left MBM in 1971 when I sensed that my future did not lie there. But if not there, then where? Did I have enough by now of church schools and church programs? Enrolling at AMBS nearby appeared somewhat attractive, but initially I found myself continuing to resist the idea of exploring pastoral ministry.

Thus for a while I concentrated on finding employment with a travel agency but ended up with Snelling & Snelling Employment

Agency in a position that lasted only nine months. There I learned what it was like to dislike a job and to dread going to work. I was not cut out for a sales job and earning a commission salary.

In autumn 1972 I enrolled in AMBS's MDiv program for one semester. Getting back to the books was not that hard, I found. What I remember from that first semester is Howard Charles' New Testament course, which introduced me to critical questions surrounding biblical studies, such as the synoptic problem when looking at the Gospels. On the reading list was Stephen Neill's classic, *The Interpretation of the New Testament, 1861-1961*. The first chapter was "Challenge to Orthodoxy." Howard's faith commitment to the Scriptures came through while making room for the importance of critical thinking. I was learning the meaning of "faith seeks understanding."

I spent spring semester 1973 delivering travel trailers and recreational vehicles to RV dealers around the country. I remember thinking that while this was fun and a source of income in the short term, it could not ultimately be a career. By that fall I was back in seminary with renewed resolve. I sensed that persons in my Sunday school class at Prairie Street Mennonite were far more affirming of my attending seminary than of my driving truck. My idea, hardly a dream, of finding a career in trucking died easily as I dusted off my Greek New Testament and took up the study of biblical Hebrew.

The most influential Old Testament course for me was with Millard Lind in which he put the Genesis materials alongside a range of ancient Near Eastern texts, to show the differences between the polytheistic, warring belief systems of the Ancient Near East and the monotheistic faith of ancient Israel that ultimately gave us the Old Testament. Again, I did not find myself resisting these observations while reclaiming the Old Testament for myself.

AMBS in those days was strong on the importance of small groups for the fuller expression of church community. Kass and I participated in several groups over the course of my student days. People like Ross Bender, C. J. Dyck, J. C. Wenger, and Gertrude Roten provided role models. I sang in seminary choir as well as in a community-based Bach Choir directed by Orlando Schmidt, a seminary professor. The use of inclusive language and the increasing role of women in pastoral leadership were coming to the fore. It all made sense to me if we wanted to be faithful people of God.

## Notre Dame University

In the 1970s there was a comfortable back and forth between Notre Dame University in nearby South Bend and AMBS. My own decade-long involvement with Notre Dame began in 1974, when as an AMBS student I took several classical Greek courses at Notre Dame that involved reading Homer and Plato in the original. By the time the 1975-76 school year rolled around, I had been accepted into the doctoral program in the department of theology at Notre Dame on a full scholarship with a stipend.

The department promoted its doctoral program as one to prepare teachers of undergraduates in universities and colleges. This focus for further graduate study suited my career aspirations at the time, and so I became one of the first Mennonite graduate students to be accepted as a doctoral student in the department of theology at Notre Dame. I declared a major in biblical studies, both Old and New Testaments, with minors in the biblical languages, Greek and Hebrew, plus systematic theology.

My Notre Dame experience was successful—to a degree (no pun intended); I received a ThM in 1980 after successfully completing comprehensive exams in fall 1979. By then we had already relocated to Harrisonburg for a teaching position in the Bible department at EMC, with the understanding that along the way I would complete my dissertation for a PhD. However, as it played out, teaching trumped work on the dissertation. Furthermore, I soon sensed a measure of incompatibility between myself and my dissertation director. It seemed that my selected dissertation topic dealing with aspects of the book of Isaiah, a subject of great interest to my director, was overly ambitious for me. Consequently, in 1985 I reluctantly, yet decisively, ended the dissertation process with Notre Dame, believing that I had career options other than academia.

My years on the Notre Dame campus aided me in discerning further direction for my life as a teacher-pastor-scholar. I'll be forever grateful to Notre Dame for introducing me to life in Israel-Palestine as a junior scholar at Tantur Ecumenical Institute. And it was there that I learned to value systematic theological thinking as essential to the eternal quest for a faith that seeks understanding.

## Teaching at EMC and Beyond

As indicated earlier, we moved from Elkhart to Harrisonburg in 1979, after having been away for nineteen years following graduation in 1960. I joined the Bible and Religion Department at EMC to teach Old Testament-related courses. Many students expressed appreciation for introducing them to a liberal arts approach to the Old Testament along with a faith perspective. A few others took issue with the approach and found their way to my office to express concern.

The highlight of my EMC teaching years was organizing and leading EMC's cross-cultural study tour of the Middle East—including the countries of Jordan, Egypt, and Israel-Palestine—in the fall semester of 1984. This allowed me to introduce a group of twenty college students to some of the fascinating features and issues related to the Middle East, things I had experienced earlier. Academic activities included lectures, field trips, test taking, and journaling. In addition, I recall making a special effort to expose students to the adverse effects of the Israeli occupation upon the Palestinians, and particularly the plight of Palestinian Christians. From that group of students, several went on to serve with MCC in the region.

In 1985, while engaged in teaching at EMC, Kass and I were approached by MBM, my former employer from VS days, to consider overseas service in Israel-Palestine starting the following year. I informed EMC that the 1985-86 academic year would be my final year of teaching. The understanding with MBM was that I would resume academic study in Jerusalem—Modern Hebrew language, along with Jewish history, culture, and religion—as preparation and orientation for the possibility of longer term ministry in that setting.

In July 1986 we said good-bye to EMC; the condo was sold and the bags packed. Once again, this time from Dulles International Airport, we took wings to Jerusalem. I recall sitting in the Dulles airport, awaiting a flight to Vienna, thinking that I was without a key ring—neither the first time nor the last to reflect thusly in some airport awaiting passage to the Middle East. One day later, Paul and Bertha Swarr met us at the Tel Aviv airport for another ride *up to* Jerusalem, again to Tantur where we again settled in temporarily until a suitable apartment could be located in West Jerusalem, the Jewish-Israeli sector of the city.

I enrolled at Hebrew University, renewing my study of Modern Hebrew, taking courses taught in English, and auditing several taught in Hebrew. Again Kass found herself involved at Bethlehem University. On weekends we found church fellowship with messianic Jews and Palestinian Christians. We associated with MCC as well as other MBM personnel. Bruderhof friends came from North America to live on Israeli kibbutzim, where we visited them. Deepening friendships developed in the Palestinian community. In keeping with our original understanding with MBM, we were conscious of striving to live in both worlds and to move across the divides in Israeli-Palestinian society as much as possible.

But with the onset of the first Palestinian *intifada* (uprising) in 1987, I found it increasingly difficult to continue my studies at Hebrew University, given the intense suffering going on in the Palestinian setting. Likewise, our strong peace and justice perspective made it seem increasingly difficult to cast our lot with the Jewish messianic folks, a priority for MBM in that setting.

In May 1989, with plans to come back to Jerusalem, we returned to the U.S. to close out a three-year term making contacts with church under MBM auspices. While in the States, we anticipated in-depth consultations with MBM on how to continue our presence in Israel-Palestine, and initially it appeared that we would return to Jerusalem. However, our return was not approved by MBM because we appeared to have given too much attention to Palestinian concerns and inadequate attention to working within the context of messianic Jewish fellowships.

While there were other complicating factors, such as how to obtain an Israeli visa to continue living in Jerusalem, we felt that the decisions we made grew out of our peace and justice values. For instance, how could we continue to support messianic fellowships in Israel when some messianic Jews live in settlements in the West Bank and provide personnel for the Israeli military that runs the West Bank occupation? While our categories may have been too rigid and our goals too unrealistic, at the time it was extremely disappointing that MBM stakeholders did not support our vision. In all fairness to our initial understanding with MBM, I must accept responsibility for having dropped academic pursuits in Jerusalem.

The years 1986-1989 spent in Jerusalem were important for the opportunities we had to mingle with both Israelis and Palestinians. We formed rich friendships in both communities and drank deeply from both cultures. Unfortunately, neither MCC nor MBM were able to fit us into their programs at the time. Perhaps the greatest benefit growing out of these three years was that of being able to share Middle East understandings in numerous congregations in North America.

After several months of speaking in churches under MBM auspices, we accepted an assignment with Franconia Conference in church development in Burlington, Vermont's largest metropolitan area. The early '90s was an era of "church planting" among Mennonites—a term I never made peace with, by the way. Burlington, a university city, seemed a likely location for a developing Mennonite fellowship or church plant, as some would insist on calling it. When we arrived there during the Easter season in 1990, the Quaker Meeting welcomed us warmly and demonstrated a lively interest in our presence for strengthening the peace church witness in the area. We also found fellowship with a Presbyterian-affiliated church meeting on the University of Vermont campus nearby.

We rented office space along a busy city street and hung out a sign letting it be known that the Mennonites had come to town. Certain people passing by became curious but, finding no horse and buggy parked behind the office, quickly lost interest. Others queried, "Are you the home school people?" Mennonite House of Friendship in Montreal, Quebec, along with established downstate Mennonite congregations at Bridgewater Corners and Taftsville, provided welcome fellowship.

Bringing together a critical mass of persons interested in forming a new congregation was essential. Individuals and families with Mennonite-Anabaptist roots and sympathies were scattered throughout northern Vermont. Such folks were interested in meeting periodically for Mennonite cultural fellowship, but forming a core group in the interests of establishing an organized faith community was not on their agenda. In fact, some had likely been attracted to Vermont to escape what they considered Mennonite baggage. Nonetheless, we persevered. A group calling itself Burlington Peace Mennonite Fellowship did coalesce with a dozen charter members in June 1994. The group remained in existence for the next decade, but eventually dissolved due to lack of pastoral leadership and key people moving away.

Over the course of several years leading into the mid-1990s, conference funding for the Burlington project and several like it elsewhere were drying up. Furthermore, I was never totally consonant with the church development philosophy, strategies, and methodologies some conference leadership persons were encouraging us to adopt, such as setting up a phone bank to make thousands of phone calls inviting people to a new church that was about to commence.

Likewise, the inconstancies of conducting church in this environment, as well as making a living with the conference threatening to pull the funds, strengthened my growing desire to pastor an established congregation somewhere. Meanwhile, an interest in chaplaincy led me to take several units of clinical pastoral education at the University of Vermont Medical Center in Burlington. I also recognized that units of clinical pastoral education would enhance my résumé when applying for pastorates, a process I began early in 1994.

In the fall of 1994, we left Burlington in response to an invitation to work temporarily in the Franconia Conference office in Souderton, Pennsylvania, while exploring pastorates. There I helped to launch a conference-sponsored project dealing with racism as well as to coordinate conference efforts related to peace and justice. During this interim year in Souderton, I was in contact with numerous pastoral search committees.

Candidating for the pastorate in half-a-dozen instances proved interesting on one hand and stressful on the other. Before coming to Souderton, I had already lost the vote in a sizeable Indiana congregation. My guess is that I was perceived as having too much education and being too open to looking at gay-lesbian issues. I can now see the hand of God in closing the door to pastoral ministry in that congregation. In several other candidacies, search committees sized me up as too peace-and-justice oriented—too Anabaptist, in other words.

In the end, the match turned out to be on the other end of the country in the Central Valley of California, specifically First Mennonite Church in Reedley, twenty-five miles east of Fresno, within sight of the Sierra Nevada Mountains—on a clear day. Their only concern was the fact that I had not previously pastored an established congregation. I began pastoral duties at First Mennonite Church on November 1, 1995, and was officially installed early in January 1996.

Thus, after nearly two years of exploring with a variety of congregations, I became the pastor of a former General Conference Mennonite Church, now part of Pacific Southwest Mennonite Conference.

This congregation of 300 consisted mostly of members with Russian Mennonite background. It also included several war veterans and four sets of parents with openly gay sons, although the sons were no longer part of the congregation when I arrived.

It turned out to be a good match that lasted nearly nine years. I learned to engage with veterans in the congregation and welcomed occasions to offer support and acceptance to families with gay members. These years in Reedley were good ones. There was much appreciation for my abilities in preaching-teaching, pastoral care, and support of the music program. I visited the elderly and sick, met with church committees, and prepared sermons. The congregation supported a Hispanic ministry, and with Reedley being 70 percent Hispanic, my orientation to Spanish language and Hispanic culture was a plus. Going beyond the congregation to the level of Pacific Southwest Mennonite Conference, I was privileged to serve as chair of the conference ministerial committee for several terms.

A number of things from the Reedley years stand out. In 1998 a dozen persons from the congregation accompanied us on a TourMagination Lands of the Bible tour. On a different note, a number of adults—persons who had written off First Mennonite Church—found their way back to the congregation, attracted to the Anabaptist-oriented peace-and-justice emphasis now openly espoused. These folks joined the congregation and were instrumental in starting a weekly Friday evening program of sharing peace-and-justice concerns, a program of witness and outreach to the broader community that continues to this day.

In October 2003 I took a few days away from Reedley to attend a Mennonite mission and service consultation on Christian-Muslim relations at EMU and to visit my parents then living in Virginia Mennonite Retirement Community. I returned to Reedley acknowledging to my late wife, Kass, an inner stirring to return to the Middle East yet again, a sentiment she had been expressing for some time.

We discovered that MCC had an opening for country representatives for the country of Lebanon. We applied for a five-year term and were accepted. I announced my resignation to the congregation. We sold our house and many furnishings, while storing some essentials with a parishioner. When we left for the Middle East in 2004, the congregation gave us a tremendous send-off saying, "We're not surprised to see you head back to the Middle East again at age sixty-six," parishioners our age said. "You are doing what we ought to do, but our families and our possessions keep us here."

## BACK AGAIN TO THE MIDDLE EAST

Yet again, this time in the Philadelphia airport, we awaited a flight to the Middle East, not to Tel Aviv, but to Beirut. We found the situation in Lebanon fairly stable as we came on the scene more than a decade after the end of the civil war in 1990. Damaged cities, particularly Beirut, had been rebuilt, although structural and societal scars were still in evidence. Partnering with Muslim faith-based peacebuilding and development organizations in Lebanon afforded new understanding and appreciation for shared convictions for ministry among the needy. MCC's involvement in Lebanon consisted of numerous peacebuilding programs with Lebanese partner organizations, both Christian and Muslim. Efforts were frequently directed toward bringing the youth of Lebanon together across religious and clan divides.

Maintaining the fully computerized MCC office with due attention to program planning, reporting, and managing a budget of several hundred thousand dollars, along with supervising a Lebanese employee, presented a steep learning curve. It was rewarding to be back in the Middle East, but our having lived in Israel previously was a story we could not tell in Lebanon inasmuch as Lebanon was still technically at war with Israel—even after Israel's withdrawal from Lebanon in 2000. We enjoyed church fellowship with the English-speaking branch of the National Evangelical Church of Lebanon. It was always a pleasure to visit MCC-funded projects throughout Lebanon and be able to explain that such monies were generated in North America by freewill offerings, thrift stores, and relief sales—not money from USAID.

In summer 2006 Israel and Lebanon engaged in a thirty-four-day war during which time Israel bombed South Lebanon, including the southern suburbs of Beirut. Although our part of the city was relatively unscathed, the airport was bombed by Israeli planes and consequently closed. We were scheduled for home leave during this time. We turned the MCC flat over to Bassam Chamoun, MCC's local employee and his family, who needed to come to Beirut to escape the bombs falling in their South Lebanon neighborhood. Our departure from Beirut is itself a story: evacuation from Beirut by the U.S. Embassy to a chartered ship headed to Cyprus; from there a flight to London's Heathrow Airport, and finally Dulles.

When we returned to Lebanon after our home leave, MCC implemented specialized relief efforts that continued well into 2007. Another development at that time had to do with combining the Lebanon and Syria MCC programs into a regional effort. Consequently we became MCC country representative for both Lebanon and Syria. This assignment necessitated occasional travel to Damascus to meet with MCC personnel and partner groups there. Obviously, this was happening in the years before the current upheaval and disintegration of Syria began.

In June 2009, having come to the close of our five-year term, we flew from Beirut to London and on to Los Angeles where we were met by Reedley church friends. We spent two weeks visiting with former parishioners and gathering our belongings, which we loaded on a U-Haul truck for a one-week cross-country drive to Virginia. In July 2009 we arrived in Harrisonburg and unloaded the U-Haul in Park Village on the Virginia Mennonite Retirement Community (VMRC) campus to begin retirement living.

Thus end thirty years in and out of the Middle East relating to a variety of agencies: Notre Dame University, Eastern Mennonite College, TourMagination, Mennonite Board of Missions, and Mennonite Central Committee. Service, learning, and sharing with others along the way has been my lot. Thanks be to God!

## Conclusion

How does one characterize this multi-faceted career? Perhaps "career" is not the right word; a better word, as I see it is "vocation." I have always understood myself to be called as a disciple, a follower of the Jesus way; hence that is my chief vocation. In living out that vocation I have manifested a strong interest in church-related ways of making a living. Mine has been the blessing to keep body and soul together in the context of church institutions and associated ministry endeavors.

I consider myself deeply committed and loyal to the Mennonite-Anabaptist expression of the Christian faith. In that regard I am extremely grateful for the variety of ways I have been blessed to work in numerous church programs and institutions: Mennonite mission and service, higher learning, and pastoral leadership. As it turns out, my working years are somewhat equally divided between (1) service, (2) academia, and (3) pastoral work. Somehow, in my experience, the three, which might well have been three separate streams, have converged as one stream and complemented each other. The streams have informed each other to the degree that, looking back, I do not view them as distinct from one another. I felt comfortable moving from one to the other.

If, however, you were to ask me whether one or the other took priority, I would have to opt for pastoral ministry, particularly given those satisfying years at First Mennonite Church in Reedley, California, which ultimately trumped academia. If it must be stated in such terms, I may have been tardy and somewhat resistant toward getting into the pastoral ministry earlier in life. But to say that I neglected the Lord's leading for my life in doing so would be going too far.

Living and working in the Middle East for longer and shorter periods of time likewise carried overtones of academia and pastoral concerns. Apply then a deep passion for peace and justice over the whole and you have the satisfying salad of a life well lived under God's blessing despite bumps in the road here and there.

## Afterword

I have said very little about the importance of marriage in my life. "We" throughout these reflections refers to my late wife Kathryn (Kass) Hunsberger from the Franconia Mennonite Conference in Pennsylvania, whom I married in 1959. She had her own career in education and taught in classrooms ranging from kindergarten to university settings in the various states in which we lived as well as in the Middle East.

Somehow we melded our individual careers into common career goals and the many moves reflected, for the most part, mutual interests, although Kass always felt a greater pull toward public, rather than private, educational settings. She was a strong supporter of peace and justice values, particularly when it came to the Palestinians.

When we returned from Lebanon to Harrisonburg in July 2009, Kass was already ill. Within a week we received the official diagnosis of multiple myeloma, an aggressive blood cancer. Massive treatment lengthened her life about one year. She died in 2011, and her ashes were buried at the Mt. Clinton Mennonite Church cemetery.

In 2012, Audrey Metz, also with roots in Franconia Conference, whom I had known in grade school, reconnected in the context of church choir at Park View Mennonite Church in Harrisonburg. We married. While raising a family in Sarasota, Florida, Audrey was involved in Mennonite congregational life. After leaving Florida in 1999 she moved to Washington, D.C., to share in ministry at International Guest House and Church of the Savior. Later she traveled to India to serve short term in one of Mother Teresa's ministries in Calcutta.

Now in retirement Audrey and I are actively involved in the Park View Mennonite Church. We volunteer around VMRC and MCC's Gift and Thrift and relate to Audrey's adult children and two young grandchildren.

April 2010
Revised June 2015

## Acronyms

EMBM—Eastern Mennonite Board of Missions (now Eastern Mennonite Missions)
FMC—Franconia Mennonite Conference
FMCR—First Mennonite Church, Reedley, Ca.
MBM—Mennonite Board of Missions (now Mennonite Mission Network)
MCC—Mennonite Central Committee
ND—Notre Dame University
VMRC—Virginia Mennonite Retirement Community

**PART V**

# Re-Envisioning Service ... as Peacebuilders

*Paul W. Roth*

---

**Visionary for Peace**

*A gentle, welcoming man, Paul Roth is pastor of the congregation at Linville Creek Church of the Brethren, home congregation of the late M. R. Zigler, the influential post-World War II Brethren peacemaker. Paul's passion for history made him a strong proponent of CrossRoads (Valley Brethren-Mennonite Heritage Center) and of ways to tell the story of Bishop John Kline, the Brethren elder and martyr who crisscrossed the Valley on horseback with his biblical message of peace during the bloody Civil War.*

**PAUL W. ROTH**

# *A Journey of Identity*

Paul Roth is a good Mennonite name. In my adult years the Mennonites have tried to place me among "the favored ones" in their genealogy games. I'm often amused and intrigued by this name association among Anabaptist friends. But I am also honored and humbled by this inquiry. The Paul Roths that Mennonites have known have been faithful, respected leaders in their tradition. And I am being asked to share my story from non-Mennonite beginnings. What an offer of grace this is.

I must say that this is a fearsome task to recount my life and faith to a public audience. I do not think my story is especially extraordinary, nor do I consider it worthy to be among the several who have shared their stories in this gathering. And yet, I believe it is the testimony of our common journey of faithfulness to Jesus Christ that gives each one of us the courage to follow this different way of living and believing. We have the audacity to believe that our meager lives *do* make a difference in our world. So, with trepidation and humility as well as with deep gratitude, I share this story of my life.

## MY FAMILY

At the outset, I wish to tell you about my family. My wife, Linda, worked as an English Language Learner tutor for the Rockingham County Schools for about eight years. She is now a supervisor of housewares and crafts for Gift and Thrift in their remodeled store.

As of this writing, our oldest son, Nathan, was in his second year of graduate studies at New York University's Tisch School of the Arts, seeking a master's degree in interactive telecommunication. Our second son, Aaron, graduated from The College of William & Mary with a business administration degree in marketing. He lives in Richmond and works for a large accounting firm as a marketing technician. Amber, our youngest child, also graduated from The College of William & Mary. For a number of years, she served as the program director and administrative assistant for Camp Still Meadows, a therapeutic, enrichment center for handicapped adults. She has also volunteered in Guatemala, working with children of the poor at a student center beside the largest dump in Central America.

I have just returned from the tenth Church of the Brethren National Older Adult Conference in Lake Junaluska, North Carolina. (I'm still trying to come to terms with being old enough to attend this conference!) The theme drew me to attend my first conference there: "Legacies of Wisdom." With my mother's death, I have wondered about the environment in which we grow, receiving and passing on these legacies of wisdom from our faith tradition. Here is how I understand my own legacy.

## My Birth Family

I was born the fifth child and fourth son of Mark and Madeline Roth, who lived near Carlisle, Pennsylvania. My father was asked to give a pint of blood on that July 11, 1947, not knowing that his wife was carrying twins. When another son was born fifty-five minutes after me, he tied the knot at the end of a family of six children. Our only sister cried that day, thinking that our mother had betrayed her prayers for a sister to change the male dominance in the household.

My siblings include Kenneth, who had Down syndrome and lived at home into his mid-fiftys when dementia eroded his life and increased his care. He died at The Brethren Home at Cross Keys, New Oxford, Pennsylvania, in January 1994 at age sixty-one. He taught us much about simple joy and trust, unflagging honesty, and ready love.

My sister, Anna Mae, was married to Vernon Belser of Elizabethtown, Pennsylvania, until his death in 1996. She retired as a public school nurse in the Dauphin East School District and is now active in the Elizabethtown Church of the Brethren. Her youngest child and only son, Andy, is professor of theater at Juniata College in Huntingdon, Pennsylvania. In addition to him, Anna has three daughters, seven grandchildren, and one great-granddaughter.

My brother Eugene is a retired elementary school teacher. In the late 1950s, Gene served in Brethren Volunteer Service (BVS) at a settled migrant workers camp in Fresno, California, before going to college at McPherson in Kansas. He bought the home place in Boiling Springs, Pennsylvania, taking care of our mother who had dementia for the last two years until her death at ninety-eight. He volunteers at a local food bank and is now the only family member to attend the Carlisle Church of the Brethren.

My brother, Dale, is retired from Penn State University, where he served as director for recreational services. He is a member of the University Baptist-Brethren Church in State College, Pennsylvania, has served as moderator for his congregation, president of the Camp Harmony Board, chairperson of the Middle Pennsylvania District Leadership Team, coordinator for disaster relief services in Louisiana, and on the denominational discernment committee for the Brethren Service Center in New Windsor, Maryland. Dale and his wife have two sons and five granddaughters.

My twin brother, Phil, lives with his partner Jim in Indianapolis, Indiana, where he served for thirty-four years with the Indiana State Education Offices. Phil is active in North United Methodist Church, is fluent in Spanish, and sings in the Indianapolis Gay Men's Chorus.

## FAITH VALUES, A LEGACY

The values I learned at home were very instrumental in forming my own faith and direction and that of my family. My father was the third of seven children, five of whom, including my father, raised their families around Carlisle and attended Carlisle Church of the Brethren. Even though we were related to many others in church, we carried a sense of belonging to all who worshipped there, including the youth from the District Children's Home in town.

My brother, Kennie, felt at home in the congregation but chose his own friend, a man who owned a furniture store in Carlisle, to sit with each Sunday. Another mentally challenged woman also felt at home in the congregation. Her father still wore the plain coat and often called us to prayer (kneeling, of course) to ask for God's wisdom regarding some issue. Our membership included an unmarried woman, Grace Ditmer, who kept the children in the nursery or in church as if they were her own; a missionary to Nigeria; a couple of BVS workers; farmers; factory workers; teachers; business owners; and a funeral director.

From the proud and the prominent to the diminutive and diminished, we met regularly for worship and faithfully attended love feast in the church basement, finding our common place around the table. Jesus welcomed us all at his table. And when we sang the beloved hymns, each face radiated a love for Jesus and a commitment to be his people in this place. It was my experience of *Gemeinschaft*.[1]

My father was a tenant farmer, having labored with a brother and then farmed on his own, but again without being the owner of the land. He had an eighth-grade education, attended a business school in the 1920s, and then returned to the farm during World War II. He sang in the church choir, taught Sunday school, and served on several church committees.

My mother sometimes complained to her father, who lived with them before I was born, when Dad had gone to yet another meeting. her father said, "Madeline, when the church calls, it is as if the Lord himself were calling. Don't complain about his service with the church." That surely was an Anabaptist understanding of working for the sake of the faith community who does the work of Jesus.

And my mother's own church work followed her father's legacy of wisdom. She taught Sunday school for over fifty years, served on the district board and was its representative to the Pennsylvania Council of Churches, sang in the church choir, and led congregational singing. Both my parents were deacons in the church.

When Phil and I were three, my parents welcomed Paul Herzog to our home on the farm located along the South Mountain in the Cumberland Valley. Paul was part of the Church of the Brethren youth exchange after World War II. He was tall, handsome, Catholic, and German. Mother said that many family and church members thought it was a mistake for our family to take in a Nazi youth. But Mother would engage Paul in conversation about American life and Protestant faith. He worked on the farm, helped create a raised flower bed, and built a four-leaf coffee table for us. He also introduced us to the Advent wreath, which had hemlock branches and red candles to represent God's sacrificial love in Jesus. This was the beginning of my ecumenical and foreign relationships. We moved off the farm in the early 1950s, when Phil and I were four. Dad found work at the Farmers and Trust Bank in Carlisle where he had worked before the war. We bought a large two-story house on Fourth Street in the small town of Boiling Springs. My parents rented the upstairs apartment to an immigrant German couple, Kurt and Marianne Voigt.

Phil and I often went to the Methodist church across the street for Wednesday evening club where we learned gospel praise songs. Summers we attended vacation Bible school in the Lutheran and Evangelical United Brethren churches. In that small town we belonged to each other regardless of faith traditions. At Halloween we enjoyed dressing up and visiting neighbors, even several streets away, as they, guessing who or whose we were, welcomed us as "their own."

We lived a couple of blocks from the railroad, whose train whistles announced the assuring rhythm of life beyond and for the community. From the railroad, hobos came to our back door asking for food. Phil and I stared at these desolate strangers as they sat at the back porch on the old wood box which kept our yard toys and waited for the meal our mother brought them to eat. The parable of Matthew 25 became realized as we saw our mother's graciousness. However, we forgot such hospitality one time when we snooped in a single man's old house off a side street while he was away. When our parents found that we had entered his home, we learned a hard lesson on respect, even for the most destitute.

Mother baked for three markets in Carlisle each week to bring in more income for her growing family. We children had to help with household chores. The brothers regretted that there wasn't another sister to appease our sister's prayer and relieve us of this weekend drudgery! When our mother allowed us to visit her stall at the market, we watched with curiosity as a man deformed by cerebral palsy peddled his cart around the market, selling candy from his basket. We were already sensitized to living with Kennie, but he was family. Now we had a lesson in relating to others with different disabilities.

Eventually, Mother left the market to work at a day care training school in Newville for mentally challenged adults. It was here that she was invited to get certification in special education to teach in a new school in the area. She went back to college at night to complete her degree. She became the first special education teacher in the Cumberland Valley School District and taught there for twenty-one years. She modeled dedication and compassion for those often ignored and abused in our culture of able-bodied and self-willed.

Our life on Fourth Street also taught me about stewardship. Our family didn't have much money. Yet, every week Mother and Dad took out their tithe and put it in the offering at church. We learned that our lives and our resources are not our own, but a responsibility entrusted to us by God. In addition, my home church distributed Brethren Service Cups to each family for a monthly or quarterly offering. And we learned early on about the work of Heifer Project. In addition, I remember going to the Brethren Service Center in New Windsor, Maryland, with our church to sort clothing. Service, we learned, is a significant part of faith expression.

Phil and I were baptized in the Carlisle First Church of the Brethren baptistery with the image of the descending dove overhead. Coming up out of the water we were greeted by our parents, deacons (to whom we were related) and our Sunday school teacher. It was a reminder that baptism is not a singular event for one's personal salvation only. Rather, in the Anabaptist tradition, it is a communal event shared by those who nurtured us in faith since the time of our birth. We belonged to each other in this public confession of faith in Jesus Christ and in our common witness to his presence. And we would hold each other accountable to this confession of faith in Jesus.

## SEARCHING FOR MY LIFE WORK

In high school in the early 1960s, our young pastor, fresh from Bethany Seminary in Oak Brook, Illinois, urged us to meet with the NAACP (National Association for the Advancement of Colored People) youth of the African-American church down the street from our church. We shared day camps and youth gatherings. On August 28, 1963, we rode together on buses from Carlisle and York to join the March on Washington for Jobs and Freedom. I remember that hot August day and the excitement of being part of something both historic and prophetic. Hundreds of thousands of people—black and white—

marched to the Lincoln Memorial to listen to some preacher named Martin Luther King Jr. give an inspirational address, "I Have a Dream." That was another signal event in my young life that changed me forever.

As a junior in high school I was invited to write a speech for the Church of the Brethren National Youth Speech Contest. The winner would give the address at Annual Conference in Lincoln, Nebraska. I won the district contest in York and went on to the regional event at the Gettysburg Church of the Brethren, placing second to Anita Smith, who addressed the Annual Conference as the speech winner. Anita Smith Buckwalter, pastor of the East Lansing Church of the Brethren in Michigan for thirty-five years, and I are still the best of friends. She and I initiated a listening session at one Annual Conference that was the start of Voices for an Open Spirit, a group that keeps the progressive voice before our denomination, including openness to persons of varying sexual identities.

Also in high school, Phil and I sang in several choirs and formed a quartet with two girls of another family to sing at churches. I suppose we took on our mother's singing role, since she sang in ensembles at family reunions and in the church choir. Later in college Phil asked me if I would consider going professional. I told him that I loved singing too much to have to earn my bread by it!

We graduated from Boiling Springs High School in 1965. I had already been accepted to attend Elizabethtown College, but it was too close to home for me, and I wasn't confident in my academic abilities (even though I graduated in the top 10 percent of my class). Besides, I wanted to learn who I was as Paul, rather than the collective "Paul-n'-Phil," or "P. W. and P. W." as our aunts called us, or the "Roth twins" as our friends referred to us. My brother Gene encouraged me to apply to McPherson College in Kansas, which I did. I was accepted, received a scholarship, and went there sight unseen. That move would expand my provincial eastern Brethren sights immensely.

I majored in philosophy and religion—perhaps because I had told a junior high football coach that I was thinking of the ministry when he asked me what I wanted to do when I grew up. (I later learned that my Grandmother Roth secretly hoped one of her grandchildren would become a minister.) The first people I met on campus were Roger and Carolyn Schrock, who later went to Nigeria in BVS.

My roommate was Ron Adkins from Long Beach, California, who later went to seminary, where I introduced him to his wife, Alice Martin (both now Brethren pastors). I sang in the McPherson College Acapella and Madrigal choirs. During the summers, I was an Earn-n'-Serve worker in Auburn, Indiana, and Waka, Texas, testing the waters for service in ministry.

I returned home after graduation (mostly because of nagging kidney stones that interrupted the fall semester of my senior year). Feeling directionless, I worked in a Kinney Shoe warehouse and with the farmer cooperative (AGWAY), eventually becoming assistant manager of the cooperative. I worked with my father, who had retired from the bank and was working at AGWAY. To find direction for my life, I lived in Grantham, took classes at Messiah College, and sang in a small ensemble. J. Stanley Earhart, district executive for Southern Pennsylvania District, lived nearby and was my spiritual mentor. I was youth leader at church, directed the choir, and led congregational singing for evangelistic services, mostly for the Methodists. (Perhaps I was honing skills for later ministry.)

Warren Eshbach, a pastor in the district, told me I was wasting my time and gave me a nudge ("kick in the pants" were his words) to go on to Bethany Seminary. In 1975 I took a Bethany extension course offered at Elizabethtown College and followed that with ten days at Bethany Seminary for their Summer Lay Institute. It was there that I felt a formal call to ministry. Two years later I enrolled at Bethany Seminary in Oak Brook, Illinois.

## Following the Call to Ministry

I was at Bethany only five days when I was called home for my father's funeral. He had lymphoblastic leukemia which came on rapidly after retirement from AGWAY. He died on his and my mother's forty-sixth wedding anniversary. I remember talking with Eugene Roop, the Old Testament professor at Bethany, about his death. He said to me, "Death is serious, but not all that serious." It was my introduction to a journey of probing more deeply into my faith to find God in the most unlikely places.

It was during a summer pastorate after my middler year that I met my wife Linda at the East Chippewa Church of the Brethren near

Orrville, Ohio. She was visiting her college roommate before entering BVS. Paul and Ella Mae Fike, pastor and wife at East Chipp, both encouraged me to explore this relationship further after Linda left for BVS. Later I visited Linda in service at a Bureau of Indian Affairs School in Brigham City, Utah. We got engaged Christmas of 1979 and married at the seminary after my graduation in June 1980.

Uncertain of my identity as a pastor, I chose a simple, rural congregation where I could make mistakes and pray for grace. Linda wanted to go south so I chose southern Minnesota! We followed Roger and Carolyn Schrock, whom the Church of the Brethren called to a mission in Sudan. Our small congregation had a global connection!

While at the Lewiston congregation in southeastern Minnesota, our sons Nathan and Aaron were born. Perhaps it was the rugged winters—sometimes dipping to forty degrees below zero, with wind chill of 100 degrees below zero one winter—and the dedicated farm life of members that honed our spirits. We loved these humble, rural folk, and they loved us. I wrote new words for hymns I couldn't find to fit my sermons, and I created children's stories with puppets to engage the growing number of children there. I felt God's Spirit nudging me to be creative in ministry and realized it wasn't a sin to try new things in worship.

This was also my first introduction to our Brethren heritage. While pastoring the Lewiston congregation, I planned a 125th-anniversary celebration of the congregation's founding. I invited beloved seminary professor Dale Brown as guest speaker. Little did I know this experience in coordinating a Brethren heritage event would prepare me for planning a seventy-fifth anniversary of the church building at the South Waterloo congregation in Iowa and, later, a John Kline Bicentennial Celebration at the Linville Creek congregation in Virginia.

As a novice pastor I immersed myself in church and district life, leading singing for district conferences and camp counseling three-and-one-half hours away at Camp Pine Lake in Eldora, Iowa. My wife and children suffered from my many "Yeses" beyond home. "When the church calls, it is always the voice of God." I have wondered many times since then if Grandfather Wolfe's words to my mother could become license to abuse family life for the sake of the church. It is still a discipline of discernment nearly thirty years later.

In 1984 I was called from Lewiston to the South Waterloo Church of the Brethren, a larger church with a demographic mixture within the congregation. This was a Brethren stronghold in the Northern Plains District. I began to experiment with creative writing for sermons and plays. At the same time, I walked the tight line between a patriotic, cultural faith and a radical witness to the way of Jesus. When seminary colleagues Phil and Louie Rieman became pastors of the Ivester Church of the Brethren, thirty-seven miles to the southwest, we stood with them on a cold January day as their VW van was auctioned for payment of unpaid income taxes they withheld to protest paying for war. I participated in the Iowa Peace Network activities, even withholding taxes for a couple of years as war protest, and at the same time tried not to offend some parishioners who insisted that we have a flag in the sanctuary.

Our daughter Amber was born in October 1985, the first child born to a pastor while living in the South Waterloo parsonage. During this time I also experienced my first spiritual direction from a Catholic theologian. Connie May helped me to listen to God's call within and nurtured me along the path of spiritual formation, inviting me to join her for a silent retreat at a monastery. Her weekly ecumenical Scripture encounters nourished my personal and preaching soul. I was discovering a different, unique person within, a new identity as a follower of Jesus.

In 1990 I was called by the Highland Avenue congregation in Elgin, Illinois, to interview to become their pastor. Linda and I struggled with this call, knowing that my growing pastoral leadership caused others to take notice. We yielded to the repeated invitations by the search committee. That was a mistake. The congregation, although filled with denominational staff and retired ministers, was reeling from the retirement of a beloved pastor, Sam Flora. The leadership convinced me that I was the person they were looking for to lead them into the twenty-first century. However, from the outset there were several unresolved issues over fractured relationships and residual distrust that undermined my ministry. I realized too late that I should not have left Iowa.

I went through vocational counseling at the Midwest Career Development Center, hearing from the director that I should consider the pastorate in Elgin as a long-term interim. I painfully resigned in

December 1994 (I don't like failure!) and became a teacher's aide in the special education department at a large high school north of Elgin.

### A MOVE TO THE SHENANDOAH VALLEY OF VIRGINIA

We came to the Linville Creek Church of the Brethren in June 1995. I knew that this was the home congregation of Elder John Kline, but it was the people and their yearning for a "cheerleader" that enticed me to enter pastoral ministry again. I prayed this would bring healing to my wounded soul. While here I have honed my yearning for spiritual direction and taken courses for spiritual formation at Eastern Mennonite Seminary. I have served as spiritual director for persons in my congregation and beyond.

It was also here in the Valley where I was called by On Earth Peace to serve on its board of directors and to help with developing a calling and training process for teachers, consultants, and facilitators for the Ministry of Reconciliation. Since then, I have served as a facilitator for Matthew 18 workshops as well as for Ministry with Difficult Behaviors. I have also helped in interventions in congregations experiencing conflict.

It was early in my pastorate here that I had an immersion into Brethren and Civil War history. When I learned that John Kline's 200th birthday was coming up in 1997, I asked my church board if they wanted to have a celebration of his life. They encouraged me to plan a weekend event. The celebration brought nearly 2,000 people to hear twenty lectures at the church, take tours of the cemetery, the John Kline House, The Tunker House, and the marker where John Kline was killed. We had children and youth activities, a dinner theater on "The Final Journey of John Kline," and baptisms, including two of my children, in the Linville Creek.

### INVOLVEMENT WITH THE
### VALLEY BRETHREN-MENNONITE HERITAGE CENTER

This heritage event propelled me into the circles of the local Mennonites who were seeking to create a Mennonite heritage center here in the Valley. I was invited, along with Emmert Bittinger of Bridgewater College, to be part of a steering committee chaired by Cal Redekop. I have continued to serve on the board of directors of CrossRoads—the Valley Brethren-Mennonite Heritage Center.

When I learned of the sale of the John Kline Homestead, I wondered whether we should save this place from which John Kline began his missionary and herbal medical visits as well as his peace witness on behalf of the Brethren and Mennonites during the Civil War. Does it really matter to anyone that this place may be lost and John Kline's voice for following the radical way of Jesus be silenced? I have told my congregation, "We did not have a choice in receiving this heritage, but we do have a choice with what to do with it."

I confess that this venture of preserving a heritage place for the Brethren has been a demanding and exhausting experience. But I believe that unless we save the historic places of our forebears, we are in danger of losing their legacies of faith and our connection to the core faith values they honed addressing the issues of their day. And, we potentially lose our grounding for faithful witness in our time.

My mother once told me of her Royer ancestry (her mother's family line) in Maryland. I learned that her great-grandfather, Christian Royer, was a free minister in the Black Rock Congregation just over the Pennsylvania line. When he built his house on a farm in Carroll County in the mid-1820s, he noted that preachers came from far away, including one from Virginia, Elder John Kline. There's a strange destiny in my serving in John Kline's congregation and working to preserve his home so that others might learn of his faith and find contemporary connections to this common faith we hold in Jesus Christ. Who would have thought that this twin from a humble Pennsylvania Brethren family should find the focus of his ministry in this place of heritage in the Shenandoah Valley?

There is an anthem that perhaps best describes my role as a pastor and leader in this Anabaptist/Pietist tradition known as Brethren. The anthem, reflecting the words of the writer to the Hebrews, calls attention to the "cloud of witnesses" surrounding us and inspires us to therefore run with perseverance the race that is before us.[2]

September 2009<br>
Revised February 2013

## NOTES

1. Donald F. Durnbaugh and Desmond Wright Bittinger, eds., *The Church of the Brethren: Past and Present* (Elgin, Ill.: Brethren Press, 1971). Vernard Eller defines the German word *Gemeinschaft* as "the intimate sense of union that comes as a group shares some deep commitment in common" (43).

2. Words and Music: Jon Mohr, copyright 1988 by Birdwing Music/ Jonathan Mark Music.

*Pat Hostetter Martin*

### Embodiment of the Spirit of Justice and Peace

*Across the world and back again, Pat Hostetter Martin has always embodied the same mission—of walking the way of Jesus, reflecting the spirit of Christ (and the Buddha), and exemplifying the church's witness of justice and peace. And behind and between all the formal roles she has carried, the home of Pat and Earl is an example par excellence of Judeo-Christian hospitality and the richest and best of table fellowship here on Planet Earth.*

**PAT HOSTETTER MARTIN**

# Braiding the Strands of Life

## STRANDS OF FAMILY

Oblivious to World War II and the beginning of gasoline rationing in the United States, I was born on December 16, 1942, to Grace Brackbill and Benjamin Charles Hostetter. I have few memories of Manheim, Pennsylvania. My father, having been ordained by lot at age twenty-two, was serving as pastor of his home congregation, Manheim Mennonite. In 1946, when I was three, our family of five (my parents, older sister Miriam, younger brother Doug, and I) moved to Harrisonburg, Virginia, where my father finished his last two years of college at Eastern Mennonite School (eventually Eastern Mennonite College, now Eastern Mennonite University). Five younger brothers were born in Harrisonburg over a period of nine years.

I attended my first six grades at the three-room Park View Elementary School that was standing where the Eastern Mennonite University Physical Plant is now located. Grades seven through twelve were offered in several buildings on the Eastern Mennonite College (EMC) campus. Our parents paid our education costs through high school, but we were expected to pay for our college education. Given the reduced cost of being a day student and living at home, I decided to begin my college at EMC.

But by my junior year, I was beginning to look at some of the advantages of going to Goshen (Ind.) College. Goshen had a social work major in which I was interested. But perhaps more important to me at the time, I would be able to play intercollegiate sports at EMC's sister college. I transferred for my senior year, changing my major from languages to social work and playing varsity basketball, softball, and tennis.

My maternal grandparents, Milton and Ruth Haldeman Brackbill, were significant influences in my life during my growing-up years. They bought the forty-acre homestead of Cornelius and Fannie Haldeman, my maternal great-grandparents, thus providing a home for Grandpa and Grandma Haldeman, both of whom I remember well until they died. When Grandpa Brackbill was ordained by lot at the Frazer Mennonite Church near Paoli, Pennsylvania, he and Grandma began converting the spring house, the carriage house, and other farm buildings into small cottages to rent out to tourists to make ends meet. For more than twenty years, the fourteen-room, 200-year-old stone farmhouse along the Lincoln Highway, where George Washington once slept, was the center for extended family life.

My mother and her four sisters brought their families "home" for all the holidays—Easter, Thanksgiving, and Christmas—and when husbands were gone, such as when my father and Uncle John Shenk served as chaplains for men in Civilian Public Service and when the support of family was needed. In addition, we older granddaughters spent our summers helping out at the Brackbill Motel—hanging sheets and towels on the line to dry, ironing pillow cases on the hot mangle, cleaning out toilets and ash trays, making up beds with the proper hospital corners, and helping to put up corn, tomatoes, beans, and apple sauce. The older grandsons worked at Uncle Harry Brackbill's Farm Markets that sold eggs, milk, meat, and fresh produce along the Philadelphia Main Line.

The Brackbill home was a center of warmth, laughter, hospitality, music, work, play, and spiritual conversations. People from many walks of life passed through this blessed milieu, and some stayed. Anita Purugganan, the Filipina schoolmate of two of my aunts, chose to live with the Brackbills instead of with her foster family. Max Thode, once a Prussian army officer, worked as a landscaper in Paoli, and in his old age, moved into a small cottage on the Brackbill farm, breaking up the soil in the flower gardens every spring with his hands. Luther Cummins, a former Freemason, was an excellent craftsman, but by the time I learned to know him, he was quite paranoid. Miss Goddard, a proper and elderly English woman, lived in a one-room apartment above the kitchen, and to my childhood amazement, took a dozen vitamin supplements every day. Aunt Katherine Rohrer was a Presbyterian-turned-Mennonite nurse, whose hands and practical skills touched many. They and countless others were all a part of the Brackbill extended family.

In Harrisonburg our family attended the College Mennonite Church on campus, which included Eastern Mennonite College students during the school year and shrank to a congregation of fifty or less during the summer. Understandably, I found the Frazer Mennonite Church, with its active youth group, a more satisfying church experience. In fact, it wasn't until I was overseas working with the Mennonite Central Committee that I realized how much my grandparents' home and church were my spiritual center. Almost all of my dreams, until my mid-thirties, took place in that old stone farmhouse with all its rooms, nooks, and crannies. It was a child's paradise!

But while there was this rich, nurturing aspect to my life as I was growing up, I was also very curious about the world beyond my "Mennonite womb." I remember one day at the Brackbill Motel when a tall, sophisticated woman came into the house to pay for her night's stay. Towering over my five-foot Mennonite-garbed grandmother, she reached down to pat my grandmother's caped shoulders and said, "You Mennonites are so wonderful, but I could not be like you." I started thinking about why, if we were so wonderful, would she not want to be like us?

## STRANDS OF SERVICE

My first significant foray into another culture came between my junior and senior years of college. During my junior year, I had taken several physical education courses at Madison College (now James Madison University) in Harrisonburg. One of my teachers told me about a summer program in New York City for underprivileged young people, called Youth Development, Inc. (YDI). She encouraged me to apply to be a counselor, which I did. In June 1963, I found myself heading to New York City to work with an organization started by Jim Vaus, who was a wiretapper for the mob before his conversion.

Living in a dormitory of Union Theological Seminary on 49th Street, I took the subway to the YDI storefront clubhouse at Hell's Gate Station in Harlem. Alternating with the boys' club, the girls' club spent two weeks in the city clubhouse, then two weeks at a wilderness camp in Lake Champion, New York. That summer, the mostly Hispanic and African-American girls taught me to sing the latest popular songs, to play cards and pool, and to tap dance. I taught them how to swim, to feel safe in the woods, and to sleep without lights and noise. Together we learned about Love and God (maybe they are the same). I kept in touch with a number of these girls until I went to Vietnam three years later. Several years ago, I got an e-mail, out of the blue, from one of them, who had gone on to become a teacher in New York City and had just retired! She had found my e-mail address on the web.

The year after graduating from Goshen College, I spent traveling with the last of three Life Teams sponsored by the Mennonite Board of Missions and Charities in Elkhart, Indiana. The Life Teams consisted of five Mennonite young people (two women and three men) in their twenties who traveled together for a year, visiting Mennonite Youth Fellowship (MYF) groups in the United States and Canada. Our team visited youth groups from Colorado west to Oregon in the U.S., from Saskatchewan west to Alberta in Canada, and from Phoenix, Arizona, north to Calling Lake, Alberta.

During the first weekend at each church, we did a lot of sharing and singing and Bible study and, before we left, we would introduce the "Thirty-Day Experiment," a program that suggested ways that youth might nurture and share their faith with others. Then in a month, we would return for another weekend to see what they had learned about themselves and their faith with the Thirty-Day Experiment.

Over the years since then, I have met some of the young people we stayed with during our year on the Life Team. For many of them, particularly for those in small, isolated congregations, probably most transforming was the opportunity to meet other Mennonite young people who were cool, fun-loving, and serious about living out their faith. For the five of us on the Life Team, it was a pretty tough year. Living so closely for that period of time with four other young people was challenging. We had our share of interpersonal issues and yet had to keep going, keep giving our testimonies about how Christ transforms us, and keep encouraging young people in the faith. Sometimes it made one feel a bit dishonest. But in the end we all remained friends and were perhaps more realistic about what it took to lead a life faithful to one's understanding of God.

The year following Life Team, I was asked to join the staff at Goshen College, to serve as director of recreation and as head resident of West Lawn dormitory. It was a difficult year. The Life Team had stirred up many theological questions. I was approaching age twenty-four, with plenty of suitors but none I wanted to marry. I continued to be interested in some kind of service opportunity overseas but had not found an open door. During my junior year at EMC, a Mennonite Mission Board representative, when I had expressed interest in overseas mission, kindly told me that they liked young women to be married before entering mission work.

It was during my year on staff at Goshen College that Orie Miller's son Bob came to the campus to recruit for Mennonite Central Committee (MCC). He encouraged me to think about service in Vietnam, which was appealing because it would give me a chance to really test my faith and my beliefs about peace in a setting of war and conflict.

## STRANDS OF LIFE IN VIETNAM

In June 1966 this young, idealistic Mennonite woman boarded a plane in Philadelphia that would take me halfway around the world to Saigon, Vietnam. That same month, U.S. bombers made their first attacks on the industrial outskirts of North Vietnam's two largest cities—Hanoi and Haiphong. The war was clearly escalating. By the end of 1966, the U.S. would have 385,000 troops in Vietnam.

I threw myself into two months of language study, determined to learn the language well. By September, I was assigned to work in a unit of Vietnam Christian Service (a coalition of organizations, including Mennonite Central Committee, Church World Service, and Lutheran World Relief) in Quang Ngai province in central Vietnam where bombing by U.S. and South Vietnamese forces had created thousands of displaced people. Our Vietnam Christian Service (VNCS) team of eight was to work in the "refugee camps" that were being set up around Quang Ngai City for the farmers being displaced from their land. We daily cooked CSM (corn, soya, and milk) porridge, responded to health needs, distributed blankets and used clothing, and did a bit of English teaching.

Because of nighttime curfews, we spent the evenings together in our unit house. The team was very ecumenical—from Mennonite, Brethren, Quaker, Methodist, and Church of God backgrounds. Our conversations during those first months together were typical of Christian college students—asking sophomoric questions like who came first, God or humans; whether only Christians will get into heaven; and why God allows suffering. Within six months, however, our unanswered questions fell silent as we witnessed the tremendous suffering and death around us, the complicity of our own country in what was happening, and the lies and deceit of our leaders.

As our innocence dropped away and our political education began, we also saw more clearly how we and our work in the refugee camps were being used to further U.S. and South Vietnamese political aims. And so our work and presence began to take different forms. We no longer bought U.S. commissary goods or used U.S. military transportation. We restricted our social life to Vietnamese and American civilian friends and requested U.S. military personnel not to come to our unit house. We ceased using and distributing U.S. commodities such as oil, flour, and milk. And we changed our work in the camps to technical training—sewing and nutrition classes for women and girls and training in small motor mechanics for men and boys—which would provide skills to the displaced farmers and help them earn a livelihood.

In the VNCS unit in Quang Ngai was another Mennonite volunteer, Earl Martin, from New Holland, Pennsylvania. We found ourselves riding bike together every day to the refugee camps and discovered that our personalities and passions were very similar. But how does one "date" when living together in the middle of a war? We found ways, perhaps risky but memorable—walking downtown at night to eat *ram*, a Quang Ngai delicacy of marinated pork wrapped in rice paper and grilled over a charcoal fire; climbing Tieng An Mountain to talk with the monks in the Buddhist pagoda; swimming in the Tra Kuc River as curious children stood and watched; and we often wandered to the perimeters of safety around the town.

There was definitely attraction, but as a Paxman, Earl was not to marry during his three years of service. Halfway through our three-year term we asked permission to marry. Paul Leatherman, the VNCS Director, came to Quang Ngai and talked personally with each team member to make sure that our marriage would not detract from our work. Being assured it would not, we were given a special dispensation to marry. What Paul Leatherman didn't know was that there were two other couples-in-the-making in the unit at the time, who were hoping they also might marry down the road, and in fact they did!

Earl and I planned our wedding for early February 1968, but unbeknownst to us, the Viet Cong (Vietnamese Communists) had their own plans. On January 31, 1968, the first day of Tet, the traditional, lunar New Year, they launched what became known as the "Tet Offensive," striking military and civilian command posts and control centers in South Vietnam, hoping to spark a general uprising among the population.

A squad of Viet Cong guerrillas occupied our town, the provincial capital of Quang Ngai province, effectively turning it into a battleground. Some were barricaded in the post office just up the street from our unit house. Others holed up in the Catholic High School, and still others entered the local jail, releasing prisoners. Helicopter gunships, with their autocannons, machine guns, rockets, and guided missiles roared overhead as we all ran for our bunkers. By evening, the grounds of the provincial hospital were filled with injured and dying people, and the bodies of the Viet Cong fighters were left in the streets for all to see.

This scenario was repeated in many provinces throughout South Vietnam. Many historians now point to the Tet Offensive as the turning point in the Vietnam War. It was also a juncture for many international organizations and personnel. Some organizations sent all of their international workers out of the country. Others, like VNCS, gave their workers the choice to leave or to stay.

Earl and I decided to stay, even though we had to postpone our wedding for a couple of months. When our three-year terms ended in 1969, it was clear that we were not yet finished with Vietnam. But we felt that the most important thing we could do to help the people of Vietnam, whom we had come to love, would be to go back to the U.S.

to help end the war. From 1969 to 1972, we were in school in California—Earl in an Asian Studies program at Stanford University and I in a graduate certificate program in occupational therapy at San Jose State University. It was a time of much ferment on university campuses. Earl and I did a lot of public speaking on campuses, in churches, and in communities. MCC sponsored us on a tour across the U.S. with the documentary, "Inside North Vietnam." It was an opportunity to humanize the "enemy" with our own stories as well.

In January 1973 the U.S. signed the Paris Peace Accords with North Vietnam which called for a withdrawal of U.S. ground troops within sixty days and a negotiated political settlement between the North and South. People displaced by the war were to be able to return to their homes. In October that same year, Earl and I headed back to Vietnam with our almost two-year-old daughter, Lara Mai. Since I was seven months pregnant with our second child, we stayed in Saigon until after the birth of our son, Minh Douglas, and then returned to Quang Ngai. As refugees began returning to their home villages and agricultural land that had been fought over for more than a decade, our assignment was to survey the problem of unexploded ordnance in those areas and to explore what technology might be available to safely detonate the munitions.

Some family members and friends questioned the wisdom of our having two small children in a war zone, but I had few qualms about our decision to return. We were going back to a town and people we knew. I had always assumed that if Jesus meant that women were to be disciples, he would know that we weren't going to be able to leave our "wives" and children behind to follow him! But thankfully, I didn't know when we arrived back in Vietnam in 1973 that in a year and a half I would be leaving Vietnam alone with my children and entering into one of the darkest times of my life.

As often happens with peace agreements, the Paris Peace Accords were not upheld. While U.S. and other foreign ground troops were no longer on Vietnamese soil, the ideological conflict between North and South Vietnam was not resolved and fighting continued. MCC had left decisions about whether and when to stay or leave up to individual workers. Earl and I decided we would stay in Quang Ngai as long as our Vietnamese friends thought it was safe for us to do so, and that if and when we decided it was time to leave, we would do so together.

In March 1975, when it became clear that the Viet Cong were about to take over our province, Earl and I decided that it was time for us to take our children and leave, anticipating that there would be major fighting. Since there was no way out of the province at that point, except by Air America, we had agreed to leave together as a family the next day. But in the wee morning hours, Earl wakened me to say that he very much wanted to stay in Quang Ngai. There was little time to protest or process since by daybreak friends were coming to the house to say their good-bys. And it became clear that I would be flying with our one- and three-year-old to Saigon alone.

The next days and weeks were intense. Three days after the children and I had left Quang Ngai, the Viet Cong took over our town, essentially without a fight. The Saigon soldiers had fled the town and the Viet Cong soldiers had marched in. The next day in Saigon a friend I knew from Quang Ngai came to tell me he had heard that an American and two Japanese had been shot and killed in Quang Ngai. After a sleepless night, I decided that while I didn't know whether that news was true, I needed to focus on our two small children who were experiencing the anxiety and uncertainty of leaving their daddy and the only home they knew or remembered. I embraced the possibility that I would be leaving Vietnam as a single parent.

On April 10, three weeks after the children and I had left our home in Quang Ngai, the MCC office in Saigon received a cable from the MCC International Headquarters in Akron, Pennsylvania They had received word via the Provisional Revolutionary Group (PRG) delegation in Paris that Earl and Hiro, a Japanese MCC worker who had joined Earl from a neighboring province after I left, were "well and working hard."

With the assurance that Earl was alive and no indication that he would be leaving soon, the children and I flew to Bangkok, Thailand, where we stayed in the YMCA until the end of April. When we got word that Earl would likely be staying in Vietnam for another three months, we flew to Lagos, Nigeria, where my folks were working with an African Independent Church, the Church of the Lord (Aladura). In August, four months after the Communist take-over, Earl finally left Vietnam and joined us in Nigeria.

Earl and I had much to talk about and a relationship to mend. We returned to the U.S. and settled in a house in the woods near my

Brackbill grandparents' home. We spent time with our children, cut our own firewood, planted a vegetable garden, raised animals, and picked apples. I worked part time in a famers' market while Earl wrote a book, *Reaching the Other Side*[1] about his experiences in Vietnam during the five months after the children and I left. During this time, our youngest son, Hans, was born at home. Little by little, over the next four years, the rhythms of life together as a family began to heal the trauma of our Vietnam experience.

## STRANDS OF LIFE IN THE PHILIPPINES

In 1979 we felt ready to once again consider an assignment overseas with MCC. With children Lara (six), Minh (four), and Hans (two), we headed off to Mindanao, the large southern island of the Philippines, where a conflict brewed between the Moro Liberation Army and the Armed Forces of the Philippines. We partnered with the Social Action Center of the Catholic Diocese of Malaybalay, Bukidnon, under the leadership of a progressive Jesuit Bishop from Bontoc, Francisco Claver. He was an outspoken opponent of martial law and a proponent of nonviolent resistance against any activity promoted by either the Philippine government or the New People's Army that adversely affected the livelihood of subsistence farmers in the barrios.

Believing that Jesus' life modeled a preferential option for the poor, the Social Action Center (SAC) monitored multinational companies operating in the province. This included Delmonte with its 30,000-hectare banana and pineapple plantation plus smaller coffee and sugar plantations persistently trying to take the land of poor farmers, many of whom did not have titles to their land. SAC also followed up on any threats, arrests, or military action in the barrios.

Earl and I found ourselves writing to American audiences about the ways that U.S. history and influence in the Philippines contributed to the poverty—both physical and spiritual—of its people. As we traveled around the islands, we looked at the role of U.S. agribusinesses and military bases in the Philippines. I narrated a video, *The Bases of our Fears*, which explored the lives of women working as "hostesses" in Olongapo and the plight of Amerasian children. And we engaged with the various political factions in the Catholic

Church as they attempted to address the causes of violence in their society.

As MCC Country Representatives, Earl and I were also administrators for MCC's programs and personnel in country. Some MCC workers were involved with Reconciliation House, a center set up to help Muslim families displaced by the conflict in Mindanao. Others were relating to the women and children in Olongapo, the sprawling town outside the U.S. Naval Base in Subic Bay. The 262-square-mile Subic Bay Naval Base, just north of Manila, was at the time the largest U.S. military installation outside the U.S. mainland. Almost 15,000 women worked in the bars and clubs used by U.S. servicemen on leave for R&R (rest and recreation) or waiting as their ships were being repaired or resupplied.

Our children thrived in the small-town setting of Malaybalay, where they were quickly adopted by the warm and generous families in our neighborhood. The laboratory school at the Bukidnon State (teacher's training) College was an ideal place for our children to begin school; they quickly picked up the local language and made friends. It was difficult for all of us to leave our Filipino friends at the end of our three-and-one-half year term in 1982.

## STRANDS OF LIFE IN THE UNITED STATES

Back in the U.S., we settled in Washington, D.C., where Earl worked at the MCC Washington Office and I worked as an occupational therapist at a center for multiple-handicapped, low-income children. Our children fit happily into our diverse neighborhood school, Janney Elementary, excelling as "immigrant" children often do. So when MCC called in early 1984, inviting Earl and me to consider sharing the job of administering MCC's programs and personnel in East Asia, we were not overly enthusiastic.

Ten-year-old Minh said we could leave but he was going to stay in D.C., even if it meant he had to sleep on the street. Lara, then a wise twelve-year-old, said that she would be willing to move one more time, but we had to agree that we would not move again until she graduated from high school—a promise that we kept.

Using the Quaker discernment process, and with much thought and prayer, we finally agreed to take the job in Akron, Pennsylvania, with both of us working half-time. During the spring before our move, I spent two months in Cambodia as interim country representative, a wonderful opportunity for me, but a very difficult time for Earl, who had to juggle a job and three children. When I returned home in June, Earl, who had just celebrated his fortieth birthday, was in a full-blown, midlife crisis. For him, the job in Akron was a return to his Lancaster County roots and raised the prospect in his mind that he might never be able to do all the things he had hoped to do with his life. The concern for me was how Earl and I, with our very different working and relational styles, would be able to share a job.

But move we did, settling into a "wooden tent" (the house had no insulation) along the Cocalico Creek in nearby Ephrata. We deliberately chose a low-income neighborhood and imagined ourselves creating community, much like we did in Asia, with our neighbors in the trailer park next to our property. But we were to discover that poverty in the U.S. was unlike poverty in Asia. It was more a poverty of spirit, of imagination, of supportive networks.

We also discovered that the Mennonite communities of our childhood were very different from the communities of popular culture to which our children were being exposed. We did not always share the values of parents of our children's friends. So parenting in the laissez faire methods of our parents and grandparents did not always provide adequate guidance for our "third culture kids" who were trying to sort out identities in a mostly white, rural community where Mennonites were "dumb yonies" (which we figured out later probably referred to Earl's great-grandfather, Jonas Martin, the Old Order Mennonite Bishop who in 1893 led his conservative followers out of the Lancaster Conference, forming the Weaverland Conference).

Our lives, which during our MCC years in Asia were part of an integrated whole—where family, community, church, school, and friends overlapped—were now fractured into many, often competing parts. We lived in the community where our children went to school, but our friends and associates were a part of other communities. We traveled twenty minutes to a church in Lancaster City and our work was focused 6,000 miles away in East Asia. Earl and I each traveled to Asia separately two times a year for three or four weeks at a stretch. And as often happens, our one full-time job, to be shared equally between us, demanded more and more of our time.

After eight years as co-secretaries for MCC's East Asia program, Earl and I decided in 1992 that it was time to do something else. MCC Vietnam needed interim country representatives for six months and we were both eager for a chance to experience life in the northern part of the country. Our two older children, Lara and Minh, were already in college. Hans, a high school sophomore, eagerly joined us in this adventure, attending an international school in Hanoi for the second half of his tenth grade.

When we returned to the U.S. in summer 1993, I took my GREs and applied to the MA program at the Institute for Conflict Analysis and Resolution (ICAR) at George Mason University in Fairfax, Virginia. Peacebuilding as a field of study was about a decade old, and I was interested in learning more about it. It felt like we needed peacebuilding skills in much of the work we had been doing with MCC, so I was ready to bring my stories and experiences to the classroom. While the Conflict Transformation Program at EMC was not yet up and running, John Paul Lederach encouraged me to take some of the courses he was teaching. In fall 1993, I took nine credit hours with John Paul—an undergraduate course (with graduate reading and writing requirements), a seminary course, and an independent study.

By the spring semester of 1994, I had been accepted into ICAR at George Mason and began commuting to Fairfax for my courses. I also started working part time at the Lancaster Mediation Center. As their training coordinator, I went into schools to give training to students in peer mediation. I also did some mediation of interpersonal conflicts, some training in mediation skills to adults, some specialized training of youth who were in trouble with the law, and some intervention in church conflicts. My life was again very full.

## STRANDS OF MENTAL ILLNESS

In February 1995, during his senior year of high school, our youngest son had a psychotic break. Hans had had a rough readjustment when we returned to the U.S. from Vietnam in summer 1993. He did not reconnect with his old friends at Ephrata High School and did not take up basketball, a sport he had loved. He began spending his time writing dark poetry and hanging out with kids on the fringe.

By the beginning of his senior year, his teachers were observing that this bright, talented, and gentle young man was isolating himself, skipping school, not completing assignments, and obviously troubled.

Hans' psychotic break was the beginning of our family's introduction to mental illness. During the next nine years, Hans was in and out of hospitals and treatment centers, spent time in homeless shelters and jails, and hitchhiked around the country fleeing the unrelenting voices in his head. On his twenty-eighth birthday, Hans was released from Hopewell, a therapeutic community in Ohio for people with long-term mental illness.

After three months in this supportive community, Hans seemed finally ready to accept responsibility for his own recovery. That meant taking his medications as prescribed, staying away from street drugs and alcohol, seeking out support groups, finding steady work, nurturing the spiritual part of himself, and learning how to manage the negative voices in his head.

Earl and I were also on a steep learning curve during these years, so much of it seemingly counter-intuitive. We had to learn how to let go and allow Hans to make his own decisions, even when they were destructive. We walked ourselves through Hans' probable early death many times. We had to learn how to set boundaries and to pay attention to our own needs. We had to learn how to be gentle with ourselves and with each other. The sometimes competitiveness in our marriage was tempered by something that we both wanted more than anything else—healing and well-being for our son.

During the first several years of Hans' illness, Earl was storytelling for MCC and was sometimes away from home for two to three weeks at a time. It soon became apparent that I would need to drop out of school to be more available for Hans, which I did. But when we moved to Harrisonburg in January 1997 for me to continue my MA studies in the newly operational Conflict Transformation Program (CTP) at EMU, Earl agreed to find work that would make him more available for Hans. His work as a self-employed carpenter was such that Hans was able to learn carpentry skills as he worked with Earl and his fellow sub-contractors.

## STRANDS OF THE SUMMER PEACEBUILDING INSTITUTE AND THE OPEN TABLE COMMUNITY

In 1998 I finished the requirements for an MA in Conflict Transformation and began working as co-director of the Summer Peacebuilding Institute (SPI). One of my goals in getting my MA in conflict studies was to work internationally again, this time using my skills in conflict transformation. Hans' illness made that impossible. Working with SPI, however, was the best job imaginable for my skills, interests, and experiences. As director of SPI, the world came to me!

*Pat in Summer Peacebuilding Institute, 2004.*
Photo by Eastern Mennonite University

In summer 1997 another CTP student, Tammy Krause, and I decided to look around for a large house that would have enough space for international students to live together with us. There were several male, foreign students in our class and we realized how difficult it was for them to feed themselves, get around on foot, manage phone bills, find meaningful social interactions, etc.

We found the perfect house at 1013 College Avenue, just one block south of the campus. The Jacob and Lucy Shenk house had five bedrooms and two baths. The upstairs had already been renovated and had a kitchenette. It was a perfect boarding house and the rent was affordable, so Tammy, Earl, and I moved in. We had our first renters that summer—two Intensive English Program students from Taiwan. In the fall, two CTP students from Africa—a Muslim woman from Somalia and a Methodist pastor from Mozambique—moved in with us. Together we shared meals, costs of living, and upkeep of the property. We named ourselves the "Open Table Community."

By 1999 the two apartments in the Shenk Hatchery next door to our house were vacated, and we asked the Shenk family if we could sublet those apartments to students as well. In 2000, the living community had expanded to fourteen residents and a special dining table with eight boards that could seat twenty-four people was made by one of the residents. By this time we were taking turns preparing an evening meal to share together as a community. In 2002, when a Pakistani Muslim family of five moved into the upstairs of our house, we started sharing only one meal a week together.

From 1997 to the present, about 120 people have lived in the Open Table Community. More than half were MA students at the Center for Justice and Peacebuilding. The rest were EMU and JMU (James Madison University) students or recent graduates, family members and friends of residents, transfer students, Fulbright research scholars, SPI participants, and a few locals needing temporary housing. There have been three marriages in the Open Table Community and four babies born while their parents lived in the community.

These years have been rich in learning and sharing. We have consciously been an interfaith community. One fall semester, we had three women living upstairs—a Buddhist from Sri Lanka, a Muslim from Kurdistan in Iraq, and a Christian from Korea. Then as now, we take turns preparing the community meal, and whoever cooks is also invited to bless our food and the gathering in whatever way and in whichever language they choose. As we linger over meals, often with additional guests, our conversations turn to religion or politics or humor or family stories or events of the day. Nothing is off limits. And I can't remember a time when any of us left the table with an empty stomach or spirit. Shared meals are a time of sacred communion, perhaps not unlike what Jesus had in mind in saying that When you break bread and share a cup of wine, you do it in remembrance of me.

## STRANDS OF LIFE IN RETIREMENT

In summer 2008 I retired as director of the Summer Peacebuilding Institute. I felt the need to be more active physically, and I craved more time to reflect on all that has transpired in my life and in the life of our family the past years. There has certainly been trauma and anger and doubt. But with our son Hans now at a stable place in his recovery, there has been a renewal of faith and a bubbling of joy in life once again. Our children are all finding meaningful work and relationships.

Our daughter Lara, age forty-one, lives in San Francisco, California, and works in restoration of the San Francisco Bay for the Audubon Society and for San Francisco State University. Our son Minh, age thirty-nine, lives in Charlottesville, Virginia, and works as a glassblower. He is married to Anna Shapiro and has one child, seven-year-old Sophia. Our son Hans, age thirty-six, is presently living in Mesopotamia, Ohio. He is working as a volunteer at Hopewell, the therapeutic farming community where he was a resident in 2004.

We have been through the fires of hell and have hopefully become more thoughtful and compassionate people in the process. I have always wanted to be a healer, but I didn't realize how much work was needed to get me to a place where I was ready to be a channel of healing, to be truly alive to the compassion that stirs in the depth of my soul.

Since my retirement, I have found chaplaincy to be a wonderful way to connect me with people in this community. After two years of clinical pastoral education training, I have been working as a chaplain at Rockingham Memorial Hospital with Hospice, and in the Harrisonburg/Rockingham County Jail. It seems like a gift to be able to touch people's lives with spiritual care at times of uncertainty, of transition, of crisis, and on occasions of birth, illness, incarceration, and death.

I have never felt called to pastoral ministry in the church. Perhaps because in earlier years, the Mennonite church was not ready for women to be pastors, but perhaps, not unlike Simone Weil, I have, in recent years, felt called to stand "at the intersection of Christianity and everything that is not Christianity."[2] I want to be with people who feel that God has forgotten them. I want to share bread with the hungry, water with the thirsty, freedom with the captives, sight with the blind, healing with the sick, good news with the poor, and hope with the oppressed.

## STRANDS OF RELIGIOUS EXPERIENCES

The roots of my Mennonite ancestors go back to the Anabaptists of Europe. I remember spending time in the EMC library as an eighth grader, pouring over the stories and pictures of the *Martyr's Mirror* and wondering when it would be my turn to suffer for my faith. I was a very conscientious child who always tried to do the right thing. And when I told a lie or did something I knew was wrong, my conscience would bother me until I sought forgiveness.

During the era of my childhood, there was a strong evangelistic movement in the Mennonite church, which created anxiety for me as a sensitive child trying to do the right thing. One of the few memories I have of Manheim, Pennsylvania, where I lived the first four years of my life, was being in church when a minister gave an invitation, asking for a show of hands if anyone wanted to confess their sins. I was scratching my head at the same time that the minister said, "I see that hand." He then invited all those who raised their hands to come to the front of the church when the service was over. I was so afraid that I went immediately to our car after church, closed all the windows, locked all the doors, and got down on the floor so I couldn't be found!

Some years later, after our family moved to Harrisonburg, I remember one Sunday evening when our youth teacher was telling us the story of how lambs were used in Old Testament times to carry the sins of the people away into the desert, whereas in New Testament times, Jesus became the lamb of God who would take our sins away. Then she asked her class of grade school children how many of us wanted Jesus to take away our sins. In innocence, I raised my hand, assuming that we would all want Jesus to take our sins away, but I quickly became aware that our teacher put special meaning into my raised hand. She asked me after the class whether that night I would tell my parents what I did that or whether she should. I felt terrified and assured her that I would tell them.

I was baptized at nine years of age, I suppose because I wanted to be in the same class with my older sister. I also thought that baptism would make me perfect, "even as our Father in heaven is perfect." How sadly disappointed I was when I realized the next day that my feelings of irritation at my brothers continued, that baptism hadn't really changed me as I had expected! But I was a seeker and kept learning more about what it meant to be a follower in the way of Jesus.

Living in Vietnam as a young adult was a time of exposure to new experiences, new ideas, and new religious expressions and beliefs. I observed our neighbors paying respect to the ancestors every first and fifteenth day of the lunar calendar. I watched as people left bowls of rice for the spirits (and birds) to eat. I was touched by the Buddhist monks and nuns who took to the streets during the war to make a plea to leaders on both sides of the conflict to cease the shedding of blood of brothers and sisters. I was also aware that many of the Vietnamese Protestant pastors we knew supported U.S. involvement in their country's struggle and were eager to get as much money and material aid as possible for themselves and their churches. I struggled with these contradictions.

I began to read books on Buddhism and was particularly drawn to Zen Buddhism, which tends to emphasize the discovery of the Divine through direct, experiential knowledge gained through meditation and religious practice, rather than through the study of religious texts and theological discussions. It appealed to a deeply intuitive and spiritual part of me that was barely touched by the emphasis on correct beliefs and works of my Mennonite faith.

On our way home after our first three years in Vietnam, we spent time in France at Plum Village, where Zen Master Thich Nhat Hanh lives. As we washed dishes together one evening, he talked about the importance of mindfulness, of paying attention to what you are doing at every moment. When you wash dishes, you smell the soap and feel the water temperature, the patterns on a dish, the texture of cloth. Mindfulness means not rushing through washing dishes to do something else. When you wash dishes, you simply wash dishes. I have found this Buddhist concept of mindfulness to help me connect the inner life of Spirit with the outer life of service and action.

There were many other people during our time in Vietnam who helped to open up my world view, who helped me take God out of the Mennonite box. Trinh was one such person. During our second term in Vietnam, we tried to live like the Vietnamese around us—in a simple house with no indoor plumbing or electricity. With two small children, it was clear that we would need help to go to the market every day, cook meals, carry water, wash clothes, and care for the children. A friend recommended Trinh, a young woman who lived in one of the refugee camps near town.

Trinh was nineteen years old with a fourth-grade education. She had grown up in rural Quang Ngai province where we lived. Her father had died of small pox, leaving her mother with five children. Some years later, Trinh's mother was killed when an American napalm bomb was dropped on their village. The children were forced to leave their ancestral land. Her older brother joined the Communist guerrillas and went to North Vietnam for military training. Her older sister married a South Vietnamese soldier.

Trinh and her younger brother and sister went to live in one of the refugee camps near Quang Ngai City. Her younger brother laid low in the camp so as not to be drafted by either army. Her younger sister was permanently crippled by a Viet Cong mortar fired into the camp. And Trinh had stories of being detained by American soldiers, of rubbing her face and arms with charcoal so as not to look attractive to them, for fear of being raped. But despite the traumas and losses of her life, this young peasant woman, darkened from life in the sun and standing not more than five feet tall, was one of the most joyous people I had ever met. At a time in my life when I often felt overwhelmed, her spirit was a daily lift to my soul—another contradiction to my childhood belief that only Christians were truly happy!

I have also been deeply influenced by Quaker persons, worship, and thought. The American Friends Service Committee had a hospital in the town of Quang Ngai where we lived. The hospital offered rehabilitation and prosthetics for Vietnamese who had lost limbs during the war. We grew quite close to a number of the Quaker volunteers staffing the hospital over the years. So when we were in school in California between our two terms in Vietnam, and far from any Mennonite congregation, we attended a silent Friends Meeting.

I found the time for listening, for reflection, for prayer to be just what my spirit needed, but I sorely missed the music of my Mennonite upbringing. We found others who liked to sing and began gathering to sing a half-hour before the regular meeting. I have become aware over the years of how central music is to worship for me. But I also often long for more silence and fewer words. During our three-and-one-half years working in the Philippines, we attended the large Catholic cathedral in town. Again, it was the music that appealed to me. I can still sing many of the songs of the mass we learned in Cebuano, though I have lost most of my ability to speak the language.

I had a "conversion" experience in this Catholic Church as well. One sultry Sunday afternoon, as I was in the line moving slowly toward the front of the church to receive the Eucharist (the bishop had given us permission to do so), it occurred to me that I might be communing with people who were enemies of the farmers we worked with in the barrios—the military and paramilitary who harassed the farmers, the jailers who tortured people they considered political prisoners, and the landlords and town fathers who sided with the wealthy.

But then, as the rays of afternoon light touched me (or was it light from farther away), I began to think how very appropriate that this Mennonite woman—whose people have historically separated themselves into communities of faith to preserve their purity and to be a "light on the hill"—was now sharing the body and blood of Christ with such people since she is in as much need of God's grace as they are.

My years of working in Asia and with the Summer Peacebuilding Institute have awakened me to the richness of interfaith exchanges. I have learned so much from the religious cauldron of Asia and from the many students who have lived with us. Not only do I understand more about the beliefs and values of other faiths, I now understand my own faith better. For instance, in visiting Iran several years ago, I observed the fundamentalism of Shia Islam in that country and became aware that the reason I could understand Islamic fundamentalism so well was because I was exposed to Christian fundamentalism as I was growing up, listening to my grandfather discuss premillennial and postmillennial views with people around his dining room table!

Thich Nhat Hanh has written many popular books on Buddhism. The one I most like is *Living Buddha, Living Christ*. He enhances my understanding of my own faith by the fresh ways that he approaches many Christian concepts through his understanding of his own faith. Sometimes we can see ourselves best through the eyes of others. Gandhi is quoted as saying to missionary Stanley Jones, "I love Christ. It's just that so many of you Christians are so unlike Christ."[3]

I have come to the conclusion that true religion, wherever it may be found, manifests what Christians call "the fruits of the Spirit." Perhaps Menno Simons, an early Anabaptist leader, says it best:

*True evangelical faith ... cannot lay dormant; but manifests itself in all righteousness and works of love; it ... clothes the naked; feeds the hungry; consoles the afflicted; shelters the miserable; aids and consoles all the oppressed; returns good for evil; serves those that injure it; prays for those that persecute it.*[4]

And so the braiding, strand by strand, continues to bring meaning to the journey.

March 1, 2010<br>Revised May 2013

## Notes

1. *Reaching the Other Side: The Journal of an American Who Stayed to Witness Vietnam's Postwar Transition* (New York, N.Y.: Crown Publishers, Inc., 1978).

2. Simon Weil, *Waiting for God* (New York, N.Y.: Harper Perennial Modern Classics), 32.

3. James Edward Stroud, *The Knights Templar and the Protestant Reformation: The Case for a Modern-Day Monk* (Maitland, Fl.: Xulon Press, 2011).

4. Menno Simons, 1539, "Why I Do Not Cease Teaching and Writing," *The Complete Writings of Menno Simons*, trans. Leonard Verduin and ed J. C. Wenger (Scottdale, Pa.: Herald Press, 1956), 307.

*Earl S. Martin*

---

**Prophetic Peace Advocate**

*Vulnerable compassionate service encapsulates the story of Earl Martin's entire life. Earl was in Vietnam in the 1960s and '70s during and after the war; MCC administrator and story-teller in the '80s and early 90's; then carpenter and prophetic peace witness—always remaining a parachurch traveler, an ambassador of justice, and a riveting teller of tales. Too bad he's not Catholic, for if Earl's ecumenical mennonitism practiced the religious art of beatification, Earl would be destined for sainthood.*

**EARL S. MARTIN**

## Bread Boys and Woodcutters

What prompted him to awaken so early we cannot know. But the almost six-year-old lad felt the excitement of a new experience coming on. The oft-creaky farmhouse lay dark and silent with its seven sleeping children and two parents—or so he thought. The young boy, sharing a bed with his next older brother Bob, threw aside the covers and jumped out into the chilly room. He made his way down the creaky steps, relishing the excitement of entering the kitchen, indeed, entering the new day, before anyone else had stirred. He was the first!

But when he pushed open the kitchen door at the bottom of the stairs, he discovered, with some amazement and a touch of disappointment, that perhaps he had not been first to rise. The kitchen light was on. The boy scanned the scene. Everything was in its place. The wood cook stove sat cold along the north wall. The new Philco, recently replacing the old ice box, stood shining on the east wall. To the right, the kitchen table, where the brood ate all their meals, sat covered with the familiar red-and-white checkered oilcloth.

But wait! At the far end of the table lay the family Bible. Open! That was weird. Normally the Bible was perched up on the clock shelf right above the far end of the "little boys' bench." Right above the place where he usually sat. But now it lay open . . . on the table.

And yet no one was around! Strange indeed. He tiptoed toward the front room, still dark, to investigate this conundrum. The rocking chair, the stuffed chair, the coal stove, the hassock all sat silent . . . and empty. Who could be up at this hour?

The parlor! How about the parlor? The parlor was a special room. You mostly went to the parlor to sing around the piano as sister Mary played. Or to look through the few, old, grey-covered books in the corner bookcase, such as, *What Every Boy of 16 Ought to Know*. Or when company came. The parlor's double doors were now shut. But you must remember how the warped main door never latched quite properly. Now the curious boy tiptoed over and peeked through the crack between the doors. There in the half-light of early morning he saw a dim silhouette that remains etched forever in his memory—a great man kneeling at the davenport in prayer. Could it be? That every morning before he would head out to milk Sooky or to hoe long hours in the corn field, this bronze-skinned farmer would rise and kneel before his Maker, communing—one on one—with the Great God of the Universe?

### From Certainty to Questioning

My childhood brimmed with goodness and well-being. Work abounded: washing dishes, mowing the yard, hanging up wash. Most often the work was domestic, for I was the "baby boy," following oldest sister Mary and four older brothers who would be chosen to work with Pop in the fields. But we played too—homemade games like "Chicken," when we "hens" would lay eggs (the little early apples from the smokehouse in the back yard) in our hidden nests, then cry, "cut-cut-cadocket" and run off before the designated "rooster" could come and find our nest.

Despite the goodness and security of the community in which I grew up, there was always an element of mystery in this world as well. There were train tracks just north of our thirty-five acre farm. Where might they lead? And who were the "road walkers" who showed up at our farm to sleep in the loose hay in the barn after feasting on Mom's egg sandwiches and smokehouse apple sauce? What adventures might they store under their warm stocking caps?

And who dropped those latex balloons we found filled with slime along the woodsy stretch of gravel road on our way to Maple Grove, my one-room school house? What were they all about? I sensed even then that a wondrous, intriguing world lay outside of my secure Mennonite and Amish community in New Holland, Pennsylvania.

There were, however, occasional touches of anxiety that invaded my consciousness. In my adolescence, I remember noticing, with some relief, days that were cloudless, because I could be sure that the Lord—who would come "through the clouds in the sky"—would not be appearing today for an accounting of my days! What does a touch of fear do to a child's formation?

But by my halcyon years at Garden Spot High School, any theological uncertainties were left behind and I became a prime candidate for the certainty-producing ethos of Youth for Christ. YFC seemed zippier, more demanding of spiritual zealousness, than my Mennonite Youth Fellowship of the more staid New Holland Mennonite Church. I became an ardent Bible quizzer—my team winning in Lancaster, then in regionals at Ocean City, and finally to national competition at Winona Lake, the fundamentalist haven of evangelist Billy Sunday. I was impressed with movies at YFC like *Communist Encirclement*, where in fear-inducing scenes, we witnessed one country after another on the world map suddenly engulfed in a sea of red. "Bloop!" There went Russia. "Bloop!" There went Eastern Europe. "Bloop!" There went China. "Bloop!" North Vietnam. "Bloop." Cuba. "Bloop!" "Bloop!" "Bloop!" They would soon be at our borders!

So during the presidential campaign of 1960, I piled into a car with some high school buddies to drive twelve miles west to Lancaster. After chasing the visiting motorcade around the city for a while, we finally caught up with them at the Lancaster airport, where I ran across an open field toward the slow-moving convertible to thrust my hand into the outstretched hand of the man who would save the U.S. from its first Catholic in the White House: Richard Milhous Nixon.

But I resisted the attraction of continuing the YFC trajectory of going to Moody Bible Institute or Philadelphia College of Bible immediately after high school and instead stayed out of school for a year. A merciful year later, I hitch-hiked to Hesston College in Kansas, with a duffle bag filled with my red Bible, a picture of my high school sweetheart, and a few boxer shorts.

The feasts of such freedom were sumptuous. Bible study and prayer groups. Good-hearted debates about the ways of God and humans in our world. Gospel Teams off to the Ozarks. And being elected president of the campus Young People's Christian Association

(YPCA), the leading expression of what seemed to matter most at Hesston.

But it was also a heady time of exploration. Hitch-hiking to a bar in Newton with a date one night to discover a world outside the Mennonite cocoon. The drinks, I tell you, were nothing more than Cokes and Pepsis, but those experiences were no less intoxicating for the adventure of tasting that world beyond. But most inebriating of all was the permission to graze theological and cosmological pastures that I had never before encountered.

Strangely perhaps, I believe the most life-changing course I was ever to take in school was none other than Clayton Beyler's Survey of the Old Testament. Beyler invited us to see the Scriptures not as a compendium of dictums and immutable instructions but as a gathering of stories of a people who sought to know and understand, however imperfectly, their world and their God. So far was this from my high school inclination to view the Bible as a normative catalog of aphorisms for human behavior that I was emboldened to begin questioning many assumptions that had once seemed so very rock-sure.

By the second year at Hesston, this orgy of questioning and doubt led me to place on the bulletin board by my desk a three-by-five card with my ultimate sophomoric question, "Who came first—God or man?" The dissonance between being expected to be a spiritual on campus in my YPCA role and the spiritual wringer washer tossing and battering my soul was at times excruciating. (John A. T. Robinson's *Honest to God* treatise made some sense to me during this time.)

Wandering in this spiritual wilderness, I decided to enroll at Penn State for my junior year, thinking a secular school might provide less discord for my search. But though my Jewish, Unitarian, and Christian dorm-mates were endlessly kind to me, I found myself standing outside a student lounge one night looking in on the throng of my fellow students dancing and laughing to the hard beat of the latest rock stars and had to face my isolation: I didn't know how to dance—at least not to that music!

## Walking into War

Plan B. Now's the time! I had known forever that someday I would set sail for the great world beyond. Ever since childhood preacher Noah Sauder spoke of communicating by "signs and wonders" when he visited Israel. "We made signs and they wondered." Ever since older brother Aaron mounted a world map on our front room wall which he wired with lights indicating all the Mennonite Central Committee relief and Mennonite mission positions around the world. Ever since Junji Yamamoto from Japan lived with our family for a summer. Ever since older brother Luke joined Pax Service to build houses for refugees in Bachnang, Germany, and Brother Ray worked with camel herders in Somalia.

My letter of inquiry to the Mennonite Central Committee in 1965 brought a quick reply. They needed relief workers in Vietnam and the Congo. If my theological certainties had now become more uncertain, perhaps a war zone would give opportunity to help define what truly mattered most to me. My parents supported this move. Pop always said that he felt his sons, as conscientious objectors, should be open to the same kinds of risks and dangers as Frank Ludwig, the neighbor boy who was drafted into the U.S. Army.

After expeditious processing and orientation, I landed in Saigon in January 1966, as the United States government was drastically escalating the war. Oh the utter thrill of tasting strange, new foods, of cruising the city streets and country roads on motor scooters, of twisting my tongue around new sounds like, *"Toi cung khong cam on Chi Ba."* After two months of language study, I headed 500 miles north to the backwater province of Quang Ngai where fighting had been especially heavy.

As I was going to bed that first night in Quang Ngai, a cannon blast, "WHOOMH!" seemed to nearly blow down our house. And again, "HA-WHOOM!" It became a nightly ritual that we would have to get used to. U.S. servicemen, at the artillery base on the edge of town, would fire their 105mm and 155mm howitzers every evening as "harassment and interdiction." "H&I fire," the army captain later explained to me, "is just to keep the enemy in the countryside off balance." But the countryside was precisely where the farmers lived. Often in the mornings we would see farmers with bamboo poles and stretched hammocks over their shoulders, carrying wounded neighbors into the hospital in town.

\* \* \*

One evening soon after I arrived in Quang Ngai, I kicked off my sandals and climbed into my cot under the mosquito net for the night. Soon from out on the street I heard the plaintive cry: *Banh mi day! Banh mi nong gion day.* "Bread here! Hot, crisp bread here!" I couldn't resist. I slipped back into my sandals and hurried out to the front gate. I could hear the H&I fire: HA-WHOOM. HA-WHOOM. From our front gate, by the light of a flickering, florescent street light, I could see the lad coming down the street, bread bag swinging across his back like a flare on a tiny parachute.

*Earl swapping stories with Vietnamese bread boys in Quang Ngai Province, 1966.*

*Em oi, lay day, toi muon mua banh mi!* I called to the boy. "Lad, come here, I'd like to buy some bread." He came toward me, pulling the bread bag off his shoulder. We exchanged greetings and I told him I'd like to buy a loaf of bread. As he dug into his bag, I tried to make conversation:

"Where do you live?"

*O dang kia,* "Down that way," he replied.

"And where do you go to school?" I inquired.

"How can I go to school without my parents to pay the fees?" he said with some pain in his voice.

"And where are your parents?" I asked.

*Mat.* "Gone."
*Mat sao?* "How gone?" I asked.
*Ca-nong.* "The cannons."

I swallowed hard. I understood all too well the fate of this lad before me. I paid him for the bread, and begged him to return often. Then I watched him go, off into the night.

*Banh mi day. Banh mi nong gion day.*

I hear him still, all these decades later. I hear this little priest—in all the homeless shelters, in all the war-torn streets of the world—call out to us: *Banh mi day.* "Come, this is my body, broken for you. Come, eat, in remembrance of me."

\*\*\*

Amid this warfare, I came to know people who had lived under the artillery blasts, under the rockets, under the 200-pound bombs, under the blazing jellied gasoline of napalm, and yet had found a way to go on. What amazed me most was the apparent lack of bitterness that I witnessed from our friends and neighbors in the refugee camps. One refugee woman explained to me that when they still lived in their countryside homes, the fighter planes or the helicopter gunships would appear without warning. To survive they had to dig a deep bunker room and live under ground. They had to do their farming at night time to avoid the spotter planes that circled overhead in the day, always watching and ready to call in a rocket at anything that moved in this "free fire zone." Still, these dislocated farmers were ever so kind to us as Americans even though they knew those bombers came from our country.

The other amazing feature of those early months in Quang Ngai came in the heart-quickening form of a young woman from the Shenandoah Valley in Virginia. Pat Hostetter had also volunteered to serve in this war zone and joined our Quang Ngai team six months after I had arrived. With her dark, attractive features and long, braided hair, many Vietnamese insisted that Pat must be *Viet-lai*, half Vietnamese. As fortune would have it, Pat and I began taking daily trips on our bicycles the six kilometers out to the Rung Lang or Bau Giang refugee camps to distribute food or blankets, or to teach English, or to organize sewing and motor mechanics classes for the youth who were forced from their countryside homes because of the fighting.

Well, over the next year-and-a-half we took just one too many bike rides together and on March 23, 1968, we two innocents abroad were joined in holy, hilarious matrimony, with Vietnamese friends jamming our house, helicopters flying overhead, and the neighborhood children cheering at the windows.

## Where Is God?

Pat and I, together with our teammates in Quang Ngai, would sometimes gather in the kitchen at night to eat hot French bread smeared with home-made peanut butter or jam and discuss the events of the day: the bus that hit a mine—intended for an American tank—planted on Highway One by the Viet Cong, spewing the bodies of dead and wounded over the road, or a burning white American phosphorus flare that had been launched in the middle of the night, but a faulty parachute sent it crashing through the tile roof of the house of Thay Chi, a high school teacher friend of ours, and onto their sleeping one-year-old son, burning him to death. The village of My Lai lay only six miles from our house where on March 16, 1968, just days before our wedding, American soldiers of Charlie Company entered the village and within four hours 504 unarmed villagers—men, women, children, and babies, as later testimony revealed—lay dead.

Where was God in all this?, we would implore each other. Why do the innocent suffer? Was God asleep? Did God not care? Was God powerless to stop this?

Over time, as we noticed in retrospect, we seemed to stop discussing these unanswerable questions because, well, perhaps precisely because they seemed so unanswerable. The only thing that seemed answerable was this: Given the suffering around us, how were we going to respond to that suffering? We did less theologizing and more walking closely in solidarity, in grief, in anger, in celebration with the people we met from day to day.

And so on the morning of the death of Thay Chi's son, when I visited their home and learned the heart-breaking news, I happened to notice under a banana tree in their front yard the charred block of the murderous flare. In anguish and rage I picked it up and noted its olive drab casing was stamped "U.S. Navy Lot No. 624847914" or some such number. I strapped that flare onto the back of my bicycle and went pedaling off furiously toward the American military command post. Without stopping at the guard gate I stormed into the office of the captain and set that death-dealing flare down on his desk, crying, "You've got to stop this war. This war is killing innocents."

## Living Within the Empire

When we came back to the U.S. after those initial three years in Vietnam, our hearts burned within us. How could our nation, professing such lofty principles, wage such a cruel war against a people halfway around the world who had never threatened our country? And how could Christians, even our fellow Mennonites, who claimed to be people of peace, blithely pay taxes without protest to fund the killing of our friends in Vietnam?

We wrote articles. We poured out our stories in churches all across the U.S. We knocked on doors of Congress and sat down with officials in the National Security Council and the White House to plead for an end to this devastating war. While studying for three years in California, we spoke in campus-wide "teach-ins," sharing the simple stories of the Vietnamese people we had come to love. One night we were on the Stanford University campus. Antiwar radicals were lined up to throw rocks at the Electronics Lab which had a Pentagon contract; the Police Tac Squad was lined up by the building to fire their tear gas and swing their batons. We found ourselves, together with friends in the Gandhian nonviolence house, standing between those two lines of rock-throwers and tear gas-throwers.

Were we being theologically pure? Frankly that was not a question we were asking then. When friends are burning, when friends are bleeding, we are not called to be pure. We are called to be engaged. Step up to the line. March through the streets. Tell the emperor and his officials that we will not support their war on the innocents.

And no, we cannot willfully give our money to the emperor to buy napalm and Agent Orange poisons to drop on our friends in Vietnam. We cannot pay for war anymore! To willfully pay the tax the government claims for war-making would be tantamount to having a man rush into our kitchen and demand a butcher knife so that he can go next door and kill our neighbor . . . and we would give him the knife! No, no way.

Sure, come and seize our car and sell it for your tax, as you threaten. Sure, place a lien on our house until you find a way to seize the money. That's okay. But giving you this money without protest—without calling you, Mr. Official, to responsibility for the killing of our brothers and sisters? No. A hundred-fold No!

Ah now, were we a bit self-righteous during those days? Did we often unload our passions on our families and friends who felt they were in little position to affect the war? Did we become so outraged at our own nation's crimes of war that we may have downplayed the killings by the other side in this war? Yes. Yes. Probably yes.

Happily, we came to learn that within the church a small but significant number of folks were writing letters against the war. Some were even refusing to pay war taxes. And when we stopped to listen, we discovered that most of our friends and family members did cry in their souls and in their prayers for an end to war.

## Vietnam Reprise

After the Paris Peace Accords were signed in 1973 and the U.S. ground troops returned home, Pat and I returned to Quang Ngai with our two small children. Many of the refugees we had known were returning to their homes and fields in the countryside after ten years of war. Of great concern to everyone were the millions of unexploded munitions left lying in the soil. Our MCC assignment was to do research and come up with options for cleaning up some of the unexploded ordnance left lying in the farmers' fields.

Mr. Quang, a local farmer who had spent nine years in a refugee camp, went back to his home in the countryside as the war was winding down. He knew there might be grenade duds in his field because the M-79 grenade launcher was a favorite weapon of the Americans to defend their nearby artillery post. Mr. Quang first went down on his hands and knees and combed through the grass with his fingers. There! He felt its smooth side. Ever so carefully, he dislodged the unexploded grenade from the soil and carried it over and dropped it into a dry, abandoned well. Boom! The explosion hurled a spray of dirt and stones up from the bottom of the well. He combed with his fingers through all the weeds in his field, the size of a basketball court. He dislodged twelve dud grenades and dropped them into the well.

Only then did he swing his broad-bladed hoe into the soil to turn it so he could plant rice for the first time in a decade. He didn't hoe even five minutes before his hoe found the thirteenth grenade.

The explosion threw him on his back, ripped off his conical hat, and broke his hoe handle. But, thank God, Mr. Quang shook himself and discovered he was still alive. When I talked with him two days later, Mr. Quang concluded with a chuckle, "Since then, I've been really lazy. I haven't done any hoeing in the last two days!"

After completing our research, MCC bought a tractor which we planned to arm with steel plates to protect the driver, then to plow up these fields laced with grenades. Before that could be implemented, however, the revolutionary armies were beginning to take over the country, province by province.

As the revolutionary forces came closer to our province of Quang Ngai, Pat and I were faced with the most trauma-filled decision of our lives. Shall we stay or leave? We desperately wanted to stay. Here were our friends of five years. Here was our calling of standing in solidarity with the people of Vietnam. The revolutionaries were not our enemies, even though our government had declared them the enemy.

On the other hand, we now had two small children. And it appeared there would likely be heavy fighting and perhaps bombing of our town as there had been in other provinces that had been taken over. Could responsible parents keep children in such a place when they had opportunity to leave? In the end, we did what we had promised each other we would not do: we separated. Pat left with three-year-old Lara and one-year-old Minh. I stayed.

In two days the revolutionary forces took over our town and found me and a Japanese co-worker who had joined me in Quang Ngai at the last minute. Because in previous months we had communicated with them about trying to clean up unexploded munitions, these "enemy" forces knew about us Mennonites and welcomed our presence after the take-over. Suddenly we were "behind the lines" and communication with our families and friends became difficult.

We were not only treated well but given travel papers that allowed us to go anywhere in our province. One day we traveled past My Lai, the village where one of the massacres of the war had taken place seven years earlier. While waiting for a boat to cross a canal near My Lai, a boatman appeared up the banks of the canal. When he saw me, he started to scream, "American! Grab him. Tie him up! Get him!" A Vietnamese friend traveling with us tried to persuade the boatman that this American was friendly and wanted to help the people of Vietnam. But the boatman waved his arms and shouted, "But look what they did to our village!" pointing to My Lai. "Arrest him, I say!"

Finally our friend persuaded the boatman that we were different from the soldiers who destroyed his village. In the end, the boatman scratched his head and said, "All right, if what you say about this American is true, then let me carry his bicycle into my boat and take him across this canal."

In the coming weeks and months, we met scores of "the enemy," the National Liberation Front fighters who saw themselves in similar light to American revolutionaries who fought against the British at the outset of the United States. In years following, I recorded many of the stories of this tumultuous time in the book *Reaching the Other Side*.[1]

The decision for some MCC workers to stay when nearly all other Americans were fleeing the country seemed to communicate two messages: to the American public, it declared that we did not accept our government's definition of the enemy. We believed that with an open hand and spirit, we were ready to see humanity in people whom the war propaganda had so dehumanized. To the Vietnamese people and officials, MCC workers' staying communicated that we were ready and eager to work with the people of Vietnam regardless of which government was in control.

## PILGRIMS STILL

Back in the U.S., Pat and I retreated to the woods near Phoenixville, Pennsylvania, for a few years to nurture our family, birth a third child, write the book on Vietnam, sell meats and cheeses at a farmers' market, and pick apples at a local orchard. We lived on Jug Hollow Road. In the house we rented, we found an old Mason jar of home-made wine, so we dubbed our house "Pilgrims Still." Aside from any moonshiner allusions, however, it was indeed time for these pilgrims to be still for a stretch. If our marriage was ever in crisis, it was during these years. How does a married couple balance "call" and "family" commitments? Pat would remind me that the prophet who said "unless you turn your back on . . . your wife and children . . . you cannot be my follower" was himself never married. Perhaps more than we realized at the time, the trauma of the war and our four months of separation as a family had taken a heavy toll.

## New Hope in Mindanao

Alas, after four years of such retreat, we were again eager to explore new commitments to people in Asia. We learned, through friends in MCC, of church activists in the Philippines who were raising their voices against the injustice of American military bases in that country and against the American agribusiness corporations that were squeezing local farmers to get their land for growing pineapples and bananas for export. So, once again, we packed up the family, this time landing in the Philippine's southern island of Mindanao.

Our three-and-one-half years in the Philippines became a time to restore more deeply our trust in the church as an instrument of healing and justice. For there we joined with a team of Catholic laypersons and clergy who courageously defended marginalized farmers against the onslaughts of U.S. fruit corporations and the martial law government of Ferdinand Marcos. One priest friend, who regularly was accosted by the military officials, inspired us deeply when he told us, "I do not seek to hate so much that I would be willing to kill. Rather I seek to love so much that I would be willing to die."

We would visit the two largest U.S. military bases outside of American soil: Clark Air Field and Subic Naval Base. Eventually MCC assigned several women to work with the young Filipina women who were lured into the sex trade surrounding these bases. Sitting with some of these women, Pat recorded and presented their stories in a video called *The Bases of Our Fears*.

We also joined with the efforts of many Filipino activists to close down the bases. In 1992 the Philippine Senate finally took up whether to renew the agreement to host these bases which the United States had tenaciously maintained over fifty-five years. MCC sent an expert on "base conversion" from the University of Texas to discuss with Philippine officials ways the bases could be transformed to productive commercial enterprises. In the end, the Philippine Senate split ten to ten on the bases vote, and it fell to our friend, Jovito Salonga, president of the Philippine Senate, to cast the vote which expelled those centers of militarism and prostituted economy, thus ending ninety-four years of American military presence in the Philippines.

## Home Again, But Where Is Home?

When our family returned home from the Philippines in spring 1982, MCC invited me to serve as justice advocate and researcher for two years in the Washington Office on Capitol Hill. There were many opportunities to visit officials in the Congress, the State Department, and the Pentagon. On various occasions I was able to give testimony in congressional hearings drawing from our grassroots experiences in Asia. MCC workers generally had a great deal of credibility in these settings, because it quickly became clear to officials that we had entered deeply into the lives and cultures of people.

One morning I met with a busload of students from Eastern Mennonite University who had come to Washington for the day to get a taste of the world of government. During my meeting with them, I explained how we and other MCC workers had tried to address the tragedy of unexploded mines and grenades left behind in the war in Southeast Asia. I showed the students a model of an anti-personnel bomblet the U.S. had dropped in profusion in Vietnam and Laos. Unthinkingly, I stuffed that bomblet in my overcoat pocket at the end of that session, and we all scrambled onto their bus for our next appointment at the State Department. Only after we had entered the lobby at State did I notice the metal detectors we would need to pass through. Whoops. What do I do with this bomb?, I asked myself. Ditch it in a phone booth? Hand it over to the person at the information desk: "Would you take care of my bomb for the next thirty minutes?"

In previous years, I had smuggled such bomblets (all without explosives in them) into the White House and National Security Council to impress upon officials the gravity of the problems facing our friends in Asia. But this was the first I had encountered a metal detector. Now, in desperation, after all the students had gone through the detector, I knew no choice but to walk through as well. Glory be! No buzzer! Close call!

Despite—who knows, perhaps because of—this advocacy work for peace, during the latter part of my Washington sojourn, I experienced a time of gloom descending on my spirit. For the next months I went through a season of depression like I had never before—nor since—encountered. I could not sleep through the night. I felt alone in the universe. I felt worthless, of no consequence. All our efforts for bringing peace in the world seemed of no avail.

One afternoon I rode the Metrobus home from the MCC office and disembarked at Fessenden Street near our home in northwest D.C. As I walked up Fessenden Street, I noticed coming toward me a jaunty looking man in tank-top shirt, pushing a two-wheeled cart loaded with gallon paint cans. A cigarette hung from the corner of his mouth. I also noticed that between us a raucously flowering forsythia bush was leaning out and claiming half the sidewalk, making it one-way traffic at that point. On drawing close to the bush, the painter and I both paused for a moment. Then he looked at me and laughed, "Imagine this. Here we've been walking for blocks, and where should we meet but at this bush!"

Though touches of the depression stayed with me for nearly a year, since that time, if ever I feel alone in the universe, I remember the tank-topped painter at that burning bush of forsythia. We are not alone in the world. I remember the line from Goethe: "To know of someone here and there whom we accord with, who is living on with us, even in silence—this makes our earthly ball a peopled garden."

## BUT DO I WANT TO GO HOME?

In 1984—I was forty—MCC invited us to move to their headquarters in Akron, Pennsylvania. Pat and I were asked to jointly administer the MCC programs in East and Southeast Asia. The opportunity had its allure. This work would allow us to visit Asia regularly and keep in touch with many of the people who had inspired us most over the previous two decades.

But for me, this meant going back to Lancaster County where I had grown up. After swimming in the oceans of the world and on finding Godspirit and inspiration for life in people of many cultures and beliefs, this felt like asking us to go back and swim in the cultural ponds of our childhood . . . a regression, perhaps.

\*\*\*

Years before, in the heat of a Saigon noontime, I had experienced what I can only describe as a vision. I saw a hearty young man grow up living deep in the forest. In this isolated setting the young man performed his work, becoming especially skilled with the axe. He learned to fell a tree and split it into logs or rails with unsurpassed deftness. Rarely did any visitors come that deeply into the woods, save for the occasional tinsmith who entered seeking to sell his wares. And the tinsmiths also brought their stories. Stories of the market places in the far off town. Stories of the shops, the lights, and best of all, the fairs where the hale and hearty could compete with their skills.

Eventually, this young man could not resist any longer. He packed a small bag, threw the axe on his shoulder, headed out of the woods, and in time came to the fabled market town. And, ah yes, the shops, the laughter, the raucous stories over ale at night, the lights and—best of all—the fairs. There, the young woodman was able to demonstrate his dexterity with the axe, besting all with his extraordinary skill. And the applause! Oh, the sweet nectar of the applause!

But soon someone told the young woodman, "You think this market town is great. You haven't seen anything yet. You must go to the bigger market town." This the young man did. And oh, the bigger shops, the brighter lights, the more challenging competition at the fairs and the ever louder applause. Yet again, someone told him, "Oh, there are bigger towns; you've not seen anything yet." And so on and on, he went, to ever more alluring towns.

Until finally, he came to a fork in the road. The young man knew that one path led to an even bigger market town. The other path circled a long way back and would lead him back to the place in the woods from where he had started. In the vision, it was not given for me to know which path the woodcutter took at that time. But it was clear that *at some time* he would return to the place of his beginnings and there he would live in peaceful fulfillment.

\*\*\*

Despite the power of that vision for me over the years, my fear was that returning to Lancaster in my early forties was far too early. That disconsolate thought troubled me deeply.

Soon after our arrival back in Lancaster County, one morning I jogged the three miles from my mother's home to the Weaverland cemetery where my father (and nearly all my ancestors for seven generations) were buried. With fevered spirit, I lingered by Pop's grave and communicated with him my anxious thoughts. In that moment it was as though Pop spoke to me calmly, "Do not trouble yourself about returning here to the homeland. You are not coming to stay. You are just coming to 'tag up,' and then you will go out again." It was an allusion to a childhood game called "Prisoners' Base," where tagging up at base gave a player power to go out and capture players on the other team. The message gave me hope.

## Seeking Passion Amid the Ordinary

For about a decade Pat and I gave leadership to MCC's East Asia programs. We lived in Ephrata near the headquarters of MCC International. Whenever we would make a major transition in life like that, we would phone Atlee and Winnie Beechy in Goshen, Indiana, to consult with them. We knew them from Vietnam days and had come to respect their wisdom, quiet gutsiness, and affirmation of the best in every person. And sometimes we would gather friends in our home and do a Quaker Clearness Session to discern the wisdom of a prospective move.

Indeed, the first months in Pennsylvania did feel somewhat confining. Working office hours and being surrounded by an utter world of Mennonite-ness felt a bit claustrophobic. But the opportunity for travel to Asia and the growing of a daughter and two sons through high school brought plenty of challenges and excitement. Pat and I did our share of grousing over work schedules and parental responsibilities. Pat was often more assertive than I in naming irritants that needed attention in our relationship. When she would state firmly her feelings, I would frequently recoil silently and retreat for a few days until we could come back to the issue more dispassionately.

But our rhythms also gave us much energy and mutual respect. I remember, for example, one afternoon at a park bench in Akron when I watched as Pat engaged some friend in animated conversation. I fell in love with her all over again. What a stimulating, engaging—yes, say it—what a sexy woman! Sexy in the sense of making you feel so totally alive, and loving that aliveness. At that time, we wrote an anonymous article which ran on the front page of *Gospel Herald* celebrating the beauty of such sexual loveliness. What a lucky man I am!

I soon discovered that while I enjoyed the international travel and reconnecting with friends in Asia, I did not enjoy administration. I had to find ways to keep my creative spirit alive. Finding other lovers of poetry, we started meeting regularly and challenging ourselves to memorize poetry. It was during this time that I rediscovered Hopkins, as in Gerard Manley. Willard Conrad had first read a few Hopkins poems from our salmon-colored *Exploring Literature* text at Hesston College decades earlier. And now to find Hopkins again:

> THE WORLD *is charged with the grandeur of God.*
> *It will flame out, like shining from shook foil;*
> *It gathers to a greatness, like the ooze of oil*
> *Crushed....*

Ah yes, for Hopkins, "all things are charged with love, are charged with God. And if we know how to touch them, bring forth sparks and take fire...."

Indeed therein lay our profoundest commitment to nonviolence, to loving even the enemy. For even that enemy is charged with love, is charged with God. Or as the Quakers would say, "There is that of God in every person." Hence, to strike another would be to strike a creation of God.

## Pain and Discovery Like No Other

Our world suddenly changed one winter night in 1995. On that night our youngest son—a bright, creative, sensitive young man about to graduate from high school—dissolved in anguish on the living room sofa before our eyes. He spoke of receiving painful messages in his mind. In the coming days in school, this widely beloved student perceived that his classmates and teachers were all screaming condemnation and judgment on him. Eventually, he could bear to go to class no more.

A psychiatrist friend from our Community Mennonite Church in Lancaster came and visited with us. While he cautioned against being too quick to make a diagnosis, he suggested that what Hans was experiencing looked much like symptoms of schizophrenia. The distress for Hans, and the fear and confusion for us his parents, were like nothing else that we had encountered in our lives. To witness a child in utter torment. . . .

After a month of trying to stumble along, Hans finally agreed to go to Philhaven, the Mennonite psychiatric hospital nearby. Upon consulting with the doctors, he was admitted. That night we were able to visit Hans on the unit. There he was, surrounded by patients who obviously were going through their own mental crises. After talking with Hans and meeting his big roommate, it was time to leave. Waving goodbye to our beloved son, we heard the door lock behind us.

That night I was so exhausted I quickly fell asleep, as is my wont. But within an hour I awoke with the terror of grief and fear seizing my soul. I pulled my journal from the night stand and, perhaps in the mode of the Old Testament writers, heaved my cries of despair and anger onto the written page. "God, why? In our lives, we have sought to serve you. To serve your people. To stand for justice. To walk with the downtrodden. Yet now you strike down our son with this mental torment. God, you're sick. You're the one who needs a doctor. You're the one who should be in that hospital, God, because you are a terribly sick God."

I lay spent on the bed. Broken. Afraid. But strangely, my pen kept moving on the journal page. "Yes, Earl, you're right. I am sick. I am terribly sick. You're right. I do belong in that hospital. In fact, I am in that hospital. Actually, my son is in that hospital. He's in there together with your son. They're both sick. They're both in there together."

Our journey with Hans transformed my understanding of God. God is no longer the Omnipotent One who can independently fix the broken world. I now know a God who comes and sits with us. A God who weeps with us. A very weak and broken God who gives me strength and courage precisely because in this brokenness, we are one. I am not alone.

The following years, as Hans bravely journeyed toward recovery, were the most wrenching years of our lives. But in many ways, the most inspiring years as well. For despite the debilitating "voices" with which he was wrestling, we witnessed in Hans a purity of spirit, a totally genuine search for spirit of the Divine. As we read Scriptures and devotional passages together, as we prayed together, Hans' prayers would still the very streets of heaven with their utter openness and spontaneous goodness.

Happily, today Hans and I are often working together in carpentry, my work of these last fifteen years since we moved to Harrisonburg. We sometimes sing together some of his favorite songs: "The Love of God" and "Wonderful Grace of Jesus."

We have learned so much from our children. Our daughter Lara, who spends much time in her wetsuit in the San Francisco Bay seeking to restore the health of the Bay's ecosystem, helps us to respect and care, not only for humans but for animals and all the earth. Our son Minh, a glassblower, and his wife Anna, a fiber artist, teach us to love the arts and have helped us—with their buoyant spirits—to move beyond the burden of *helping others* to the joy of just *being with others* in an uplifting celebration of life. Helping granddaughter Sophie learn to ride bike and grandsons Indigo and Kiran have fun in the snow gives joy beyond measure.

Lucy O'Meara, my spiritual director in past years, invited me every month or two into a sacred place of laughter and tears as she helped me see the tracings of the finger of the Divine in my life. My mother, who lived independently until her death at 102 at Garden Spot Village in New Holland, showed me the path of true serenity in life. A few years ago, we laughed when my mom, who never talked politics, was so engaged in speaking to my sister Grace of her excitement about the election of Barack Obama. In her enthusiasm, she forgot she had a pan on the stove and the maintenance men banged on her door to respond to the smoke alarm!

My life has been blessed. I love this life. My greatest teachers have been those whom society considers broken. Those who, from struggle in their own lives, know how deeply we need each other. And I am lucky enough to live with a woman who loves me and creates spaces of wholeness and well-being for many around us.

Thanks be to God.

## NOTE

1. *Reaching the Other Side: The Journal of an American Who Stayed to Witness the Vietnams' Postwar Transition* (New York: N.Y.: Crown Publishers, Inc.), 1978.

*Edgar Metzler*

---

**An Unfettered Menno: Servant of Church and World**

*The saga of the life of Edgar Metzler—reared among powerful Mennonite personalities—is an intriguing account involving many peoples of many faiths under administrations both secular and sacred. It is no fluke that Goshen College in 2006 gave Edgar and his wife Ethel a Culture of Service Award for their lifelong commitments to service in its many forms. But perhaps most significant has been Edgar's quiet demeanor, brilliant mind, and compassionate involvement in the ethical and political evolution of Mennonite peacemaking from passive nonresistance to engaged peacebuilding.*

**EDGAR METZLER**

# An Autobiographical Stroll Through Sixty Years of Mennonite Peacemaking

On December 7, 1941, a sixth-grade classmate and I were roller skating on the sidewalks of Scottdale, Pennsylvania, when suddenly a woman burst out of her back door, shouting to a neighbor in the next yard, "The Japanese have bombed Pearl Harbor. We'll be at war soon." She was right. By the time I entered seventh grade, the country's war efforts were in full mobilization. This extended even to Scottdale Junior High School where we were urged to sell war stamps to family and neighbors. My parents vetoed my participation as it violated the teaching of the Mennonite church on nonparticipation in war.

But I wanted to be part of some response to the war. The Civilian Air Patrol recruited students to help identify German warplanes. This ability would be useful in the case of a Nazi attack on U.S. territory. Interested in aviation, I thought this seemed a good way to satisfy that curiosity. The large posters with silhouettes of various planes in the Luftwaffe fleet intrigued me. My parents, skeptical, had long conversations with me about whether I should participate. Finally they consented, and I became skilled in differentiating between the Nazi Messerschmitt fighter and the USA's P-51 Mustang.

## Mennonite Nonconformity

As I remember and reflect on those discussions with my parents, the main point did not center on the immorality of war or the biblical injunctions to peacemaking. Rather, it centered on the issue of being nonconformed to the world. The world went to war; we didn't. Our nonconformity included nonresistance as a subset under the first priority of being different from the world. In later discussions with my father, I realized that he felt a lot of pressure as a bishop and a denominational leader to make certain that his children exemplified, in some measure, the church's standard of nonconformity.

Our next-door neighbor, Daniel Kauffman, one of the church's stalwart defenders of nonconformity, wrote the widely used book, *Bible Doctrine*.[1] The chapter on nonresistance follows the chapter on nonconformity. Despite the stern image that stares out from all his photographs, I remember Daniel Kauffman quite differently. At age five or six, on Sunday mornings before church, I would walk across the quiet street between our house and the Kauffman's. Uncle DK, as we called him, would take me on his knee, open his roll top desk, reach into a drawer, and find a piece of hard candy to give me. This may have been one reason I never felt the onerous restrictions of nonconformity which Kauffman advocated and which burdened some of my friends.

Growing up in Scottdale, I did not develop a strong sense of Mennonite ethnicity. Paul Peachey, a sociologist, helped me to understand why. At a conference on Mennonite ethnicity at the University of Waterloo, Paul and I shared a lunch table with four Russian Mennonites from western Canada. They were dumbfounded when I said, "If for any reason I decided to give up my Christian faith, I would no longer consider myself a Mennonite."

Paul commented, "That's because you didn't grow up in a Mennonite community."

"What do you mean?" I responded. "Scottdale was one of the centers of the Mennonite church."

"Let me ask you a couple questions," Paul continued. "When you were in the sixth grade, how many other Mennonites were in your class?"

"None."

"In junior high school, who were your three best friends?"

"Ted Vinzani, an Italian Catholic; Max Blagovich, a Polish Catholic; and Tom Owens, a Scotch Presbyterian."

"And where was the closest Mennonite congregation?"

"At Johnstown, about fifty miles away."

Perhaps that is one reason why, throughout my life, I have found it easy and inviting to relate to persons of cultures, races, religious affiliations, economic status, and sexual orientations different from my own identity.

My first trip overseas, at age sixteen, took me on a UNRRA (United Nations Relief and Rehabilitation Administration) ship carrying horses to Poland. I suppose the only reason my parents consented to such an adventure was that the crew had been recruited and was led by my father's friend, Melvin Gingerich. Although I did not articulate my motivation at the time, that experience was my first step toward a lifetime vocation of service work. It undoubtedly fueled my interest in other cultures and other lands as had my favorite subject in school, geography.

Between high school and college, I joined a voluntary service unit at the General Hospital of Kansas City. Working one month each in the burn unit, the surgery rooms, and the psychiatric ward encouraged my fascination with medicine and certainly gave me a close personal encounter with human need.

## MENNONITE NONRESISTANCE

At Goshen College, the doctrine of nonconformity did not exert the oppressive dominance I had experienced at Eastern Mennonite High School in Harrisonburg, Virginia, where I did my last three years of high school. My understanding of nonresistance as something much more than an aspect of nonconformity expanded as I studied with teachers such as Guy Hershberger, H. S. Bender, and Melvin Gingerich. During my junior year I worked as a student assistant to Gingerich in the office which was preparing *The Mennonite Encyclopedia*.

If I thought of nonresistance as a unique characteristic of Mennonites, that idea was certainly debunked by my participation at a Conference on the Church and War in Detroit in May 1950. I traveled together with Harold Bender, C. L. Graber, and Roy Umble in

Graber's big, new Chrysler. Twenty denominational peace fellowships, including MCC, sponsored the conference.

The conference was inspired by the 1948 Amsterdam Assembly of the World Council of Churches, which had stated that there are those in the churches who "refuse military service of all kinds, convinced that an absolute witness against war and for peace is for them the will of God, and they desire that the Church should speak to the same effect." The summary message of the conference was a dramatic appeal "to the Church of Christ throughout the world to break with war—to repent of war making now." It asked the church to "support the use of the methods of reconciliation and nonviolent action, such as Gandhi has demonstrated in our time." I returned to Goshen and read everything I could find about Gandhi and had many conversations with Guy Hershberger, who raised critical questions about my enthusiasm for exploring this model for Mennonite peacemaking.

## SOME REFLECTIONS ON HAROLD S. BENDER

Why did Bender invite me to accompany him and Guy Hershberger to the Detroit peace conference? Since I was active in the Peace Society at Goshen College, perhaps he wanted to encourage me to pursue that interest. Bender had a reputation for directing students he thought promising in their choice of graduate schools and area of study. Some of my peers, and those slightly older, experienced Bender's heavy hand as oppressive. I did not. Bender opened doors for me, but I never felt pressured to walk through those doors. They led to possibilities for service which were in line with my interests.

I had known Bender since I was six years old. Bender would come to Scottdale on church business and to visit his wife's parents, John and Christine Horsch, who lived just two doors from my home. He was a friend of my father, A. J. Metzler. The two had many common, and sometimes conflicting interests, in the church's publishing activities. I distinctly remember an instance of differing opinions.

The Mennonite Publishing House was a block from my home, and the Pittsburgh Street School, where I was in sixth grade, was two blocks. I would go home for lunch, often stop in my dad's office, and then walk home with him. If he was on the phone or in conversation with someone, I would wait in one of the many chairs in his office.

One day, when I came to the office, Bender was meeting with my dad. Bender's interest was the publication of a book on some aspect of Mennonite history. My dad pointed to the bookshelves near his desk. On one shelf were all the published books in chronological order. On the other shelf the books were arranged by category. Dad pointed to the extensive array dealing with church history and doctrine, then to the few volumes relating to evangelism and missions. "Don't you think we should have more balance?" he asked Bender. I don't know how they resolved that but I do remember walking down the hill toward home and Bender asking me about what I was studying in sixth grade.

When I started my junior year at Goshen College, Bender asked if I wanted to work as a student assistant to Melvin Gingerich in the preparation of *The Mennonite Encyclopedia*. I learned much from that association with Gingerich and also with Bender's wife, Elizabeth, who did research, writing, and editing for the project. In the middle of my seminary studies, Bender, as chair of the Mennonite Central Committee (MCC) Peace Section, asked me to coordinate MCC efforts in Washington to protect and expand the rights of conscientious objectors. Several years later the First Mennonite Church in Kitchener, Ontario, was searching for a new pastor. They sent their church board chairman to Goshen to interview Bender, who recommended me. I found the pastoral experience deeply challenging and satisfying. But six years later Bender again came into my life in the form of an invitation to take the place of Elmer Neufeld as director of the Peace Section at the MCC International headquarters in Akron, Pennsylvania.

Bender died in 1962 as I was beginning the work at MCC. But his influence continued in a serendipitous contact that led to my seven years' service on the Peace Corps staff in South Asia (see later section on Mennonites in government service).

## MENNONITE WITNESS TO THE STATE

My engagement with the challenge of nonresistance took a new twist when halfway through my MDiv studies, Harold Bender, who served as chair of the MCC Peace Section, asked me to go to Washington, D.C., to become the Associate Executive Secretary of the National Service Board for Religious Objectors (NSBRO).

Again my ecumenical horizons broadened. NSBRO represented forty faith groups, including all the major Christian denominations, the Rabbinical Assembly of America, and groups I had never heard of, such as the Pentecostal Fire-Baptized Holiness Church and the Essenes of Kosmon. The mission of NSBRO was to assist with individual conscientious objectors (COs) in the member groups and to monitor government actions affecting freedom of conscience.

During those years at NSBRO, 1954-56, I began to realize that Mennonites had no compunction about witnessing to the government about their own beliefs and interests, but they did not yet have the vision that they could do that for the benefit of others. I spent much of my time advocating for the recognition of conscientious objectors from different faith traditions. I also began to recognize that there are people of no professed faith who have conscientious scruples against killing another human being.

Another pioneer effort was working with the Department of Defense to draft procedures for the military to follow when a member of the armed forces developed a conscientious conviction that he could no longer serve. This undertaking was triggered by a young man from a Hutterite colony who ran away from the colony and joined the Navy. After several months, he realized he had made a mistake and asked to be discharged on grounds of conscientious objection to war. At the time, the military had no provisions for such discharge. The Navy finally adopted regulations and later these were made the policy of all the armed forces. Yet even today, a member of the armed forces seeking recognition as a CO faces a difficult challenge.

When members of Congress, or even the usually cooperative director of Selective Service, General Hershey, pushed proposals that would have jeopardized the privileges of conscientious objectors, I often arranged for Mennonite church leaders to testify before Congress or to make visits to key legislators. Clearly, Mennonites had no hesitation witnessing to the government on behalf of our own rights. That much was widely accepted. But going beyond that narrow agenda was not yet acceptable.

In 1937 the Mennonite church, assembled in General Conference near Turner, Oregon, adopted a statement on "Peace, War, and Military Service," including our usual message of gratitude to government for recognition of conscience. But it also added that "we desire to endorse the policy of neutrality and nonparticipation in disputes between nations." At least one district conference took exception to this reference when it endorsed the Turner, Oregon, statement. The Virginia Conference stated:

> We favor making appeals to the government in regard to our constitutional privileges for religious liberty and freedom of conscience and commend making contact with government officials to explain to them our position on nonresistance but we do not favor giving advice to the government in any way.

A significant broadening of Mennonite witness to the state occurred with Harold Bender's testimony to the House Committee on Armed Services in March 1955. In a more prophetic witness against the growing militarization of the time than usually articulated by Mennonites, Bender stated, "I am not here to suggest Mennonites know better than the members of Congress how to provide for the necessary defense of this nation.... We do plead with you, however, that, whatever the pressure of this moment, you do not take even the first step toward any type of Universal Military Training."

Bender described the failures of militarism in Germany and Japan, ending with a statement of responsibility rare for Mennonites: "We can win the battle for the allegiance of those not yet committed to the Communist system ... " by shifting our emphasis from the

> purely military approach to security to an approach which will employ all the various and effective methods of aid to needy and underdeveloped areas of the world such as relief, use of surplus foods, technical assistance, Point Four programs, peaceful diplomacy, peace leadership.

Bender had shared his testimony with me at breakfast the day he was going to Congress. I felt positive about what he would say to the Armed Service Committee but commented that it did go beyond the usual witness limited to the rights of COs. He reminded me that in 1927, after the Peace Problems Committee of the Mennonite Church General Conference had almost been discontinued, a new committee adopted a three-point program of "aggressive peace work." The second point concerned witness to the state, not only about the traditional concerns "affecting our status as nonresistant citizens" but also "to encourage officials whenever possible in a wider application of the policy of good will rather than that of force of war."

## Mennonite Service

The Mennonite understanding of its role in the world and its practice of nonresistance was expanded by the impact of World War II and alternative service. We now consider *service* a central element of Mennonite identity, but this is a recent development. Even MCC, which many now identify as the primary expression of service, originated as an instrument of mutual aid to the Mennonites of Russia. The Civilian Public Service (CPS) experience of many young men broadened their awareness of needs in the world beyond that of their fellow members. Addressing those needs was a positive expression of nonresistance. They were engaged in the world rather than withdrawn, active rather than passive.

The result was the explosion of service activities and organizations, such as Pax, VS (Voluntary Service), TAP (Teachers Abroad Program), Mennonite Mental Health Services, MDS (Mennonite Disaster Service), and MEDA (Mennonite Economic Development Association). These organizations and activities pushed the horizons of Mennonites to include other Christians and needs outside our ecclesiastical boundaries.

MCC service expanded beyond postwar reconstruction in Europe to many parts of the so-called two-thirds world in Asia, Africa, and Latin America. The experience of many of these MCC workers led to the conviction that some of the problems confronting their partners were caused, or at least exacerbated, by the policies of the U.S. government. In 1956, I wrote: "We have observed that the Mennonite Church in recent years has responded to the needs of the world through missions and relief. Could it be that the next step in our growing outreach is a greater prophetic witness to the State?"

## Prophetic Witness to the State

In 1961, the Mennonite Church General Conference adopted a statement on "The Christian Witness to the State," drafted by the Peace Problems Committee. The committee had recently added two younger members, Albert Meyer and myself. We were appointed, along with the secretary, Guy F. Hershberger, to draft a statement on witness to the state. The statement moved beyond the classic two-kingdom concept to posit the lordship of Christ over both church and state. I was once asked what the intellectual provenance of that statement was. I replied that the intellectual stream to the committee was via Al Meyer, from John Howard Yoder, and back to Oscar Cullman.

The draft we brought back to the committee for approval stirred wide-ranging discussion. Finally one of three bishops on the committee, I believe Amos Horst of Lancaster County, said, "I think the young men have showed us the biblical basis and we should approve it."

For me, further immersion in the issue of church and state came in late 1961. Harold Bender, still chair of the MCC Peace Section, asked me to travel from my post as pastor at First Mennonite Church in Kitchener, Ontario, to meet him and Elmer Neufeld at Buffalo, New York. They wanted me to consider taking Elmer's place as director of Peace Section at the MCC International headquarters in Akron, Pennsylvania. When I started that assignment in 1962, I was often asked to arrange visits to government officials in Washington, D.C., for MCC workers returning from overseas assignments. In this way, legislators and other officials could hear first hand observations of conditions in other countries where a change of U. S. policy could make a difference.

Following several years of discussion, a decision was made, though with some reservations, to establish the MCC Washington Office. The Church of God in Christ Mennonite representative on the Peace Section, Harry Wenger, took me aside during a coffee break and said, "My church will probably not approve this officially, but I can assure you we will not oppose it." Under leadership of Washington office directors Delton Franz and then Daryl Byler, the office proved to be a valuable component of Mennonite service and peacemaking.

## MENNONITE CONCERNS FOR JUSTICE

In his 1958 doctoral dissertation, J. Lawrence Burkholder lamented that the Mennonite ethic had a "complete neglect of justice as a Christian goal. . . . justice has virtually no place in the Mennonite vocabulary." Burkholder wanted to persuade Mennonites "that love must take the form of justice if it is to be effective."

When I returned to the States in 1975 after seven years in Asia, I felt woefully behind in the current issues of ethics and theology. A friend gave me a new publication, *Marx and the Bible*, by Jose Miranda. The book captivated me. Miranda, a biblical scholar with a liberation focus, simply exegetes the Bible's focus on justice (the provocative title is misleading). I read it a second time more carefully, again impressed with the author's passionate vision of God's concern for justice. I found myself pondering how this biblical mandate could add to the Mennonite understanding of peace.

I soon discovered that Mennonites were already discussing the idea that justice needed to be incorporated into our peace and service ideals. There were two reasons for this: one, a growing awareness of liberation theology, sparked not so much by Mennonite academic theologians as by Mennonites serving in Latin America having grassroots exposure to the plight of the oppressed. The second reason was the sympathetic response of many Mennonites to the civil rights movement to correct the injustice of America's (including Mennonites) treatment of racial minorities.

By the late 1970s, interest was developing among MCC personnel, in the Mennonite Church and in the General Conference Mennonite Church to draft a position statement on justice. In 1983, at a joint meeting of the two denominations in Allentown, Pennsylvania, a lengthy statement was adopted, "Justice and the Christian Witness." Later a widely used study book provided a solid resource for congregations to do their own study and discernment. Burkholder's wish that Mennonites include justice concerns as central to their peacemaking has at least been partly fulfilled.

## **MENNONITES AND GOVERNMENT SERVICE**

In the mid-1960s, the duties of the MCC Peace Section director included sponsorship of the Mennonite Intercollegiate Peace Fellowship. I found meeting with students from all the Mennonite and Brethren in Christ colleges challenging and fun. Students asked about the possibility of serving with the government as a Christian vocation and as an expression of peacemaking. I did a brief survey of Mennonites working with the federal government and couldn't find many. Those I could identify were technocrats with training and skills in a specific area. Today many Mennonites work with federal, state, or local governmental units, but still not many at a higher policy level.

The 1965 conference of the Mennonite Intercollegiate Peace Fellowship met in Washington, D.C. Participants heard from Christians working in government, trying to influence government. The questions and aspirations shared by students were in the background of my thinking the next year when I took a study leave from MCC to pursue graduate studies at American University's School of International Service in Washington, D.C. Many of my fellow graduate students were in government service, mainly with the diplomatic service or the military. The professor for a seminar on communism in Asia invited us to his home for the last session before the Christmas recess. He said it would be mainly a social evening and invited some of his friends.

The first person I met at the party was the Latin American director for the Peace Corps, on a two-year leave from his work as an assistant dean at Harvard. Within the first few minutes, he discovered I had attended Goshen College. He asked me if I knew Harold Bender. The former assistant dean at Harvard had worked for Bender's brother Wilbur, who was dean of the college at Harvard. He had often met Harold Bender when he visited his brother at Harvard. For the next hour, we talked about H. S. Bender and Mennonites. At the end of the evening, he suggested I take off a couple more years and work on Peace Corps staff. I told him that was unlikely, but after Christmas he called me and invited me for a series of interviews, which led to an offer to go to Nepal with the Peace Corps.

Only later did I learn about a Mennonite statement on the Peace Corps, agreed to in May 1961 at a meeting of the MCC Executive Committee, the Council of Mennonite Colleges, and the Council of Mennonite Mission Board Secretaries. They concluded that "it appears inadvisable for MCC and its constituent agencies to enter into contract with the Peace Corps program." The group concluded that any Peace Corps program would be "administered under firm and detailed government control."

Three particular reasons were given that would prevent church agencies from collaborating with Peace Corps:

> 1) the stated policy against proselytizing with its implied restriction on Christian witnessing, 2) the recruiting policy which de-

nies the church agency a satisfactory measure of selectivity in choosing candidates, and 3) the policy of operation which constitutes the agency as an arm of government.[2]

I had similar concerns at the time I was offered a staff position in May 1967. At my final interview with the Peace Corps Director, Jack Vaughn, it became apparent that he would approve my nomination. Pointing to my thick application file open on his desk, I asked him if he had seen the articles I had written protesting the Vietnam War and the arrest record from an antiwar demonstration. Vaughn leaned back in his chair, took a suck on his pipe, and said, "Ed, I want you to know that I don't want anyone working for the Peace Corps who thinks what we are doing in Vietnam is a good idea."

Soon after I arrived in Nepal in fall 1967, the Peace Corps volunteer newsletter interviewed me. The article highlighted my work with conscientious objectors, resulting in a flood of inquiries from volunteers about the draft and how to request CO status. The Peace Corps did not qualify as alternative service; it only postponed the draft obligation until the completion of Peace Corps service. In my first year in Nepal, I did more draft counseling than in my five years at the MCC Peace Section. At no time during my seven years of Peace Corps service in Nepal, India, Thailand, and Iran did I ever confront a situation in which I could not openly share my Christian commitments, nor did I ever feel the need to compromise my ethical principles.

I recall two possible tests of those principles. At a Peace Corps directors conference in 1970, a major subject was the use of local staff in selected positions instead of Americans. There was consensus that this was the right direction but disagreement as to how far it should go. I argued that even the country director might be local staff. Richard Holbrooke, on leave from his State Department career to be Peace Corps director in Morocco, argued passionately against my position, asking me, "Don't you know that the Peace Corps is part of the U.S. government and therefore the country director must be a part of the ambassador's country team. Only a U.S. citizen could do that." I shared alternate ways requisite communication with the ambassador could be maintained. Apparently I didn't satisfy his concerns. Several years later he met MCC director, Bill Snyder, at a conference and asked if he knew Ed Metzler, "a guy who never understood that the Peace Corps was a useful tool for the government's foreign policy."

Another occasion was the first and only meeting of Peace Corps country directors from around the world. Nixon had been elected president, and it was no secret he wanted to downgrade the Peace Corps; he resented its positive and popular identification with the Kennedys. Nixon appointed a new director and relabeled the Peace Corps the overseas arm of a new agency called Action. We met in Washington and the last session was to be on a Saturday morning. But that morning we were all invited to the White House for the Sunday morning worship service, followed by brunch with the president. These weekly services had been started by Nixon, and he would invite well-known religious leaders to speak at the services.

In the discussion that followed that invitation it became clear that we were all expected to attend. A few strong dissenters questioned whether the White House should be used for public worship. In addition, the few African American directors did not want to appear in solidarity with the Nixon regime because of the views put forward by Nixon staffer Daniel Moynihan in a speech we had heard earlier that week. He had elaborated on his policy suggestion that the best way forward on race relations would be "benign neglect." Of course the Vietnam War was part of the discontent most of us felt.

At an informal caucus over lunch of those who questioned the White House invitation, I was asked to carry our concerns to the Peace Corps director. The next morning most of us did go to the White House and when shaking hands with the president to make a quick witness regarding the policies being pushed by the administration.

Working for the Peace Corps may present many opportunities and a few challenges for Mennonites. Government service becomes more problematic in any position involving use of force or competing demands of justice posing intractable dilemmas. The experience of Paraguayan Mennonite Ernst Bergen, serving in that country's presidential cabinet, illustrates. We still have not adequately addressed the challenge of power—namely, that love must take the form of justice to be effective—raised by Lawrence Burkholder fifty years ago.

## MENNONITES AND CIVIL DISOBEDIENCE

We know that witness to the government seldom produces the results we hope for. What do we do then? Political scientist and philosopher John Rawls suggests that civil disobedience, which he describes as "a public, nonviolent and conscientious breach of law undertaken with the aim of bringing about a change in laws or government policies.... Persons who practice civil disobedience," Rawls notes, "are willing to accept the legal consequences of their actions."

Our faith tradition began with a radical act of civil disobedience, adult baptism, when Zwingli and the City Council would not move in the direction demanded by the conscience of Conrad Grebel and his colleagues. In the centuries that followed, Mennonites in some places became part of the political authority (Netherlands and the Ukraine) and in other places maintained sufficient distance from the political order that they seldom encountered challenges of conscience that might lead to civil disobedience. In the buildup of preparations for the U.S. entry into World War II, Mennonites, along with Quakers and the Church of the Brethren, secured a compromise on conscription with the government so that young men had an alternative to disobeying an order to report for military service.

In the 1950s, the United States reinstated conscription as part of the Korean War effort and the massive military buildup in the Cold War with the Soviet Union. Some believed the 1-W Alternative Service Program was a convenient concession by the government to silence witness against the growing domination of the military in U.S. policy. The November 17, 1959, issue of *Gospel Herald* carried a front-page article advocating civil disobedience by nonregistration.

Several months earlier, I had come to this conviction, had torn up my draft registration card, and had sent it with a letter to my Selective Service local board. Soon thereafter, I was talking with *Gospel Herald* editor Paul Erb at a conference. When he heard what I had done, he asked me to write an article explaining my reasons. I wrote, "The only Christian reason (for non-registration) would be the deep conviction that this was a matter of obeying God rather than man and that by this act an urgently needed witness would be made."[3]

As soon as that issue of *Gospel Herald* reached Goshen, Indiana, I received a phone call from Harold Bender expressing his displeasure both with me for advancing the argument for nonregistration and with Editor Paul Erb for putting it on the front page. Two months later in the January 20, 1960, issue of *Gospel Herald*, this argument was answered by Bender with these words:

Now one may refuse to register in the belief that by so doing he is testifying against military conscription with all its evils and dangers for the state and for those who accept military service. But the intent to give such a witness is not sufficient ground for disobedience. When disobedience is engaged in for such purpose alone, it becomes sin. It is on this ground that the Mennonite Church has not agreed that it is legitimate for a CO to refuse registration.

*Edgar with Washington, D. C., police officer who has arrested and handcuffed him for participating in a rally for banning nuclear weapons tests.*

How quickly attitudes can change. Bender died in 1962. Nine years after he condemned nonregistration, the Mennonite church officially sanctioned it. In summer 1969, young Mennonites went to Turner, Oregon, to engage their elders about this. The manners, appearance, and, according to one delegate, smell of the young Mennonite radicals did not make conversation easy at the Mennonite Church General Conference meeting. But apparently there was significant interaction, as reflected in this conference statement:

> We are grateful that a group of young people have come to this assembly at considerable personal sacrifice to speak their Chris-

tian convictions regarding the evils of conscription. . . . In response to this message we take the following action: 4. We recognize the validity of noncooperation as a legitimate witness and pledge the offices of our brotherhood to minister to young men in any eventuality they incur in costly discipleship.[4]

I am grateful that my supervisors at MCC and at the Mennonite church offices allowed me to engage in civil disobedience even when they disagreed. Two of those actions resulted in brief jail time. One was at the Soviet embassy in Washington, D.C., in connection with efforts to secure a nuclear test ban, which resulted in a very educational night interacting with inmates at the crowded District of Columbia jail. The other was at the American nuclear test site in the Nevada desert. This time the overnight jail stay was in a crowded small room with several peace leaders, including Jim Wallis. The conversation during that long night was, by turns, deeply personal, issue focused, and at times, humorous. The fellowship that night and the next day until we were released was as significant as I had ever experienced.

## Mennonites and Active Peacemaking

The desire to do more than protest verbally to end violence and oppression led Ron Sider to make a daring proposal to the Mennonite World Conference in Strasbourg, France, in 1984. He urged Mennonites to form a nonviolent force of thousands who would interpose themselves between conflicting parties with the aim of stopping the violence and building a foundation for peace. Sider's appeal was passionate and, some would say, grandiose:

> Unless we . . . are ready to start to die by the thousands in dramatic and vigorous new exploits for peace and justice, we should sadly confess that we never really meant what we said and we dare never whisper another word about pacifism to our sisters and brothers in those desperate lands filled with injustice.[5]

The response of the Mennonite denominations resulted, eventually, in the formation of Christian Peacemaker Teams (CPT). Incidentally, the response was picked up not by MCC but by the Council of Mennonites, and Mennonite Brethren and Brethren in Christ denominational executive directors. As chair of the first steering committee of CPT, I struggled with my own reservations about the approach. My experience overseas made me skeptical of short-term teams entering a culture new to them with admirable motivation but limited acquaintance with its history and the nuances of the local social, economic, and political situation. Also, what priority should CPT have on a denominational agenda already pulled in many directions?

Despite these reservations, CPT moved forward, although with much more limited activity than envisioned by Sider. The steering committee hoped for one hundred participants for the first training program, but the number was actually twelve.

I would characterize CPT as a learning organization, meaning that it has reflected on its experiences and modified its approach in positive ways. The term used to define its peace efforts, "nonviolent direct action," complements other peacemaking efforts such as mediation and witness to government.

Kathleen Kern's book, *In Harm's Way: A History of Christian Peacemaker Teams*,[6] is quite brief on the origins of the organization but describes in rich detail the various projects they have undertaken.

## PEACEMAKING ON THE INTERNATIONAL SCENE

The term *nonresistance* refers mainly to the behavior of an individual reacting to a threat. On the personal level this means refusing to do evil in response to evil. On the national level, nonresistance is impossible if the nation state needs to be preserved. Does this mean that nonresistant Christians have nothing to contribute to peace between nations or peace between conflicting groups within a nation? This question elicited more attention as Mennonites, post-World War II, became involved with worldwide needs.

The question also arose from another source. Building skills in mediation and conflict resolution suggested there were other ways to demonstrate positive expressions of nonresistance. The success of Eastern Mennonite University's Center for Justice and Peacebuilding has shown that training in nonviolent methods of conflict resolution can impact, sometimes dramatically, conflict in the larger society.

A modest but necessary step in the reduction of conflict is to learn more about our "enemies" by personal interaction. Programs of student exchanges, efforts to bring ordinary citizens together, service in cross-cultural contexts; all these can help us understand and empathize with others, a significant benefit of these activities.

The most challenging international conflict of the 1950s and '60s was the Cold War between the Soviet Union and the U.S. In that context, there was increased interest in MCC circles to reestablish contact with Mennonites in the Soviet Union. The Mennonites there had been absorbed into the umbrella organization Stalin had created to satisfy President Roosevelt's demand in connection with the Lend Lease arrangements for more religious recognition of nonorthodox groups, the largest being the Baptists. The Baptist World Alliance (BWA) had begun negotiations that led to the first group of Soviet clergymen visiting the United States.

MCC began talking to the BWA about the possibility of a small delegation visiting Mennonite communities in the Soviet Union. The driving force for this initiative may have been primarily to contact Mennonites, but it was also an opportunity to demonstrate love for enemies in the context of anti-Soviet extremism in the U.S. That extreme sentiment was expressed as soon as the delegation of four Baptist pastors from the Soviet Union became public knowledge. I had the privilege to accompany the visitors to various Mennonite communities. Everywhere we went there were demonstrations and picket lines protesting the visit and questioning the authenticity of the pastors who lived in an antireligious communist state. A prominent Christian anticommunist, Carl McIntire, claimed credit for the protests and appeared at several locations to lead the crowds he had recruited through his daily radio program. The *New York Times* described him as "a fiery radio evangelist who preached an amalgam of fundamentalist Christianity and hawkish patriotism."

Several times I walked out to the demonstrators to talk with McIntire but he refused to discuss issues and rallied his followers to a higher volume of protest. When we ended the tour by returning to Akron, McIntire met us at the Philadelphia airport. I walked out through the signs to make one last effort to dialogue. McIntire introduced me to a visitor with him that day, Ian Paisley, the firebrand Protestant defender and anti-Catholic activist in Northern Ireland. McIntire immediately returned, in very loud voice, to the pep talk for his followers protesting the visit of the Soviet Baptist ministers.

After our Soviet Baptist guests returned home, I raised the question at MCC if we could do anything to communicate with Rev. McIntire at a level other than shouting matches on the picket lines. The result was a visit to McIntire at his church across the river from Philadelphia by C. N. Hostetler, MCC board chair; William Snyder, MCC executive director; and myself. McIntire welcomed us into his spacious office, asked his secretary to bring tea, and settled us around a table to talk. In this context, McIntire was a different person. He spoke in a conversational voice, asked questions, and listened, a welcome change from the person I had encountered on his protest lines.

Did this cross-cultural dialogue make any difference? It was a meeting of two different cultures, let alone different theologies. Afterward, McIntire's radio program references to Mennonites were more restrained and less frequent. On the MCC side, the visit of the Soviet Baptists was a major step in an initiative that led to exchange visits and to contacts with Mennonites who had been gathered under the Soviet engineered umbrella of one church organization.

## Conclusion

I feel enormously blessed by the opportunities offered me to be a small part in the evolution of Mennonite peacemaking over the past sixty-five years. Evolution is the right descriptor. Change has not been sudden. Gradually, however, our understandings and practices have evolved from a basis of refusal to be part of the military to engaging in a wide variety of actions that challenge violence in our world and foster peaceful relations at all levels, from interpersonal to international. For much of Mennonite history, the test of our peace witness came when government authorities imposed conscription. Now with the changing nature of war, particularly with the use of technology, we may never again see a military draft.

At the beginning of World War II, when I was twelve years old, the doctrine and practice of nonresistance was seen as one aspect of the dominant teaching of nonconformity. The world goes to war, but we do not engage in such "worldly" activity. At least that is how I perceived it from my experience in the heart of the "Old" Mennonite Church. I realized later that my peers from the General Conference Mennonite Church had a different perspective which focused more on peacemaking and less on separation from the world. That difference has largely disappeared as we together seek to be nonconformists in a world threatened by violence at many levels.

I began our story with nonconformity, and now it may behoove us to return to it. We live in a society where the dominant culture is riddled through and through with the use of force and violence in ways far more subtle but no less destructive than war itself. The challenge is to live nonconformed to that ethos and to demonstrate the Jesus way of relating to others nonviolently amid differences and conflicts.

I am grateful to my family, teachers, colleagues, friends, and to many peacemakers from other traditions who have taught me by their words and deeds the way of peace. It has been an exhilarating and challenging journey. I hope in the years ahead I will find ways to continue to be part of God's peacemaking adventure.

April 2009<br>Revised September 2015

## Notes

1. *Bible Doctrine: A Treatise on the Great Doctrines of the Bible, Pertaining to God, Angels, Satan, the Church, and the Salvation, Duties and Destiny of Man* (Scottdale Pa.: Mennonite Publishing House, 1914).

2. Here, as at a number of later points, aditional documentation might be desirable. However, we decided that because of the very close involvement of the author with the events being recorded, we would retain the quotation marks and the exact wording of the document as we received it. —The Editors.

3. See explanation note 2 above.

4. See explanation note 2.

5. See explanation note 2.

6. Kathleen Kern (Cambridge, UK: Lutterworth Press, 2009).

CALVIN W. REDEKOP AND RAY C. GINGERICH

# Appendix: Re-Examining Our Call to Service: The Geography of Our Faith[1]

The Steering Committee of the Anabaptist Center for Religion and Society (ACRS), which approved appendices for Volumes 1 and 2 of *The Geography of Our Faith*, thought it prudent to continue the practice in Volume 3. These appendices, unlike any of the essays in the body of the volumes, reflect on the spirit and dynamic of the Anabaptist Center for Religion and Society that has nourished and hosted the "ACRS Monday Morning Breakfasts," the locus in which each of these "stories" was originally shared.

ACRS attempts to be aware of itself and of the socio-political milieu that informs it while also critiquing the church and our society's self-justifying injustices in our culture and institutional structures. We begin with our own Anabaptist-Mennonite tradition and the institutions to which we ourselves are deeply indebted and for which we seek to be responsible and faithful progenitors.

Students of history know that the need for being critically self-aware is a noble tradition that has, nonetheless, been woefully neglected in most epochs, especially in our most recent one, with its massively destructive ideologies, conflict, and chaos. Abraham Lincoln, referring to perhaps the greatest threat to survival ever faced by the United States, described the challenge profoundly in his June 16, 1858, "House Divided" speech: "If we could first know where we are, and whither we are tending, we could better judge what to do, and how to do it."

Thus ACRS, even in the re-examining of our own service, seeks to keep alive the dialectic (as with a weaver's shuttle) of the progenitors' voices of the past with the prophet's voice calling forth the future, ever weaving our present.

It is this orientation—shall we call it a joyous, audacious, epistemological cynicism—that undergirds ACRS's motivation in the struggle not to be overtaken by the opiates of culture, in its attempt to be aware of "where we are, [and] where we are going, so we can better decide what needs to be done."[2] We believe this stance may make ACRS somewhat unusual. It also explains, in part, why emphasis has been placed on telling our stories, reflecting on them together, and collecting them in these volumes for posterity to ponder, to judge, and, humbly said, to help both us and our posterity to know "where we are, and whither we are tending."[3] Does this not explain the somewhat daring (some might say arrogant) vision, structure, and activities initiated by ACRS—a group of persons who at this stage in life now have no institutional mandate, lack major financial support, and are keenly aware of the contingencies of life—both the physical and the institutional?

Some answers among its members have been proposed for this audacity: 1) we in ACRS have no status that needs to be protected (even though at times we forget this); 2) we believe that experience is probably the best basis for wisdom (even though outside observers might ask, "Whose experience?"); 3) we believe that wisdom is sorely needed to critique the present generation (even though the source of that wisdom may be disputed); and 4) ACRS members are freer than many of our compatriots to contemplate the dictum that Lincoln states so well (an affirmation that has been expressed in various ways by colleagues from our sister institutions).

Evidence that ACRS is at least partly succeeding in self-critical analysis can be accessed by reading appendices in the two preceding volumes of *The Geography of Our Faith*. The appendix in Volume 1, entitled "An Unfinished Story," by Calvin Redekop, notes that from the outset we were not clear whether the effort might indeed be too audacious and diffuse. The essay provides some specifics on the dynamics of the origins. The order of business in the first several meetings basically focused on what to call the movement, resulting in "chaotic meetings attempting to define ACRS's identity."[4] ACRS became the identifying moniker which is quite enigmatic. "Anabaptist Center for Religion and Society" seems too broad to delineate clear boundaries; and yet, paradoxically, that breadth includes specifically Anabaptism, religion, and society, freeing the members to range across the entire "intellectual geography" while remaining remarkably focused, as subsequent developments have shown.

In the appendix of Volume 2, Ray Gingerich continues this self-critical stance and evolutionary development by stating, "Today's Anabaptist Center for Religion and Society represents a growing vision for . . . the integrative re-imaging (critique) of faith and life in contemporary academia and church. However, what really does ACRS represent? And who exactly belongs to it?"[5] The essay then proceeds to list and describe the variety of problems, activities, and programs that emerged. The key activities include an amazing variety—memoirs, forums, seminars, colloquies, and conferences—that need not to be repeated here.[6]

In keeping with the self-critical stance, Gingerich includes several paragraphs on "Setbacks, Losses and Challenges,"[7] among which were the death of a key founding member, Al Keim; the inability to engage and critique the larger church and its leadership as we had originally hoped; and the seeming loss of the vision to move beyond the Mennonite tradition, such as the Church of the Brethren. Gingerich believes the megachallenge for ACRS remains: "What will the political shape and theological texture of the Anabaptist heritage come to be in this century? ACRS is attempting to raise a critical perspective essential to negotiate the shift to the new millennium." Gingerich opines that in pursuing these goals, ACRS has "to date been all too ineffective."[8]

Volume 3 now provides some new information on how well the original perspective (the critical self-evaluation) has fared. One of the institutionalized self-critical practices, (which itself seems to be an oxymoron) was the establishment of an annual meeting intended to put a personal face on the organization's structure via a community gathering including a potluck (what else?). Secondly, but equally important was an "open mike" format which invited all those attending the annual meeting to share their perceptions of ACRS—what it had done right and what was still needing to be realized.[9] The minutes of these annual meetings provide the gist of the concerns that follow: It is clear that the "self-critical stance" is operating, but some concerns will become obvious. The success of self-criticism in ACRS will allow it to be more effective in its goal of critiquing the larger Anabaptist movement.

Yet, self-criticism and audaciousness are not unique to ACRS, and we need to be careful not to claim a unique endowment of these qualities. More importantly, however, self-criticism and audaciousness—both intellectual and socio-political stances—cannot be "stand-alones" and are of little value unless we give them some "substance"—a socio-historical reality embodying these existential phenomena. In reviewing the past four years, the following developments within ACRS help to provide the necessary embodiment for audacity and self-criticism:

1) We have for the first time succeeded in recruiting women to be on the ACRS Steering Committee. We now have three women as regular members of our SC and a fourth one (formerly president of Mennonite

World Conference) waiting in the wings. This might not exactly be audacious, but at least it is a result of being self-critical. It reflects an attempt to embody Anabaptist values in our own organization, namely: diversity and gender equality.

2) We are no longer a group that can even remotely claim to model itself after the self-critical thought of Princeton's high-brow Institute of Advanced Studies (see Redekop, volume 1, 315). For a few of us, particularly those founding members who were motivated by this vision, this lowering of academic rigor appears to come at considerable cost. Others would disagree. So perhaps this is an illusion. Does "the PhD" continue to be a measure of audacity and intellectual curiosity? Or is it rapidly becoming a dinosaur in a digitalized age? How are we to measure this shift in the context of what is happening at EMU and in the larger society that we seek to serve? Might it be more audacious if ACRS sought to apply the functional equivalent of an Anabaptist norm to its own structures, as for example: Are we modeling a more horizontal, participatory, nonviolent understanding of power (not to be confused with gender equality) than we have inherited from the medieval university? Time will enhance any critical assessment that we may seek to make today.

3) Now, more to the deficit side: ACRS has—at least for the moment—lost the vision for a distinctive institutional geography (note the title in each of these volumes). A goal in earlier years was to be a group of academics sharing a common space (such as the entire first floor of the Weaver House) doing our research and writing in geographic proximity with each other, "provoking one another unto love and good works" (Heb. 10:24 KJV), i.e., being an audacious, self-critical intra-community of provocateurs and catalysts daring to think "outside of the box" (see Gingerich, Vol. 2, 360). This would be of lesser importance if this critical function were being carried forward by other segments of the EMU community. But in the humdrum of routine, under the pressures of efficiency and the necessary appeasement of a conservative public, even our more creative professors seldom find room for this in their workload. Yet without this (what in establishmentarian terms might be called a "think tank"), EMU and ACRS are in danger of losing their prophetic edge.[10]

4) The Monday Morning Breakfast Stories, originally intended to be a kind of mid-level bonding activity that would outwardly give ACRS some publicity and inwardly serve as glue that binds us into a community, has become the flagship of ACRS. The publication of these volumes, this being the third, ipso facto runs the risk of turning ACRS from a movement at the edge of an institution into yet another institution flying its own flag—not particularly audacious or self-critical, particularly when we realize that our Monday Morning Breakfasts seldom draw an audi-

ence with an average age below fifty-five, and even more seldom do they find their way into the classroom. And lest we have forgotten, our Foreign Scholars in Residence Program, with its immense potential for providing an on-campus awareness-raising presence, has slipped out of existence—at least for the time being.

5) Creation care/climate change is a phenomenon that permeates our presence on a daily basis. We are living in this environmental change. Whether we will live through it will largely be determined by our response. EMU has made significant advances in this arena, both at the operational level and at the structural level. ACRS, particularly Cal Redekop, has over the past two decades, published significantly in this arena, grounding his studies in our Anabaptist heritage.[11] Increasingly this "theme" is being tied inextricably into an already dominant pursuit on the EMU campus—peace-with-justice. It might be audacious, but not too audacious, to claim that ACRS must and will make this its major focus in the immediate years ahead. Whether such a focus could become the flagship of ACRS remains to be seen—but it would seem to be most appropriate.

6) Finally on a most positive note—three major events initiated, or shall we say impregnated, by ACRS are about to be born: First, a major film on *The Mennonites* (projected to be shown on one of the three national networks) is in its earliest stages of development. A presentation by filmmaker Burton Buller in a Monday Morning Breakfast sparked the notion—not merely that a film of this magnitude was needed to update earlier Mennonite films (done largely by Buller)—but that in Burton and his wife Mary lay unique talent (given their cultural and intellectual grasp of Mennonites and their professional experience in filmmaking) that needed to be resourced. If this project moves beyond its present pollination stage into full bloom and to eventual fruition, it will serve as a near-perfect model of ACRS's minor role of being a visionary, audacious catalyst—minor, yet one of ACRS's most important functions.

Second, the publication of a biography of Orie O. Miller took place in May 2015.[12] The history of this production is most fascinating and illuminating, beginning with the untimely death of Al Keim and the realization that without Keim on our steering committee, ACRS would be unable to "pull off" a larger conference on H. S. Bender building on Keim's definitive biography of Bender.[13] We recognized at the same time that in the life of Bender's contemporary, O. O. Miller, lay a story that may be of equal or greater significance to the present and future Mennonite church than that of Bender. It would seem to be a humble, factual statement to say that in no group other than among the elders of ACRS could the vision for the Miller biography have emerged.

Third, inspired by the work of the O. O. Miller biography, a major conference on leadership from a life-giving, Anabaptist perspective was planned. The well-received event, with other sponsors ultimately joining ACRS and Eastern Mennonite University hosting, was held in April 2016 and titled "Leading into the Common Good: An Anabaptist Perspective." This event took one of ACRS's initial goals from a thought and transformfed it into the world of political reality for the first time![14] But much more, with regard to ACRS, is happening here: The structure for this conference involved multiple institutions and organizational work well beyond anything within ACRS's potential. All doubts about the mutual benefits between ACRS and its host institution, EMU, must herewith be laid aside.[15] And this is as it should be!

September 2016

## Notes

1. The ACRS Steering Committee originally asked Calvin Redekop to write the Appendix. He accepted only on the condition that other steering committee members would also contribute to the self-critical "reflective" approach. However, only Ray Gingerich responded to Redekop's general introduction to the discussion, and he responded with such an extensive and relevant review that the present essay is the continuation and integration of two contributions.

2. The self-awareness and self-critique of the person *and* the social structure has received massive analysis in recent times, beginning with Marxist "dialectical theory," followed by "critical theory," which produced conflict theory" now ending with "ethnomethodology" which focuses "attention on how people in interaction go about maintaining the presumption that they are guided by a particular reality"—in other words, a highly self-conscious mode of analysis reaching near total cynicism (Jonathan Turner, *The Structure of Sociological Theory*, 405). ACRS responds by stating we believe the Anabaptist faith and Anabaptism's geographical stance as a people on the margins of mainline society protects us from becoming totally cynical about the human prospect, hence our audacity.

3. In stating it thus, we are not claiming that each of the authors in this volume (or in previous ones) necessarily demonstrates this critical stance. Rather the genre of "telling our stories" and sharing them with each other is an essential step in self-analysis and critical cultural awareness—of discovering "where we are, and whither we are tending."

4. Vol. 1, "Appendix," 318.

5. Vol. 2, "Appendix," 359.

6. Ibid., 360 ff.

7. Ibid., 364.

8. Ibid., 366.

9. Gingerich's note on the agenda for the April 12, 2006, ACRS annual meeting suggested we conduct an "annual review" as part of the annual meeting.

10. The simplicity of this concept bedevils us in our individualistically oriented educational institutions. Ironically, it is "Anabaptist" and subconsciously it may have roots in certain Silicon Valley models.

11. Cf., e.g., Calvin Redekop, ed., *Creation and the Environment: An Anabaptist Perspective on a Sustainable World* (Baltimore, Md.: Johns Hopkins Press, 2000). It should be noted that this particular work was published prior to the beginnings of ACRS and that ACRS claims no credit for it. Nevertheless, I (Gingerich) wish to claim that it represents the audacity still present in ACRS.

12. John S. Sharp, *My Calling to Fulfill: The Orie Miller Story* (Harrisonburg, Va.: Herald Press, 2015).

13. Gingerich, "Appendix," vol. 2, 364.

14. Redekop, "Appendix," vol. 1, 318.

15. In our early gatherings, referred to above as "chaotic meetings attempting to define ACRS's identity," one of the agenda items rigorously debated was the question of ACRS's structural relationship to EMU—the elderly sociologist among us arguing for near-total autonomy lest the prophetic flame of ACRS be neonatally snuffed out! In fairness to this ever-cynical founding member (perhaps carrying the inflictions of institutional neurosis contracted from EMU in an earlier age), his was a mind that refused to be numbed by the opium of either chronological age or institutional environment (see note 2 above).

## NOTES ON CONTRIBUTORS

**Bertha Beachy** grew up in an Amish farm family in Iowa. By the time she reached fifth grade, she knew she would become a teacher someday, but she also knew that she would not be able to go to high school. At age nineteen, she attended the first Amish Mission Conference and felt called to mission. By taking GED tests and working several jobs she finished a bachelor's degree in elementary education in five years without any debt.

After graduation in 1958, she set sail for Somalia. Thus began her journey with education, overseas mission work, and Islam. During furloughs she had additional training in Arabic, Islam, literacy, English, and journalism. She started an English elementary school in Jamama, ten miles from the equator, and opened an English bookstore in Mogadishu. Later she taught English in Somali secondary schools, but when Americans were no longer welcome in Somalia, she moved to Kenya where she organized the writing of three elementary Somali literacy books which were translated into Swahili.

After returning to the U.S. in 1978, Bertha managed a Provident Bookstore in Goshen, Indiana, for fifteen years. When she retired in 1995, she was asked to manage a small Somali office in Nairobi, Kenya, on behalf of both Eastern Mennonite Missions and Mennonite Central Committee. Wherever Bertha has lived she has found ways to share her experiences with Somalia and Islam with churches, students, and other interested community groups. Bertha is now living at Greencroft Goshen, a continuing care living community for older adults.

**Emmert F. Bittinger** (PhD, University of Maryland) was born into a Church of the Brethren minister's family which nurtured the values of peace, justice, and racial equality. At age seventeen he was elected to the ministry. He earned a master's degree from Bethany Theological Seminary, following which he served as pastor of several churches in West Virginia and Maryland. After earning a PhD at the University of Maryland, he taught at Bridgewater College from 1963-1988. He spent 1982-1983 in Germany teaching for the overseas program of the University of Maryland.

During his retirement years he researched Anabaptist family lines and wrote *Allegheny Passage: Churches and Families, West Marva District, Church of the Brethren, 1752-1990*. He was also a contributor to and co-editor, with Norman Wenger and David Rodes, of six volumes of *The Unionists and the Civil War Experience in the Shenandoah Valley*. His love of church history is reflected in numerous articles published in *Mennonite Family History*, *Pennsylvania Mennonite Heritage*, *Messenger*, and *Brethren Roots*.

For eleven years he served on the board of the Valley Brethren-Mennonite Heritage Center (CrossRoads) during its formation. He and his wife, Esther M. Landis, served with several volunteer projects, including Brethren Archives, Disaster Response, and church camps. Emmert currently lives with his wife at Bridgewater (Virginia) Retirement Community.

**Earle W. Fike Jr.** (ThM, Bethany Theological Seminary) was ordained to the ministry in 1952 and served as pastor in Church of the Brethren congregations. He taught preaching and worship courses at Bethany Seminary and was the executive for the Parish Ministry Commission of the Church of the Brethren General Board. He served on the Juniata College and Bethany Seminary Board of Trustees.

In 1972, Bridgewater College recognized his service by awarding him the Doctor of Humane Letters, and in 1982, he was named distinguished alumnus of the year. In recognition of his athletic contributions as a student, he was selected to the Bridgewater College Athletic Hall of Fame in 1997.

In 1949, Earle married Jean Kiser of Dayton, Virginia, a relationship which lasted sixty-two years, during which time she was a pastor's wife, a public school teacher, and an administrative secretary to college personnel. Their marriage produced a daughter and two sons, three remarkable spouses, and five grandchildren. Tragically, Jean succumbed to an incurable infection in October 2011.

In July 2012, Earle remarried to a retired Bridgewater College graduate and honored alumnae, Dr. Anne Haynes Price of La Verne, California. Anne died of cancer in 2014. Earle now lives in the Bridgewater (Virginia) Retirement Community.

**Margaret Jantzi Foth** (MS Education, Canisius College) grew up in western New York. After attending Mennonite schools in Virginia and Indiana, she worked in the Mennonite Publishing House in Scottdale, Pennsylvania, and in the Mennonite Central Committee (MCC) headquarters in Akron, Pennsylvania. At MCC she met Donald Foth from Hillsboro, Kansas, who was doing his 1-W service in the accounting office, and they married following their service terms.

For the first twenty years of marriage they lived in western New York, near Margaret's parents, while raising four children and attending the Clarence Center Mennonite Church. Margaret's interests included education, music, theology, and drama. With the limitations on women's participation in the ministry of the Mennonite church at that time, she chose to major in English and communication at Goshen College, later securing the MS in education to find an entry into teaching.

Margaret's life work and experiences continued to use this variety of talents and interests in parenting, teaching, writing, and producing radio programs, administering a local mediation center, and training others in mediation settings. Throughout her life she was active in the Mennonite church, both in local congregational life and in church institutions. In retirement Margaret worked for the Center for Conflict Transformation at Eastern Mennonite University. She says that hosting and listening to the international participants in this program have been a most enriching and blessing experience—her newest education!

**Daniel Hertzler** (PhD in Religious Education, University of Pittsburgh) went to Europe twice on cattle boats—in 1946 and in 1947—followed by five years at Eastern Mennonite College where he graduated with a ThB in 1952. In July that year he married Mary Yoder from Streetsboro, Ohio, and in September he began work as an office editor at Mennonite Publishing House. In 1960 he became editor of *Christian Living* magazine and was editor of the *Gospel Herald* from 1973-1990.

Along the way he graduated from Goshen College Biblical Seminary (BD 1955) and the University of Pittsburgh (PhD, 1966, with a major in Religious Education). He drafted a committee report, "Mennonite Education: Why and How?" (Herald Press, 1971). During a sabbatical in 1980, he and Mary traveled around the border of the U.S. and western Canada, compiling material for *From Germantown to Steinbach* (Herald Press, 1983). Following retirement in the mid-1990s, he became instructor for Unit 2 "The Biblical Story" in the five-unit Pastoral Studies Distance Education, retiring from this assignment in 2015. He has written two memoirs, *A Little Left of Center* (Dreamseeker Books, 2000) and *On My Way: The View from the Ninth Decade* (Dreamseeker Books, 2013).

**Carl S. Keener** (PhD, North Carolina State University) graduated from Eastern Mennonite College (EMC) in 1957. Raised on a farm in northern Lancaster County, Pennsylvania, he found the woods and meadows full of interesting flowers and eventually pursued graduate studies in plant systematics. Carl was an assistant professor of biology at EMC from 1960-63. Following his doctoral work, he joined the faculty at Penn State University from which he retired as professor emeritus in 1997, after thirty-one years of teaching, curating the Herbarium, and serving in various departmental, college, and university roles.

Most of his research in plant taxonomy focused on the mid-Appalachian shale barren endemic flora, the buttercup family of the southeastern United States, and the flora of Pennsylvania. In addition to his numerous professional papers and book reviews, he won the Jesse M. Greenman award of the Missouri Botanical Garden in 1967 and the Henry Allan Gleason Award of the New York Botanical Garden in 1984.

Carl's other interests include philosophy, natural history, music, and genealogy. Married to Gladys Swartz in 1955, this year will mark their sixtieth wedding anniversary. Carl and Gladys have three children, four grandchildren, and six great grandchildren. Carl has been a member of the University Mennonite Church in State College since 1966.

**J. Kenneth Kreider** (PhD, Pennsylvania State University) was born and raised on a dairy farm in southern Lancaster County, Pennsylvania. He served over three years in alternative service, first as a DHIA (Dairy Herd Improvement Association) tester and then as a volunteer in Brethren Volunteer Service (BVS). As a BVSer he was a guinea pig for medical research at the National Institutes of Health in Bethesda, Maryland and in the Metabolic Research Unit of the University of Michigan Hospital in Ann Arbor.

He was then assigned to Kassel, Germany, where he became visitation representative of Heifer Project International. When the Hungarian revolution broke out in 1956, Kreider was transferred to Linz, Austria, to coordinate the work of BVSers in the various refugee camps. He completed his work in Europe by originating the refugee resettlement program on the island of Sardinia, Italy.

When he returned to the U.S., he earned his BA degree from Elizabethtown College and his MA and PhD degrees from Penn State. As Professor of European History at Elizabethtown College, he organized various groups to participate in national antiwar demonstrations in Washington D.C. He has also conducted educational tours to many parts of the world—traveling in fifty states and 110 countries on all seven continents.

He has written two books: *A Cup of Cold Water: The Story of Brethren Service*, and his autobiography, *From the Buck to E-town: An Awesome Journey*. He is a lifelong member of the Church of the Brethren and is still active in his local church. Kreider has been married to Carroll Hall Kreider (Professor of Business, emerita, Elizabethtown College) for fifty-years years. They are parents of two daughters and have six grandchildren and one great-grandson.

**Earl S. Martin** (MA, Stanford University) is currently a carpenter in Harrisonburg, Virginia, after trying to save the world. (His son says he is doing the reverse of Jesus, who worked as a carpenter then tried to save the world!) Earl worked with the Mennonite Central Committee (MCC) for over two decades, starting with five years in Vietnam, then several years in the Philippines with his wife, Pat Hostetter Martin. Together they directed the MCC programs and personnel in East Asia. He also spent two peripatetic years storytelling for MCC and two more years working in the MCC Washington Office. Earl studied two years at Hesston College and completed his BA and MA in East Asia Studies at Stanford University.

He authored the book, *Reaching the Other Side*, a firsthand account of his experiences in Vietnam, including his five months in Vietnam after the change of government in 1975. He also co-edited with his wife Pat the book, *World Winds: Meditations from the Blessed of the Earth*, a collection of short reflections written by volunteers living and working in countries around the world. His passions include learning from folks on the margins including persons with mental health concerns, storytelling, and reading and performing the poetry of Gerard Manley Hopkins and others. He enjoys interaction with his three children and three grandchildren.

**Pat Hostetter Martin** (MA in Conflict Transformation, Eastern Mennonite University) spent twenty formative years working for the Mennonite Central Committee. Half of those years she lived in Southeast Asia, learning from and sharing life with the people of Vietnam, Cambodia, and the Philippines. The other half was spent overseeing MCC personnel and programs in Vietnam, Laos, Cambodia, Thailand, and Burma.

In 1994 Pat began to pursue conflict studies, beginning at George Mason University then transferring to Eastern Mennonite University. Upon graduation, she served as director of the Summer Peacebuilding Institute (SPI) at EMU for ten years. During that time, she and her husband Earl also opened their home to international students studying at the Center for Justice and Peacebuilding and at SPI. More than one hundred students have lived with them over the years, enriching their lives with humor and hope. Since retirement, Pat has been working as a chaplain at Sentara RMH Medical Center in Harrisonburg, Virginia. Pat and Earl have three children and three adorable grandchildren.

**Edgar Metzler** (MDiv, Associated Mennonite Biblical Seminary) began to explore the wider world through the many international visitors who shared his parents' hospitality while visiting the Mennonite Publishing House in Scottdale, Pennsylvania. At age sixteen, he traveled to Poland on a boat carrying horses for farmers recovering from World War II. His ongoing interest in a global perspective is reflected in his old passports with visas stamped from more than fifty countries.

After completing his schooling, Ed represented Mennonite Central Committee (MCC) in Washington, D.C., moved to pastoring for six years in Ontario, Canada, then returned to MCC to direct the Peace Section. A study leave to complete a PhD in international relations was interrupted by seven years on the staff of the Peace Corps in Nepal, India, Iran, and Thailand. A year of teaching at Goshen College was followed by the challenge of helping a mental health center develop programs for addiction prevention and treatment.

After several years as the Mennonite church staff person for peace and justice concerns and director of New Call to Peacemaking, a request came for him to return to Nepal as CEO of a large multi-factor development agency supported by forty church related organizations from seventeen countries. Nine years in Nepal and his final three years of service as International Program Director for MCC pulled together the experiences and skills of a life time. Ed's variety of assignments over the years developed from his basic conviction that peace and justice for all is the calling for Christians in the world.

**Paul W. Roth** (MDiv, Bethany Theological Seminary) traces his faith ancestry to eighteenth-century German Lutherans and Swiss Anabaptists who immigrated to Pennsylvania and became Brethren in the new country. Until his recent retirement, he served Church of the Brethren pastorates in Lewiston, Minnesota; South Waterloo, Iowa; Elgin, Illinois; and Broadway, Virginia He has served on the Church of the Brethren Annual Conference Program and Arrangements Committee and on the Committee on Inter-Church Relations. He has been district moderator for the Northern Plains and Shenandoah Districts.

After receiving an associate's degree from Eastern Mennonite Seminary in spiritual direction and formation, he served as both pastoral mentor and spiritual director in the community. He has served on the board of directors for the Valley Brethren-Mennonite Heritage Center since its inception in the late 1990s. He also formed the board of directors for the John Kline Homestead, Broadway, Virginia, and serves as its president. He and his wife Linda have three young adult children: Nathan, Aaron, and Amber.

**Paul M. Schrock** (1935-2011) loved words. This passion proved to be a hindrance to working on his childhood farm in Oregon but launched him into a forty-one year career in Mennonite publishing. A venture across the continent to Bible school at Eastern Mennonite in 1954 put him on a path toward the Mennonite Publishing House in Scottdale, Pennsylvania, where he first served as assistant to the editor of *Gospel Herald*. Subsequent roles saw him as editor of children's magazine *Words of Cheer* (later *On the Line*), founding editor of *Purpose* magazine, book editor and vice president of publishing for Herald

Press Trade Books. As book editor, Schrock shaped the publication of more than 750 books, including the best-selling *More-With-Less Cookbook*, award-winning *The Upside-Down Kingdom*, and the *Believers Church Bible Commentary* Series.

During a two-year stint in Harrisonburg, Virginia, he produced radio programs "The Mennonite Hour" and "Way to Life" and taught at Eastern Mennonite College (EMC). He also operated a stock photo business for many years. Schrock was born in Tangent, Oregon, graduated from Western Mennonite School in 1954, from EMC in 1958, and earned a master's degree in journalism from Syracuse University in 1963. He was married for fifty-three years to June (Bontrager) Schrock. He was the father of three children and the grandfather of five grandchildren. In his retirement he enjoyed volunteering with Booksavers of Virginia and the Menno Simons Historical Library at Eastern Mennonite University.

**Kenneth L. Seitz Jr.** (ThM, Notre Dame University), grew up in eastern Pa. and in Harrisonburg, Virginia. He married Kathryn Hunsberger in 1959 and, until her death in 2011, they served the Mennonite Church together in many capacities: domestic and overseas service work, administration, college teaching, and pastoring. His overseas experience was in the Middle East where he studied, led tours, directed service ministries, and related to indigenous churches. In doing so, he lived in both Jerusalem and Beirut. His pastorates were in Burlington, Vermont, and in Reedley, California.

In 2012, he married Audrey Metz, likewise with roots in eastern Pennsylvania. They live in the Virginia Mennonite Retirement Center and are members at Park View Mennonite Church. "I've been blessed," Ken says, "to have been privileged to serve the church I love in so many different settings."

**H. Dwight Swartzendruber** grew up in rural Iowa. At the end of World War II he volunteered to go to Europe with the Mennonite Central Committee (MCC). His first assignment was at a children's home in France, where he learned to know a coworker, Françoise Quirin, who later became his wife. Later he worked as a logistician in a refugee camp in Germany. At the end of his MCC term, he and his wife returned to Iowa to start a family.

In 1957 H. D., Françoise, and their two small children moved to Karachi, Pakistan, where he began a twenty-one year career with

Church World Service (CWS). As a CWS Country Representative, H. D. worked closely with Catholic Relief Services and CARE in setting up a countrywide feeding program and documenting their successes and failures. Following the Pakistan assignment, H. D. and his family served with CWS in India, Algeria, and Brazil. In 1969 he was relocated to the United States to fill the post of CWS Regional Program Director for East Asia and later for Latin America and the Caribbean.

After leaving CWS, he continued providing consulting and contract services to the United Nations, to USAID, and to the many new NGOs that were entering the field, but were lacking experience in international relief operations. While retired in Arizona in 2007, he lost his wife to cancer and moved to Virginia to be near to his family. He has since remarried and now lives with his wife Faye in the Virginia Mennonite Retirement Community in Harrisonburg, Virginia.

**R. Jan Thompson** (1935-2015) grew up in a Church of the Brethren family in West Milton, Ohio. He attended Manchester College for a year and a quarter before registering for the draft as a CO. He served for two years with Brethren Volunteer Service in Vienna, Austria, assisting in the rebuilding of the Evangelisch KarlsSchule. When he returned to the U.S., he married a fellow BVSer, Roma Jo Mickey, and resumed his schooling, this time at Miami College (now called Wright State University), and sold life insurance part-time to support his growing family. Jan would eventually get two master's degrees—one in counseling and one in human development relations.

Over the years, his passions led him to teach school, coach sports teams, work as a "lay churchman" and houseparent to missionary children in Hillcrest School in Jos, Nigeria, serve as dean of men and director of housing at Manchester College, direct disaster response teams and refugee resettlement programs, among other things. Jan died of a brain tumor on January 12, 2015. Jan and Roma Jo were married for fifty-seven years. They have three sons, two daughters-in-law, and two granddaughters.

**Dale V. Ulrich** (PhD, University of Virginia) served on the Bridgewater College faculty in the field of physics (fifteen years), as dean of the college (fifteen years), and as provost (nine years). He was reared on an apple ranch in Wenatchee, Washington, attended La Verne College (BA) and the University of Oregon (MS) before entering Brethren Volunteer Service with his wife Claire. The Ulrichs served in Baltimore Inner City in 1957-58 before Dale joined the Bridgewater College faculty. His experiences include responsibilities in the Church of the Brethren as well as numerous other professional involvements.

For thirty-one years he has served as secretary of the board of directors of Brethren Encyclopedia, Inc. He is the co-editor of Volume 4 of *The Brethren Encyclopedia*. His international experiences include participation in a two-month Seminar in India for U.S. College Deans (1972-73) and three months as interim director of the Brethren Colleges Abroad program in India (1999-2000). He and his wife are the parents of three children.

# THE INDEX

## A

Alternative service. *See* I-W service
Amish Mission Conference, 253
Amish and Muslim cultures compared. *See* subhead under Muslim
Anabaptism, Anabaptist
    began as "radical act of civil disobedience," 370
    "a communitarian, non-creedal" movement, 107
    confessions of faith
        "modeled on the Sermon on the Mount," 107
        reflect "the ways of peace and nonviolence," 107
Anger, status and role of, 167, 327, 342, 353
Arab-Israeli conflict. *See* Palestinian-Israeli conflict
Augsburger, Myron, 127, 146, 149, 154

## B

Baptism in Brethren and/or Mennonite traditions
    adult baptism marked beginning of movement(s), 370
    Brethren mode of baptism "led my family to the Brethren," 24
    communal event shared by those who nurture in the faith, 302
    not a "singular event for one's personal salvation," 302
    total immersion required "to make the baptism stick," 172
Beahm, William, 177, 180
Bender, Harold S., 191-2, 359-71, 381
    chair of MCC Peace Section, 361
    opened doors for graduate studies, 360
Bender, Urie, 126
Bethany Theological Seminary, 46, 56-60, 73, 78, 161, 169-70, 174-5, 209-10, 304
    centennial celebration, 180
Bible school (winter, summer, vacation), 120, 142, 187, 199, 253, 280
Board of Congregational Ministries
    new in 1971 reorganization of Mennonite Church, 194
Bolt, Eberli
    first Anabaptist executed, 184
Bowman, Carl F., 61
Brethren Colleges Abroad, 56-7
*Brethren Encyclopedia*
    conception of, 58-60
    constituent Brethren groups involved in creating, 60
    primary editor, Donald Durnbaugh, 61

Brethren *Haus* (in Kassel Germany), 29, 31
Brethren Service Center, 27, 47-50, 59-60, 212-16, 222, 299, 302
Brethren Student Movement, 48, 63
Brethren Volunteer Service (BVS), also Brethren Service, 18, 23, 27-28, 46-55, 207, 299-305, 388, 393
  in Austria, 35
  in migrant workers camp, 299
  origins of, 46
Brethren World Assemblies, 62-3
Bridgewater Church of the Brethren, 55-6, 63
Bridgewater College, 44-8, 53-8, 62-4, 69, 72, 80, 168, 386-7, 393
Brown, Dale, 305
Buddha, The
  Buddhist, 316
  one spirit with Christ, 310, 331
  on mindfulness, 329
  Zen Buddhism, 329

C
Capon, Robert Farrar, 180
Catholic Relief Services (CRS), 232-3
Cattle boat, 187-8
CEPAD (Council of Protestant Churches in Nicaragua), 245-6
Children's Disaster Services, 213-4
Christian Peacemaker Teams (CPT), 372-3
Church, church life
  a given for those in "service," 18, 25, 276-7
Church of the Brethren Disaster Response, 212
Church planting, also church development, 280, 288-9
  in Mexico City, 280
Civil disobedience, 369-73
  adult baptism as radical act of civil disobedience, 370
  definition of by John Rawls, 370
  Mennonite church counters to civil disobedience, 370-1
  non-registration for military, 370-2
Civilian Public Service (CPS), 17, 120-1, 190, 252-3, 264, 312
Civil War in Shenandoah Valley, 64, 82-3, 296
  and Elder John Kline, 83, 307-8
Clan
  both cohesive and conflictive, 256, 263, 266, 291
  elders of, 266
Clinical pastoral education, 289, 327
Community Mediation Center, 132-3
Conflict Transformation Program (CTP and its successor Center for Justice and Peacebuilding) at EMU, 133-4, 324-5.
Conscience as moral guide, 328, 370
Conscientious objectors to military service (COs), 24-6, 72, 121, 361
  based on Scripture, 47
  COs with no preferred faith or religion, 262
  should be open to dangers just as are military persons, 339
  testifying before Congress, 362
Consciousness
  origins of, 110
  role of clan consciousness, 256
  and religious anxiety, 337

Consensus, 368
  versus voting, 235
Conservative Mennonite, Conservative Amish Mennonite, 116, 118, 127, 254
Creationism versus science
  in biblical interpretation, 76-8
  at Eastern Mennonite College/University, 94-6, 111
  at Liberty University, 54-5
CrossRoads. *See* Valley Brethren-Mennonite Heritage Center
Cutrell, Ben, 150, 193

**D**

Depression, Great. *See* Great Depression
Disaster Child Care Program, 86, 212, 216
Disaster Response Program, 204
Discipleship (MCC service) in military zones
  Jesus' intent for women and children questioned, 318
  effect of mission presence on military presence, 316
Doctrinal exam given by Eastern Mennonite Board of Missions (EMBM) to mission candidates, 255
Doctors without Borders, 12
Dordrecht Confession, 143
Down's syndrome persons
  wisdom and acceptance of, 298
Draft board, 26, 47-9, 169
Drescher, John, 152, 156, 194
Dress code, plain, 68, 118
Dunker Church on the Antietam Battlefield, 78
Dunkers. *See* German Baptist Brethren
Durnbaugh, Donald F., 60-2, 82, 161, 221, 309n1
Dyck, C. J., 154, 186, 284

Dyck, Peter, 17

**E**

Earlham School of Religion, 57, 120
Eastern Mennonite Board of Missions and Charities (EMBMC), 18, 255-66, 270-6, 294
Eastern Mennonite College (EMC), 18, 88, 91, 99, 140-5, 127, 155-66, 254, 245, 270-5, 292, 311-13
Eastern Mennonite University (EMU), 14, 19, 57, 63, 88, 91, 118, 133, 154, 158, 188, 281, 307-13, 348, 373
Eby, Omar, 130, 154, 263
Elder John Kline. *See* Kline, Elder John
Elizabethtown College, 31, 37-40, 60-2, 68-9, 85, 178, 303-4
Erb, Alta Mae, 130
Erb, Paul, 98, 143-7, 154, 370
Evangelistic meetings. *See* Revival meetings
Evolution. (*See also* Creationism versus science), 76-7
  as intellectual faith challenge, 94-9
  process theology and evolution, 102
  and the early C. K. Lehman, 95

**F**

Family devotions practiced, family worship, 23, 252, 277-9
Fellowship of Reconciliation (FOR), 73
FEMA (Federal Emergency Management Agency), 155, 313
Food distribution guidelines, 240-2

"Free minister" (non-salaried), 73, 166, 308
Friends, Society of, Quakers, 13-15, 25, 63, 206, 352, 270
Fulbright Grant, 54, 326

## G

Gandhi, Mahatma, 14, 57, 360
 as model for Brethren and Mennonite peacemaking, 40, 360
 disputed by Guy F. Hershberger, 360
Gandhian nonviolent house on Stanford U. campus, 343
General Board of the Church of the Brethren, 176-7, 214-5
General Conference Mennonite Church, 154, 158, 289, 366, 375
Geography of our faith, the, where is home? 348-9
 the loss of "soul" and the search for a place to belong, 319-20
German Baptist Brethren. *See also* Dunkers, 59-60, 67-8, 78
Gingerich, Melvin, 359-61
God, view of, vision of God
 beyond any vision based on ancient cosmologies, 108
 in Christ, Christocentric, 103, 108
 classical, theistic, 100-2
 from enforcer of moral rules to lover of all people, 135-7
 as the great relativizer and humanizer, 105
 as passionate concern for justice, 366
Goshen College, 18, 120, 135, 187, 265, 314-5, 356-61, 367
*Gospel Herald*
 editors of, 147, 182, 194, 370
 as a moral voice for Mennonites, 352, 370
 a quasi-official voice of the Mennonite Church, 182, 194-5
Great Depression, the
 the economic-cultural parental background of contributors to current volume, 23, 45, 116
Grove, Merlin
 EMBMC missionary assassinated, 259
Guerrillas, 237-8, 317, 330

## H

Habitat for Humanity, 220
Hammar, Howard, 253
Head covering, 25. *See also* Plain dress
Heifer Project, heifers, 18, 29-34, 43, 49-50, 188, 207, 302, 389
Herald Press, 150-8, 264
Hershberger, Guy F., 92, 145, 190, 199, 359-60, 365
Hertzler, Dan
 begins editorship of *Gospel Herald*, 194
 on leadership styles, 194
Herzog, Paul
 COB youth exchange, 300
 German Christmas symbols, 30
Hobos, "road walkers"
 and hospitality, 23, 301, 336
Holocaust, 11, 33
Horst, Amos, 365
Horst, Kurt
 official "closer down" of Mennonite Publishing House, 197-8
Hymn writing, 305

## I

Institute for Conflict Analysis and Resolution (ICAR), 323

Intercollegiate Peace Fellowship, 367
Islam. *See also* Muslim, 256-71, 331
  Islamic fundamentalism like Christian fundamentalism, 331
  restrictions on teaching, 257
  taught in mission school in Somali, 258
I-W service, 24-6, 42-50, 94, 121, 364-70

## J
Juniata College, 46, 160, 176, 180, 299

## K
Kauffman, Daniel
  *Doctrines of the Bible*, 94
  on lack of proof for evolution, 94
  *One Thousand Questions and Answers*, 90
  stalwart defender of nonconformity, 358
Kaufman, Gordon, 103-7
Keim, Al, 13, 29, 154, 379, 381
Khan, Abdul Ghaffar Khan, pacifist Muslim, 40
King James Bible (KJV), 119, 135, 192, 252
Kline, Elder John, 83-4, 169, 296, 305-8
  bicentennial celebration, 305
  Kline Homestead, 308, 391
Kraybill, Paul N., 195, 260

## L
Landis, Hans, 66, 184
La Verne College, 18, 44, 47-9, 55, 209, 387, 393
Lederach, John Paul, 133, 323
Life, aphorisms of
  "a journey in love, faith and unrelenting courage," 111
  "life is too short to miss today," 114, 132
  "like a river with many small tributaries," 90
  "unfinished, incomplete, boundless," 97
Lind, Millard, 153, 190-3, 274, 284
  editor of *Christian Living*, 193
  joined faculty at AMBS, 193
  *Yahweh is a Warrior*, 153
Linville Creek Church of the Brethren, 305-7
  celebration of 200th anniversary of Elder Kline, 84, 169, 305
  home congregation of Elder John Kline, 84, 169, 307
  M. R. Zigler's church home, 169, 296
Lobbying government
  for self-interests, 362
  witnessing to government beyond self-interest not acceptable, 362
Longacre, Doris Janzen, 132, 152
Lordship of Christ,
  basis of peace statement to transcend two-kingdom dualism, 365
Love feast, 300
Lutheran World Relief (LWR), 218, 233, 239, 315

## M
Mack, Alexander, 58, 65
McCarthy, Coleman, 40
McPherson College, 46, 48, 303-4
Mahatma Gandhi University, 57
Manchester College, 61, 120, 207-13, 393
March as political protest, 52, 132, 302-3

march on Washington with
  Martin Luther King, 303
Marshall Plan, 230
*Martyrs' Mirror*, 66, 251, 328
MennoMedia, 158, 178
Mennonite Board of Missions
  (MBM), 18, 114, 129-30, 136,
  235, 255, 264-9, 275-88, 292,
  314
  personnel vision of occupying
    Israelis, 275, 287
Mennonite Brethren, 121-2, 154,
  372
  limited roles for women, 122
  representative of a collectivist-
    type culture, 12
Mennonite Central Committee
  (MCC), 18, 29, 59, 114, 121,
  130, 152, 218, 237, 257, 275,
  292, 313-5, 339
  added "service" to its tagline,
    17
  sponsor of *More-with-Less*
    cookbook, 152
  MCC Washington Office, 275,
    321, 348, 390
  valuable component of Men-
    nonite service and peace-
    building, 365
Mennonite Church/church
  as change agent, 130
  non-accommodating to busi-
    ness, 191
  nonconformity trumps non-
    participation in war, 358-60,
    375-6,
  owned *Your Time* radio pro-
    gram, 139
  and its tribal God? 198
  views on sexual orientation,
    107
  women in leadership, 263-64
  women in professional
    roles, 120

Mennonite Community Association, 190-1
*Mennonite Community* periodical,
  142, 189
  Grant Stoltzfus editor, 189
Mennonite Disaster Service, 155-6,
  212, 216, 364
Mennonite ethnicity, 198
Mennonite Graduate Fellowship,
  origins of, 97
Mennonite Publishing House
  (MPH), 119, 140, 142-42, 189-
  91, 260
  brief history of factors leading
    to its demise, 191-8
  vigorous organization in '50s
    and '60s, 191
  geographic decentralization of
    offices, 194-5
  downfall of books and curricu-
    lar division, 157
Mennonite Voluntary Service
  (MVS), 277
  operated under Mennonite
    Board of Missions, 282-3
Mennonite women in ministry,
  130, 265, 389
Mennonite World Conference,
  130, 200, 269, 272
Mennonite Youth Fellowship
  (MYF), 314, 337
Menno Simons on "True evangeli-
  cal faith," 332
Messianic Jews, 287
Metamorphosis through "service"
  of Brethren and Mennonites
  like a Monarch butterfly leav-
  ing its cocoon, 2
Metzler, A. J., 191, 260, 360-1
Meyer, Albert, 365
Military bases,
  Clark Air Field, 347
  Subic Bay Naval Base, 321, 347
Miller, Orie O., 25, 121, 224

founding executive secretary
of Mennonite Central Committee, 121, 257, 381
Mennonite co-leader with
Brethren M. R. Zigler and
Quaker E. Raymond Wilson,
25
Mission(s)
Amish mission conference
held in Iowa, 253
mission focus versus MCC in
tension in Israel-Palestine
work, 275
Mother Teresa, 54, 294
Mow, Sister Anna, 180
Munitions, unexploded, 318, 348,
344-5
Muslim(s). *See also* Islam
community building with
Muslims in U.S., 268-71, 325-6
compatibility of Amish
women in Muslim world,
250ff., 279-1
Eastern Mennonite Board of
Missions and Charities missionary killed by Muslim,
259
Pakistan as Muslim majority
nation, 231
preached nonviolence to Pashtun tribesmen, 40
violence instigated by Muslims from "outside," 259
My Lai, massacre of a Vietnamese
village population, 342, 345-6

## N

NAACP (National Association for
the Advancement of Colored People), 19, 52, 302
Napalm, jellied gasoline, 330, 341,
343

National Service Board for Religious Objectors (NSBRO),
361-2
New English Bible (NEB), 192
New International Version of Bible
(NIV), 192
New Windsor, Md., 27, 29, 47, 50,
59-60, 188, 207, 212, 299, 302
Brethren "intellectual center"
to balance relief and service,
59-60
Brethren Volunteer Service
Center, 27
Center for "On Earth Peace"
program, 59
Nonconformity, Mennonite. *See
also* Nonresistance
in dress, 100
immorality of violence is
trumped by nonconformity,
358
nonresistance was subset of
nonconformity, 358
today takes on new meaning
where the dominant form of
culture is violence, 376
Nonresistance, nonviolent resistance, 100
under Guy Hershberger,
Melvin Gingerich, and H. S.
Bender, no longer a subset of
nonconformity, 359
debunked as a unique characteristic of Mennonites, 359

## O

One-minute radio sermon, 171,
174, 177
One-room schoolhouse, 90, 117,
225, 253, 336,
Open Table Community, 325-6
Ordain, ordination, 79, 141, 162,
186, 209
lends special privileges, 269

by lot, 311-12
of women, 136-7, 177

## P

Pacifist, 71
  CPS as pacifist alternative to military, 190
  on being a young pacifist Brethren, 168
  men of draft age, 15, 17
  Muslim, 40
Palestinian-Israeli conflict, 32-4
Paris Peace Accords, 318, 344
Parker, Alice, 130
Pax (MCC), Pax service, 28, 208, 212, 221, 257, 339, 364
Peace church(es), Historic Peace Church, 15, 17, 72, 288
Peace Corps, 12, 260-1, 361, 367-9
  Mennonite statement advising against entering Peace Corps, 367-8
Peace Problems Committee (of the Mennonite Church), 144, 363-4
Plain dress, 25, 68, 118-19, 300
Poverty
  in Appalachia, 282
  contrasting phenomena between Asia and U.S., 322
  Johnson's War on Poverty, 125, 282
  in Philippines, 320
  poverty of spirit and imagination, 323
Preheim, Vern, 236
Provident Bookstore(s), 151-8, 264-6
Psychotic break, 323-4

## Q

Qur'an (Koran), 156, 162

## R

Race, race relations, 74, 98, 173, 178, 236, 289, 359, 369
  race riots, 282
Ramer, Robert, 152
Red Cross, 213-8, 236
Reforestation program
  in Algeria, 237-8
  staffed by former guerrillas, 237
Retreat center, spiritual retreats, 63, 268-9, 275
  at Benedictine convent, 266
  The Hermitage, 266
  silent retreat, 306, 351
Revised Standard Version (RSV) Bible translation
  Mennonite Publishing House became flashpoint for Sunday school materials, 192
Revival meetings, 90, 119, 143, 253, 277
Ruth, John, 97, 155, 184-5

## S

Salvation
  baptism, prayer covering... convinced my grandmother that "only Brethren would go to heaven," 25
  transformation of character, person and communal, 107
Sawatsky, Walter, 153
Scharzenau, Germany
  origin of Church of the Brethren, 41, 58, 61
  venue of 300th anniversary celebration, 62
Schizophrenia
  and the brokenness of God, 253
  is God a schizo? 253
Schleitheim Confession, 184
Scripture

as basis for refusing war, 76, 82
not a compendium of dictums but a gathering of stories, 338
created controversy in Mennonite Church and at Publishing House, 192
ecumenical encounter with Scripture, 306
and the gathered community, 184-7, 191
"inerrancy"—not a useful hermeneutic concept, 193
inspiration of, 119
use of Revised Standard Version, 192
and the Way of Jesus, 53
"Seagoing cowboys," 168, 206
Searle, John, 93
    intellectual offering a contemporary non-sociological basis of reality, 106
Second Vatican Council, 273-4
Sermon, preaching
    preparation, 161-4
    purpose, 162ff.
Service
    as central element of Mennonite identity, 13, 364
    as discipleship, 15
    Pax and TAP, 364
    service inflicted trauma, 319-20
    as transformative for those who serve, 2, 11, 43
Shar'ia law, 256
Sudan Interior Mission (SIM), 262, 270
Suffering
    of Brethren movement, 66
    of Palestinians, 287
    of veterans, 270
    the theologizing of, 312, 316, 342

and the weakness of God, 353
Summer Peacebuilding Institute (SPI), 114, 134, 325-31

**T**
Tantur Ecumenical Institute, 273-5, 285-6
    study center in Jerusalem that has attracted Mennonite scholars, 274
Taxes for war. See War taxes
Tet Offensive, 317
Theology of service,
    adequacy for expressing an Anabaptist faith, 18
Thich Nhat Hanh, 329, 331
Training in organizational development, leadership, 57, 130-4, 176-7, 289

**U**
Unexploded ordinance. See Munitions, unexploded
Unionists and the Civil War, 64, 82
"Universal military training"— Mennonites advise government against, 363
USAID (United States Agency for International Development), 232, 239-42, 261, 291

**V**
Vacation Bible school. See Bible school
Valdoie—Mennonite-owned children's home in northeast France, 228-9
Valley Brethren-Mennonite Heritage Center. See also Cross-Roads, 64, 86, 296, 307-8
Vatican Council II
    and impetus to establish Tantur Ecumenical Institute, 273

"preferential option for the poor" in the Philippines, 320
Vietnam Christian Service (VNCS), 315-7
Vision of healing and hope, pursuing a, 12

**W**
War stamps
   and nonconformity, 357-8
   and nonparticipation in war, 357
War taxes
   Gandhian nonviolent resistance to war, 306
   resistance to payment of disputed, 343-4
*Weather Vane*, 140, 146
   on purple ditto paper, 146
Weaver, Ken, 127
West Bank, 274
   settlements built on, 274
   Israeli occupation of, 287
Women
   encouraged to continue in traditional roles in *Heart to Heart* program, 129
   in leadership, 284
   in transition from homemaking to professional roles, 19, 129
   given broader outlook on life in MennoMedia's *Your Time*, 129-30
   limited roles for women in MB churches, 122
   National Women's Conference in opposition to nuclear war, 132
   ordination of women in Brethren churches, 177
   ordination of women in Mennonite Church, 136-7, 327
   and prescribed attire, 119, 122
   role of women in third-world societies, 241
World Council of Churches (WCC), 18, 129, 243, 246
   in Algeria, 235
   and Decade to Overcome Violence, 267
   in Geneva, 59
   1948 Amsterdam Assembly: "Peace is... the will of God," 360
Worldview, world view, 95-9, 120, 153, 230, 282
   Christian worldview and evolution stand "diametrically opposed," 95
   religious versus scientific, 76-8

**Y**
Yake, C. F., 142
Yoder, John Howard, 154-5, 227, 274, 365
Young People's Christian Association (YPCA), 189, 281, 338

**Z**
Zigler, Jesse, 46
Zigler, M. R., 25-6, 31, 36, 58-60, 169, 296
Zook, Elrose, 142, 147

www.ingramcontent.com/pod-product-compliance
Lightning Source LLC
Chambersburg PA
CBHW050241170426
43202CB00015B/2873